# How to Ski the Blues and Blacks

# (Without Getting Black and Blue)

*by*

Craig McNeil

Blue Willow, Inc.
Littleton, Colorado

**This book belongs to:**

Name: ......................................................................

Address: ..................................................................

.............................................................................

Phone: ....................................................................

.............................................................................

In case of emergency, please notify:

.............................................................................

Copyright 1998 by Craig McNeil

1st Edition, 1st Printing - November 1998

If you find errors in this book or have suggestions, please notify:

Blue Willow, Inc.
P.O. Box 621227, Dept. 101
Littleton, Colorado 80162
Phone (303) 932-1600
Toll Free (888) 932-1600
Fax (303) 932-1800
World Wide Web home page: .bluewillow.com

Printed in the United States of America

Library of Congress Catalog Card Number: 98-074214

ISBN 1-889796-08-5

# Preface

This book would not have been possible without the love, support and encouragement of my entire family. It is to my beautiful wife, Amy, that I am most deeply indebted. Without her constant encouragement and guidance I would have given up on the idea of ever writing this book a long time ago. Also I must acknowledge my son, Sean, and daughter, Moira, who served unknowingly as my Guinea pigs, and who have allowed me to share with them the deep love I have for the mountains and skiing. They are my pride and joy and the true treasures of my life.

I owe a dept of gratitude to my mother, Ellen, who has always been an example to me. She gave me the gift of unwavering faith and showed me what it meant to have a never-ending love. I have learned much from and will be forever thankful to her.

Also to my sister, Lauren, and brother, Edward, who have taught me so much throughout my lifetime. They are as talented as they are gifted. They both display the true meaning of the indomitable spirit.

Bill Clossick, my uncle and father figure, who took me skiing as a boy and who continues to ski with me whenever he stops by for a winter visit. He is skiing better now at 73 than at any time before and continues to serve as an example and confidant. He keeps a pace and a lifestyle that most men half his age would find hard to keep up with.

Bob and Dorothy Glover, for their encouragement and willingness to proofread the early incarnations of this manuscript. Their love and dedication to one another serve as an example to me.

Harald Harb and Diana Rogers for their help and insight in putting this book together. Harald, thanks for having the courage to step "outside the box" and give us this evolutionary system of skiing.

George and Eric Friedman, ski students from my days at Vail, who gave me the seeds and the inspiration to write this book.

Joe Hardy and Joe Bouchard, my first ski school directors at Mt. Southington, CT.

John White, a long time friend and one who believed in the idea and encouraged and supported it from the beginning.

Larry Forbis, Kevin Huhn and Steve Campbell of the Rocky Mountains News for giving me the chance to write for such a distinguished paper.

3

**Mary Miller**, my editor at Blue Willow, for her patience, direction and insight into the whole process which transformed this manuscript into a book.

**And**, most importantly, to Tom & Mary Glover & everyone else at Blue Willow Publishing, for the helpfulness, motivation, support and dedication it took to bring this book to life.

### Special Acknowledgments:

Mount Southington, CT: Joe Hardy & Joe Bouchard (my first ski school directors), David Wells & David Sause.

From Hotdoggers West: Rossi Moreau, Mike Conlin & Lou Duby

Keystone: Jerry Jones, Lois Barr, Rod Carney, Tom Grossi, Jon Reveal, Gene & Ina Gillis, John Howe, Bob Gleason.

Copper Mountain: Jerry Muth, Floyd Bashant, Dean Jones, Ed Jones Sr., Christy Sports and Keith Van Velkinburgh, Bob Lange, Sandy Mortensen.

Fathers Ed Poehlman & John Kaufman, Gene & Joan Biehl of Frontier Sports.

And to all my skiing buddies who hold a special place in my heart: Ron "Boomer" Colson, Mike & Vicki Wood, Mark Whittaker, Mark Uglesich, Craig Sabina, Dean Watkins, Bob Kuha, Steve Fasino, Bill McNice, Bruce Ruff, Eric Pielstick, Jeff "Snakes" Jakelich, Lance Wood, Brian Bennet, Mark "Honeylamb" Sandmeyer & Bob Feyerherm.

Tommy Doran (Elan Skis, Boots & Boeri Helmets), Joe Decker of Tecnica Boots, Larry & Patti Schmidt ( Ice Ski Poles & Revo Sunglasses).

Roger Klingerman of Smith Sport Optics, Keith Van Velkinburgh & Al Paniccui of Christy Sports, Kenny Gart of Colorado Ski & Golf.

And a special dedication to all my many ski friends and students who are far to numerous to mention, who have helped formulate the thoughts and ideas that became this book.

*Craig*

Portrait by Jake Williams
Based on Photo by Eric Weber

## About the Author

Craig McNeil is a nationally-syndicated ski columnist who has been with the Denver Rocky Mountain News in Denver, Colorado for more than nine years. McNeil has taught skiing full time for more than twenty years at some of the most prestigious ski resorts in the country including Vail, Copper Mountain, Keystone and Breckenridge Ski Resorts. McNeil began skiing at the tender age of six, and teaching at age fourteen at Mount Southington in Connecticut.

McNeil is a fourth degree black belt and former International Taekwondo Federation/United States Taekwondo Federation sparring champion. Besides his biweekly ski columns, McNeil works as a feature film producer. He lives in Littleton, Colorado with his wife, Amy, and two children, Sean and Moira.

# Acknowledgments

Aspen Skiing Company
Berthoud Pass Ski Area
Copper Mountain Resort
Crested Butte Mountain Resort
Adrian Crook
DalBello Sports, LLC
Descente Ski Apparel
Dynastar
Elan Ski Company
Harald Harb and Harb Ski Systems
Loveland Ski Area
Monarch Ski and Snowboard Area
Nordica (Prince Sports System)
Steamboat Powder Cats
Steamboat Ski and Resort Corp.
Silver Creek Resort
Sunlight Mountain resort
Tecnica
Telluride Ski and Golf Company
TLH Heliskiing
Vail Resorts (Beaver Creek, Breckenridge, Keystone and Vail)
The Volant Ski Company, LLC
Winter Park Resort

*Some of the information in this book was collected from numerous sources and if not properly acknowledged, Blue Willow would like to express its appreciation for those contributions. The author and publisher have made a serious effort to provide accurate information in this book. However, the probability exists that there are errors and misprints, and that variations in data values may also occur. Information included in this book should only be considered as a general guide. Skiing can be a very dangerous sport and the author and publisher both encourage you to seek training from professionals.*

# More Blue Willow Books

***Measure for Measure*** · · · · · · · · · · · · · · · · **$14.95**
by Richard A. Young and Thomas J. Glover
ISBN 1-889796-00-X, 4"x 6" soft cover, 864 pp
The most complete conversion factor handbook
ever written. Contains over 39,000 conversions for
more than 5,100 different units.

***Pocket Partner*** · · · · · · · · · · · · · · · · · · · · · **$9.95**
by Dennis Evers, Mary Miller and Thomas J. Glover
ISBN 1-889796-02-6, 3.2" x 5.4", soft cover, 576 pp
An amazing shirt-pocket reference book for law
enforcement personnel. Everything from hazmat to
web sites.

***Seldovia, Alaska*** · · · · · · · · · · · · · · · · · · · **$24.95**
by Susan Woodward Springer
ISBN 1-889796-03-4, 8-1/2"x11", soft cover, 240 pp
An historical portrait of life in the town of Seldovia,
Alaska.

***Troubleshooting Your Contracting
Business to <u>Cause</u> Success*** · · · · · · · · · · **$39.95**
by Charles Vander Kooi
ISBN 1-889796-04-2, 5"x 8.5", soft cover, 640 pp
A comprehensive collection of tips, tricks and
experienced advice from a nationally recognized
expert in construction and business management.
A must for anyone in a contracting business.

# Figures, References and Trade Marks

## Figures, Photos and Illustrations:

Credits for all Figures, Photos and Illustrations are listed in a caption with each individual item.

## References:

*Pocket Partner* by D. Evers, M. Miller, and T. Glover
Cold Weather Safety Chapter
ISBN 1-889796-02-6, 576 pp, soft cover

*Anyone Can Be An Expert Skier* by Harald R. Harb
ISBN 0-9661282-0-6, 214 pp, soft cover

*The White Book of Ski Areas 1997-1998*
by Robert G. Enzel
ISBN 0-931636-22-1, 116 pp, soft cover

## Trademarks:

Blue Willow Logo is a registered trademark of Blue Willow, Inc.

Inflex™ is a trademark of Inflex Corporation

Kevlar® is a registered trademark of E.I. Dupont de Nemours and Company

Sno-Cat® is a registered trademark of Tucker Sno-Cats Corporation

Teflon® is a registered trademark of E.I. Dupont de Nemours and Company

Labiosan® is a registered trademark of Labiosan, U.S.A.

Salomon® is a registered trademark of Salomon Corp.

# Table of Contents

Preface and Acknowledgments....................................3, 6
About the Author..................................................................5
More Blue Willow Books......................................................7
Figures, References, and Trade Marks................................8
**Chapter 1: Preparation**........................................................13
   Starting a New Season ..................................................14
   "Ski Legs" ......................................................................17
   Early Season Lesson ....................................................20
   "CANI" ...........................................................................23
   Intention .........................................................................26
   Beginner Skiing .............................................................29
   Ski Safety ......................................................................31
   "Inflex" ...........................................................................39
   Ski Awareness ..............................................................42
**Chapter 2: Accelerated Skier Performance System**.45
   Accelerated Skier Performance System (ASPS)..........46
**Chapter 3: ASPS Part 1: Alignment And Ski Boots**.49
   Alignment.......................................................................50
   Ski Boots........................................................................49
   The Right Boots: Rotary vs. Lateral..............................57
   The Worse for Wear.......................................................60
   Custom Insoles..............................................................62
   I Can If I Cant................................................................65
   Feeling Unsure..............................................................68
**Chapter 4: ASPS Part 2: Primary Movements**........71
   Introduction....................................................................72
   Balance..........................................................................75
   Phase I: Beginner Exercises.........................................80
   Phase II: Beginner Exercises With Skis.......................86
   Phase III: The "Phantom Move".....................................92
   Balance in the Turn.......................................................98
   Phase IV: The "Phantom Turn" ....................................102
   Phase V: "Phantomizing" .............................................105
   Phantomizing on Advanced Terrain.............................107

**Chapter 5: Hourglass Skis** ...........................................**111**
   What Are They? ...........................................112
   Making Them Work for You .......................113
   To Carve or Slide ........................................115
   Advanced Skiing ..........................................118

**Chapter 6: The Six Steps To Effortless Skiing** ...**121**
   Introduction .................................................122
   Step One: "Lift and Tilt" ...........................123
   Step Two: "Right Ski, Left Ski" ................126
   Step Three: "Control Your Speed" ...........128
   Step Four: "Exhale on Every Turn" ..........132
   Step Five: "Look Ahead" ...........................136
   Step Six: "Keep Your Rhythm Constant" ...138

**Chapter 7: Open Your Mind** .................................**143**
   Be Present in The Moment .........................144
   Start Your Day ............................................ 146
   Mentoring ....................................................148
   Be Kind to Yourself ...................................151

**Chapter 8: Making Breakthroughs** ....................**155**
   Expert Improvement ...................................156
   Overcome Your Fear ...................................158
   Attitude .......................................................161
   Think Ahead ...............................................164
   Relaxation ...................................................167

**Chapter 9: Intermediate Lessons** ......................**170**
   Smooth Transitions .....................................171
   Work Into Your Skiing ...............................173
   "Easy Run, Hard Run" ...............................175
   Unlock the Leg ...........................................177
   Sliding Right ...............................................179
   Use Your Hips ............................................182

**Chapter 10: From Intermediate to Expert** ...........**186**
   Intermediate Skier ......................................187
   Common Problems in Intermediate Skiing ...189
   The Pole Plant ............................................192

**Chapter 11: The ABC's of Mogul Skiing** .................199
  Keys to Success ...........................................200
  Skiing on the Edge .......................................205
  Turning in Moguls ........................................210
  Ski the Line .............................................213
  Keep Your Rhythm .........................................217
  Phantomizing in The Bumps ................................221

**Chapter 12: Powder Skiing** ..............................224
  Powder Skiing for Beginners ..............................225
  Advanced Powder Skiing ...................................229
  Fat Skis for Powder ......................................234
  Snowcat Powder Skiing ....................................237
  HeliSkiing ...............................................241

**Chapter 13: Extreme Conditions** .........................245
  Keys to The Steep ........................................246
  Breakable Crust ..........................................250
  Hard Snow ................................................251

**Chapter 14: Spring Conditions** ..........................255
  Spring Skiing ............................................256
  Spring Skiing Preparations ...............................259
  Inconsistent Spring Snow .................................261

**Chapter 15: Something For Everybody** .....................265
  Getting the Kids Started .................................266
  Skiing With the Kids .....................................269
  Shape Skis for Kids ......................................274

**Chapter 16: In Closing** .................................279
  Avalanche Awareness ......................................280
  It's Not Too Late to Ski .................................283

**Cold Weather Safety and First Aid** ......................287
  First Aid Priorities .....................................288
  Hypothermia ..............................................291
  Frost Bite ...............................................290
  Wind Chill Chart .........................................293
  Ice Thickness Safety .....................................293
  Altitude Sickness ........................................294
  Cold Water Survival Times ................................296

## Ski Areas of the United States

Alabama...................................................................298
Alaska....................................................................298
Arizona...................................................................300
Arkansas................................................................None
California................................................................302
Colorado................................................................312
Connecticut............................................................324
Deleware...............................................................None
Florida..................................................................None
Georgia..................................................................326
Hawaii..................................................................None
Idaho.....................................................................326
Illinois....................................................................331
Indiana...................................................................333
Iowa......................................................................334
Kansas..................................................................None
Kentucky...............................................................None
Louisiana...............................................................None
Maine.....................................................................336
Maryland................................................................341
Massachusetts.........................................................342
Michigan................................................................347
Minnesota..............................................................362
Mississippi.............................................................None
Missouri.................................................................None
Montana.................................................................368
Nebraska...............................................................None
Nevada..................................................................373
New Hampshire.......................................................374
New Jersey.............................................................381
New Mexico............................................................382
New York...............................................................385
North Carolina.........................................................401
North Dakota...........................................................405
Ohio......................................................................406
Oklahoma..............................................................None
Oregon..................................................................409
Pennsylvania...........................................................412
Rhode Island...........................................................424
South Carolina.........................................................None
South Dakota...........................................................424
Tennessee..............................................................425
Texas....................................................................None
Utah......................................................................425
Vermont.................................................................432
Virginia..................................................................437
Washington.............................................................439
Washington, DC.......................................................None
West Virginia...........................................................443
Wisconsin..............................................................446
Wyoming................................................................456

**Index**.................................................................**461**

**Notes**.................................................................**479**

# Chapter 1
# Preparation

Photo © Jack Affleck, courtesy Vail Resorts

# Starting a New Season

It's the beginning of another ski season and you are getting ready to ski. The time to get your equipment together is long before you walk out the door on the day you plan to ski. It may seem obvious, yet many wait until the last minute to find all the stuff they'll need for a day on the slopes. The excitement mixed with the adrenaline and anticipation of your first day skiing means you inevitably over look or forget something.

## The Night Before

As a ski pro, I gather my equipment the night before I ski. When you put your equipment together the night before, it allows you to make a mental checklist in preparation for your day of skiing. This method will also help keep your enthusiasm in check while you figure out what you will need for your upcoming ski day.

If you are like most people I know, you wait until an hour before you walk out the door to make sure you have everything and that it is in good working order. That's a mistake! Prepare yourself for your first day of the season well before you walk out your front door!

## Skis Tuned and Waxed

If you have not looked at or touched your skis since last season, it is a good idea to take them to a local ski shop to have your skis tuned and bindings checked. A ski that is tuned has had its base:

- P-texed to fill any holes
- Stone ground for an even base
- Flat filed for a sharp edge
- Waxed for a smooth slide and more efficient turn.

A well-tuned ski gives you better performance from your equipment and is safer. Tuning and waxing the ski bottom reduces drag or friction. Beginner thinking is that drag is good because it keeps you from going too fast. Wrong. A ski that is not tuned is dangerous. Friction from the ski base can hang you up and put stress or torque on your legs and knees when you attempt to turn. The smoother the glide, the smoother the ride.

The ski edge should be free from any burrs or nicks. A ski coach from my early race days told me it's not the sharpness of the edge but its smoothness that allows for making a precise turn. Run your finger lightly along the edge to check its smoothness. The smoother the edge, without any burrs, the better

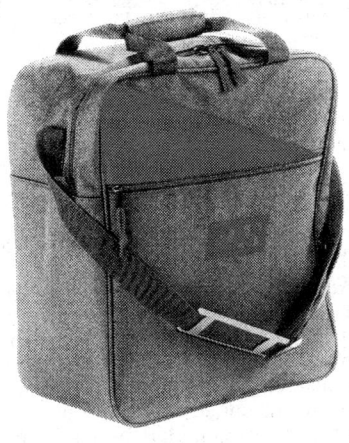

Boot Bag

your edge control and hold on the snow. You can buy a "stone" at your local ski shop made especially for de-burring the edge. Carry it in your ski jacket and use it when you need to remove any rough spots.

## Have Your Bindings Checked

Before your first day on the hill, make sure to have your bindings checked, too. Bindings can deteriorate over time, and road grit, salt and dirt (which may accumulate on your skis while driving to and from the ski area) will affect the inner workings of the bindings. Together, these factors will compromise the function of the bindings. Have them checked at your local ski shop to make sure they will release properly for your height, weight and skiing ability. Use a binding cover to protect the bindings when skis are carried on a rack, especially if you are only making day trips to your favorite ski area. It is a small price to pay to extend the life of the binding and ensure your safety.

## Check Your Ski Boots

I find it's also a good idea to try your ski boots on before you head to the hill for the first time each season.

- Put the boots on with the socks you intend to wear when you ski.
- Make sure your sock is smooth over your foot and there are no wrinkles where your shin contacts the front of the boot. Socks that are bunched or wrinkled between your leg and the tongue of the boot can cut off the circulation or create pressure points on your feet.
- If your feet are uncomfortable inside your boots, isolate the pressure points and work them out with your fingers.

- If the problem is not with your socks, check the liner inside the boot to make sure it is not wrinkled. If you can't adjust or manipulate the problem by hand, you may need to take them to the ski shop for surgery.

## Get Your Season Off on the Right Foot

There is nothing more frustrating than getting to the hill your first time out, and wasting the first two hours adjusting equipment while everyone else in your party is skiing.

Once you know your skis and bindings are tuned and your boots fit properly, you can concentrate on everything else you will need. Most pros keep all their ski paraphernalia, i.e., goggles, a hat, gloves, socks, long underwear, and neck gaiter, in a boot bag. When you have everything in one place it's easy to go through a visual checklist as you pack the night before. Next day, all you have to do is grab your skis, poles and jacket along with the boot bag as you head out the door.

Start your ski experience with a feeling of fun and excitement, not frustration. Preparation will save you time and needless worry, and is the key to a smooth, carefree downhill ski experience!

# "Ski Legs"

Ski legs. If you plan to ski, you need to get yourself a pair. "Ski legs" is the often-used industry term for getting your feet under you the first few times you ski. "Ski legs" also means developing your timing and rhythm, synchronizing your breathing with your movement, and learning to flow from one turn to the next.

Whatever your ability level, you need to give your legs a chance to get back under you your first few times out each season. You need to develop a flow and a feel for the snow as you go from turn to turn and make your way down the hill. This is important not only at the beginning of the season, but for the first few runs each day you ski.

## Prepare Body and Mind

Because skiing is a leg sport, the stronger your legs are, the better you will ski. I recommend an exercise program that combines weight training and aerobic exercise two or three times a week.

The weight work will increase your strength and muscular endurance. The aerobic work will increase your lung capacity, efficiency of movement and overall stamina. The combination of the weights with the aerobics will make a noticeable difference in your ability to handle the hill. A regular exercise program will prepare your mind as well as your body. Working out will result in more energy and vitality with less overall fatigue once you are on the mountain.

All the elements of conditioning come into play when you ski: balance, timing, rhythm, breathing, muscle flex and engagement. Hence, the importance of being in good shape. Besides the demands on your body, you are thinking about and feeling your skis, feet and snow for the first time since last ski season.

## Overcoming Off-Season Rustiness

Many of these things, both physical and mental, become second nature after you have skied a handful of times. But it's not so your first day out! Add all this to the excitement of being on the hill again and . . . Whew! You've got a lot to think about.

Though you might find yourself in reasonably good shape at the start of a new ski season, some circumstances will always be challenging after being away from skis for six months. Timing will be off and thigh muscles will fatigue simply from making lots of turns during a run.

Photo © Ben Blankenburg, courtesy of Vail Resorts /Keystone

**Keystone Resort offers terrain
for skiers of all levels.**

When timing is off, it means you have to work harder. This creates fatigue. When your legs are tired, they are less likely to respond to your mental commands for control. Stop more frequently (off to the side of the trail, out of the flow of traffic) to let all the nerve synapses and impulses catch up to the excitement and adrenaline coursing through your brain. Use your breathing (or at least do not hold your breath) to help you create flow and let your body get a feel for moving downhill.

Also important is the sensitivity of your feet to the edge of the ski under your foot. Your feet are the sensors for the terrain. Variations and undulations of the hill are felt with the feet. The more sensitive you are to the pitch, steepness, quality and consistency of the snow, the less you have to work. This initial feedback comes from your feet and legs.

Once you have skied a couple of times this sensitivity to your terrain will become second nature. That's when you know you have your ski legs back.

# Early Season Lesson

Each new ski season brings excitement at the thought of hitting the slopes. When we think about being on the hill and making turns, the adrenaline begins to pump. Letting the excitement get in the way of our know-how is easy. We tend to forget where we are and what we are doing. For this reason, I think ski lessons are a good idea. A ski lesson will give us the skills we need to ski safely. It also cuts down on the time it takes to learn the same technique alone.

## Getting What You Want from a Lesson

We all want to polish our current technique as well as acquire new skills. Taking a lesson is more than just showing up and saying, "Teach me." Give some thought to what you want to get out of your lesson. Maybe you want to learn to ski more efficiently, or look graceful or have more control on steeper runs. Maybe you want to hone or improve your technique and make breakthroughs to the next higher level. It's a good idea to know where you want to be or what you want to get from a lesson.

If you do not know specifically what you want to get from a lesson, that's okay too. There is no such thing as a dumb question when it comes to your growth or improvement. Most instructors have a game plan or idea of what they will teach for a certain level or class. Don't be afraid to ask or let your instructor know what you want to get out of your time together. Also, during the lesson, make sure you get the kind of feedback or attention you want from your instructor. Most will be happy to give you additional thoughts or suggestions if you ask for them. This kind of communication will help create a successful outcome for your lesson.

Photo © Ben Blankenburg, courtesy Vail Resorts/Keyston

**Skiers taking a lesson at Keystone Resort**

# Early Season Extras

Every ski area offers incentives and special ski deals. For example, an early season ski package might combine lift tickets for consecutive days or weekends and ski lessons at a discounted price. The early season usually runs from the date the area opens until just before Christmas. Because the season is not yet in full swing, you may luck out and get the top-ranked or most experienced instructors. These individuals are much in demand and are booked solid with private lessons most of the season. Chances are you couldn't get them even if you wanted. Here's an opportunity to get the most for your money.

# Have Your Equipment Ready

Once you have decided to take a lesson, make sure that your equipment is in good working order before reporting to your class or instructor. There is nothing more frustrating than to have your binding pre-release or your foot slide around inside your boot when you are on the hill with an instructor. Not being prepared is a waste of time and money for you, your instructor and the others with whom you ski. Eliminate any surprises.

Taking a lesson early in the season will give you a chance to pick up where you left off last year. Your skill level and progress are equivalent to how much you know and how well you apply what you know. It is about using your body effectively to get your equipment to work for you. The sooner you get in touch with your ability, the sooner you set yourself up for the breakthroughs necessary to be an effortless skier.

# "CANI"

Some time ago, I read the book by motivator Tony Robbins called "Awaken the Giant Within." I was impressed with his energy, enthusiasm and the passion that seemed to leap off the page. The one thing that really stood out was his philosophy of "CANI." CANI stands for "<u>C</u>onstant <u>A</u>nd <u>N</u>ever-ending <u>I</u>mprovement." Skiing, like life, should be about growth and improvement. I feel it appropriate to apply "CANI" to skiing.

All of my ski life I've felt that improvement in skiing is a process. It's a journey, not a destination. The past few years have brought revolutionary advancement in ski technology. Recent innovations in ski design and boot technology allow skiers of all ages and abilities to break through to new levels of skill and experience new levels of enjoyment. These opportunities are available to everyone, but you have to look for them.

## Questions are the Key

If you are a serious skier or a skier who is serious about learning, CANI is the attitude with which you should approach your ski season. *The way to improve is to ask yourself questions about where you want to be.* How you get there will depend on the QUALITY of questions you ask. The more specific your questions, the better the results. By asking specific questions you direct your mind to think about the kind of skier you wish to be.

## Questions to Ask

*You can ask questions about the upcoming ski season:*

- Am I planning on skiing seriously this year?
- How many times will I commit myself to skiing each week? Each month?

- What means or methods will I use to improve my skiing?
- Will I take a lesson, clinic or workshop to brush up on my skills and prepare myself for the coming year?
- With whom do I want to ski with this season?
- Is there someone who can support me in my enthusiasm to ski?
- Is there someone with whom I can ski who shares my passion about the sport, and can help me to improve?

### Or questions about your physical condition:
- Am I mentally and physically prepared to ski?
- Am I doing or have I done any exercise to prepare me for the hill?
- Am I in shape?
- Will the level of conditioning support my ability-level as a skier?

### Or questions about mechanics:
- Is my equipment ready?
- Are my skis properly tuned?
- Are they waxed and sharpened?
- Have I had my bindings checked for proper function and release?
- Do my boots fit properly?
- Do I have any movement of my foot inside my boot when I make a turn?
- Am I perfectly aligned?

### Or questions about technique:
- Do I know how to tip or tilt the skis on edge to get them to come around?
- Do I know where or how to stand to make this happen?
- Do I control my speed on every turn I make?
- Do I know how to make my skis work for me?

- Do I know how to use the edge under my foot when making a turn?
- Do I use my breath, or do I hold it during a run?

Much of what you get out of the hill will depend on the type of questions you ask yourself about your skiing, and whether you are serious about your own improvement.

## A New Attitude

CANI is an attitude that relates to your performance. It means:

- Looking for the techniques or skills that allow you to be in control.
- Making your skis and boots work for you.
- Mastery of the terrain despite steepness or snow condition.
- Learning the idea of flow as you move from one turn to the next.
- Creating breakthroughs that will propel you to new and higher levels of performance.

CANI is knowing that your equipment works for you and allows you to get the most from your technique. CANI is committing yourself to a course of action and following through. With an attitude of CANI you will find yourself reaching new levels of excellence that you never thought possible.

# Intention

In the last section I talked about Tony Robbins philosophy of CANI, and how improvement can come about through the quality of the questions we ask ourselves about subjects ranging from the number of times you will ski during the season, to the type of skier you want to be, or the ability level you wish to reach.

## Have "Something in Mind"

Most skiers I talk to are serious about their skiing. Those who progress the most in the shortest period of time are the skiers who know what they expect from the time they spend on the hill. Whatever their level of ability, these individuals want results when they ski. Skiing well is important to them. I call this the "discerning skier." This is someone who wants to progress and recognize gains.

That is why I feel it is important to have "something in mind" when you go to the slopes. By that, I mean not just a goal, but what you intend to gain from each ski experience.

I think of the goal as the outcome, and your intention as the mental process it takes to reach that goal. As I mentioned in the last section, getting results from your skiing will depend on the quality of the questions you ask yourself. Asking a question focuses your mind on finding the answer. This puts the focus of your attention on where you want to be and how to get there. The more specific and particular you are with the question, the more specific and particular the answer will be.

Once you start skiing, set your intention for the results you want to achieve. When you set an intention, it programs your mind to work toward a finished product. When I teach a student to ski, I always ask "What do you want to accomplish?" or "Where would you like to be with regard to ability?" or "What would you like to be able to do because of this lesson?" The student then sets an intention for the outcome. Right up front the expectations of the student are clear. That way, it is not what the instructor wants for the student, but what the student wants for him or herself that becomes the focus for both instructor and student.

## Phrase It as a Question

When you set an intention that takes you toward your goal, it should come in the form of a question. And it should be as simple and specific as you can make it. What do you want to accomplish when you ski? Do you want more control on each turn? Do you want to ski more difficult runs with greater confidence? Do you want to feel the edge of the ski working under your foot? Do you want to make effortless, graceful turns and look good doing it? Or do you just want to have fun and forget the pressures of life for a while?

I find it important to ask a positive question rather than a negative one. For example, instead of asking yourself, "Why do I fall down every time I make a run?" or "How come I always go too fast?", you might ask "What can I do to have more control over my skis and feet on each run?" or "How can I control my speed on each turn?" Using a positive approach sets you up for a positive response.

## Be Mentally Engaged

Very often we don't set an intention because we don't know that we should, or we're afraid of not getting the results we want. We want our skiing to be a fun, mindless activity. That's when we get into trouble. Yes, skiing should be fun, but never mindless.

This is the equivalent of mentally "checking out." That is, not being "present" where you are or what you are doing. It's a dangerous state of mind. I call this the "sun on the face, wind in the hair syndrome." It shows up in the skier who is completely unaware. When distracted by another skier or obstacle, this skier is set up for a fall or injury.

If you are not mentally engaged or thinking specifically about your technique (i.e., your turns, where your weight is, how to engage the edge, controlling your speed, etc.) your mind goes blank when you get into trouble.

If you are serious about skiing and your personal progress in the sport, what you think about or focus on will largely determine how well you do. The more you know about what to do and when to do it, the more breakthroughs you will experience, taking you to new levels of ability.

# Beginner Skiing

If you have never skied before and plan to do so, take a lesson with a qualified professional.

## The Need for A Beginner Lesson

I was skiing recently with my son at a local area. I headed for the beginner slope and was dismayed at what I saw when I got there. First time beginners were trying to learn to ski without an instructor. These novice skiers, who had never been on skis before, would ride the short chairlift to the top and attempt to ski without knowing what to do. It was a dangerous situation, as they were all over the place with no idea of how to turn, slow down, avoid other skiers, or stop. I avoided a collision more than once with someone who was out of control.

If you are going to go out your first time on skis and "just wing it," think again. If you don't know what you are doing, there is a good chance you will hurt yourself, and an even greater chance of hurting someone else.

Am I saying there is no room to play, have fun or experiment without taking a lesson? Not at all. But your first time out, a ski lesson is a must. In the analogy of driving a car, if you don't know how to turn, use the brakes and stop, you're going to have an accident. The same applies to skiing. This is why a first-time ski lesson is a must - it will give you the fundamentals to slide, glide, change direction and stop. It's the best investment you can make for yourself and others who share the hill with you.

## What You'll Learn

The cost of a lesson is a small price to pay for what you get out of it. You will learn:

- The basic techniques for control

- About your equipment and how your skis are designed to work for you
- About balance - how to stand over your feet
- About the edges and the role they play in achieving control
- How to change direction, control your speed and stop
- The right way to get on and off a chairlift
- The right way to fall, and how to get up after you do. Learning how to get up correctly after a fall can mean the difference between having the energy to keep skiing, and being too exhausted or hurt to continue.

Photo by Byron Hetzler, courtesy of Harb Ski Systems

Harrison Harb (not a beginner) shows his stuff

Every resort that I know of offers a beginner lesson package that includes equipment rental (skis, boots and poles), lift ticket and cost of the lesson, all for one very low price. The reasoning behind this is that once you learn to ski you'll be hooked for life, so the low cost is the enticement to at least try it once. It's worth it.

A ski lesson is designed to be fun while learning, with an eye on safety. That includes the safety of others, too. If you know how to turn, control your speed and stop, you'll be able to avoid other people and objects. The worst way to get hurt is to run into someone or some thing (or vice versa). Learn from a professional ski instructor what you need to do to control yourself. You'll have a better first-time experience, and set yourself up for a great future in skiing.

# Ski Safety

Each year I start the season writing about preparation, fitness, technique, equipment or things to think about when you're on the hill. All of these subjects are really about ski safety. Ski safety is about responsibility and common sense. Each time I ski I see a number of people who have hurt themselves being carried off the hill in toboggans by the ski patrol. This is not my idea of a good time, especially when it's early in the season or it's your first time out on the hill for the year.

## Physical Preparation

Skiing is a physical sport. It requires effort. The better prepared you are mentally and physically, the better you will do.

Doing some kind of physical activity will get you ready for the coming season. Even if you have done nothing until now, it's not too late. A little bit of preparation will go a long way when you're on the hill. Getting your lungs and muscles working together will give you an "edge" both literally and figuratively. It will also reduce your chances of injury.

Photo by Craig McNeil

Craig prepares for the upcoming season

## Early-Season Snow

When ski areas open in October or November skiing tends to be limited, so use caution. Most resorts open select runs with man-made snow. Because man-made snow contains more water than natural snow, the ski runs get icy faster. Although the quality and consistency of the snow itself will be very good, it will become hard as more people use those runs and the snow gets skied off or pushed to the side. When the snow is hard or icy, make sure you maintain your balance over your feet and control your speed on each turn you make. The sharper the edge of your skis, the more control you'll have in these conditions.

As natural snowfall increases, more runs will open. Be careful: these runs can be deceiving. First, the quality and consistency of natural snow will be different from the runs with man-made snow. Natural snow is softer and therefore easier to ski. The danger lies in what's underneath. Even if the runs appear to have adequate coverage, there can be debris, i.e., rocks, grass, twigs, stumps or other obstacles, beneath the surface that can trip you up. If you are skiing a run that has been recently opened and has had little skier traffic, watch out. Sometimes there is a layer of air between the ground and the upper crust of snow. Unless the run has been boot or ski packed, it's easy to hook a tip under this layer. If you are carrying any kind of speed and you bury a tip, you can do serious damage.

The typical scenario on an early season ski day is that all runs are prepped and groomed the night before. This means the best skiing is found early in the day. When the snow has been groomed, it is more consistent. This consistency allows you to feel your skis and edges evenly on the snow as you go from turn to turn. By late morning more skiers will fill the slopes. With this increase in skier traffic, the snow will get skied up or scraped off. Late afternoon brings hard, icy conditions.

## Start the Season Safely

Use your first couple of ski days each year to do two things:

1. Get your "ski legs" under you.
2. Become familiar with your equipment again.

If you have skied fewer than three seasons, do yourself and the other skiers on the hill a favor and take a lesson. This will enable you to review the basics and establish your confidence and control from the start.

Early in the season, skiing will be limited to mostly green or blue runs. Use this time to concentrate on your turns and technique. Start your day early when there are fewer people on the hill and the snow is best. Take a break midmorning to gather yourself and give your muscles a rest. To avoid the crowds, eat an early lunch or ski until 1:00 p.m. or 2:00 p.m., then quit early.

Rest when you are tired and stop when you've had enough. Fatigue slows your reaction time. If you continue to ski when you're tired, you're setting yourself up to get hurt. Once you know you're tired, don't push it. I've seen skiers too exhausted to make a turn or control their speed turn around and go up for "one last run." This is foolish and dangerous. It's not worth getting hurt trying for one more run. When you need to rest, stop on the side of the trail. When you take off, look uphill so you can merge with the skiers coming downhill. Be aware of the other skiers around you. Sometimes it's the other guy you have to watch out for. Look out for skiers who are obviously out of control. If they hit an icy spot when trying to stop, they will take out anybody who's in their way.

## Know Your Limits

There is a sense of anticipation, wonder and excitement that comes with every ski experience. But out-of-control levels of energy and enthusiasm are cause for concern. Lately, I've noticed an attitude of "throwing caution to the wind" at numerous ski resorts.

Use common sense and good judgement. Don't be stupid. Peer pressure, skiing terrain or conditions beyond your ability, or skiing with friends who force you to keep up, are all acts that qualify as stupid.

Advanced skiers who expect beginners or intermediates to keep up with them should know better. It should be the other way around. *The advanced skier should always ski at the pace of the skier with less ability.* It is absolutely foolhardy to expect a less experienced skier to try to keep up with someone who is more advanced. And this is even more true when skiing with a group of people. This is not golf, and the ski slopes are not fairways where a foursome can play together well despite their different handicaps and abilities. *Ski at your own pace on ski runs suited for your ability.* Offer to meet the more advanced members of your group in the lift line or where the runs converge if you choose to ski an easier trail.

## Which Runs can You Handle?

Next, know your ability. If you are not sure of your ability, take a lesson to find out what you know (or don't know) and which runs you should be skiing.

Skiers of all abilities enjoy skiing
the groomed runs at Keystone

There are four different levels of difficulty you can choose to ski: green (circle), blue (square), black (diamond) or double black diamond. The following are general guidelines:

- If you make a wedge and turn to both sides, try the beginner hills.
- If you slide your skis at the end of each turn after making a wedge, you can handle most green runs on a mountain.
- If you make a wide track parallel turn, steer both feet and slide the skis through your turn, you can handle all green runs and most smooth, easy blue runs.
- If you make a quick parallel turn and have good edge control, you will probably be comfortable on most blue and groomed black runs.
- If you are comfortable in moguls and are sure of your feet, skis and edges, you can probably handle most black and double black diamond slopes.

## Hazards on Groomed Slopes

If it is still early in the season, the best skiing will be found on the runs with man-made snow groomed the night before. The groomed slopes will have the most consistent snow over the run. However, once the groomed snow is skied off or pushed to the side of the trail, the run will get hard or icy. With these conditions, it is easy to go fast and lose control. If you fall on such hard or icy surfaces you can slide just as fast as if you were standing up. This is dangerous and can be deadly.

For some reason, momentum seems to dictate that, once you fall and start sliding, you may end up going head first down the hill. And, if you go off the trail carrying any speed at all, you are headed (pardon the pun) for serious injury. Witness the number of injuries and deaths related to skiing each season and you will find that many are a result of this "slide for life."

# How to Avoid Injury

So, how do you avoid putting yourself in such a situation?

- First, use common sense. Don't leave your brains with your shoes.
- Know which slopes you can handle and ski only those runs.
- Check which runs have been groomed for that day. A groom sheet or list of groomed runs will be found either at the top or bottom of the chairlift. These runs will give you the most consistent snow over the course of your run.
- If it has been three or more days since the last natural snowfall, chances are the runs that have not been groomed will have hard or icy conditions.
- Keep your speed constant. You need to keep your speed under control, especially when the conditions are limited. Your speed should remain consistent on each turn. You should be going the same speed into the turn as when you finish. If you make wedge turns your overall speed will be slower. If you make parallel turns your overall speed will be faster. Find a speed that is comfortable for you and maintain it.

With a little bit of technique, common sense and courtesy you'll not only have more fun but keep yourself from getting hurt.

Adrian Crook demonstrates his flexibility

# "Inflex™"

The better your physical condition, the better you'll perform on skis. For this reason I recommend an exercise program to prepare you for the coming season.

A few years ago I injured my lower back lifting weights improperly. I've been working out most of my life so I should know better. Since the injury, I've had recurring back trouble on a regular basis.

Never before in my life have I had any back problems. Not until I had the injury. Suffice it to say I've been looking for a program to alleviate my chronic back problems and increase my flexibility.

## Meeting Adrian Crook

In early November I had the opportunity to ski with the Professional Ski Instructors of America (PSIA) demo team at Copper Mountain. It was there that I met Adrian Crook, movement specialist and consultant to PSIA. Adrian has been working with professional athletes for a number of years using his movement program called "Inflex™."

The first thing that strikes you about Adrian is his remarkable flexibility. For a man in his mid-forties his degree of stretch is extraordinary. "But," says Crook, "the flexibility is a by-product of the Inflex™ Program. This program is designed to increase your range of motion and maximize your movement regardless of your sport."

Indeed, this is evident from his client list, which ranges from the Detroit Lions and San Diego Chargers to professional golfers and other world-class athletes.

## The Inflex™ Program

"The basic fundamentals of movement will always apply regardless of the sport," says Crook. The Professional Ski Instructors of America picked up Adrian as a movement consultant after hearing about and experiencing the positive results of his program.

"Regardless of an athlete's ability, they will eventually reach a plateau. In order to continue to grow they must enhance that foundation so it will support that growth," says Crook. "Inflex™ does this by focusing on the natural range of motion of

*Preparation*

the body while incorporating balance and flexibility." The Inflex™ Program brings an athlete closer to optimizing his or her full potential.

Inflex, as PSIA has discovered, is ideally suited for skiing. Most athletes work from what they know and are trained to do, and, although they may be accomplished in their given sport, tend not to use their full range of motion. Many PSIA D-team members have found that working the body through a full range of motion that includes flexibility is an ideal form of conditioning for skiing.

Adrian's philosophy is that life is movement and that we are all athletes no matter what we do for a living. The same things that will make you a stronger skier will also make you stronger in the workplace, at home or just around the garden.

## Inflex™ and Injuries

Inflex™ also works for those who have injured themselves and are looking for a nonthreatening way to grow stronger after an injury. Crook has documented case after case in which people who were scheduled for surgery to repair an injury, have been able to forego the surgery because of using the Inflex™ program. Crook's feeling is that to be healthy, you must have healthy movements. The goal of Inflex™ is to optimize the potential for those movements and achieve longevity.

## Personal Experience

Since meeting Crook I've done the program on a daily basis. Within a week, my re-occurring back spasms were gone. Within three weeks I had already seen other noticeable improvements. I plan to keep it up. I'll report back and let you know how I'm doing!

*For more information about Adrian Crook'*
*Inflex™ program, call 1-800-463-5393.*

# Ski Awareness

Ski awareness is one of the most important yet leas talked about or understood concepts in skiing Awareness is simply *being conscious of where you are and what you are doing when you are on the hill.*

## Be Conscious of Yourself and Others

Because of the excitement and adrenaline rush tha skiing brings, it's easy to put common sense on hold and leave your brains with your shoes. The

---

### SKIER'S RESPONSIBILITY CODE

1. Ski under control and in such a manner that you can stop or avoid other skiers or objects. Excessive speed is dangerous!

2. People ahead of you have the right of way. It is your responsibility to avoid them.

3. You must not stop where you obstruct a trail or are not visible from above.

4. When entering or merging onto a trail or starting downhill, yield to others.

5. All skiers shall use devices to prevent runaway skis.

6. Observe all posted signs and warnings. Keep off closed trails and out of closed areas.

7. Prior to using any lift, you must have the knowledge and ability to load, ride and unload safely.

---

exhilaration and sensation of moving downhill with the sun on your face and the wind in your hair becomes too much when you realize, too late, that you're out of control, and you end up hurting yourself or someone else. Ski Awareness is more than common sense, although that's not a bad place to start.

When you are conscious of yourself and your surroundings you can be responsible for the well being of yourself and those around you. It's a safety issue. You don't want to run into anybody or anything and vice versa, and yet, sadly, it happens all the time.

## Manage Technique and Terrain

Skiing is about know-how. If you don't know what you are doing or when to do it, you can hurt yourself or someone else very seriously. This is why the Skier's Responsibility Code exists. You have to know how to manage yourself with regard to both your technique (how to turn, slow down and stop) and your terrain (skiing runs or trails that are within your ability level).

If you haven't skied since last season and it's your first time out, or if you're just plain rusty with regard to know-how, take a lesson. It's okay to admit you've forgotten or it's been awhile. A qualified instructor can do wonders for your skiing in a short period of time. He or she can help point out what you may be doing wrong, show you the right technique and build your confidence at the same time. Avoid being taught by a well-meaning friend or spouse. Although their intentions are good they don't have the knowledge, expertise or language to give you serious help.

# More Safety Tips

Here are a few more safety tips for managing yourself and the mountain safely.

- **Avoid tunnel vision.** Be aware of other skiers and snowboarders in your peripheral vision. This eliminates the surprise if someone skis in front of you.

- **Stop or stand to the side of the trail when catching your breath or waiting for others.** I've seen more people get bowled over because they stopped in the middle of the trail and someone behind them did not (or could not) stop.

- **Look uphill when trails merge.** Skiers on the trail moving downhill have the right of way when trails intersect. It could be hazardous to your health if you cut in front of someone (who has tunnel vision) and doesn't see you until it's too late.

- **When skiing with children, ski behind them.** This is best when it's crowded or congested or when you are coming down off the hill at the end of the day. Skiing behind them allows you to run interference and minimizes the risk of someone running into them from behind. ◆

# Chapter 2

# Accelerated Skier Performance System

Harald Harb, creator of the
Accelerated Skier Perfomance System

# Accelerated Skier Performance System

Back in 1992, I predicted that the face of ski instruction would be changed forever. Well, that prophecy has finally come true. Recently I had the opportunity to visit Telluride Ski Resort where I caught up with my old friend, Harald Harb. Harb is the man I predicted would change ski instruction as we know it for the better.

After serving in Winter Park and Aspen, Harb has landed in Telluride, where he works as a trainer and consultant for the ski school. According to Harb, this is "the first completely integrated biomechanical teaching and alignment system." Telluride is the first area that has completely embraced the "Accelerated Skier Performance System" as he calls it.

## A Fully-Integrated Teaching and Alignment System

I wasn't clear what Harb meant by "fully-integrated" until I had the opportunity to experience it first hand. I watched a beginner go from a "never ever" skier to a solid parallel skier in little more than an hour.

Harb's primary emphasis is that balance in skiing must be redefined. Lack of balance can hold a skier back from his or her next breakthrough. "We don't use a snowplow or wedge with the System, we use the Primary Movements to teach balance and edge control. Standing on two feet in a wedge, or using both feet to turn, is not balance," Harb says. "Two footed skiing is the reason for the skier's rut. It's dead-end skiing that leads to frustration and lack of progress. The more you stand on two feet to make a turn, the deeper your rut."

## The Two Parts of the System

The Accelerated Skier Performance System is a complete system that encompasses the entire ski spectrum from your equipment to your technique.

It's broken down into two major areas:

1. Alignment
2. Primary Movement Patterns.

*Alignment* deals with your ski boots; the right boots with the right fit, custom insoles and canting, and how you stand on your skis when in your boots.

*The Primary Movement Patterns* are the movements you use to make a turn.

"Both the Alignment Process and the Primary Movement Patterns are designed to help an individual ski at an optimum level," says Harb. "The purpose is to bring a skier to a higher skiing level in a shorter period of time. These movements allow the body to work in the simplest, most efficient and effective manner when making a turn."

Harb created the Accelerated Performance Skier System after a lifetime of work with ski racers including Olympic gold medalist Tommy Moe, U.S. Ski Team member Hillary Lindh, and World Extreme Skiing Champion Kim Reichelm. The System is based on the science of how the body moves.

## The Importance of Balance

When you use the Phantom Move, also known as the "Lift and Tilt," you establish balance and use it to make your turn. You bring the skis to the edge in the most efficient manner by moving your feet laterally instead of steering or rotating the foot or lower leg. Rotating or steering your skis will disrupt your balance. And once your balance has been disrupted, you must regain it before you can find your edge and make a turn.

## Advantages of the System

"Traditional ski teaching systems are not based on balance," Harb says. "The skills taught by these systems create terminal intermediates and stagnate skiing. Skiers reach a level of frustration and either get tired or give up. The purpose of this system is to create an experience of quality that you can't get anywhere else." I attest to this in that I have seen noticeable improvement in my own skiing each time I work with the Primary Movements.

The folks at Telluride Ski Company are sold on the System. Everyone from ski and rental shop technicians to upper management are supportive of it. "I was very impressed with how effective and efficient the Accelerated Skier Performance System was," says Annie Savath, Director of the Telluride Ski School. "All our instructors are training to become Accelerated Skier Performance ski teachers."

The beauty of the Accelerated Skier Performance System is that a skier learns more quickly, and is up enjoying the mountain in a shorter period of time. Because the movements are more efficient, you use less energy, resulting in a safer ski experience that puts less demand on your body, especially your legs.

Without further ado, let's look at Part 1 of the Accelerated Skier Performance System, Alignment and Ski Boots. ◆

**To order Harb's book** *"Anyone Can Be An Expert Skier,"* **call 1-800-553-4040**.

# Chapter 3

# Alignment and Ski Boots

Photos © J.D. Quakenbos, courtesy of Dalbello Sports Manufacturing

DalBello TX 808 Ski Boots

Bow Legged Skier

# Alignment

Alignment is a critical part of the Accelerated Skier Performance System. In the same way that you align the tires on your car for maximum mileage and performance, you align your knees over your feet to maximize ski performance. Skiing with perfect alignment reduces the amount of tension, torque and fatigue in your hips, knees and legs for

*Alignment and Ski Boots*

peak performance regardless of age, ability or experience.

## Structural Imbalance

Do you stand perfectly flat on both skis or do you favor one side? Most skiers naturally favor one side. That is, we get more edge from one ski than the other, and use this stronger side each time we need to slow down, control our speed or stop. The problem with skiing this way is that you expend a tremendous amount of energy. And once you are tired you set yourself up for getting hurt. You also put a great deal of unnecessary stress on your legs and knees.

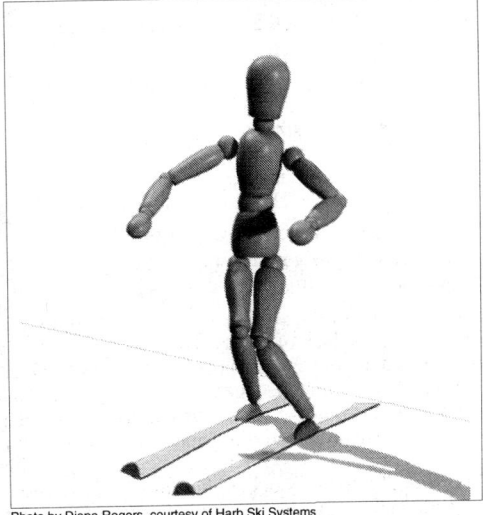

Photo by Diana Rogers, courtesy of Harb Ski Systems

**Knock-kneed Skier**

The reason a skier favors one side is because of *structural imbalance*. In a lifetime of skiing, I've only known one or two skiers who were naturally in perfect alignment. That means the rest of us must do something to compensate for this imbalance and put us in the best position for skiing. And that something is "alignment."

## The Alignment Process

Alignment is a process that puts your knees in a neutral position over your feet, so you can edge the skis equally from side to side. A skier who has been aligned and is able to stand with both skis flat is in the most desirable (and capable) position for skiing. Once you are aligned, skiing is as easy as it is effortless to tip or tilt the ski to engage the edge and make a turn.

Alignment encompasses five areas and consists of:
- Having the right type of boot
- Proper sizing
- The right fit
- Custom insoles
- Canting (also called "alignment strips").

This five-part process is designed to eliminate any imbalance and put you in a neutral position so you have equal edging from both skis.

It is common for the average skier to blame himself or herself for a lack of ability. And yes, experience does play a major role in ski performance, but that's not all there is. In experimenting with this process for myself and others, I have seen changes that were immediate, definite and recognizable.

In the following sections we'll break down the alignment process and take our first step at learning *How To Ski The Blues And Blacks (without getting black and blue)*.

# Ski Boots

Ski boots are your single most important piece of equipment in skiing. Think of the ski as an extension of your foot. Your boot is the link between your foot, the ski and the snow. The more control you have over your feet, the better performance you'll have with your skis on the snow. The better the fit of your boot, the more responsive will be your turns. It is your ski boot that will, to a large extent, help you grow or hold you back as a skier.

Photo courtesy Tecnica

The Tecnica Explosion boot

## How Ski Boots Should Fit

Your ski boots should fit tightly or snugly without hurting your feet. There should be no pressure points or sore spots when your feet are in your boots. **You should not have to "get used to"** any foot cramping or discomfort, and there should be no pain or pressure points whatsoever. If there is, see a good boot fitter or think about changing boots.

If you are trying them on, start with boots that are a full size smaller than your street shoe. If they are too snug, go up a half size until you find the ones that seem right. Make sure you seat the heel in the pocket of the boot to alleviate pressure on the toes. (It's a good idea to trim your toenails to alleviate any discomfort or possible bruising that might occur if they are too long.)

## Renting "Demo" Boots

You apply tremendous pressure to your feet when you make a turn, so it's difficult to know how a boot will perform until you actually try it on the hill. Most ski shops offer a "demo" program that will allow you to try a performance boot and will deduct the price of the demo from the purchase price of the boots. This is the best way I know to find the boot that will work best for you. However, since a ski boot liner will pack out differently for each foot that skis in that boot, be aware that you'll have a more accurate fit once you purchase your own boots. I look at the right ski boots as an investment that should last you a number of years. It's critical to your ski performance that you get boots that are going to work for you.

***Most, if not all, beginner boots <u>do not work</u>, especially rental boots!*** Ironically, the boots that are made for the skier who needs them the most are the least reliable. While they may feel good on your feet, they do not help your skiing. Rear-entry boots give the least reliable performance, while front-entry boots are better in terms of comfort AND increased performance.

## The Right Fit

The number one rule of skiing is that <u>your feet should not move inside your boots</u>. Any excess movement of the foot inside the boot will result in a lack of edge and ski control. It's the biggest problem for the average skier, but most are not aware of it. If your foot slips or slides around inside the boot, it diminishes your balance and your ability to effectively use the edge of your ski. The tighter and more secure the fit of the boot, the better your ski control and performance.

Photo courtesy of Nordica

Nordica Grand Prix racing boots

## Custom-Fit Boots

The foot can move inside the boot in a number of ways: heel lift, up and down, movement over the top of the foot, and sliding back and forth from heel to toe. When it comes to ski boots, there are two factors that will enhance performance: one is the right boot with regard to size, the other is fit. A custom fit includes orthotics or insoles as well as working with a boot fitter to eliminate any excess movement. (I'll spend more time talking about the importance of custom insoles and how they affect performance on page 62). You can eliminate excessive movement with heel pads to secure the heel, or adhesive foam strips over the top of the foot (put them between the shell and the liner).

## Why Fit is Important

When you move your foot, the ski should respond. As we will learn in the upcoming chapter on Primary Movements, you start a turn by tipping or tilting the inside ski to engage the edge of the outside ski. As you begin to move down the hill, you increase the pressure of your foot inside your boot against the edge of the ski. If your foot moves inside your boot, you will lose your balance and the ability to hold the edge when you tip or tilt at the beginning and most critical part of your turn. Instead of engaging the edge, you'll twist your body or shoulders to make the turn and bring the skis around.

It is the pressure from your entire foot (the arch, ball and big toe) that allows you to hold the edge through the turn after you tip or tilt the ski on edge.

Once you get the fit of your boots right, you'll be surprised at how much more sensitive your foot feels on the snow. You'll have more control of your skis and edges than you ever thought possible.

# The Right Boots:
# Rotary vs. Lateral

Rotary boots or lateral boots? If you read any of the ski magazines lately these are the terms used to describe boots or, more accurately, how certain ski boots perform. As tends to be the case within skiing circles, these ski boot descriptions can be confusing for most skiers.

**A rotary boot** describes *how a skier has to move* in order to make the boot perform. With a rotary boot, the ski will skid or twist before it comes to an edge. This action puts torque on the knees and legs.

With **a lateral boot** the skier is standing in a neutral position over the foot. Rather than twisting or steering as with a rotary boot, tilting or tipping laterally to the edge of the ski is all that is needed to engage the ski and make a turn.

The difference between the two types of boots comes down to efficiency or economy of motion. The less energy you expend to put the ski on edge and have it come around, the easier it is to make a turn. It's also less taxing on the legs, especially the knees. *Proper alignment in conjunction with a lateral boot can completely eliminate the knee problems which plague many skiers.*

Two criteria mark the difference between these two types of boots:

- Amount of forward lean or flex built into the upper cuff
- The "ramp angle."

The **ramp angle** is the height or lift of your heel, measured in degrees, on a plane from the heel to the toe. A high ramp angle puts your foot in a position similar to wearing high heels.

## Rotary Boots

The higher the ramp angle and the greater the forward lean of the upper cuff, the more "rotary" or skidding movements will result when you try to turn the ski. This boot style is a remnant of the days when you would turn by driving the knee into the boot to make the ankle flex, to load the front of the ski, to make the ski bend, to steer the foot, twist the leg or roll the knees to put the ski on edge, and ride it through the turn. That is a rotary boot.

## Lateral Boots

A lateral boot has a lower ramp angle and a cuff with less forward lean, if any at all. All that is needed to put the ski on edge is a tipping or tilting. Gone is the effort or force needed to make the boot flex to get the energy or weight on the front of the ski.

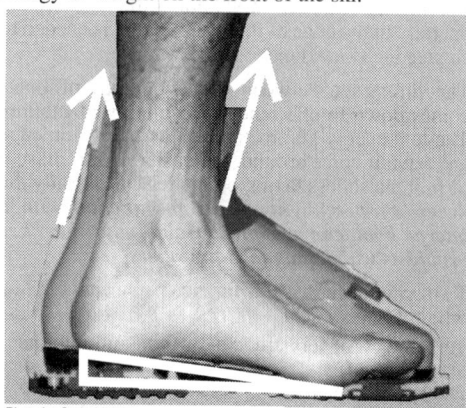

Photo by Craig McNeil

Cross section of foot inside a ski boot. The white triangle represents the ramp angle of this boot. The white arrows show the angle of the boot's cuff.

*Alignment and Ski Boots*

# How to Tell the Difference

So how can you tell the difference between the rotary boot or a lateral one? Most people don't know how.

- Start with the footboard - the removable piece that sits under the liner inside your boot. You can take it out and measure the height of the heel over the toes. Five degrees or less is considered a low ramp angle, more than five degrees a high ramp angle.
- A boot with a lot of forward lean contributes to the rotary motion of a high ramp angle boot (regardless of the ramp angle or whether you are knock-kneed or bowlegged). The higher the ramp angle, the more cant or shim you will probably need under your binding to bring you to a neutral position (or a flat ski) if you are knock-kneed.
- Most rear-entry boots (where you put your foot into the back of the boot) and most older ski boots are rotary boots. What they offer in the way of comfort or fit, they lack in performance or ski response.
- Some newer boots, but not all, are lateral boots that put a skier in the most desired position for skiing.

Try on different models and compare. You can tell which ones have you stand flatter and more erect than others.

# The "Worse For Wear"

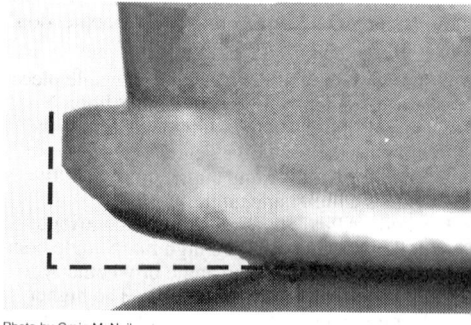

Photo by Craig McNeil

Worn Ski Boot. Black line shows original contour.

I was in a neighborhood ski shop recently, checking out the latest equipment, when in walked a lady with an older pair of boots and a brand new pair of skis. As I stood at the counter, I couldn't help but hear the conversation and notice her equipment, particularly her ski boots. They were a pair of 10-year-old Salomons. She wanted to have her old ski boots adjusted to fit her new skis. The problem was the bottoms of her boots - the toe and heel were so worn down that they resembled the shape of a rocking horse. I think the ski shop mechanic did a good job of explaining the potential danger of these boots. It is definitely something I feel needs to be addressed.

We've already talked about the importance of your ski boots. They are the link between your foot, your ski and the snow. Boots that have extensive wear cannot help but perform poorly, and can be dangerous as well.

## Why Worn-Out Boots Can be Dangerous

If you look at your ski binding, the plastic area where your toes will rest on the ski is called the "AFD" or anti-friction device. It is like a smooth piece of Teflon® that helps the boot release from the binding during a fall. Ideally, the AFD on the binding and the bottom of the ski boot should be smooth, without wear, so as not to inhibit the action when the boot releases from the binding. Hence, the name anti-friction device.

Over time the bottom of the boot gets worn, picks up gravel or dirt and scores or scuffs both boot bottoms and the AFD. The wear and tear can have the bottom of your boot looking more like the bottom of a canoe than a flat surface (as was the case with the lady mentioned above). Ski boots with soles as worn as this can fail to release when you take a fall.

## Problems with Old Bindings

If you are skiing on skis with bindings as old as your boots, you may compound the danger. Road grit and salt can erode the springs of your bindings and inhibit their ability to function. What you have is a combination of boot and binding that will fail to release when you fall.

## Some Solutions

It is a good idea, therefore, to have your boots and bindings checked to make sure they are in proper working order and will release when needed. This means having the binding adjusted not only to your boots, but for your current weight and skiing ability.

Many models of ski boots have replaceable parts for both the toe and heel once they wear down. If yours are well worn, you might think about replacing the worn toe and heel areas. It's a good idea to order those parts when your boots are new. The older your boots are, the less likely it is that the manufacturer still makes those pieces or that you can find them.

# Custom Insoles

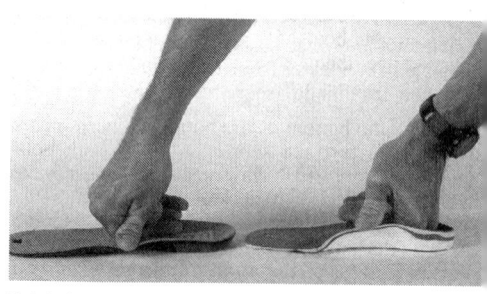

Photo by Carl Scofield, courtesy of Harb Ski Systems

Custom insoles, semi-rigid vs. hard

I have said that your boots are your single most important piece of ski equipment. Alignment starts with boots that fit properly, are snug to your feet and allow no excessive movement within them.

The best way to secure the foot and eliminate movement inside the boot is with a custom insole or orthotic. Using an insole is the second step in the alignment process. Most insoles (also known as "footbeds") are made of plastic, foam, silicone or cork, are molded to your foot and sit inside the liner of your boot.

A good custom insole does four things:

- Supports and distributes your weight over your entire foot
- Increases the response when pressure from the foot is applied to the ski or edge
- Allows for the natural movement to occur within the ankle when applying the pressure from foot to ski
- Makes your boots more comfortable.

If you want to excel at skiing, you must have a custom insole in your boots. All the pros and top competitive skiers have them. It can help take you from a frustrated intermediate to a confident advanced skier, and move you from the blue runs to the black ones. Having the true fit that only an insole can provide can improve your skiing by 50% or more.

## Types of Custom Insoles

There are two varieties of custom insoles, hard and soft (which is actually semi-rigid). I favor and recommend the softer insole, usually made of foam or a lighter plastic.

The softer version supports the foot, but has more give when you stand on it. The give allows for the natural movement of the ankle and is something you NEED to have when you ski. It increases the sensitivity under the arch and ball of your foot as you stand on the foot through the turn. Another benefit of the softer or semi-rigid is that it gives you better shock absorption with more even weight distribution of the foot inside the ski boot.

When your foot is supported by a rigid or super hard insole, it locks up the ankle and deprives the foot of the natural ankle movement you need to engage the edge and ski. This can also be true if you have a soft insole that's been built up or excessively "posted" under the foot so as to inhibit this ankle motion.

The insole should give under the arch without flattening out.

## Where to Get Custom Insoles

Custom insoles are available at most specialty ski shops or custom boot fitters and run from $50.00 to $200.00 or more. These usually last for many years and are interchangeable if you switch boots. I recommend working with a ski shop specialist who can help maximize your fit with your insoles. They are well worth it and will make a noticeable difference in your skiing.

If you have problem feet or past injuries relating to your feet, knees or hips , you might want to consult a podiatrist. They can help design a footbed or orthotic that will take into account any special problems you might have or have had in the past. Although they are more expensive, you can minimize or alleviate most knee or ankle problems with the right insoles.

If you don't currently have a pair of custom insoles, look into getting some. They can help skiers of all levels and abilities. If you've already put down the money for a hard insole, don't worry about it. A custom insole, whether hard or soft, is better than no insole at all. As I mentioned the harder insole limits the foot to some degree, but will still serve the purpose. If you are shopping, try a softer version. You'll be pleasantly surprised at how much more effective your skiing will be from such a simple process. If you've been in a rut, want to make serious breakthroughs or are looking to take your skiing to new levels, think about custom insoles. They might be the answer you've been looking for!

# "I Can If I Cant"

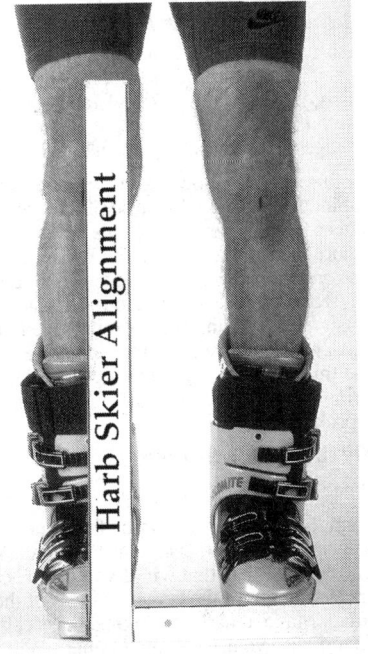

Photo by Carl Scofield, courtesy of Harb Ski Systems

Neutral alignment as measured in ski boots.

Canting is the fourth and final step, and brings the process of alignment full circle. Canting is what you do to bring about a neutral stance that allows you to stand perfectly flat on both skis. This is the method in which *the foot is shimmed under the binding to bring you to the desired position.*

## The Importance of a Neutral Stance

To be a masterful skier, in command of yourself, your skis, your boots and the mountain, you must be balanced, from a neutral skiing stance on each ski. When you make a turn you want to be able to get equal edge from the right ski as well as the left.

Most of us are either bow-legged or knock-kneed (or a combination of both). Because of the way our legs and knees line up over our feet, we tend to favor one side more than the other. We use what we consider our "stronger" side and to do most, if not all, of the skiing work for us. We use our stronger side to establish our rhythm, control our speed or stop. Because we have an easier time engaging the edge, we use this side in our skiing for everything we do. Favoring one side over the other is the root cause of most problems in skiing.

## Analyzing Your Stance

The knee is the key to analyzing your stance.

- Find the center of the mass of the knee, (not the center of the kneecap, necessarily). You can buy calipers that will give you an accurate measurement of the center of mass of the knee. Make a mark at the knee mass center. Stand with your feet slightly apart. With a carpenter's framing square, line up the mark you have on your knee and see where it falls in relation to your boot.
- Look at the toe of the boot and you will see a ridge in the center of the toe from when it was molded. Ideally, the straight line of the framing square from your knee should be one-quarter inch *inside of the toe center when*

*standing on a perfectly flat surface.* (This is the only accurate way I have found to measure cant.) I know it's hard to believe, but one degree or even one half degree can make a big difference in your skiing.

## How Adjustments are Made

If you are inside of that one-quarter inch mark, you need canting to build up the inside edge under the binding. Outside of that mark, build up the outside edge. Adjustments are made with "cant" or "alignment strips" that look like a wedge are thicker on one side than the other and are accurate to one-quarter of a degree. The question is whether you have been properly measured and if you know whether you need the cant strip on your inside or outside.

## Where to Get Help

A good boot fitter or specialty ski shop can help you with canting. Call ahead first and ask how they measure and what they charge. *Some ski shops use a platform device that "rolls" you to that neutral position.* **These don't work.** I've yet to find one that could give me an accurate measurement (and I'm as bow-legged as they come). You must stand on a perfectly flat surface in your ski boots when you take the measurement from the knee to the floor with a straight edge. This is the most effective, if not the only, way I've found to accurately take this measurement.

Although canting is technical in nature, it's one of the best things you can do to improve your skiing. There is no greater feeling in the world than being able to stand in a neutral position and tilt your ski to the edge and have the ski respond with little or no effort.

## A Note On Canting The Boot Cuff:

Do not confuse canting the boot cuff (the upper part of your ski boot) with making an adjustment with a shim under the binding. We are talking about two different things here.

Many companies make ski boots with an adjustable cuff that you can adjust to tilt or lean inside or out. This adjustment is meant to follow the shape of your leg. It is not enough to adjust only the cuff of the boot. Some unknowledgeable boot fitters try to use the boot cuff alone to affect the angle your leg strikes the ski boot. The cuff adjustment itself will not bring you to a neutral position in your stance. You must make the cuff adjustment *in conjunction* with the shim under the binding. *The adjustments you make with the cuff are meant to complement your stance, not alter it.*

The cuff adjustment should be made to follow the contour of your leg. If you are bowlegged, the cuff should tilt out; if knock-kneed, tilt the cuff in. A good boot fitter at a custom shop can help you get this adjustment right. This is the only way I recommend using the cuff adjustment.

# Feeling Unsure

If you are a beginning or intermediate skier do you ever feel shaky or unsure when you make your turns? In the last few sections I talked about the importance of boots that fit properly, and how you can customize and neutralize your stance with insoles and canting. But what happens when you get to the hill and you have rented equipment for your ski vacation, or you are using second-hand boots and you don't feel comfortable with your turns? What do you do then?

## Problems with Rented or Second-Hand Boots

I was skiing at Keystone Ski Resort in Summit County, Colorado recently, and I was surprised to see the majority of skiers making weak, unstable turns. It was common to see a skier make a turn where the skis would "flutter" or wobble throughout. I use this term to describe the way the skis appeared to move through the turn. It almost looked like the skis were waving. It is this activity that can leave you unsure of your ability to control your speed or turn at all.

Most lower-level skiers don't have enough experience to know what should happen or when they are "doing it right." So they feel good on some turns and not so good on others. The good turns come haphazardly and are not as consistent as they would like them to be. The first thing you want to do is *tighten your boots.*

## Tightening the Buckles Increases Control

Remember that the ski is an extension of your foot and your boot is the connection between the two. When getting fitted for ski boots in the rental shop, Skiers often buckle their boots loosely so they are comfortable while walking around, standing in line and riding the lift. They may forget about their feet when they arrive at the top of a ski run and begin down the hill.

But, when they start down the hill, that comfortable buckle adjustment backfires. The boots must be buckled more tightly for skiing. How the boots fit and how tightly they are buckled determines how much control you have over your skis and the quality of your turns.

You apply tremendous pressure to your feet when you make a turn. The simple act of tightening your boots prior to your run will give you greater control. And that is what skiing is about - more control.

## Proper Fit and Adjustment of Rental Boots

If you have to tighten your buckles to the last catch, your boots are too big. There is not much you can do once you are on the hill, short of renting a smaller pair at the rental shop.

Your feet should not fall asleep, and there should be no pain or discomfort when you tighten the buckles. If there is, loosen the buckle to relieve the pressure in that area. Once your boots are tight, you should have more control on each turn.

Ski instructors need to be aware of this, too. I am amazed to see students who are having a tough time who simply need to buckle their boots a notch or two tighter.

Skiing begins from the ground up, and most problems begin and end with the feet. So the next time you are feeling insecure or unsure of your turns, check your boots. You will be surprised at how a simple adjustment can make all the difference. ◆

# Chapter 4
# Primary Movements

# Introduction

Primary Movement Patterns are the second half of the Accelerated Skier Performance System. Alignment works with your stance and how your knees line up over your feet, while *Primary Movements are the movements you use to bring your skis to the edge and make your turns.*

The Accelerated Skier Performance System is a movement-based system that activates the *kinetic chain* to achieve results.

## The Kinetic Chain

The various parts of the body are linked together sequentially, very much like the links of a chain. If you shake one end of a chain, the energy is transmitted from one link to the next until it is absorbed or dissipated. Basically, if you shake the chain at one end, the other end moves as well.

Now, say the chain has links that are small on one end and become progressively larger toward the opposite end. If you shake the small end, the movement doesn't go very far up the chain before all the energy is absorbed. But, if you shake the chain at the large end, the movement transfers to the small end quickly and suddenly.

In his book *Anyone Can Be an Expert Skier*, Harald Harb says, "The body reacts similarly in many ways... If you use the upper body you will create large movements. Many skiers must use their upper bodies to make skiing movements. This causes constant disruption of balance to the smaller links. The foot and ankle are small, fine-tuning joints with tremendous balancing and adjusting capabilities. If configured properly, they allow balance to be controlled from the base up. The upper body won't

have to make large balancing adjustments, because
t can absorb the movements of the lower leg
without losing stability."

When the kinetic chain is used in skiing, it allows
the foot and ankle to be the primary control center.
The Accelerated Skier Performance System
incorporates the principles of the kinetic chain into
what are known as "Primary Movements."

## Primary Movements

These movements have never before been linked
together to produce a parallel skier from scratch.
Experts and good racers use these movements,
although they may have never consciously learned
them, since the movements are not taught in
traditional ski teaching systems. It may be the
reason you've never heard of Primary Movements
before. While you may not necessarily want to ski
like a racer, these movements have proven to be the
most effective and efficient way to achieve
maximum results in the shortest period of time.

With Primary Movements, the basic movements
you learn as a beginner are the same ones you will
use as an expert skier, only with more precision and
refinement of your balance and edge control. I
should also mention that you don't have to be
aligned for the Primary Movement Patterns to
work, but alignment in combination with the
Primary Movements will bring you to the highest
level of skiing in the shortest period of time.

## Use the Same Movements from Day One

The "Phantom Turn" that we'll talk about on page
102 is, in my opinion, what the Primary Movement
Patterns are all about.

Traditional methods of ski instruction have, until
now, taught dead-end skills. You learn a skill or

maneuver only to discard it in favor of a different technique or skill as you progress and develop in ability.

With the Primary Movement Ski Teaching System you use the same movements from day one through your entire ski career. Think about it: most sports or activities always refer back to the basics, even at the most advanced level. You use those basic techniques as building blocks that take you to higher levels. Martial arts, gymnastics, tennis and golf are but a few examples. It is through constant practice, honing and refining those initial skills and movements, with each step taken, that eventually brings you to the advanced levels. Now for the first time in ski teaching history is such a method of instruction revealed.

As you become more skillful and adept at using the Primary Movements, you will learn to refine them. And once refined, you'll make faster, quicker and more dynamic turns than you've made before in your life.

# Balance

Why do people fall when they ski? More often than not it is because they lose their balance. So, finding and keeping your balance should be your prime objective as you make your way down the hill.

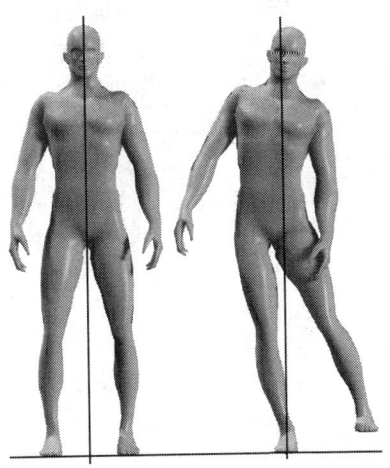

Effects of wide stance on balance

Now, you might think this whole topic is rather silly. Lose your balance and you fall. But I don't think it's that simple, nor am I trying to be patronizing. I see skiers of all ability levels who fall. They may catch an edge, drop a hand, sit back or simply mentally let up, and then it happens. They lose balance and fall. So balance is critical, not only in maintaining but making breakthroughs in your level of skill. Balance should be the number one goal for skiers of all abilities.

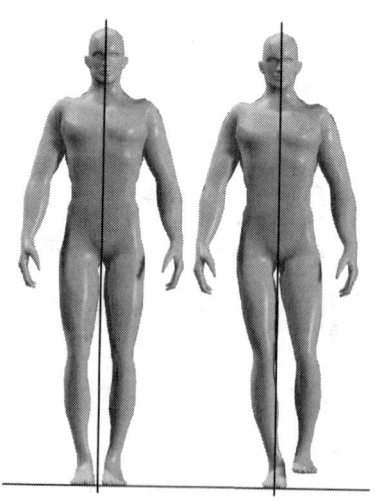

Effects of narrow stance on balance

## Not Taught in Traditional Instruction

Balance is not taught in traditional ski teaching methods. While individual instructors may talk about or even teach balance exercises, balance for the most part is not considered. I know, because after 25 years of ski teaching, balance was something taken for granted and rarely, if ever mentioned.

Let me state that standing on two feet to make a turn is not balance, nor does it teach you skills for balancing. I'm the first to admit that in the past when I taught skiing, even I emphasized a two footed stance, steering the feet with weight on the outside ski as the means to make a turn. I used the argument that lifting the inside ski was wrong and created an *imbalance at the most critical part of the turn.*

Better, I thought and taught, to stand on two feet and steer the feet and drive the knees, and in the seventies and eighties that was how you skied. But with the technological advances of skis and boots the way you learn to ski has changed as well. Standing on and steering both feet to make a turn is a thing of the past. Let me show you what I mean about balance.

## Balance Exercise

Try this exercise:

- From a traverse going across the hill, lift the uphill ski off the snow and *balance on the downhill leg.*
- Traverse the full distance from one side of the slope to the other. (Look uphill and make sure you don't cut in front of someone skiing downhill).
- Keep the uphill ski completely off the snow without setting it down.

If you've never done this before you will be surprised. One, how difficult it is to do and two, what little balance you have. But there is hope. Balance is a skill and each time you use your balance in a concentrated manner it will improve.

This balance exercise is also used to indicate whether you stand in a neutral position over your feet. Rare is the person who can stand on the downhill foot, stay balanced and track straight across the hill. If your alignment is off and you are not standing in a neutral position, your balance ski will not track straight in the traverse.

- If you are knock-kneed or pronated with your feet and not in alignment you'll be standing on the big toe edge and your ski will track into the hill.
- If you are bowlegged or supinated with your feet and not in alignment you'll be standing on the outside or little toe edge of your balance ski where your ski will want to track or steer down the hill.

The goal is to have the ski track straight across the hill in your traverse without any variation.

## Imbalanced Stance and Canting

Most of us will find that we have an easier time doing this exercise with one leg than the other. The leg that is easier for us is what we may consider our "strong" or "favored" leg. We use or favor this leg over the other because of an imbalance in our stance.

The balance exercise that we just talked about is the way to tell where and how you stand on your skis. This is also the first indication that you might need "cants" to correct your imbalance and help put you in a neutral stance. As I mentioned on page 65, one half or even one quarter of a degree can make a considerable difference in the skiing of those who are that discerning and sensitive.

If you are knock-kneed, put a cant under the inside edge for less edge and a more neutral position. Put it under the outside edge if you are bowlegged and need more edge. Play with it and see what works for you. The kind of boots you ski in and how your legs line up over your feet will determine how much cant you need. With older ski boots, because I'm extremely bowlegged, I was off a neutral position by as much as three degrees. In skiing, that's a lot. With modern technology and newer ski boots I'm down to one degree or less.

I usually carry a pocketful of canting strips of varying thicknesses with me when I ski. If you don't have access to the canting strips, you can make a shim out of a yogurt container or similar plastic. The top of a yogurt container measures about one quarter degree. With a yogurt container I cut each shim two inches long by a quarter inch wide. I place the strip under the heel, either on the inside or the outside edge, between the boot and the binding. You can use different material and play with the degrees of thickness. Make sure the boot sole is clean and there is no ice or snow buildup.

## A word of caution

I only use these strips to "dial myself in" and give me an indication of the most neutral stance for my own skiing. You may want to put duct tape on the yogurt strips to hold them in place. If you put more than two degrees between the boot and the binding it can affect or load your binding for pre-release. Once you are sure of what degree cants or alignment strips you need, they should be mounted <u>under your binding</u>.

# Phase I: Beginner Exercises

*The movements in Phase One are designed for first time beginners and are to be done in ski boots without skis.*

There are three movements a beginning skier will learn in ski boots on the snow, without their skis. They are:

- Tipping or tilting,
- Side stepping and
- Walking the "S" line.

All skiing action starts with the feet, so building awareness of the foot is important. The more precise and accurate you are with only your ski boots, the better you'll do wearing skis.

## Tipping or Tilting:

- Stand on a flat surface in ski boots and start tipping the boots from one edge to the other. Always start by tipping to the little toe side first.

- It is important to feel the feet and what happens when tipping or tilting the ski boots from one edge, to the flat and then to the other edge. Starting with the feet will move the whole body. This is the basis for lateral movements.

- Make sure you don't pivot or twist your boots.

- Do the movement slowly and feel what happens to the feet inside the boots when you tilt from side to side.

- Try it standing on one leg. Keep your balance on the stance leg as you tip from inside to outside boot edge.

Photo by Darren Jacklin, courtesy of Harb Ski Systems

**Tip as far to one side as possible without losing balance**

## Side Stepping:
- Move to a point on the hill where you have a slight incline.
- Position both boots going across the hill.

- Next, tilt or tip the boots toward the hill and use a side-stepping motion to move up the incline.
- While standing with the ski boots on edge (and in comfortable balance) flatten the boots to the snow. This is the precursor to using the feet to edge or flatten the skis.
- Make sure you keep the angles of both boots the same when you side step.
- Try this exercise on both sides.

## The "S" Line:

Next, you will learn to walk the "S" line. This is one of the most important series of movements in skiing and it is the foundation of all future skiing movements. Walking the "S" line will help you feel the boot as a platform under your foot as your walk in the snow. The exercise is designed to have you tip or tilt from one edge of the boot to the other. See the photo sequence on pages 84 and 85 to help visualize these movements. The idea is to alter your balance from your little toe edge to your big toe edge in order to make an "S" line.

- With a ski pole, draw an "S"- shaped line, down the hill, in the snow.
- Stand with your feet on either side of the line at the top of the "S." (Fig. 1 two pages ahead)
- Tilt your right ski boot, , along the little toe edge of the free (downhill) foot as you follow the top of the "S." Your left boot (stance foot) tilts toward the big toe edge and follows the lead of the other leg. (Fig. 2 two pages ahead)
- Take small steps as you follow the line with your feet.
- Shifting the direction of the edges of each boot starts you into a new turn. Shift your balance

to the other edge of your boots on the lower half of the "S." Your right ski boot tilts toward the big toe edge and your left ski boot tilts towards you little toe edge.

## Additional "S" Line Notes:
- You may want to use your ski poles to help keep your balance and aid your movement.
- Try to work the movements laterally along the boot edge rather than with large steps forward.
- Start every tipping move towards the little toe edge. (See Fig. 2, 2 pages ahead)
- Feel the pressure changes inside the boot with your feet as you follow the line.
- Avoid standing or tipping on the big toe side.
- Focus on the tipping or tilting action of the foot and ankle inside the boot as you follow the "S" line. (As in Fig. 4, 2 pages ahead).
- Be aware of the little toe side of the boot of the inside foot as you "walk the line."
- Don't rush the movement, but feel the pressure of the foot against the inside of the boots and how it shifts from one side to the other as you follow the line.
- Allow the upper body to tip or tilt in direct proportion to your ski boots.

Once on skis, these stepping movements will create the edge change from one side of the boot edge to the other and provide the sensations you will need once you have your skis.

Photo by Darren Jacklin, courtesy of Harb Ski Systems

Figure 1 - Standing in middle of "S" with
feet in neutral position. This is the
critical point in the exercise.

Photo by Darren Jacklin, courtesy of Harb Ski Systems

Figure 2- Lift right foot and tilt it
toward its little toe side.

Figure 3 - Take small steps

Figure 4 - Tipping laterally as you
follow the "S" line.

# Phase II: Beginner Exercises **with** Skis

*These movements are designed for first time beginners and are to be done on skis.*

These next movements, which you learn with skis on, are designed to teach balance and edge awareness. It is important to start these basic walking exercises (once your skis are on) by using very small steps, just as we did in ski boots.

Again I need to emphasize that the Primary Movements in Phase One and Two are designed for first time beginners. These are the fundamental movements you will use once you start skiing. The same movements you are learning here will stay with you your entire skiing life, even through advanced or expert levels.

Note: There are two terms with which you should be familiar, traverse and fall line.

- *Traverse* is the position you take with your skis going across the hill.
- The *fall line* is the path along which gravity would pull a ball down the hill if it were released.

# 1) Circular Movement:

- On a flat surface, move your ski tips to the right, one ski at a time.
- Keep the tails of your skis stationary.
- Continue stepping the skis around until you have completed a circle. Notice that the ski you move is on a slight edge.
- Now do the same movement in the reverse direction. Always focus on moving toward the little toe edge and match it with the other ski.

See photo sequence on the next two pages to help you visualize this movement.

Photo by Darren Jacklin, Courtesy of Harb Ski Systems

Circular Movement, starting position

*Primary Movements*

Circular Movement, ending position

## (2) Stepping up the slope, releasing to a traverse:

- **Side stepping:** Side stepping up the hill is the same that we did on the flat, only now with skis.
- The difference is that the ski that moves uphill has to be rolled or tipped to the little toe or outside edge.
- Take five or six steps uphill. Using the poles for balance as you do this, extend the lower (downhill) leg to move your body over the uphill ski.
- Place the downhill next to the uphill ski when you step and make sure you keep both skis going across the hill to prevent sliding forward or back.
- Practice this in both directions.
- **Gliding Movement:** This is where we first learn to change direction.
- After you can move up the slope a few steps, come back to the flat by stepping the tips only slightly downhill.
- Use your poles to hold you in place as you step your tips downhill.
- Release the poles and allow yourself to glide forward toward the flats.
- As you move toward the flats, step your skis back up the hill until you stop.

# (3) From a Traverse, Stepping Up and Down to make a Turn:

- Now let's step back up the hill and build on that gliding movement.
- From a traverse, move the tips down the hill.
- Slide for a few feet, then step back up the hill to slow down.
- When you have almost stopped, begin to step down the hill again. Do this until you feel comfortable with your forward movement.
- This time step ten or fifteen feet up the hill from the flat.
- Use your poles to hold you in place as you step the tips downhill and in the fall line.
- Pick up the poles and start down the slope.
- As you approach the flat, step your skis into the hill until you stop.
- Make the steps as small as possible, until you stop.
- Practice this to both sides.

Do not hurry your movements. Be precise with your steps and *focus on the <u>quality</u> of your movements as you do these exercises.* The Primary Movements we've done in phases one and two are primarily for beginners, but are just as important and critical for experts. The lack of understanding of these simple principles demonstrates why we have developed generations of terminally intermediate skiers. Up until now, no one has focused on the **quality** of movement for beginners. A very simple movement, or movements done well can make all the difference in learning, especially when you refine them.

# Phase III: The Phantom Move

Primary Movements are the movements that you use to make a ski turn. These Primary Movements teach you skills that build on one another. The skills and movements you learn as a beginner are the same ones you use as an expert, obviously with more precision and refinement. The "Phantom Move" is really what the Accelerated Skier Performance System is all about.

When you first try the "Phantom Move," do it from a traverse. See the figures on the next two pages to help you visualize this movement.

- Use a slope that is smooth and gentle in pitch so you don't go too fast.
- Release the edges and flatten both skis to move forward across the hill.
- As you traverse, lift the tail of the uphill ski (Fig. 1 - upper right)
- Tilt the ski and boot toward the little-toe side. (Fig. 2 - lower right)
- Keep the tip of the uphill ski on the snow (Fig. 3 on page 94). The downhill leg is the "balance" or "stance" leg and the uphill ski is the "free" foot.
- Try to keep the feet closer together and the lifted ski as close to the snow as possible (See Fig. 3). Focus more on the tilt than the lift.
- Stand so that your weight is evenly balanced over the entire foot of the "stance" leg.

Photo by Grafton Smith, courtesy of Harb Ski Systems Fig. 1

Photo by Grafton Smith, courtesy of Harb Ski Systems Fig. 2

*Phase III: The Phantom Move* 93

Photo by Grafton Smith , courtesy of Harb Ski Systems  Fig. 3

Keep the tip of the lifted ski on the snow,
focusing more on the "tilt" than the "lift."

When you pick up the uphill ski and tip toward the
little-toe side, it causes you to balance on the
downhill foot, and the pressure or weight will shift
to the big-toe side of the downhill ski. Once you are
on the edge, the ski turns into the hill.

This subtle movement is all you need to make the
skis turn into the hill. Rather than force the ski to the
edge, which will cause it to keep going straight,
keep the ski flat and allow it to turn into the hill.

*Primary Movements*

If you've read any of the ski magazines you may have heard about using the inside ski and doing a "Lift and Tilt" to make a turn. The "Lift and Tilt" and the "Phantom Move" are one and the same and are patented moves from Harb's Accelerated Skier Performance System.

## How it Works

Lifting and tipping the uphill ski to the little toe side changes the angle of your hips as well as the edge angle of your "stance" (downhill) ski. You move to the edge of the stance leg in a tilting or "lateral"

Photo by Grafton Smith, courtesy of Harb Ski Systems

Stance foot firmly engaged, free foot raised

**Weight and balance over stance
leg has created arc**

motion. This is the action that allows you to turn. You don't need to twist, steer, pivot or "rotate" the downhill foot. You don't need to press the knee forward or use any pressure or force into the boot.

The beauty of the Phantom Move is that this technique will work regardless of whether you are on a conventional or hourglass ski. When you first try the Phantom Move from a traverse you haven't made a turn yet. You should finish in the same direction as you started. The hardest part of the

Photo by Grafton Smith, courtesy of Harb Ski Systems

Turn is completed using Phantom Move

Phantom Move is standing and balancing on one leg
as you turn into the hill. Work into doing the
"Phantom Move" slowly and progressively. Allow
yourself the opportunity to feel what happens when
you do "the Move." Find your balance first, before
you do the "Lift and Tilt" with the uphill ski. Each
time you do the "Phantom Move" you will find your
balance increases.

*Phase III: The Phantom Move*     97

**Benefits**

Once you begin to use Primary Movements in your skiing you will begin to see a number of benefits.

- Because you don't twist or steer your knees and legs there is less stress on your joints.
- As you learn to use the stance leg you will see your balance increase.
- As your balance increases, so will the strength in your legs due to the demand put on them to balance through the turn.
- As your stance becomes stronger you will find you are more stable on each turn.
- Because you are more efficient, you will experience less fatigue, which will allow you to ski longer. This also translates into a safer ski experience.

The Accelerated Skier Performance System uses one simple movement to combine all actions of effective skiing. This simple approach makes it faster and easier to learn to ski.

# Balance in the Turn

Balance, as we talked about on page 75, is an often neglected aspect of our skiing. It is rarely talked about or used as a critical component to aid us in our turns. Most skiers don't think about balance, or do so only after a fall.

Balance in skiing can be used to create stronger more efficient turns, and help make breakthroughs necessary for advancement. Balance isn't talked about because, on the whole, it's not really considered. Standing on two feet isn't balance for most people. But standing on one leg is.

# What Happens When You Balance

Photo by Darren Jacklin, courtesy of Harb Ski Systems

Harald Harb demonstrates the
balance exercise discussed below

Try this exercise:
- Stand up with both feet slightly apart.
- Lift one foot and ski.
- Stand and balance on the other.

What happens when you balance on that leg? Your
ankle wobbles as you search for the position that
allows you to stand on that leg without falling over.
What's going on with your leg as you stand on it, is
that the muscles in the ankle and on either side of
the lower leg work in conjunction with one another
to help you find and maintain a balanced position.

*Balance in the Turn*

## Improving Your Balance

Each time you do this and engage those muscles your balance will improve. Over time as your balance improves and gets better it becomes more precise. When you first do this one-leg balance exercise, you're all over the place. In time you are able to balance with a minimum of leg wobble or body movement.

The same thing happens when you apply these principles of balance to your skiing. Each time you force yourself to balance on your stance leg you refine your balance. Initially the muscles in your lower leg are working overtime to find your balance, but after you do it a few times it gets easier and takes less effort to maintain a balanced position.

- From a traverse, pick up the uphill ski and balance on the downhill ski as you make your way across the hill.
- Once you are aligned and standing in a neutral position, you can concentrate on your balance when you are moving.
- At first you may feel awkward and lose your balance, or only be able to keep the ski off the snow briefly.
- Do it again. Make sure you are not picking up speed or going too fast.

Your balance will improve each time you do this. As your balance improves, so, too, will your ability to feel the edge of the ski you are standing on. You will also become more aware of your feet and skis.

## Add the Phantom Move

Now try doing the Phantom Move at the end of the traverse as you turn into the hill.

- Continue to use the first part of the traverse as a balance exercise.

- At the end of the traverse tilt the free foot (uphill ski) to the little toe side.
- Maintain your balance on the stance leg until you turn into the hill and stop.
- Keep doing this from a traverse and increase the steepness (down the hill) slightly as you do.
- Maintain your balance on the stance leg. It will help if you spread the weight over the entire foot of the standing leg.
- If you lose your balance or your foot cramps from all the attention, stop and start again.

It will get easier each time you do it. You are in essence doing a "fan" (also known as a "garland"). Increase the steepness until you are comfortable doing it straight down the fall-line. Again the run should not be so steep that you have to worry about going too fast. Start and finish the balance exercise going in the same direction.As you continue to perform the Phantom Move avoid the temptation to twist, steer or rotate the balance (downhill) leg. *If you twist or rotate the upper body to force the skis to turn, you will disrupt and lose your balance.*

Balance is the critical aspect of this exercise, and the reason you begin it from a shallow traverse and gradually increase the steepness each time you do it. The more you work on your balance in this manner the more it will improve. The end result will be a stronger, more confident turn.

# Phase IV: The Phantom Turn

Photo by Grafton Smith, courtesy of Harb Ski Systems

Turning all the way into the slope

On page 92, we talked about how to do the Phantom Move. The movements that you use to do the Phantom Move are the same ones you use to do the "Phantom Turn." From the traverse we used the uphill ski , or free foot, to "Lift and Tilt" to the little toe side, creating a change of direction into the hill. Now we incorporate these same movements into a complete direction change known as the Phantom Turn.

## Initiate the Turn with the Inside Ski

When you do the Phantom Turn, you use the inside ski of each turn as the free foot to "Lift and Tilt" to the little toe side. You don't need to think about weighting (or turning, or steering,) the outside ski; even though this is the ski you stand on when you make the turn. *The inside ski initiates the turn and the outside ski is the balance or stance leg.*

When you lift the tail and tip to the little toe side of the uphill ski, it forces you to stand and balance on the downhill leg and changes the angle of your hips and the edge angle under your downhill foot.

## Beginning the Next Turn

When you finish a turn and are ready to begin the new turn,

- Stand on your downhill ski, begin to release the edges and flatten both skis. The downhill ski will now become the inside ski.
- Once you release the edges, and do the Phantom Move you transfer **balance**. *This is different than shifting your weight.*
- When you transfer balance, you create a higher level of performance and the sensation of control. As soon as you perform the Phantom Move, you engage the new inside or uphill edges of both skis. The more you emphasize the tilt of the inside ski to the little toe side, the quicker you'll come through the turn on your stance leg.

## The Role of the Stance Leg

The outside leg of the turn now becomes the stance leg. From this position you must maintain your balance over the entire foot. You are essentially creating a platform on which to stand supported by your ski and the edge underneath. This is why the alignment of your knees and feet over your skis is so crucial. If you are not in a neutral position that enables you create equal edge control from both sides, you'll have a hard time maintaining your balance and edge on the stance leg.

## Change to the Phantom Turn

What may seem confusing about the "Phantom Turn" is that you are using the *inside* ski to make the turn. This is probably contrary to everything you have heard or been taught before in ski school. It is a paradigm that is hard for most seasoned skiers to accept. After years of putting weight on the outside ski, the Phantom Move contradicts what we've learned or been taught by traditional ski teaching methods. This is what makes the Primary Movement Teaching System so revolutionary and unique.

With the "Phantom Turn" you are moving to the ski edge in a lateral motion. You don't need to twist, steer or pivot the outside/downhill foot or leg. These are rotary movements and will completely contradict the Phantom Turn. Doing these movements will cause the leg to over-rotate and force the tail to skid and cause you to lose balance and control on your stance leg.

When you first learn the Phantom Turn, the movement you use for picking up the inside ski and tilting to the little toe side will be exaggerated. As you become more comfortable with those movements you can tone them down. Once you use the Phantom Move to make your turn, be sure to keep your hands away from your body and out to each side. This will help maintain your body position and balance on your stance leg as you come through the turn.

# Phase V: Phantomizing

If you've been using the Phantom Turn in your skiing you'll agree how remarkable, and yet how simple and effective, it is for making a turn. The best part is that, not only does your balance improve, but your turns become stronger. And, the stronger your turns, the more confident you'll be as a skier. This is important if you want to break out of the ranks of the intermediate and into the realm of the advanced or expert skier.

## Refining your Moves

As you become more adept at the Phantom Turn, you will want to refine the movement of the inside or the free foot. When you "Phantomize" it is not apparent that you pick up the inside ski. At an advanced level you are still doing the Phantom Move, but without lifting the inside ski off the snow. Instead it becomes more of a "brushing" action of the ski over the snow as you tilt to the little toe side. As with the "Phantom Move," the action of tilting to the little toe side establishes proper body movement that brings the ski to the edge and allows you to ride it through the turn.

When you first perform the Phantom Turn, it's necessary to exaggerate the movement of the Lift and Tilt. As you find your balance and get a feel for the movement, let's begin to refine it.

## Breaking Old Habits

If you are a seasoned skier with many miles or years under your feet, the hardest aspect of the Phantom Turn or "Phantomizing" will be breaking the old habits you've built up over a period of time.

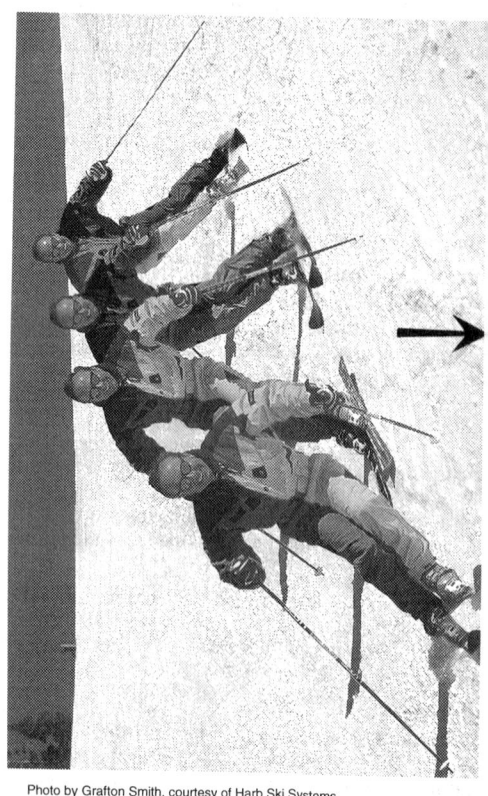

Photo by Grafton Smith, courtesy of Harb Ski Systems

Linking short-radius turns

Yes, the weight is on the outside ski, but only as the stance leg upon which you balance through the turn. It is the inside ski that you use to make your turn. Avoid the tendency to collapse the stance leg and drive the knee through the turn. There may be that old urge to steer the outside foot or leg into the turn instead of using the inside ski. Rather, lengthen or extend your stance leg throughout the turn.

### Find Your Rhythm

After you become more experienced at "Phantomizing" the turn, look for the rhythm that will result from using this technique. There is an effortlessness that will come once you begin to put your turns together with this process. Maintain a rhythm, "Phantomizing" each turn as you move down the slope. The sooner you tilt the free (inside) foot, well before you start the new turn, to the little toe side the more quickly you'll move into your turn. Continue to lengthen your stance as you tilt to the edge of the stance leg. Maintain your balance through the turn.

# Phantomizing on Advanced Terrain

In the last section we talked about the process of "Phantomizing" your turns. Now it's time to apply this process to more difficult terrain. When you ski runs that are steep or bumpy, go more slowly to get the feel of using the inside ski to begin each turn. If you learned how to ski using nothing but the Phantom Turn and Primary Movements, you are way ahead of the rest of us. If you were weaned on traditional ski teaching methods, the tendency will be to resort back to techniques that are tried and true for you, even if they are ineffective.

By the time you get to this level in skiing, you should be fairly confident in yourself and your ability. As with the Phantom Turn, begin the use of the inside ski as soon as you finish the old turn. If this sounds confusing, think of using that inside ski to begin the new turn as soon as you can. *The key to success on more difficult terrain is to keep the stance leg on the ground.* This is especially critical in moguls and we'll talk more about that in detail in the chapter on mogul skiing.

## Do Expert Skiers Need Primary Movements?

I divide the use of Primary Movements into two categories:

- Knowledge and use of the Primary Movements
- Use of these movements in varied terrain.

Photo courtesy of Tecnica

An advanced skier "Phantomizing"

After a lifetime of using and instructing traditional ski teaching methods, I recognized the effectiveness of Primary Movements at the beginning and intermediate levels, but questioned their effectiveness at advanced levels. Every time I had the opportunity to ski with Harb I would drag him out to the steepest, bumpiest terrain I could find, and grill him on the on the application of Primary Movements in critical terrain.

What I didn't know was that Harald Harb grew up in the Canadian Rockies, skiing some of the steepest and most difficult off-piste conditions imaginable. It was here that Harb would perfect and refine the techniques that became his basis for the Accelerated Skier Performance System. When I initially skied with Harb, he'd ski these conditions with a relish that I couldn't believe. It seemed he had an easier time skiing double black diamond terrain than a blue or green run. Suffice it to say he never lost his composure, and looked just as at home as if he were on easy runs.

It was here that I discovered the true essence of Primary Movements. In my search for the perfect turn, I was able to witness what Primary Movements were all about: the preparatory steps that would lead to the application of the Primary Movements for all mountain skiing.

## Importance of Balance in Advanced Skiing

In the early sections on Primary Movements we talked at length about balance; how to get, keep and improve it. Once you are secure in your use of the Phantom Turn and are Phantomizing your movements, it's time to take them to the mountain. Regardless of the conditions, whether steep, icy, crud, mush, bumps, powder or any other off-piste (ungroomed and inconsistent) condition you can find, the Phantom Turn remains the same.

On more difficult terrain, balance on the stance leg as you initiate the turn is critical. While you are still doing a Phantom Turn, it's not as obvious. Brush the inside (free) foot lightly over the snow as you tilt to the little toe side. Think of the movement with the inside foot as a "lighten-ing," without picking it up. You can almost keep the inside ski on the ground as you release the edge from the old turn and tilt to the little toe side. It is the action of tilting the free foot that is important, as the Phantom Move is almost imperceptible. Pull the free foot and ski toward the stance ski to avoid a wedge turn entry.

## Use of the Hands

The hands at this point will determine the success of your turn. Keep them up and away from the body to each side. You should be able to see them in front of you. Hold the ski poles out in front with the ski baskets held off to the side in front of you. The analogy is that of holding an ice cream cone just before you take a lick. Your hands will actually support the movements you create with your lower body. The hands must be kept up with your forward momentum. Flex only the wrist and hand to bring the pole forward. Any action with the arm or shoulders will throw you off balance.

Phantomizing the ski is a faster, more efficient, less tiring way to make a turn, for all skiers, in all terrain. Once you grasp the concept of using the inside ski, you can begin making turns that are as effortless as they are exhilarating. ♦

# Chapter 5

# Hourglass Skis

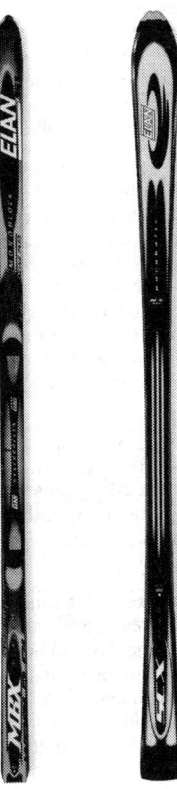

Photo courtesy of Elan

The Elan MBX Slalom on the left is a traditional ski. The SCX Mono on the right is an hourglass ski (also known as parabolic or shape skis.)

# Hourglass Skis: What Are They?

Hourglass skis are the wave of the future. Do you own a pair yet, or have you skied on them yet? If you haven't seen or are not familiar with hourglass skis, they resemble regular skis, but have a wider, fatter tip and tail, a narrow waist where the binding is mounted, and look like an hourglass. Hence the name. They are also known as "parabolic," or "shape" skis.

## Why Change the Shape?

The ski is constructed in such a way as to have the design or "shape" work for you. They are meant to make skiing and the process of learning to ski quicker and easier. They reduce the time it takes to learn how to turn and get you up on the slopes enjoying the mountain. I think this revolutionary technology has given the ski industry a new outlook on the future of the sport. These skis make skiing not only easy, but effortless.

The beauty of the hourglass ski is that it works for any level skier, from beginner through expert. How is this? When you tip the ski, the edge takes over. With little thought and no effort, the shape of the ski does the work once you put the ski on edge.

## Do They Really Work?

When I see someone skiing an hourglass model, I usually ask what they think. The response is almost the same each time - tried them one day and bought themselves a pair the next. All said that their skiing improved by at least 50% immediately. I've skied with professional skiers who said they found these skis the most versatile ever made and that they would never ski on anything else!

When these skis were first introduced they were met with a lot of skepticism. Were they another fad or gimmick, or could they do as promised? As more skiers of all ability levels began to embrace the technology, the ski industry as a whole began to take notice. Now, they've been embraced by the entire ski world!

Are you frustrated, or have you reached a rut or plateau in your own skiing? If so, the hourglass skis might be just the thing for you. It's hard to believe that a funny-looking ski could take all the work out of the sport. But they do, and without tripping you up.

If you haven't investigated them for yourself, do it now. After you've tried them you'll wonder why you waited so long.

# Making Them Work For You

Hourglass skis are here to stay. How many of you reading this book are currently skiing on hourglass or parabolic skis? An increasing number of skiers are now using hourglass skis. It seems that every article about skiing relates to learning to ski on these new skis. If you are not skiing on these new hourglass model skis, it can make you feel left out.

Whether you are skiing on conventional skis or the new hourglass shape, you still have to apply the principles of making a turn. The turn is made with the foot and ankle transmitting pressure over the entire foot, as you tip or tilt the ski to engage the edge.

## The Old Way

In previous days of ski instruction skiers were taught to do two things to get a conventional ski work for you:

- Make the ski bend;
- Ride that bend or arc through the turn.

To bend the ski, you had to drive the knee forward, flex the knee and ankle simultaneously, and load or pressure the front of the ski. This was the action you needed to make a conventional ski carve. It took a tremendous amount of physical energy and technical know-how.

## The New Way

With the hourglass design, wide at the tip and tail and narrow under your foot, skiing is simplified because the ski does the work for you. You still want to use the edge of the ski under your foot, but because of the design, you don't need to load or pressure the front of the ski. With such a dramatic arc, when you tip the ski on edge, the shape of the ski takes over for you. It's easier and takes less effort. And, I think, this is why the hourglass skis have taken off.

The hourglass skis are so popular that most ski resorts throughout the country now use them in their ski schools. They offer classes and have them available for all ability levels. The beginner will find the basics come more quickly; the intermediate skier will waste less energy managing the mountain; the expert will find quicker edge response with less wasted energy. They get a student learning and turning at a faster rate.

## Making the Change

But be forewarned, you naturally want to work harder than you have too. And that's more out of habit than anything else. The tendency is to steer the feet and force the ski into a turn. Instead, *use your Primary Movements to tip the ski on edge and let it make the turn for you.*

If you are knock-kneed and always on your inside edges, it's critical to get your boots canted to put you in a neutral position with equal edging from side to side. See page 65 for more information.

It takes a clearing of the mind and a bit of gearing down to let the ski do the work for you. So you have to start slow and feel how the ski wants to work under your foot. The sooner you let go and let the skis do the work, the sooner you'll enjoy them.

If you haven't tried hourglass skis yet, you owe it to yourself. If and when you have a chance to try a pair, by all means take advantage. You will notice the difference immediately. It will be one of the best skiing decisions you've ever made!

**Note:** If you don't ski very often, or your skiing is limited to a one or two week vacation each ski season, you might be better off renting both boots and skis for your visit to the mountains. Most of the rental ski boots made within the past few years are designed to work with the new hourglass skis. They have a lower ramp angle than your old boots, and will give you a better fit as well as increased performance. It also eliminates the need to lug your ski equipment with you from home.

## To Carve or Slide?

If you've read about hourglass skis or skied on them yourself, you know they make skiing easier. But you may get the impression that while it is easy to put the skis on edge and make them carve, that is all they can do. What most people don't know, or, at least those who are not familiar with them, is that you *can* ski them like conventional skis. It is possible to flatten the hourglass skis and make them slide just like a conventional ski, and just as effectively put them on edge and make them carve.

Photo by Grafton Smith, courtesy of Harb Ski Systems

Release to Sideslip

## The Need for Edge Control

In skiing you need to be able to do either. Edge control comes from our feet, as we talked about in Phase One of our Primary Movements. When you begin skiing more difficult terrain - steeps, bumps, trees or powder - there is less margin for error. You need to have control over your feet and edges to manage this kind of terrain. If you can't control your edge, you can't control your speed. Plain and simple!

# To Change from Edge to Flat

But the reverse is also true. If you are always on your edge without the knowledge or ability to flatten the ski, you'll have a hard time controlling your speed on steeper runs. It can be very frustrating if you cannot flatten the ski when necessary.

In Phase Two of our Primary Movement patterns we learned how to "sideslip." This is how you control your movement from the flat to the edge of the ski.

- From a static position with your skis going across the hill, release and flatten the edges of both skis. Hold the slide.
- Now, tip or tilt the edges back into the hill. Try it to both sides and feel how effortless it is to release or engage the edge.
- Keep your hands forward and upper body facing your direction of travel.
- Avoid twisting or turning the upper body when you release or engage the edges. This will create a rotary motion cause the skis to "wash out" and leave you skidding, off balance and out of control.

Now try the same from a traverse, moving across the hill. You are NOT making the turn, but simply releasing the edge, flattening the skis and tilting your feet back into the hill, going the same direction the whole time. Once you engage the edge, the ski takes over and finishes the turn.

## Practice Making the Change

Because edge engagement is so spontaneous and effortless with an hourglass ski, the challenge is to control when both skis are sliding and when you tip or tilt the ski on edge. (For those who remember early ski lessons, this is similar to an exercise called a "garland" or a "christie.") Practice will tell you how much pressure you need and how subtle you can be when making the edge change. The hourglass model you are skiing (extreme versus modified sidecut) will determine how strongly the edge of the ski wants to take over.

I find that when I ski bumps I use this method to help me manage the terrain. The sideslip can smooth out the line or path you're on when skiing down the hill. We'll talk more about skiing black diamond terrain in upcoming chapters.

# Advanced Skiing

One of the most frequent complaints I hear about hourglass skis is that, while they may be terrific for beginner or intermediate skiers, they're not that great for advanced skiers. Many critics denounce these skis because they think that, with such a wide tip and tail, the skis couldn't possibly work or be effective, especially on black diamond slopes.

I think the critics and skeptics are wrong! Hourglass skis (and I include all models when I say this) make skiing easier than ever in all terrain and in _any_ condition found on the mountain.

## Use the Ski Shape

Be forewarned! With the hourglass skis you need to ski with your feet. To move from a conventional to an hourglass ski demands that you use the ski shape instead of the ski length. By that I mean _you tip the ski on edge directly under your foot with an hourglass ski_, instead of putting weight or pressure on the front of the ski. If you don't use the edge under the ball of your foot it will take you longer to make them work for you. You DO NOT have to load the tip or apply pressure on the front of the ski to make them work for you.

## Adjust Your Stance

You have to adjust your stance so that you are centered over your feet. This is as much mental as it is physical. On a conventional ski the tendency is to load the front of the ski by driving the knee and ankle forward to make the ski flex or bend. This is how skiers traditionally learned to make the ski carve. Once the ski is flexed, you roll to the edge and ride the ski through the turn. In bumps, when skiing a conventional ski, I use the front of the ski to slow me down. I drive the tip and flex the ski to control my speed, even when I'm skiing in the fall line.

## The First Time

With hourglass skis it is ankle flex, pressure from the ball of your foot and the ski edge directly under the foot that you need. When I first tested the hourglass skis in black diamond terrain, it took me awhile to completely adjust. Whenever I tried to use the front of the ski to slow my speed, the tips would flop around like a fish on dry land.

I was in the habit of using the ski *length* for speed control, now I was forced to use the *turn shape*. By that I mean the arc that is designed into the ski to help you turn. Once I adjusted to using the ski edge under my foot, I found I could make a quicker, more spontaneous turn, with 50% less effort. It was exhilarating. After a lifetime of skiing, I was making quicker turns with half the effort. Initiating the turn with the inside ski gave me a quicker edge response. With little thought, and even less effort, I could put the ski on edge and have it come around immediately.

When I would "Phantomize" consecutive turns in the fall line, I felt a flexing and bending from the torsion of the ski, an oscillation if you will, that came with using the inside ski, a sensation that I had never felt before. Once I got a taste of this new sensation I was hooked. I hadn't been this excited and passionate about my skiing since I was a kid. I'm skiing better now than when I was skiing professionally in my 20's and 30's.

If you purchased brand-new skis recently, or you are still loyal to your old brand, don't worry. Conventional skis will still perform. But if you are thinking about getting new skis, check out these new hourglass, super-sidecut models.

## What does the future hold?

With more skiers trying and improving on hourglass skis, they are definitely here to stay. Conventional skis will all but go the way of the dinosaur. There will be less demand for them as hybrid or modified hourglass models appear. The hybrid models will offer the ease of turning with less effort as they appeal to the skiing population at large. The highest level of skiers or those experienced skiers who know and like their personal skiing style will stay with conventional skis. ◆

# Chapter 6

# The Six Steps to Effortless Skiing

Photo courtesy of Nordica (Prince Sports Group)

# Introduction

The intermediate level in skiing is the easiest level to reach, but the hardest from which to break out. With three or four days of traditional lessons you can go from a "never-ever" beginner skier to a solid intermediate. On the other hand, you may have skied for many years, yet never have progressed beyond the advanced-intermediate level.

After teaching skiing full-time for over twenty years, I've come up with six basic techniques that I feel every skier needs to know, regardless of their ability. I call these the "Six Steps To Effortless Skiing," and they are based on the Primary Movement Ski Teaching System.

## Mental Keys

The mind can only think about one thing at a time when we ski. By using each step one at a time, in succession, you apply a positive mental focus to your skiing. I think of each step as a "key." The key directs you down a path or a train of thought that brings your skiing together. In golf that key might be one aspect or element of your swing that allows you to have the best stroke possible. It might be "keep hips square to the target line" or "use light grip pressure." Using a word or phrase in this way not only helps as a focus, but acts as a "mental trigger" to give you the best possible results.

## How to Use the Six Steps

Start with step number one and work on it until it becomes something you can do without thinking about it. When number one is established subconsciously, move on to number two. Again, do this until it becomes reflexive before you move on to number three, and so on through all six steps.

After you are familiar with and can do all six steps, refer back to the step that works best for you and use that as your key. It might be as simple as saying "breathe" each time you make a turn, or "hands" to keep your hands up and your body balanced over your stance leg, or "tilt" as you stand on your foot and tip the inside ski to the little toe side.

The more familiar and the more refined you can make each step, the more sensitive you'll be with your feet and skis on the snow. These steps can be used from beginner through expert. Once you get to advanced levels, I modify some of these techniques and add certain elements to take into account the terrain you are on as well as the steepness of the hill.

The "Six Steps to Effortless Skiing" are:

- Lift and Tilt
- Right Ski, Left Ski
- Control Your Speed
- Exhale On Every Turn
- Look Ahead
- Keep Your Rhythm Constant

Let's go to step number one...

# Step One: "Lift and Tilt"

The first step in learning *How To Ski The Blues And Blacks (without getting black and blue) is* "Lift and Tilt." Step One is really the Phantom Move that we learned on page 92. "Lift and Tilt" are the words that we use to get into the movements of doing the turn.

In the "Phantom Move" we learned to do the "Lift and Tilt" initially from a traverse. Now, as you begin to make turns, use the inside ski to initiate or start the turn.

- You "lift" the tail of the inside ski and "tilt" your ski boot towards the little toe side.
- Make sure the ski tip stays on the snow as you tilt to the little toe side.
- The outside ski is the stance or balance leg for the turn.
- "Lift" and "Tilt." This is all the action you need to do to create the turn.

Photo by Grafton Smith, courtesy of Harb Ski Systems

- Say out loud to yourself "lift" when you lift the tail of the inside ski and "tilt" when you tip the boot to the little toe side.

## Say It Out Loud

*It's important that you vocalize when you do this action* in order to focus your concentration on the action you are doing, and make it a mental command to physical action. It's what you need to do to bring the mind and body together.

It's not enough to *think* of the command "lift" or "tilt," you must *say* the words out loud at the same time you perform them. "Lift" and "tilt" are the key words you use to create the action for the turn. After you engage the edge through the "Lift and Tilt," you need to balance on the stance (outside) leg and ride the ski through the turn. If you're not aligned or you have trouble keeping your balance on the stance leg, you'll have trouble holding the edge through the turn. When you finish the turn, repeat the action to the other side, pick up the tail of the new inside ski and tilt the ski boot to the little toe side.

"Lift and tilt" is designed to give your mind a focus for the action you are doing. When you can ski an entire run using this method, it's time to move on to Step Two.

> **Note:** Steps One and Two are the only steps I have modified since I came up with the "Six Steps To Effortless Skiing." I originally called Step One "Right Ski, Left Ski," which emphasized the weight on the outside ski of each turn; and Step Two, "Up and Down." "Up and Down" was used to create a flexing action with your skis and rhythm with your body. It also had to do with the weighting and unweighting of the skis from turn to turn: "up" to start the turn and "down" to finish it.

The technology behind today's ski equipment, in conjunction with the Primary Movement Ski Teaching System has made learning and turning in skiing easier than ever. The true essence of skiing is learning how to be smooth, graceful and effortless as you make your way down the mountain. This new combination of methodology and technology has made it possible to eliminate old habits and techniques with a simpler, more efficient means of turning.

# Step Two: "Right Ski, Left Ski"

Once you have the idea of doing the "Lift and Tilt" you're ready to move on to Step Two, "Right Ski, Left Ski."

In previous years, I taught "Right Ski, Left Ski" to mean that weight or pressure was on the outside ski of each turn. With the Accelerated Skier Performance System, however, Step Two takes on a new meaning. *Right Ski* or *Left Ski* are the words we use to *indicate which ski will initiate or start the turn.*

With Step One we create the action for the turn with the "Lift and Tilt." We already know from Step One that we are using the inside ski to start each turn. This is either the "Right Ski" or the "Left Ski." The ski that you "Lift and Tilt" (the inside ski) is the direction you'll turn.

## Change the Phrase, Change the Focus

From Step One we can do the "Lift and Tilt" over the course of an entire run. Now, switch to saying "Right Ski, Left Ski." When you pick up the inside ski tell yourself (out loud) which ski you are using. As in Step One it's important to vocalize at the same time you perform the action.

Step Two is a simplified version of Step One. Step One tells you how to do the action, while Step Two tells you which ski it will be. By now we can do the "Lift and Tilt" by feel. With Step Two we can *concentrate on the ski we use to make the turn.* Not only does this allow us to work on the consistency of our turns, but on the quality as well.

## Establish Fluidity

As soon as you finish one turn, start the next one. You want to establish a pattern of fluidity from one turn to the next. There should be no pause or hesitation in between your turns. If you are tired, winded, get distracted or need a break, stop and recollect yourself. But as long as you are moving, stay in concentration and keep the flow and rhythm going between your turns.

"Right Ski, Left Ski" are the key words you use for the mental command to the physical action. You use the "Right Ski" or "Left Ski" in the "Lift and Tilt" to start your turn. Once you begin the turn, the outside ski of each turn is your stance or balance leg. Although your balance and weight are the outside leg, it is the inside ski that initiates the turn. *The outside ski will follow the action that is created by the inside ski.*

- Start on a slope that is not too steep so you don't go too fast when you first try this.
- It's not enough to think of which ski you use to start the turn, you must say it out loud. Thinking about it does not allow your mind and body to work together; *you must vocalize the command* to be effective.

## The Importance of Vocalizing

I admit I've had more than one student say they felt funny when first saying this. But aside from feeling funny, it is important, necessary, and... it works. It helps you to focus your mind on the action you are doing.

As you progress from intermediate to advanced levels it is even more important to say out loud to yourself which ski you are using to begin the turn. As an expert skier, you ski more critical terrain that allows less margin for error. You may laugh at first (or hear others do it for you) when you first try this. Don't worry about it. It will pay off the next time you ski bumps or powder or ski a run from top to bottom in perfect control.

Now that you have the idea of making your turns, let's put them together with Step Three...

# Step Three: Control Your Speed

Once you know how to do Steps One and Two, you need to concentrate on keeping your speed under control. Most skiers start out on a run and, after each turn begin going faster and faster until they are out of control. The essence of ski mastery is to be able to control your speed on each turn, regardless of terrain.

## Edge Control = Speed Control

To control your speed you must know how to control your edges.

- As you start a new turn you release the uphill edges and flatten both skis.
- Once the skis are flat, use the Phantom Move (Steps One and Two) to begin the new turn.
- Balance and stand on the entire foot of the stance (outside) leg, as the ski tilts on edge. When you are on the edge of the ski, you have a platform under the foot.
- Maintain your balance and ride the ski completely through the turn.
- The edge of the ski allows you to control your speed. Feel the transition as you go from flat to edge.
- Make sure your release and engagement of the edges is smooth. Abrupt movements will

cause the skis to react unexpectedly and may throw you off balance.

- Keep your speed the same on each turn. Not too fast, not too slow.
- Feel the edge under the foot of the stance leg as you ride the ski through the turn.
- Ride your ski completely through the turn until you begin to slow down.
- As soon as you begin to slow, start your new turn. Most skiers do not allow themselves to slow down before they begin the new turn with the result that they accelerate after each turn until they are out of control. Remember, slow your speed when you turn into the hill.

## Stance and Control

Watch skiers coming down the hill as you ride the chairlift. Look at the stance they have over their feet. Look at their legs. Notice the skiers whose legs are flexed slightly forward versus those who have their legs straight or are sitting back. Look at the position of the knee, and, more importantly, the ankle position of the various skiers.

The skiers who exhibit the most control will be those who have their knees and ankles flexed. It is from this position that you are able to engage or feel the edge under your foot, and have the skis work for you. If you ski with your weight on your heels (or no flex at the ankle), you will not be able to use (or feel) the edge under your foot to get the control you need.

## Turn with Consistent Speed

Observe good skiers as they make their way down the mountain. Look at the consistency they demonstrate as they go from turn to turn. See how they maintain the same speed from turn to turn, not too fast, not too slow. Look, too, at the arc they create in the snow, see how they finish a turn regardless of whether the turn is large or small. This is how to control your speed.

Many skiers lose control right from the start. Keep control by maintaining your speed on each turn so it's neither faster or slower. Then you can concentrate on your rhythm or tempo as you make your way down the hill.

Courtesy Crested Butte Mountain Resort/Tom Stillo, Photographer

Alison Gannett powder skiing at Crested Butte

## Speed vs. Tempo

Don't confuse your speed with rhythm or tempo. Speed is how fast you physically move down the slope; tempo is synonymous with the type of turn and the speed at which you make it.

The analogy I use for rhythm or tempo is that of a metronome, the instrument that helps you keep time when learning to play the piano. The clicks of the metronome are either fast or slow, that's tempo. It's the same with your turns. Regardless of the type of turn you make and the tempo you use - a large sweeping turn or short, quick turns down the fall line - your speed should remain the same from one turn to the next.

## Experts Flow from Turn to Turn

At the advanced and expert levels, speed control is about directing the energy or "flow" from your skis. Once you know how to make your skis work for you, there is an oscillation that comes from the camber and torsion of your skis on each turn. Skiers who appear to make effortless turns are in this flow. Flow is taking the momentum from one turn and directing it into the next. It is the subtle use of your edges that keeps your speed and overall momentum the same. The idea of flowing from turn to turn takes time and practice, but it is something that everyone can experience.

## Master Speed Control First

At the beginning and intermediate levels, speed control should be your main concern. If you are not able to keep your speed under control on each turn, you are an accident waiting to happen. Keeping your speed in check is absolutely necessary if you expect to ski more difficult or advanced runs. It takes effort and concentration to keep your speed, not only under control, but the same on each turn. Once you master your speed and the flow that links your turns together, each run and every turn will be smooth and effortless.

# Step Four: Exhale On Every Turn

My knowledge of breath control and proper use of the breath in skiing comes from the days when I taught skiing during the day and Taekwondo (the martial art) at night. After a while I began to notice many similarities between the two and how they seemed to blend together.

## Use of Breathing in the Martial Arts

In the martial arts, your power comes from your breath. You can use your breathing for offense or defense. Your breath can help increase your power when you execute a technique, or likewise when you defend against an incoming blow or strike. The reverse is also true. The time when you are weakest, off-balance or most susceptible to injury is when you hold your breath. Sounds strange, I know, but it's true.

In the martial arts, you use your breath by exhaling at the same time you execute a move. This is done with a sharp, deliberate expulsion of air. You can actually increase your power if you do this at the same time you execute a technique. You can also use the same technique to protect yourself. If you exhale at the same time a blow lands, it can protect you.

## Using the Breath in Skiing

Using the breath in this manner applies to skiing as well. Although you don't have opponents trying to kick or punch you when you ski, you can still use the breath in conjunction with your movements. Proper breath control can help with your balance, rhythm, power, control and consistency.

Most skiers need to know two things about using their breathing effectively. One is knowing when to breathe; the other is holding the breath as you make a turn. If you hold your breath or don't consciously use your breathing when you ski, you put yourself at a disadvantage. This is the time when you are weakest, both mentally and physically. It's also the time you are most likely to lose your balance and fall.

## Breathing 101

- Exhale each time you tilt the inside ski on edge and ride it through the turn.
- Open your mouth and exhale, squeezing the air out from the lower abdomen.
- Vocalize the "ah" sound. This is important for the same reason you vocalize "Right Ski, Left Ski."
- Sustain the exhale as you balance on the outside ski and ride it through the turn.
- Your lungs are like a sponge. As soon as you relax in between your turns the air will come back in naturally. You only need think about a conscious effort of squeezing the air out through the exhale.
- It is not enough to puff the cheeks or blow the air out through your lips. It must be the "ah"

Photo © Loveland Ski Area

sound and you must squeeze the air out from your lower belly.

## Trying it Out

When you first try this, do it on a run that's not too steep or challenging so you don't have to worry about going too fast.

- Start slowly and make a conscious effort to exhale on each turn, squeezing the air as you do.
- Pick a point a short way down the hill and ski to it.
- See if you can breathe on each turn.
- As you make more turns or start to ski faster, check to see if you are holding your breath. This usually happens when you get excited, caught up in the moment or when everything starts to come together.

If you stop and are panting uncontrollably, you probably held your breath at some point in your run. (Either that or you are horribly out of shape.) If this happens, collect yourself and try it again. The trick is to breathe on every turn, regardless of the conditions, the terrain, or your state of mind.

## Using Step Four with Step Two

I use Step Four as an extension of Step Two, "Right ski, Left ski." When I make my first turns I vocalize when I stand on the inside ski. Initially, you start by saying, "right ski" or "left ski" each time you lift the inside ski to begin the turn. After four or five turns you can switch from saying "right ski—left ski" to "one—two," as your body picks up the rhythm for each turn. As this process becomes more natural, you incorporate it into your breathing, exhaling and vocalizing the "AH" sound instead of saying "Right Ski" or "Left Ski" out loud. This is both simple and basic and what you must do _each time_ you make a turn.

## Tips for Breathing Correctly

If you get light-headed or dizzy, you are only breathing with the upper portion of the lungs and not the belly. Concentrate on squeezing the air from the lower abdomen. If this seems awkward or your timing is off, it may be necessary to take "cheater" breaths in-between. That's okay.

The first time they try this, many students find it difficult to consciously think of breathing when making turns. If this happens, forget about your breathing all together. Release yourself from the effort of trying and just enjoy a run or two. Come back to it when your mind is clear and there is no pressure to perform. Let the breath "happen" when you make a turn.

## Applying the Technique

After you learn to use your breathing with your turns, the challenge is to apply this technique to more difficult terrain, e.g., powder, moguls, trees, or gates. As you go from turn to turn use your breathing in rhythm with your turns. It doesn't matter if your turns are fast or slow. Develop your timing and match your breath with your turns, whether you are making large sweeping GS turns, or quick, short swings down the fall line.

When you learn to exhale you'll find that you have more energy and power on every turn. You'll have more control in extreme or critical situations and be able ski longer distances with less fatigue. The breathing that moves with the rhythm of your turns will keep your muscles and body from getting tired. You'll find that you have more physical energy and can ski longer throughout the day.

It will take patience and practice for Step Four to become second nature. When it does you will notice that your skiing becomes more flowing, graceful and effortless.

# Step Five: Look Ahead

One of the most important elements in skiing is to see where you are going. All too often a skier concentrates on an area only a few feet in front of the ski tips. This narrow focus limits the ability and potential of the skier.

Ideally you should look down the hill at least three to four turns. Because of the way I like to ski, I not only look ahead, but I carefully select each turn that I am going to make. Rather than turn haphazardly, I look for the best snow and turn there. This allows me to use the terrain to my advantage while I miss any obstacles in my way.

## Why Skiers Don't Look Ahead

Most beginners or intermediate skiers will look at their tips for two reasons: not knowing where to look and lack of confidence. Skiers who are unsure

Photo courtesy of Loveland Ski Area

This skier is looking ahead correctly

of themselves or their skiing ability tend to look down at their tips or only slightly in front of them. Once you are sure that you can turn and control your speed, look up and see where you are going.

## Avoiding the "Uh-Oh" Factor

To start, practice looking down the hill at least one turn in front of where you will make that turn; two to three turns is ideal. When you know where you will make your turn it is easier to direct your flow and momentum from your skis and the turn you just made.

Looking ahead gives not only a visual perspective but a mental one as well. Using your sight gives your mind something to focus on. The mind leads the body and it's your focus that directs your mind. When you concentrate on your tips, you set yourself up for the "uh-oh" factor. When you come across a trouble spot - a steep section, a patch of ice, a rock, another skier - you get distracted. Your mind loses concentration on what you were doing and your body stops turning. You think "uh-oh," or something similar, and you freeze. You fail to respond or react because your mind stops.

Looking two or three turns ahead will give you a way out. It opens your horizons. Focusing down the hill will not only allow you to "see" where you are going, but give you a way out should you find yourself in trouble.

Looking ahead also helps your reaction time. If you see what's coming, you have more time to respond. If you only ski from one turn to the next you are moving in a cautious, hesitant manner. There is no consistency to your turns, so your mind stops on each one. By looking ahead, you develop "flow" with your skiing and your turns. Even when you come across a ridge or a pitch where you can't see what's on the other side, if you have that habit of looking ahead, your mind will direct you to where you want to go instead of stopping.

## Using Peripheral Vision

Many times skiers fall into the habit of "tunnel vision" or short-sightedness. Tunnel vision occurs when a skier is intent only on what they are doing or where they are going. It's the analogy of not being able to see the forest through the trees. This is a dangerous habit that must be overcome for safety's sake. Because you share the hill with other skiers and snowboarders, you must develop the awareness of others around you. The best way to do this is to use your peripheral vision to see everything in your line of sight. Use of your peripheral vision allows you to expand your vision and develop a broader focus or perspective when you are on the hill.

To develop your peripheral vision, find an area or slope where is little traffic. Pick an object a short distance down the hill, maybe 50 or 100 yards. Look at the object, yet see everything in your field of vision as you ski toward it. It's simply a matter of telling yourself to see everything in your area of sight and not just the object of focus. Go slowly enough so you can accomplish your objective of keeping your sight on that point downhill yet see everything in your line of sight.

By looking ahead and using your sight properly you can increase your ability on your turns and improve the overall context of each run.

# Step Six: Keep Your Rhythm Constant

This is the final step in "The Six Steps To Effortless Skiing." It is also the one most black diamond skiers use when they ski advanced trails or steep terrain.

Step Six is "Keep Your Rhythm Constant." The best way to keep your rhythm constant is to keep turning once you start turning.

## Keep Turning

Each time you tip or tilt the ski on edge, the ski flexes under the stance leg. The flexing ski creates an energy or oscillation that can help us with the rhythm in our turns. What we want to do is direct this energy from our skis into our turns. This contributes to the flow we have when going from one turn to the next.

Most skiers start with a few turns, stop turning, yet keep moving and lose their rhythm. Or they make a few haphazard turns and never seem to develop a rhythm at all.

## Find Your Rhythm

The ski is meant to work for you. Use Steps One and Two to help you establish a rhythm as soon as you start moving. If you don't start with a rhythm, you'll never get it once you are moving. You must find your rhythm on your first few turns and keep it going throughout your run. Once you lose your rhythm, when you are moving, it's hard to get it back. When you stop turning, you stop working the skis. To get the rhythm back, you need to stop and start again.

- As soon as you start moving, find the rhythm that comes from putting the ski on edge. Direct that rhythm into each turn.
- Keep your rhythm constant regardless of your speed. Skiing is about going down the hill, and a constant rhythm follows this train of thought.
- Once you start turning, keep turning. The size of your turn doesn't matter. They can be large,

sweeping GS turns or short-swing, straight down the fall line turns, or a combination of both. The most important thing to remember is that once you start this motion with your feet and skis, keep it going.

## Traversing Across the Hill

Sometimes it's necessary to use a traverse in the course of your run. Don't confuse *using a traverse in between your turns* with *adjusting your line*, when I talk about constant rhythm. There are times when you have to change your line or the path that you are skiing down the hill. You may need to adjust where you are going to set yourself up for your new series of turns.

This is different than traversing across the hill in between each turn. Traversing across the hill

Photo courtesy of TLH heliskiing

reflects a lack of confidence. It also means you are afraid to ski down the hill. If this is the case for you, go back to a run that is less steep so you can work on skiing down the hill. Practice making consecutive turns in places where you don't have to worry about going too fast.

If you mentally let up, lose control, go too fast or get tired, stop, gather yourself and begin again when you are fresh.

## Learning to Vary Your Rhythm

When you know you can make turns using a constant rhythm, play with your tempo or speed. At an advanced level, this is what I call "broken rhythm." Broken rhythm is how you vary your rhythm in the course of a run without losing your flow or momentum from one turn to the next. Sometimes you need to break your rhythm due to a person or obstacle that might be in your way. This is especially true in mogul skiing.

Watch good mogul skiers. Watch how they add an extra turn or two in the course of their run. By "breaking" up the rhythm with an extra turn or two, they are able to maintain consistency without throwing off the whole run. It is similar to adding 1/8 or 1/16 notes in music. By adding a quicker note or step you keep your run going. Broken rhythm is more about how to alter your rhythm in the course of a run without messing up the entire run. It takes strength, agility and preparedness. Your mind, body and skis must all be flowing together as one so you are not thrown off if you have to jump a rock, miss a patch of ice, or avoid another skier or obstacle on the hill.

Keeping your rhythm constant is about how all the previous steps come together. There is a flow or train of thought when you are making consistent turns. This is accomplished by:

- How you initiate and establish a rhythm with each turn.
- Proper use of your edge
- How you direct your focus and keep your speed under control.
- Knowing how to use your breath to release the body and establish your flow.

These are what I call the "Six Steps To Effortless Skiing."

## Summary: Using the Six Steps

Remember, since the mind can only concentrate on one thought at a time, I recommend working on each step until it becomes subconscious or second nature. Advance to the next step only after the previous step comes naturally. You'll know that you've got it when you begin to develop a flow and effortlessness in your skiing. ◆

# Chapter 7
# Open Your Mind

Photo © Todd Powell, courtesy of Copper Mountain Resort

# Be Present In The Moment

This is one of the most important yet overlooked concepts in skiing. "Be Present In The Moment" is what I believe it takes to be able to successfully *Ski The Blues And Blacks (without getting black and blue)*.

## Being in the Present is a Big Change

To live in the "present" is a difficult but necessary concept to grasp, especially in skiing. We live in a world that constantly bombards our senses with distractions in a demand for our attention. We spend the majority of our time and existence mentally somewhere else. In our day-to-day lives, we're always thinking about events or situations in the future. We spend a great deal of energy trying to "anticipate" the outcome of what we think will happen.

Our minds run "down the road" with our thoughts, out in front of where we are physically. "What are we going to eat for dinner?" "Who's going to pick the kids up from daycare?" "What are we going to wear to work tomorrow or to the party next week?" "What is on my agenda today?" "Will I have enough money to pay my bills this week?" "How will I make that presentation at work?" And so on.

In trying to anticipate what our lives will be like, we miss most of what's going on right now, in front of us, here in the present. When we do make it to the ski slopes, we're still in that same frame of mind. It's difficult to let go of the patterns that we've developed on a day-to-day basis.

## Being Fully Conscious of Each Action

I first learned about "being in the moment" through training in and teaching Taekwondo. Studying a martial art teaches you the discipline to be fully conscious in what you are doing when you are doing it. It's a mental state that is tied to physical or muscular effort. When you are pushing your body to the limit physically, it takes too much energy to think about anything else, energy that could help you endure where you are at that moment in time. The most important thing I learned was how, when you are totally "in the moment," the mind and body work together.

This is one of the reasons I came up with the "Six Steps To Effortless Skiing." Thinking about where you are and what you are doing brings you "into the moment." Having a key word that relates to your technique is one of the most powerful ways to direct your attention to what you are doing. You cannot be mentally absent and ski effectively down the hill. You must be in the "here and now" to be "present in the moment."

This idea represents a thought. That thought, whether you make it consciously or unconsciously, becomes a decision about where you are and what you are doing. This decision contributes to where you are "now." The act of skiing demands your attention. You can't "be" mentally somewhere else when you are making your way down the mountain. You have to be attentive to what you are doing when you are doing it, or else you'll get hurt. That's what makes it so attractive.

## Dangers of Letting Your Mind Wander

Sometimes fatigue, or loss of breath or ski control can mentally distract you in the course of your run. I see this when a skier, after doing well on a tough run or section the hill, lets up. When they get to where it's less challenging, they relax mentally and end up falling. As long as you are moving you need to stay "in the moment," whether you're on a steep bump run or skiing an easy road. Relax or let up only after you've stopped.

If you are not fully present in the moment when going twenty or thirty miles per hour cruising a green or blue run, skiing a steep face, making turns in the moguls or cutting it up in the powder, you are going to hurt yourself or worse. It takes 100% of your concentration to be in the here and now. Nothing else will do. The more you are aware of what you are doing when you are doing it, the faster you learn. The faster you learn, the more you grow into the flow of skiing.

## Start Your Day

Photo © Jack Affleck, courtesy of Vail Resorts/Beaver Creek

The start of a new ski day can often be a frustrating experience, especially if you haven't skied in a while. Too often it takes three or four runs to get

*Open Your Mind*

your rhythm, if you find it at all. Sound familiar? Here are some suggestions to help get your ski legs under you from your first run.

## Make your first couple of runs on a groomed slope.

A groom sheet or list is usually posted at the top or bottom (sometimes both) of the various chairlifts on the mountain. If you do not see one, ask the chairlift operator which runs have been groomed the night before. A groomed run is like skiing on a corduroy carpet. It gives you the most consistent snow and will help you get your feet and skis working.

## Develop a rhythm with the skis first, and then with your body.

I always start my day with a warm-up run. When I first get off the chairlift I put the ski on edge and hold it. I do this at the top of a run where it's flat or there's little pitch. I stand on the edge and ride the ski completely through the turn, into the hill. I don't let the skis slide sideways at all. This is to get the blood flowing and warm the muscles in my legs.

## Change to the Lift and Tilt

After I do this a few times to both sides, I use the "Lift and Tilt" that we talked about in Step One to begin each new turn. This gives me a feel for my skis and the edge under foot.

## Find your Balance

Once I begin the "Lift and Tilt," I look for my balance on the stance leg. I flex the knee and ankle of the stance leg while riding the edge. I feel the edge hold in the snow under my foot and the platform created by the ski on which I am standing. This gives me a chance to work my breathing into my turns as well. As I find my balance and become aware of the edge under my foot, I gradually increase the tempo, not the speed, of my turns. This puts me in a "skiing" frame of mind as I find the flow of going from one turn to the next.

## Hold your hands up and in front of your body.

This will help keep your weight centered over your feet. With your hands in front, your pole baskets should be behind your body. If you drop your hands or you can't see them, your weight is probably on your heels. This allows the weight to shift to your heels where you don't want it. You need to keep them up where you can see them.

## Feel the Edge

Can you feel the edge under your foot? How much pressure do you need to maintain control of your turn? Can you keep your balance on the stance leg? The harder you flex your ankle and tip the ski, the more the edge will respond and the quicker the ski will come around. Practice keeping your balance as you ride the stance leg completely through the turn from beginning to end. This activity focuses on your balance and edge control as soon as you start moving on your feet.

These exercises will increase your awareness, get the blood flowing, warm your legs and help get your mind on skiing. Now you're ready to ski!

# Mentoring

One of the best ways to learn to ski is by imitating. I did this when I was a kid growing up in Connecticut, and I still do it now as an adult. Each week during the season I ski with a group of former instructors and competitors. During the course of the day, I slip in behind one of my peers and follow him or her down the run. Flat or bumps, it doesn't matter. I follow them down the hill and try to mimic what they are doing.

In an athletic endeavor like skiing, one of the best ways to learn is to see someone else do it well and then imitate that action. In order to progress, sometimes it is not enough to read or hear someone tell you what to do right, you must see it for yourself. When I follow someone, I react instinctively and copy without question. Obviously this works best with someone who is technically proficient or similar in ability. This is one of the most enjoyable ways for me to ski. The person leading is doing all the work, and I'm just along for the ride.

Photo courtesy of Loveland Ski Area

The term I use for this visual imagery is "mentoring." This describes the relationship between the one who leads and the one who follows. The person who leads "mentors" the person who follows. Most ski instructors use this technique with their students. The instructor will usually ski a level or pace that is one or two steps higher than the student. This way the student can see, literally, the next level they are skiing toward. Once they "see" where it is they want or need to be, it becomes attainable. It's the faster way to learn in the shortest period of time.

## Anyone Can Be a Mentor

Although I use "mentoring" in an instructor/student relationship, it is not limited to that. You can use as a mentor any one who inspires you to new or greater levels of excellence. As in any other industry you seek out the leaders or the people who inspire you to higher levels of performance. The same holds true for skiing and it is not limited to just instructors.

So how does one go about using someone else as a mentor? It's easy. Simply find someone who skis at a level or pace that is one level higher than your own. As a kid, I would look for another person, most times it was an instructor or a ski patrolman taking a free run, and fall in behind them. I would follow this person as far as I could until I grew tired or they lost me. I would do this over and over again until I began to feel what it was I was watching and imitating. Now I do it with my peers to stay fresh and keep my skill level up. I credit this method of learning to ski with many of my breakthroughs.

## Challenge Yourself

The idea in mentoring is to create an opportunity for you to excel. By watching someone else, you focus

*Open Your Mind*

more on what they are doing and less on yourself. This is an excellent technique to use when you are feeling stuck or in a rut. It forces you to come out of yourself and see things in a different perspective.

As I was learning to ski, I would pick a hot skier and follow them down the slope. Do the same for yourself. Find a skier who skis the way who'd like to, and follow them as they make their way down the hill. Watch how they stand on their skis. Look at how they hold their hands or keep their hips as they ski the fall line. It's best if you can follow an instructor or other technically excellent skier.

You may only be able to follow them for a handful of turns. Don't worry about it. Just keep repeating the exercise, and follow for as many turns as you feel comfortable. In watching someone of a higher caliber and following them, you are looking to improve your own skiing. If it's not an instructor or patrolman, that's okay too. You can learn a lot by following someone who is better than you, even if they are not professional. The mistakes they make may or may not be obvious to you. Don't worry about it.

See if you can get a feel for what it is you are watching. It's fun because it challenges you to imitate the style of another. It does not mean you have to make that style (or their mistakes) your own.

Mentoring is one of the best ways I know of to improve on your own. Try it and see if it doesn't work for you.

## Be Kind To Yourself

Skiing is a sport that is easy to learn and something most people can do, if they have the desire. But it's how you treat yourself in the process of understanding and applying the skills in skiing that will make the difference in <u>how</u> you progress. Developing the skills and executing the techniques is the easy part. How you treat yourself while learning is infinitely more important.

## Try to Understand Each New Technique

As you learn new techniques, see if you understand what it is you are trying to do. We all learn in different ways. If you constantly belittle or berate yourself in the learning process, you will only become frustrated or discouraged. There is a perfectionist in all of us. Allow yourself to experience what you are doing without all the negative self-criticism. Clear your mind of everything except the task at hand and experience the action without self-criticism.

I find it most effective when learning if you adopt the attitude that there is no right or wrong way to do a technique. This attitude will allow you to concentrate on doing the work. Yes, there are certain techniques you need to know to balance, edge, turn, control your speed or stop. But if you are concerned with doing it right or wrong, you don't enjoy the experience of the moment.

## Allow Yourself to Experience Failure

Hidden within this attitude is the chance for you to try anything you want without self-condemnation. If you are to be truly successful, you must allow yourself to experience failure. It is only through trial and error that we grow. If you concentrate on doing the best you can, whether good or bad, you can grow from that point. Work on improving what you have done. I think this philosophy applies to every level of skier but especially those who have been skiing for a while.

## Getting Out of a Rut

If you find yourself in a rut or frustrated with a lack of results, go back to basics. The more you can understand and refine your basic technique, the more effective you will be in going beyond your current level. As you go back over the rudiments, concentrate on what you are doing, or what it is you want to have happen. If you focus on what you are doing wrong, it will only reinforce the fact you are doing it wrong and create further frustration.

Sometimes you blame yourself, and *you* might not be the problem. As we mentioned earlier, there could be technical or mechanical reasons for your difficulty. It could be that your skis are not working for you, or need a tune. Maybe your boots are too big, or you need cants. If there is something that is not working in your skiing and you cannot pinpoint it, take a brush-up lesson from a pro. For a

Photo courtesy of Telluride Ski and Golf Company

reasonable fee, you can find out what you are doing wrong and what you can do to correct the problem.

Again, don't be too hard on yourself. See if you can understand what it is you need to work on. Don't worry about doing it perfectly. Find the one thing in your technique that works for you and build from there. As you develop this kind of attitude in your skiing, you will experience more breakthroughs than ever before. ♦

# Chapter 8

# Making Breakthroughs

Photo courtesy Loveland Ski Area

# Expert Improvement

Each season I have the opportunity to ski with a number of great skiers and champions of the sport. In my coverage of skiing, I'm constantly looking for those innovators and technicians who continue taking us to new levels. I've met and skied with some wonderful and talented people as a result.

## Performance Excellence

The reason I mention this is that I find that by skiing with these champions and mentors, my own skiing improves. I call this "performance excellence." It's the state you find yourself when in the company of other good skiers. When you ski with someone who is better than yourself, your own skiing is bound to improve, much as it does when you ski with a good instructor or a group of other good skiers.

"Performance excellence" is an attitude you have about your own skiing. This is different than an "excellent performance" or "mentoring." Whereas "excellent performance" is what I use to describe a series of good turns or a great run, "mentoring" is how you mirror or imitate another to improve your skiing. When you ski with champions, certified instructors, coaches or other top level skiers your own experience is changed through this "contact energy." When you come together with great skiers their presence raises your own level of expertise. It's similar to osmosis. You can't help but improve when skiing with and watching someone who is better than yourself.

It's the same thing that happens when you ski with a group of friends. There's a camaraderie, an excitement within yourself that comes from being and skiing with other good skiers. Good skiers, or skiers who are better than you, challenge you to excel and ski at your very best.

## It's Not Intimidation

Don't confuse this with intimidation. "Performance excellence" is a state of mind that challenges you to be your best. It shows a level of confidence in yourself and your own ski ability. Intimidation is just the opposite. It shows a lack of confidence. If you are intimidated when in the company of other good skiers, you are missing the point. You are looking to create an atmosphere where you can excel, not to hurt yourself. You want to ski with skiers who are able to challenge or inspire your ability, not threaten it.

Don't jeopardize or endanger yourself by skiing outside your ability level. It would be foolish and dangerous for a green level skier to attempt to ski with someone who is used to skiing blue run moguls. Or a blue run skier to try to make the jump to skiing with someone on a double black diamond run. If you hurt yourself, you've gone beyond your own capabilities. It's foolish and there's no reason for it. Pushing yourself to the point where you get hurt or endangered is contrary to "performance excellence."

## The Importance of Confidence

You want to establish a level of confidence that comes from mastering your technique. Once you have that confidence, you can apply it to different terrain and situations. The worse thing you can do is break that confidence down. If you put yourself in a situation where you become afraid, your fear takes over. This is what you don't want.

"Performance excellence" means you must ski within your limits, yet challenge yourself. Only by skiing with proficient or more accomplished skiers who support your own improvement do you raise your own ability. If you really want to improve, you must ski with others who are better than you.

# Overcome Your Fear

Fear is the biggest impediment to any progress or breakthroughs in skiing. Fear is the roadblock you must get beyond to experience what the thrill of skiing is all about. The way to eliminate fear or anxiety is to focus on some aspect of your technique. When you know you can turn, control your speed and stop at will, it gives you tremendous confidence. Once you have the skills to do this, it becomes a matter of applying your ability to different trails and terrain. So it becomes even more important to have something to focus on mentally.

If you concentrate on the one aspect of your technique that will give you control, you develop your confidence. Use your technique to build a level of confidence for yourself.

Photo courtesy of Skis Dynastar

*Making Breakthroughs*

## Positive Focus

In much the same way, *if you concentrate on what you do not want to happen*; i.e., going too fast, losing control, not being able to stop, not wanting to go down THERE....., *it comes a self-fulfilling prophecy*. The mind cannot distinguish between a positive or negative thought, it just accepts the command of the action you are focused on. So, instead of thinking, "I don't want to go too fast," think, "Control my speed on each turn." Again, focus on the positive outcome or result you want, and work toward making that real.

If you find yourself at a loss to break through your fear, ask a question that will help direct you to a positive outcome, such as "How can I control my speed more so I don't scare myself by going too fast?" or "What part of my ski do I need to use to control my speed?"

Refer back to the "Six Steps To Effortless Skiing," and having a word or phrase that acts as a key. Fear and confidence are two different sides of the same coin. If you find yourself in the fear mode, you need to stop and reevaluate where you are.

## Take A Ski Lesson From A Pro

This is one of the reasons I advocate ski lessons. When you work with an instructor, it helps you to know what you want to do and when you want to do it. A good instructor can help simplify the process of learning to ski. They have the skills and language that will put you on the fast track for your own personal breakthroughs. The purpose is to shorten the time it would take for you to work it out on your own, and to establish confidence in your own capabilities.

## Don't Learn from A Friend

It is for this very reason that learning to ski with the help of one of your well-meaning friends doesn't work. Unless they have a background in ski instruction, they don't know what to tell you to do right, or how to correct what you are doing wrong.

On more than one occasion I've seen one slightly experienced skier tell a less experienced skier to "hunker down and cut them edges in." Although there are many people who understand this phrase, it only tells you what to do, not how to do it. To give the wrong information is one of the worse things you can do if you are trying to teach a friend or loved one. It only frustrates both parties and doesn't help the person who needs it the most. I've seen more couples head for divorce court after one tries unsuccessfully to teach the other one to ski.

I talked to someone recently who related her first time on skis to me. Seems that a "friend" offered to teach her to ski and took her to the top of the mountain. (Does this sound familiar?) In frustration her friend either left or lost her, and she inadvertently ended up on a black diamond run. Fortunately this person did not get hurt, as many do, but her tale is typical of the war stories about learning to ski. After a lifetime of skiing and teaching this story is almost a cliche. And it proves that you fall into one of two categories: those who know what they're doing and those who don't.

## One Thing at a Time

We know that the mind can only actively think about one thing at a time, and, if it is not some positive aspect of your skiing you open yourself up for what I call the "uh-oh" factor. (We talked about this in Step Five of the "Six Steps To Effortless

Skiing.") You're skiing down the hill, thinking about nothing in particular, and see a rock, hit a patch of ice, get distracted by another skier, or simply realize you are going too fast. All of a sudden you think "uh-oh." Your mind goes blank and you're in trouble. You have nothing to fall back on, to give you the control you need, because you weren't thinking about anything in particular.

Confidence in skiing comes from (1) knowing what to do, and (2) knowing when to do it. It comes from being sure of yourself and your equipment. If you do not know how to make the skis work for you, at some point in your skiing you will fall into survival mode when going down the hill.

Find the techniques that work for you and use them in your skiing. On each run, pick the one technique that gives you control of your feet and skis. Learn to concentrate on the right technique and you'll begin to see noticeable improvement in your skiing.

# Attitude

Attitude has a lot to do with your success in skiing. Although technique plays an important role, what's going on inside your head will, to a great extent determine how you ski. All things being equal, the attitude you have in your approach will affect your outcome.

## One Bad Experience

Let me give you an example. A few weeks ago, I went to Vail for an extended stay. From the time I left home, nothing went right. I drove up from Denver at night, in one of the worst blizzards I have ever been in. By the time I got to my hotel around 10:00 p.m., they had given away my room. The hotel was full to capacity, and it took most of the night to find another room. I didn't get a very good night's sleep, and when I got up the next morning things continued to go wrong. Service was slow, my hot breakfast was cold; it took forever to get out on the hill, even after an early start. I was there to cover a ski event for a talk-radio show I co-hosted in Denver. They couldn't make the connection they needed to get the show up and running. We sat around for an hour until they could work out the bugs. You get the idea.

By the time I got to the slopes later that morning, I was in a foul mood, and it was reflected in my skiing. It had nothing to do with my equipment, my technique or the snow conditions, which were perfect as there was at least two feet of snow from the storm the previous night. It was my attitude, pure and simple. I came within a heartbeat of packing it all in and going home.

## Forget About It

But then a thought came to me, "Forget about what happened and let it all go. Forget all about the events over which I had no control, and the feelings I had associated with the way I wanted things to be." Everything that happened was a result of the way I reacted to certain events in my life that I could not control. From the moment I made the mental decision that the earlier events didn't matter, and to forget about it, my day improved. When I released myself of the outcomes that did not meet my expectations, my attitude lifted and a new mind-set took over.

We have all had days when things did not go right. Sometimes it's technical; our equipment is not suited to the conditions or isn't working right; the snow is too hard, too soft, or too deep; the weather is too cold or snowy. Maybe it's our own lack of experience or know-how. It might even be physical;

being out of shape, not getting enough sleep the night before you ski, having a hangover. Maybe we feel too apprehensive or anxious about our day on the hill.

## Sometimes, It's JUST Attitude

Whatever the case might be, there are times when circumstances will not go our way. I've skied with people who've had no excuse other than their attitude. They are in a funk and everything they do only makes matters worse. During a bad day you become focused on a train of thought, maybe even without realizing it, and then it becomes a self-fulfilling prophecy. Sometimes we work ourselves into our moods. Nothing's going right, I can't do it, why bother, I'm having a lousy day, etc. Things aren't going right, and they only get worse regardless of what we do.

If this is the case but you refuse to give up on yourself and the day, mentally make the decision to CHANGE YOUR MIND. If you are having a bad day on the hill, admit it. Then forget about it and move on with your life. Eliminate all expectations of yourself, and free yourself to enjoy whatever the experience brings. Instead of wanting or forcing something to happen, release that attitude and let your skiing come to you.

## Some Other Things You Can Do

Go back to the groomers or runs that are not as steep or challenging. Look for runs that are not as crowded where you can cruise without worry. Or stop and take a break. Sometimes if you change your environment, you change your attitude as well. This way you can alter your mind-set so you can focus or concentrate on something else.

If you're having a bad day and you can't seem to shake it, call it a day and head for the lodge. That way you avoid the chance of an injury. Nothing worse than having a bad day and getting hurt too.

When you ski you are almost forced into letting go of your mental baggage just to be able to get down the hill. By changing your mind and your focus you break the pattern that your bad mood has set for yourself. It takes a willingness to let go and get out of yourself so you can enjoy your time on the hill.

# Think Ahead

In Step 5 of the "Six Steps To Effortless Skiing" (Chapter 6), I talked about the importance of looking ahead. Most beginner and intermediate

Photo courtesy of Descente Ski Apparel

*Making Breakthroughs*

skiers tend to look only a few feet in front of their skis, at their ski tips, or worse, their feet. As mentioned earlier, it is important to develop enough confidence in your ability to turn and stop that you can look down the hill at least two or three turns. In looking down the hill, you use your eyes to develop your focus and let the mind lead the body.

I recently skied with a friend who always skied from one turn to the next. Although a good bump skier, her skiing looked static and stiff, and seemed to lack flow or continuity. I recommended the idea of looking ahead. We tried this for a run or two and her skiing seemed to improve noticeably. When we stopped to talk about it, I asked for her thoughts. "When I look down the hill, it makes me think ahead," she said. She felt that if she made the effort to "think ahead," it connected her mind to her technique.

## Responding vs. Reacting

Thinking ahead is an extension of looking ahead, and is the highest form of mental alertness. It puts you in a state of mental preparedness and sets you up for "being in the moment." Rather than reacting to your terrain by skiing from one turn to the next, you respond to it by being mentally prepared. This allows the body to move instinctively.

If you do not "think" to look ahead, you end up waiting for each turn. When you wait for each turn you are forced into reacting. This reaction process is slow, and indicates a caution or timidity that will have you fighting yourself on each turn. There is nothing wrong with being cautious or timid, but if you are mentally bound by this attitude, it inhibits the flow you need from one turn to the next. It shows a lack of confidence in yourself, your technique or your ability to turn.

## Concentrate on One Thing

When you learn to concentrate on one mental thought or aspect of your technique, your skiing will come together for you. Once this becomes habit, your ski technique will become so ingrained that your thought becomes a mental command to a physical action. Skiing becomes a sensation or feeling in which you might use a key thought or word to trigger the muscle memory that allows you to be in control. This is what I do when I use one of the "Six Steps To Effortless Skiing."

While *looking ahead* demands that you focus visually, *thinking ahead* demands that you focus internally (mentally). Thinking ahead supports looking ahead. Think, and look, far enough ahead (two or three turns) to anticipate where you will be, without getting so far ahead of yourself that it becomes a distraction.

## Transcend Physical Technique

High performance skiers use this technique, and it is why they ski so well. In situations that put you on the edge, such as extreme terrain, moguls, running gates or downhill, thinking ahead allows you to be mentally prepared.

It is the same with any athlete who transcends the physical technique of their sport. Whether it be tennis, rock climbing, bike racing, martial arts, etc., you become so familiar with your sport that it is more mental than physical. When you reach this level, the world of skiing opens up to you, and within a short time you are making turns in a way you never thought possible.

# Relaxation

In skiing there are two types of tension you can encounter when you make a turn: muscular or emotional.

- **Emotional tension** is a state of mind, but it manifests itself physically. If you are afraid, scared, doubtful or hesitant, you tighten up your muscles, making your turns difficult at best. If you ski mentally "tight," it's like driving a car with the brakes on.

  Most tension of a negative kind comes from not knowing what you are doing when you make a turn. You need to replace your emotional tension with a confidence that comes from your technique; knowing what you need to do in order to turn, control your speed or stop.

- **Muscular tension** is what you need and it is necessary in most athletic sports. This is where the muscles work actively in conjunction with one another.

In order to keep from getting tired too soon, you need to find the space in between each turn where you are able to relax. As you finish one turn, you "Lift and Tilt" the downhill, or inside, ski to begin the new turn. With all sports, there is a time when you engage or disengage your muscles from one move to the next. The same applies to skiing. If you keep the muscles continuously tight on your turns, you will tire faster and wear out after three or four runs.

This is one of the reasons that it's important to find a rhythm when making turns. With rhythm comes a point of relaxation as you finish one turn and begin the next. You want to engage the muscles when you start the turn, relax as you finish and prepare for the new turn. You must find the point of relaxation in between your turns in order to be an efficient skier.

## Mental and Physical "Looseness"

If you watch a good skier on difficult terrain, they make it look easy. They don't appear to be working at all. There seems to be a "looseness" that allows them to flow from turn to turn.

Photo by Doug Berry, provided courtesy of Telluride Ski and Golf Company,

The "looseness" I speak of here is one of being prepared. It is a mental as well as physical attitude in which you are relaxed, yet ready for action. You have to be "loose" before you can be "tight." The "looseness" comes when you relax the edges and the muscles in the legs, and flatten both skis to prepare for the new turn. The "tension" comes as you engage the muscles in the lower leg as you "Lift and Tilt" to begin the new turn. The looseness and tension work together as you engage and disengage the edges from one turn to the next. As you begin to incorporate these opposing forces into your skiing, you'll notice you have more "flow" in your turns.

## Use Your Breathing

To help create this flow as you go from turn to turn, use the breath as in Step Four of the "Six Steps To Effortless Skiing." Breathing properly will help you overcome your emotional tension and direct your body as you engage the muscles.

As with any turn, you want to exhale when you tighten the muscles. Exhale using the "ah" sound as you engage the edge of the ski and ride it through the turn. Relax the muscles in your lower leg when you make the transition. This does not mean to mentally "let go," but indicates a readiness. Your thoughts are directed to where you are and what you are doing.♦

# Chapter 9

# Intermediate Lessons

Photo © Ben Blankenberg,
courtesy of Vail Resorts/Keystone

*Intermediate Lessons*

# Smooth Transitions

Every time I ski, I watch other skiers as they make their way down the hill. It's not uncommon to see intermediate or advanced skiers use a "hop" to make a turn.

## The Hop

The "hop" begins with a rotation or twisting of the shoulders as they lift their skis off the snow to make the turn. Instead of using their feet to begin the turn, they end up starting the turn with their body. They pick up the inside ski (and it's not to do the "Lift and Tilt"), as they twist or torque the upper body to get the outside ski to come around.

When I watch skiers make this kind of move, I know that it comes from anxiety. They don't have the knowledge or the confidence to make the skis work. Yes, a hop of this kind will get the skis to come around, but at what price?

The best turn begins with your feet, not your body. If you use the upper body (as in when you twist or turn the shoulders), you limit yourself, your ability and the terrain you can ski. Using your body takes a great deal of time and physical effort. Each time you torque your body in one direction, you have to repeat those same movements to make a turn to the other side. It's a lot of wasted energy. It also limits the kind of terrain you can ski. You might be able to ski a blue groomed run, but I doubt if you can ski moguls or black diamond terrain using your body.

## Turn More Efficiently

If this sounds like you, go back and review the Primary Movements we learned about earlier. We know the most efficient turn you can make comes from our Primary Movements. The more control you have of your feet, the more control you have through the turn. This goes back to your boots, as we talked about earlier. The upper body should face your direction of travel, while your feet do the work. Using your body will not give you the control that you want or need.

## Ride Your Skis Through the Turn

In most instances, it's not your skis you are worried about, but how fast you are going when you finish a turn. *Speed control comes when you ride the skis through the turn and into the hill.* It sounds obvious, but you go faster in the middle of a turn when going straight down the hill, and slower when you ride the skis into the hill until you slow down or stop. Rather than controlling your speed by hopping the skis in the middle of a turn, ride those skis through the turn and into the hill. It can be an anxious moment when you're not sure if the skis will come around, hence the hop.

Make sure you keep your speed the same as you go from turn to turn. Not too fast, not too slow. You should not be accelerating as you come out of your turn or when going from turn to turn. If you are accelerating, stop and start again. Look at this as an exercise in control. You can always go faster or slower in the context of your run, but keep the speed the same from turn to turn.

## Quiet the Upper Body

Eliminating the hop is a matter of quieting the upper body. Go back and review the "Phantom Turn." If you've been using a hop in your skiing, it will take some thought to break the habit and get the feel for how to do it right. Look at Step One in the "Six Steps To Effortless Skiing." The "Lift and Tilt" is designed to get you thinking about feet, and will take your mind off your shoulders and upper body.

Find a run where you don't have to worry about going too fast as you work on this. Concentrate on your balance and the control you feel from using the edge of your ski under your foot. Be patient with yourself. Once you have a feel for how the skis will work for you, you'll use your upper body less.

Watch other good skiers as you ride the chairlift. See how they put the skis on edge and ride them through the turn. In contrast, notice those skiers who hop or use their bodies or shoulders to make the turn. You will see that they are off balance and more likely to fall. Remember, you need to create smooth transitions to reach new heights in skiing.

# Work Into Your Skiing

Many people wait until after the holidays or even later before heading up to the high country for their first ski experience of the season. If the ski season is well under way, it is not uncommon to show up at your favorite mountain and find two or three feet of fresh powder. The first tendency is to head straight to the top of the mountain without any preparation or warm-up runs. This is foolish and potentially dangerous.

## Make Some Warm-Up Runs

If you are beginning your ski season or your vacation mid-winter, use some common sense as you make your way up the hill the first time. Start slowly, and work your way back into your technique. Find a run that has been groomed and is not too steep. This terrain will enable you to work on making turns while feeling your skis, boots and the snow under your feet. It is okay to ski a variety of runs, but give yourself the benefit of not skiing runs that are too challenging right off.

After four or five runs you will begin to get your "ski legs" under you. Warming up this way gives your body the ability to respond to the changes in terrain, and helps establish your rhythm when making a series of turns in a run. Once you've had a chance to make a few easy runs, your mind is alert and your body is ready.

## Keep Your Speed Under Control

As the day progresses, work on skiing more slowly (instead of faster), and make more turns. It is easy to go fast, especially when you are tired. If you notice fatigue in your legs or find yourself short of breath, stop in the lodge and rest for five or ten minutes. When you return to the hill, work on keeping your speed under control. Regardless of the type of turn you are making- quick, short swings down the fall line or long sweeping turns using the whole hill- keep your speed constant; not too fast, not too slow.

Photo courtesy of Skis Dynastar

## Avoid Being Mindless

Avoid being mindless in your skiing. Concentrate on where you are and what you are doing. Find some aspect of your turn, and focus on what it is that you want to accomplish. If turns are stronger or easier on one side, check to see if you are aligned. (A good boot fitter can help you here.) If you fall into being lazy, you develop bad habits that will become hard to break and will remain with you.

## Take A Lesson

If you are altogether frustrated by some aspect of your skiing, take a lesson at ski school. This will give you insight as to what you are doing in your turns, and feedback as to how you might make those turns better. It will also help you eliminate any bad habits from the start and give you something positive to think about.

Skiing demands that you develop an awareness of where you are and what you are doing. The more conscious you are of that process, the less frustrated you will be, and the better your results will be.

# Easy Run, Hard Run

Watching other skiers while you ride the chairlift is a good habit to develop. You can learn a lot simply by watching other skiers.

When you look, you'll see that most are making turns that are smooth and efficient. As an intermediate skier this should be your goal. Too often we get on a run or section of the hill that challenges our abilities, and end up traversing the hill back and forth, making turns haphazardly that have no flow or consistency. If you get in trouble, by all means use a traverse. But don't fall back on skiing that way all the time.

## Overcome "Survival Skiing"

If you find you resort to survival skiing when on a more difficult run, try the easy-run, hard-run method of progressing. This is where you alternate an easy run with a more difficult run. The idea is to work your technique on the easy run with the same attitude and intention you had when skiing the more difficult run. Then go back to the more difficult run and ski it with the same technique and concentration you did on the easy run. Try to find the correlations in your technique regardless of which run you are on. When you go back to the easy run, ski it with the same intensity and determination you did on the harder run.

## Building Confidence and Flow

As you alternate from easy to hard, you will find the hard run becoming less difficult. As that run becomes more familiar, it becomes less intimidating. Now you can concentrate on the flow. Your confidence will begin to build as you learn to control your speed and make turns on the more difficult terrain. The hard run that you ski when you try this should be only slightly more challenging in ability. If you lose your confidence, your skiing will regress. That's not what we want.

Skiing is all about flow. Flow comes from knowing how to make your equipment work for you and your technique. The challenge is to use your technique to help build your confidence. The problem most skiers face is that they ski a more difficult run purely for survival. You end up concentrating on your fear of what you don't want to happen, or on merely getting down the hill, instead of on technique. When you get back to an easier run, you concentrate on nothing at all because you are so happy to be alive. Then you fall back into the traverse rut, making turns with no rhythm or reason.

## Use the Same Techniques

Build on what you know. The techniques you use to ski a green run are the same techniques you will use on a black diamond run. The better you understand and apply those techniques, the better your performance. On green or easy blue runs, skiing is about making turns. On advanced blue or black diamond runs, you need to master your speed, while still concentrating on your turns. That's why it is important to ski a green run with the same mental concentration as you would on a black diamond. You learn to flow, or go with the mountain, instead of fighting it. As you concentrate more on your technique, you will be able to focus more on what you want to have happen. By learning to go with the flow you will be a more efficient, more graceful skier.

# Unlock The Leg

One of the biggest secrets to advancing through the beginner and intermediate levels in skiing is unlocking the leg when making a turn. Too often the novice skier will use a straight leg technique for control, edging or stopping. The problem with using a straight leg is that it relies on the strength of the hip and upper leg, and after a few runs of locked leg edging you will become tired and lose whatever control you had when you started.

## Use the Phantom Move

We know we want our skis to work for us. If you use the outside or downhill ski in this straight leg fashion, you are doing exactly the opposite. As mentioned previously, you use the Phantom Move to begin the turn. To gain control of your feet and skis:

- Bend _both_ the knee and the ankle forward slightly.
- Feel your shins in contact with the front of the boot, but avoid leaning on the front of the boot for support. Flexing the knee and ankle puts the weight forward and distributes it evenly over the foot.
- Applying pressure from the ball of the foot and rolling the ski allows you to engage the edge.
- Once you engage the edge, the ski will flex under your foot if on a conventional ski, or the shape of the ski will take over if you are on an hourglass model.

Now you're ready to ride the ski through the turn.

## Ride the Ski Through the Turn

The natural tendency for most beginners is to stand tall with straight legs that are locked and tense. Although the stance might feel comfortable, this position will give you the _least_ amount of control over your skis. It takes a conscious effort and a certain amount of physical effort to flex the knee forward. You need to think of this movement as "unlocking the leg." The return you get is in the control you gain of your feet and skis as you make your turns.

Another secret to unlocking the leg is found in the ankle. With a straight leg position you can't flex the ankles. You need to flex the knee and shin forward into the boot to make the ankle flex. The forward flex of the ankle distributes the weight through the arch to the ball of the foot. This is where you want and need the weight or pressure when you tilt the ski and put it on edge.

# Importance of the right boots

The key to this ankle flex comes from your boots. You need to have a ski boot that allows for the natural flex of the ankle.

Many low-end beginner boots are made from a one- or two-piece cast or mold, with no hinge point. These boots are made more for comfort than performance. While they may feel good on your foot, they restrict your skiing movements. The only way you can make this kind of boot flex is through the strength of your leg and knee pressing the shin forward into the boot. Pushing your leg forward into a boot that won't flex will only make your shins sore. After a few runs, your legs will either be too bruised or tired to continue, and your weight ends up on your heels. With the weight on your heels you'll find yourself resorting back to the straight leg technique.

Your boots must allow natural range of motion in both the knee and ankle. If your boots don't allow you to flex at the ankle, find ones that do. If you are not sure about your boots, but feel you can't get your weight forward, stop by your local ski shop and try a few different pair on. Once you do, you'll be able to feel the difference between boots that flex without hurting and boots that don't.

# Sliding Right

There's something I've discovered recently: it is just as important to know how to flatten and slide the skis, as it is to know how to use the edge. Many skiers know how to put the ski on edge, but don't know how to release that edge to flatten the skis. This can be very frustrating as this type of edge use will cause the skis to "rail" and track straight once on edge.

# The importance of the sideslip

Most books or magazines on ski technique, concentrate on using the edge of the ski and learning to "carve." I think the word "carve" is often misused and frequently misunderstood.

Even before the advent of hourglass skis, I taught that the ski is shaped like an hourglass, wide at the tip and tail, narrow under foot. This was true of conventional skis, and is simply more pronounced with hourglass models. You want to use the *shape* of the ski to help make your turn. That is done by use of the edges. There is a sensitivity that must occur when it comes to using that edge.

I've made turns with accomplished skiers who can engage the edge and work the skis on all terrain, but in certain situations do not have the ability to flatten their skis. This releasing movement is also known as a sideslip, and it has been around almost as long as skiing itself. It's important to know, because there are times when you want to be able to make a controlled slide.

## "Good" Slide vs. "Not So Good" Slide

But let me back up for a minute. There's a "good" slide and a "not so good" slide in skiing. Most beginners and intermediates tend to use a "not so good" slide: they twist their upper body to start a turn. This twisting or "rotary" motion creates a "washing out" and results in out-of-control sliding of both skis. It comes from using the body instead of the feet to make a turn.

When you begin a turn,
- Release the uphill edges of both skis
- Tilt or tip to flatten the skis
- Use the Phantom Move as you transfer your balance.

- Be most sensitive to the ski edge on the snow precisely at the beginning of the turn.
- Flatten your skis with a progressive, lateral foot movement. The flattening movement will start the skis and their tips moving vertically down the slope.

Sometimes you need to prolong the amount of time the ski is flat. When you control the amount of slide with your feet and edge, this is a "good" slide.

## Sliding on Advanced Terrain

As you start to ski steeper blue and black runs with moguls or deep powder, you can use the flat of the skis to control not only your speed, but also the rhythm you need to get your turns going. Feel the transition from gripping with the edges to slipping on the flats by feeling the ski-to-snow contact under your skis and feet. This will give you a smooth, balanced release. Avoid abrupt body movements which cause the skis to react unexpectedly. Moving skis are best controlled with fine lateral movements of the ankles and feet.

We've already talked at length about boots and the importance of the fit. The better the fit of the boot, the better your edge control. If your feet move too much inside your boots, you will have less ability to control your edges. On green and blue slopes you may not notice this, but on black or double black diamond runs it becomes absolutely critical. Because there is less margin for error on steeper runs, all movements must be precise. You must be able to engage and release the edge at will for absolute control. Inability to do this will result in less control on steeper runs.

# Use Your Hips

Photo by Darren Jacklin, courtesy of Harb Ski Systems

Harald Harb standing on the outside edge.
Notice where the hips are relative to the feet.

When I watch skiers come down the hill, it is apparent that only a handful know how to use their hips. The hips are important in skiing because they connect the upper and lower body and are considered the "center" of your power, especially when you ski more advanced runs.

In the Phantom Turn, we learned to do the "Lift and Tilt." When you tilt the boot, knee and ski to the little toe side, you begin the kinetic chain. Once you

*Intermediate Lessons*

change the edge angle of your skis with your feet, the tilt follows up through your body to the hips. The tilt of the feet affects the hips and changes the angle of your body when you engage the edge.

## Using Your Hips in the Phantom Move

Photo by Darren Jacklin, courtesy Harb Ski Systems

Use of Hips in Lift and tilt

When you do the Phantom Move, your body has to be balanced over the stance leg. In essence, you have used your hips to create an angle that allows you to stand against the edge of the ski. This is where your power comes from in your turn. You use your hips and engage the muscles of the leg as you brace against the edge.

When you learn the Primary Movements, you learn to center yourself over your feet. When you start the Phantom Move, your hips will be square over the feet. Standing centered over your feet puts you in the best position and prepares you for a balanced stance when doing the "Phantom Turn." If you tend to sit back, or if your hips are behind your feet, you're using the strength of your quadriceps to hold you up. This is extremely taxing and takes a great deal of energy. Once your quads get tired, you'll have a hard time making a turn.

## Extend the Stance Leg

The best use of your hips will come through your use of the Phantom Turn. As you begin your turn, you will stand or balance on the outside leg of the turn. Once you feel the edge of the ski begin to work through the turn, think of extending the outside leg through the turn. This is following the kinetic chain, that is, the movements of your body that begin with your feet.

If you've been skiing any length of time, your tendency will be to collapse or lower your hips, drive the knees forward and rotate the knees feet and skis through the turn. Instead, find your balance on the stance leg and lengthen that leg as you come through the turn. If you are sure of your balance, think of extending the leg through the turn from the hip flexors (the muscles that connect the upper leg to the hips and waist). Stand or press on the edge as you do this. As we mentioned earlier, your balance will improve the more times you bring it into your skiing in the right manner. The more quickly or more aggressively you bring the ski to the edge, the more dynamic use you'll have of hips. As you stand against the edge of your ski, feel the power that comes from lengthening the leg through your use of the hips.

*Intermediate Lessons*

Maintain a quiet upper body, arms forward, with the head and shoulders quiet. Concentrate on two things when doing this:

- Get the skis out to the side away from the body
- Using your hip for your power as you stand on the edge for each turn.

I work this technique on smooth terrain so I can play with how far I can get my skis to the side.

## Flex and Extend the Body

Once you are comfortable with your stance on the outside leg, you can now begin to flex and extend the body on each turn. You are still engaging the edge in the same manner, but now you are letting the body tilt to the inside of the turn. If your body is facing the fall-line, the skis are lateral, or to the side. On each turn, extend the skis further away from the body. When you finish the turn, relax the muscles in your leg as you shift your balance and begin the new turn.

## Skiing Critical Terrain

When skiing steep critical terrain, your skis must be able to go sideways across the hill as your body heads straight down the hill.

Two things to remember when doing this:

- Use the "Lift and Tilt" to create the angle from the hips.
- There is no up-and-down movement of the body. Because the terrain is so steep, the hill literally is falling away from you. Use the Phantom Turn for control. Watch World Cup ski racers, or extreme skiers in any ski films. You'll notice they use this technique whether on a race course or in extremely steep conditions.

If you only think of bending your knees and ankles, you limit yourself. By using your hips into your turns, you get more power and fluidity out of your skiing. ◆

# Chapter 10

# From Intermediate to Expert

Photo © Jack Affleck, courtesy Vail Resorts/Vail

# Intermediate Skier

Once you reach the intermediate level of skiing, you can probably ski all the green and most of the blue runs on a given mountain. How well you handle that terrain may be another question, however.

## Know Your Equipment

I firmly believe confidence in turning comes from knowing your equipment. The more sure you are of your equipment, the more sure you will be of your turns. I have seen individuals whom I consider intermediate in their level of technical ability handle the toughest runs an area has to offer because of how well they knew their equipment. As a result, they ski even the steepest slopes slowly and surely. For many, it is not a question of how, but where, to make the turn on difficult slopes.

## Start Your Day on a Groomed Run

Most runs at a ski area fall into two categories, groomed and ungroomed. For the beginner and beginning-intermediate skier, it is best to start out on the trails that have been groomed the night before. Skiing a groomed slope gives you a chance to practice your turns while skiing snow that is consistent over the entire run. This also gives you a chance to build your confidence, while developing a feel for the snow as well as your equipment. When you venture off the groomed runs, you are more likely to encounter variations in snow conditions and terrain.

## Learn to Handle Varied Terrain

Knowing how to approach your terrain will make you a better, wiser skier. Let me give you an example. When skiers traverse across a trail to get to another run, most will turn the skis sideways and slide up into the hill. If enough skiers do this in the same place, the snow gets scraped down to rocks or ice as a result. The best snow will be found on the downhill edge of the traverse. Instead of turning up hill with both skis, push the heel of the downhill ski out into the soft snow. This allows you to set the edge of the ski into the place where the most snow has accumulated, and give you more control as you make your traverse.

As you get off the groomed runs, you will find moguls or bumps that form with the variations in terrain. To handle smaller moguls:

- Lower your hips so your center of gravity is over your feet.
- Keep the pressure from your legs pressing into your boots. This helps to keep your weight centered and slightly forward for both balance and control.
- Make your turns on the top of the mogul where your skis have the least resistance.
- Turn or slide both skis on the back side of the mogul where the most snow has built up.
- In hardpack or icy conditions (as in when you ski down off the mountain at the end of the day), look for places where the snow has been pushed, or appears softest. If you cannot find any, head to the side of the trail where any loose snow will accumulate. Look for where the snow is softest and make your turn there.

One other thought for the icy, displaced moguls you find when coming off the mountain at the end of the day: make sure you bend your knees so that you "absorb" the mogul. Think of trying to keep your head as steady as possible so that you do not lose your balance or end up with your weight on your heels. Lack of pressure on the ball of the foot or forward into the boot will throw the weight back.

This will mean a loss of control of the skis and an inability to make a turn, especially if you are tired. The same applies when you come over a knoll where you cannot see the other side: keep the weight forward on the balls of your feet so you maintain control of both feet and skis.

# Common Problems In Intermediate Skiing

I was riding the chairlift recently watching skiers come down the hill. Without realizing it, I found myself critiquing each skier as they passed by. Here are some of the most common problems I saw.

## Number 1: Weight Back

This is the single most common problem. Most people I watch have the majority of weight back on their heels. Skiing from this position gives little if any control. To ski like this takes muscular strength and a great deal of energy. It's almost impossible to turn from this position when going slow. That's why most skiers who ski this way are going at a fairly high rate of speed. It's a dangerous way to ski. When the hips are behind the feet and the weight is back, you do not have spontaneous use of the edge directly beneath your feet. To get your weight forward:

- Bring your hips forward over your feet.
- Think of using the edge of the ski directly under your foot.
- Flex the knee forward so that the shin contacts the front of the boot without resting on it. There should be enough pressure from the leg to make the ankle flex.

- Flexing the knees and ankles together puts the weight forward, which allows the ski to work for you. People ski with their weight on their heels because it seems easy. It takes effort and concentration to get the weight forward.

This leads us to problem No. 2.

## Number 2: No Flex In The Ankle

This goes hand-in-hand with having the weight back. If your ankles are not flexed, your weight is on your heels. It is the knees and ankles flexing together that gets the weight forward. Many skiers, especially those working toward the advanced levels of skiing, tend to sit back as if in a chair. The ankles are not flexed and the hips are behind the feet. You must *keep the hips forward, over the feet, for a balanced position* as you come down the hill. Most of us know what to do, but have trouble applying what we know to our own skiing. That brings us to problem number 3.

## Number 3: Using The Shoulders To Turn

Skiing starts from the ground up. When I analyze a skier, I look at their feet, knees, hips and shoulders, in that order. The turn should begin with the feet. Most beginning and intermediate skiers will use a full motion of the body instead of subtle movements of the feet to make a turn. The skis are an extension of your feet, so begin the turn there.

Start each turn with the Phantom Move that we learned on page 92. Keep the upper body, hips, shoulders, arms and hands quiet, and let the feet and skis do the work.

Photo by Byron Hetzler, courtesy of Harb Ski Systems

It is easier said than done, and only comes from having confidence that your feet and skis will respond when you tell them to.

## Keep Your Hands In Front Of You

- Position your hands as if you were carrying a tray.
- Keep both hands up and in front of the body.
- Once you have that position, think of using them as if you were steering a Flexible Flyer sled.
- Slightly advance the outside hand each time you make a turn.
- Avoid dropping the inside hand. Dropping the inside hand will create a pendulum effect that will throw you off balance. Once you start dropping the hands you find yourself turning your shoulders to compensate.
- Both hands should remain in your field of vision and be held quietly from turn to turn.

*Common Problems In Intermediate Skiing* 191

Being aware of some of the common problems you encounter in your skiing will help you overcome them and put you on track to smoother turns.

# The Pole Plant

The pole plant is one element of skiing that most skiers either never learn or don't fully understand. It is one element of traditional ski instruction that is frequently overlooked. Proper use of your ski poles will enhance your turns, help maintain your balance and strengthen your technique. If done incorrectly, it can throw off not only your turns, but your balance, timing and rhythm as well.

## Hand Position

First, before you use your poles, you must think about how you carry your hands. The correct position is up and in front of you, with the arms away from the body. Most skiers hold the ski poles with the baskets sticking straight out in front, while the arms and elbows clutch the body.

- Relax the arms, bring the elbows away from the body and keep the hands out in front of you, above waist level where you can see them.
- Hold the hands so the knuckles face up. From this position, the pole baskets will be held out to the sides. You should be able to see both hands as you make your turn.
- Your stance should have slight flex in the knees and ankles, with the weight centered and balanced over the entire foot. The hands held up and in front of you will help maintain a balanced stance through the turn.
- If you don't think about keeping your hands up where you can see them, or you carry them at your sides, your weight will be on your

heels or have a tendency to shift back as gravity pulls you down the hill.

- As with our turns and feet, we have a stance hand and a free hand side with our ski poles. The free hand is the inside hand of the turn and the stance hand, the outside hand.

We learned that the kinetic chain begin with the feet. Simply put, all movement starts with your feet. All other movements are secondary, and that includes your hands. All secondary movements should enhance, not detract from, your skiing. What we do with the hands at this point can make the difference between great skiing and a disaster. With the hands in the right position, you are ready to make the pole plant. Think of it as a turn signal. *The pole plant acts as a trigger and is done with the free (inside) hand.* It is made at the same time you transfer your balance to the new stance foot. Timing is such that you release the uphill edges from your old turn, use the Phantom Move to transfer balance and simultaneously make the pole plant. Plant the pole at the same time you have transferred balance to the new stance or outside leg.

## Pole Plant Position

Where you physically plant the pole in the snow is also important. Think of making the pole plant on the same plane as the fall line. Instead of planting the pole up by your ski tips, make the pole plant down the hill from your ski boots. Remember the fall line is the path a ball would roll if you were to release it down the hill. The pole plant should be made on the same line, with a light touch of the basket on the snow.

Photo by Byron Hetzler, courtesy of Harb Ski Systems

**Moving the stance pole forward
to prepare for the plant.**

## Pole Movement

Watch out for stabbing the snow with your poles, as this will affect your upper body. The pole plant should be a light, sensitive touch of the pole basket to the snow. This action should come from the wrist and the wrist only. Do not "pose" with your pole forward as you anticipate your upcoming turn. Simply bring the pole forward from the wrist in one smooth motion. There should be no excess movement with the arm. The movement in the pole plant comes from the wrist and hand only.

As you plant the pole, allow the hand and wrist to roll forward over the top of the ski pole. This way only the hand and wrist are involved, and you avoid using the arm or twisting the shoulders. Plant the pole and allow it to return to the resting position as you ski past the point of snow contact. Make sure you keep the hand up and in your sight as you let it return to the ready position.

Avoid dropping the hand after you plant the pole. When you drop the hand it does two things: 1) it throws you off balance, and 2) causes a pendulum or swinging effect that makes the turn start with the shoulders instead of the feet. The turn starts with the feet through the Phantom Turn. When you lift the free foot and tilt to the little toe side, you balance on the outside or stance leg through the turn. Any extra use of the upper body or arms when you plant the pole will disrupt this balance. This is why you want the pole plant to be smooth and subtle without any extraneous motion with the arm or upper body.

Final position before the pole plant.

I find it helps to think of keeping your hands in front of you as though you were steering a Flexible Flyer sled. This way you can think of "steering" with your hands while you keep them in your line of sight.

If you carry your hands at your side, where you can't see them, you have to raise the whole arm to make the pole plant. You waste time and energy with this motion, and it causes you to make the turn with the body and shoulders. Keep the upper body quiet and make the movement of the pole plant with the hand and wrist only. This way you minimize extraneous body motion and keep your balance through the turn.

## Ski Pole Height

The height of your ski poles is also an important factor when it comes to making a turn. If you have never used your ski poles to help you turn, there are a few things you should know.

- Your poles should allow for a natural right angle (90 degrees) when you hold the pole UPSIDE DOWN, gripping the shaft under the basket (handle touches the floor when measuring this way).
- If you rent or own your equipment, avoid ski poles that are too tall. If they are, you will have to use the arm which affects your shoulder. It becomes impossible to make the pole plant from the wrist. If the poles are too tall and you use them in the manner I just described, you will feel as though your shoulder will be ripped off.

Since I like to ski steep and spend much of my time in the bumps, I prefer a shorter pole. I am 5 foot 10-1/2 inches, and I use a 46" or 48" pole. This allows me to lower my hips and extend the skis laterally, to the side, on steep bumps while bringing the pole forward in the prescribed manner. It's a personal preference but one I feel is important in helping me ski more difficult terrain.

## Improving your Rhythm

If you are having a hard time with your timing or rhythm, try going in slow motion with little or no speed.

- Practice planting the pole from a straight run without making the turn if necessary.
- Bring the pole forward from the wrist to give yourself a feel for the action pole plant.
- Once you can do this, practice with the Phantom Turn on terrain where you don't have to worry about going too fast.
- With the hands held in front of you, bring the ski pole forward with the wrist of the inside or free hand of the turn and make your turn around the pole.
- Continue going around your ski pole on each turn to get a feel for the rhythm.
- Remember the pole plant is a turn signal, and you go around the pole plant on each turn.

## On Steeper Terrain

Proper use of the hands and poles can also assist you on steeper terrain. By putting the hands in the ready position, you can anticipate the upcoming turn. On steep slopes this demands a "separation of the upper and lower body." Your feet, skis and legs go across the hill, while the hips, shoulders and hands face down the hill.

This is the position you must have for the necessary edge and speed control. Use of the hands (or lack thereof) can affect the control you have here. Keeping the hands up and in front of you will help you maintain this body position and give you the control you need. Where the tendency is to sit back on your heels, the hands can help you reach down the hill and project the upper body in your direction of travel.

With both hands up and in front of the body, only the outside hand advances. After you plant the pole, make sure the hand stays up in front of the body. Do NOT drop the inside hand. Doing so will cause you to spin into the hill and lose control. Using the outside hand this way commits the whole outside portion of the body, from the ski, boot, leg, hip and shoulder through the turn.

**Side note:** There are many new and improved ski poles on the market today. Following the technology of boots and skis, these poles are made of space-age materials (carbon composites, Kevlar®, etc.) that make them feather-light, thinner and virtually unbreakable. This light weight will help you with your timing, and reduce the time and energy it takes to bring the pole forward. It's something that may seem insignificant, but can make a difference. Although they cost more, the ligher weight and more durable poles will not only help the swing weight of your pole plant, but will last a lifetime.

# Chapter 11

# The ABCs of Mogul Skiing

Photo by Doug Berry, courtesy Telluride Ski and Golf Company

# Keys to Success

I learned to ski moguls back in the early seventies from Mike Wood, a retired university professor and former ski instructor who lives in Keystone, Colorado.

Now, at age 60, Wood not only out-skis everyone in the bumps, but does it like poetry in motion. He does not go as fast as a pro-mogul skier, but he makes a clean, quick turn better than anyone I know. And, he can keep up with the best of them.

The point is, if you ski the bumps with the right technique, you won't break your body down, strain your knees or lower back, or beat yourself up. The right technique will allow you to ski moguls as smoothly and efficiently as possible, so you can enjoy skiing steeper runs and continue doing so your entire ski life.

## The Difficulty of Skiing Moguls

Skiing on steeper runs with bumps is one of the toughest challenges in skiing. For the average skier, moguls are the most difficult and frustrating aspects of the sport. Regardless of what level of skier you are, you are bound to encounter moguls at some point in your ski life. Knowing what to do and how to handle them will make the simple difference between success and failure.

Moguls are formed into piles or "bumps" when skiers push the snow from turn to turn. The steeper the slope, the more easily these bumps form. The pitch or steepness of the slope, the irregularity of the terrain, the moguls themselves, and the snow conditions underfoot combine to make mogul skiing very difficult. On steep slopes with such conditions there is little, if any, margin for error. Is it any wonder that most people avoid moguls like the plague? But it doesn't have to be that way. Bump skiing can be one of the most enjoyable and addictive forms of skiing.

## Boot Fit is Critical

I believe all control in moguls starts with your feet. The precision you need begins here. Any excess movement of your foot inside your boot will mean less control of your skis and edges. To minimize foot movement it is important to have a boot that fits your foot properly (see page 54). Most black diamond level skiers have custom insoles or orthotics (see page 62 ) to minimize movement and maximize foot stability and edge control.

If you are a blue or beginning black level skier, it's crucial that your foot not move inside your boot on more difficult terrain. On terrain that is not as steep, control of your feet, while important, is not as critical. The steeper and bumpier the run, the more your foot control must be as precise as it is immediate. This one aspect can make the difference between being a so-so blue level skier, or a confident black level skier.

I believe successful mogul skiing involves three areas:

- Keep your skis on the snow;
- Control your speed; and
- Keep your rhythm.

I break number one, "skis on the snow" down further into three more ideas:

- Use your legs like shock absorbers,
- Edge control
- The pole plant.

## Keep Your Skis On the Snow

Only when your skis stay on the snow are you able to control your speed. Even though you will use the Phantom Turn in the bumps, you must still think about keeping the skis on the snow. When you lose ski-to-snow contact you will find yourself in trouble.

## Use Your Legs Like Shock Absorbers

Before you can ski the bumps, you have to know how to "absorb," to handle changes in your terrain and ski smoothly. Most expert or experienced skiers take this ability for granted. It is the number one skill you must have in order to be smooth and efficient when skiing black diamond terrain. Absorption is like having a glass of water on top of your head and trying to make it across the hill without spilling any. The lower body does the work while the upper body maintains a balanced and stable position. The piston-like action of the legs as they flex and extend allows the head and upper body to remain quiet.

I first teach absorption from a traverse across the hill. A blue run with small moguls is best. Make sure there are no icy spots in between as this can upset your stance and balance.

- Keep your hands up in front of you where you can see them to stabilize the upper body and further help maintain balance.
- When the skis move into the mogul, let the skis, ankles and knees flex forward as the legs "absorb" the bump.
- Keep your body and hips over your feet and maintain contact with your shin against the front of the boot by <u>flexing your ankles</u> forward.
- Keep this pressure from your leg forward to avoid getting thrown back on your heels.
- As your feet come over the top of the mogul, extend the legs to keep the feet and skis on the snow.
- Try to make the transition from bump to bump as smooth as possible.

You are doing two things simultaneously when you do this. Your legs flex and extend to act as "shock absorbers," as you keep your feet and skis on the snow. This is very important, as any time your skis come off the snow you will pick up speed or lose control.

Practice the flexion and extension of the legs by traversing (going from one side of the hill to the other) across a run covered with moguls.

- Keep the feet close together and the majority of the weight on the downhill ski while in the traverse.
- The run should not be too steep, nor the moguls too big.
- Maintain a balanced position as the legs absorb the moguls.
- Do not allow the weight to shift back or be thrown to the heels.

Remember we are still in a traverse, not working on turns yet. You are trying to create a "smooth ride" using your legs like shock absorbers to allow the skis to stay on the snow.

A turn in the moguls is made with your body and weight balanced and centered over your feet. If at any time the weight goes to the heels you'll have trouble making your turn. So balance is a primary concern even at this stage in moguls. If your weight shifts to your heels when you ski groomed blue or black runs, you can still recover. This won't be the case when you ski steep bumpy runs like Prima at Vail, Outhouse at Winter Park, "S" lift at Copper Mountain, "Kant Make 'Em" in Telluride or any other steep, black-diamond bump runs.

## Develop Your Leg Strength

The act of using the legs like "shock absorbers" demands leg strength. The stronger your legs, the more effective they will be. I recommend supplemental weight and aerobic conditioning.If you have made it to the hill and found your legs lacking the necessary strength or stamina, there is hope. You can strengthen your legs and build your stamina in a short period of time before you ski again. A work out two or three times per week on a regular basis will greatly improve your legs (and overall body conditioning), and give you greater strength and endurance the next time you ski. I've skied with friends who, lacking leg strength earlier in the season, used this approach and are now skiing stronger than ever.

It is not only the strength of your legs but also your midsection you need when skiing black diamond conditions. Strong stomach muscles will complement your overall leg strength and help your stamina and endurance. (This is not to say that just because your legs and abdomen are strong you will be a good skier, but the stronger you are, the better you'll ski). This is true not only for experts but beginners and intermediates as well. Now that you know how to absorb moguls, let's learn how we use the terrain to our advantage.

Photo © Jack Affleck, courtesy of Vail Resorts

*The ABCs of Mogul Skiing*

# Skiing on the Edge

In the previous chapter we learned how to keep our skis on the snow and let the legs absorb the terrain. Once you know how to use the legs like shock absorbers, you'll want to think about using the edges. Use of your edge will lead you to Step Number Two, Control Your Speed.

## Find the Right Terrain

It's best to learn to ski moguls on blue terrain with soft, round bumps. Beware of the many blue-level bump runs that have some of the ugliest, hard-to-ski moguls that I've ever seen. On runs such as these you have large irregular piles of snow (I wouldn't even call them moguls) with ice patches in between. These "moguls" can be harder to ski than black diamond bumps on steeper terrain. The reason for this is that the bumps were made by the actions of inexperienced skiers. It's important to find the right terrain to give you a feel for doing the technique correctly and to build your confidence. Two favorite learn-to-ski bump runs that come to mind are "Showboat" at Vail and "Engeldive" at Winter Park. Both of these runs have the right kind of pitch, and consistently have perfect bumps with soft snow. There are many other great learn-to-ski bump runs, so it's a matter of finding a run that allows you to feel comfortable while you are learning.

## Discover The Edges

In the same way you learned to absorb, you want to discover the edges. We do this with what we call the *sideslip*:

- Standing on top of a mogul, release the edges of both skis by tipping or tilting the feet downhill.

- As soon as you flatten the skis they will move forward and down the hill.
- As you slide down the back, or downhill, side of the bump, tip the feet gently back into the hill to feel the edges grip.

The sideslip makes you aware of three necessary elements for a good turn in the bumps:

- Your balance
- Placement of your weight
- Your edges.

With the sideslip, you can play with your balance or weight, moving it fore and aft, from ball of foot to the heel, when you release your edge and slide. Tipping the feet laterally controls the sideslip and when the skis are flat or on edge. Keep the movements subtle and gentle so as not to disrupt your balance. You need this sensitivity when you release and engage the edges as this gives you the smooth, subtle control you need when skiing moguls.

As you continue to practice the sideslip, you will become more aware of your edges. Now let's do the sideslip again, but this time let's incorporate Primary Movements into our technique.

- The stance (downhill) ski in the traverse becomes the "accelerator" and the free foot (uphill ski) acts as the "brake".
- Tip the stance foot to the little toe side while simultaneously tipping the free foot down the hill.
- As soon as you flatten both skis with this technique, your ski tips will seek the fall line and accelerate down the hill.
- Do not let your skis get away from you. As soon as you feel the release and acceleration, tip the free (uphill) foot to the little toe side to

engage the uphill edge of both skis to slow down.

- Try to keep the feet relatively close together so you can work both feet together.

Now let's try it from a traverse moving across the mogul field.

- Start from a narrow stance.
- When your feet pass the crest of the mogul, use the sideslip technique I just mentioned to control your slide.
- We are not doing turns yet, but simply going from one side of the trail to the other.
- Use the stance leg to release and tip the skis laterally down the hill to flatten the skis.
- Use the same sensitivity to control your edge as you did in the sideslip.
- Tip both feet laterally down the hill to flatten the skis and slide on the downhill side of the mogul.
- As your feet come over the top of the mogul and pass the crest, think of keeping your skis and feet in contact with the snow.

Avoid skiing directly into the side of a mogul, as this will throw your weight to your heels and have you fighting to keep your balance. Instead, go around any large moguls and slide on the backside. Don't worry about making a turn yet, just get the feel for the skis sliding on the backside of each bump.

This exercise is designed to give you a feel for your edges as the terrain undulates beneath your feet. The more you do this simple exercise of releasing and engaging the edges, the more comfortable you'll feel in the moguls. You can do this regardless of the size of the bumps of the steepness of the

Photo© Ken Redding, Courtesy of Beaver Creek Resort;

"Grouse Mountain at Beaver Creek is renowned for moguls that challenge even the most veteran skiers"

slope. It's the best way I know to establish a level of comfort in extremely difficult terrain

Keep your feet closer together when you practice these exercises. This will help with your balance and foot control. Skiing with a wide stance in moguls can be disastrous. It will only throw you off balance and make it harder for you to progress. If you watch good mogul skiers, you'll see they ski with their feet close together. This way they make the skis move as one. With the feet closer together you can refine your balance and the control of your edges. By now you should have control of both your weight and balance in your traverse.

Let's try the same sideslip exercise as before, only now let's use the Phantom Move. On groomed flat terrain you have the luxury of using the whole slope; in the moguls you must try to contain this action to the space of one or two moguls. In traditional ski technique what we're going to do is

*The ABCs of Mogul Skiing*

called a "garland" or a "fan." Right now we are only working the end portion of a turn.

The top or crest of the mogul is the point of least resistance with the tips and tails of the skis. This is where you begin the Phantom Move.

- As your feet pass the crest of the mogul, lift the inside or free foot and ski and tilt to the little toe side. Keep the tip of ski on the snow. Once you lift the free foot, it forces you to balance on the downhill or stance foot of the turn. It is critical that the stance foot remains in contact with the snow, on both sides of the mogul.
- As the foot of the stance leg passes the crest of the bump, press the ball of the foot forward to keep the foot and ski on the snow. Your control will come from the contact of the stance ski edge on the back or downhill side of the mogul.
- Tipping the free foot to the little toe edge will bring you to the big toe edge of the stance ski. Only now you must control the amount of edge and slide with the stance foot. If you use gross movements when you engage the edge of the stance ski, you won't have the control you need as the terrain changes under foot. This is where you use the sideslip for control from the flat of the ski to the edge.
- Keep the pressure of the stance leg into the front of the boot to avoid the weight being thrown back on your heels and your upper body, hands, hips and shoulders facing down the hill. Once the weight is on your heels, you'll have little, if any control.

The more aggressive you are with the tilt of the free foot to the little toe side, the more quickly you will come to the edge of your stance ski.

Now it's time to think about the turn.

# Turning in Moguls

So far, we've worked on two aspects of our technique to keep the skis on the snow: 1) shock absorption and, 2) the sideslip on the back of the bump for our edge control. At this point we know how to absorb our terrain, release and engage the edges, and use the Phantom Move.

Every bump run on every mountain is different, so the keys to successful mogul skiing are confidence in your technique and the flexibility to adapt to different bump terrain.

## Using The Phantom Turn

Now it's time to think about making a turn. We've worked on the Phantom Move from a traverse, now let's work it into our turn. The thought of keeping the skis on the snow may seem contrary when you use the Phantom Turn. However, the use of the Phantom Turn in the moguls will give you a stronger, more balanced and more efficient turn than before. When I first introduce the Phantom Turn in the moguls, I exaggerate the use of the inside ski when I lift and tilt. Literally pick up the inside or free foot (keeping the ski tip on the snow) as your feet pass the crest of the mogul, and tilt both ski and boot of the free foot to the little toe side. This forces you to balance on the stance leg, and will give you a quicker feel for the turn when you tilt the free foot to the little toe edge.

# One Turn at a Time

- Start with one turn at a time. Approach the mogul from a slight downhill traverse so you don't go too fast.
- Absorb the bump and make your Phantom Turn on top where your skis have the least resistance.
- Tip or tilt the inside or free foot to the little toe edge, as you press the ball of your stance foot to maintain ski to snow contact.
- As your stance foot slides forward and down the back side of the bump, pull your feet back under your body. If you push your feet forward instead of pulling the feet back, this drops your hips and will have you sitting back.
- Complete the turn on the back or downhill side of the mogul. It is the edge contact under your foot that will give you control.
- Make only one turn and stop. Try this a few times on one side before you switch to the other.

Use this one-turn technique to get a feel for the snow with your feet, skis and edges. (Later on you'll put consecutive turns together.) With the Phantom Turn you want to think of lengthening or extending the legs, rather than lowering your hips, to maintain your ski to snow contact. Flex the legs to absorb the mogul and extend the legs on the downhill side. Be as smooth as possible, and maintain your ski-to-snow contact with your stance foot on each turn.

By making one turn and coming to a stop, you become comfortable handling one mogul at a time without being intimidated by the magnitude of the entire run. You also develop a feel for the bumps, the irregularity of your terrain, and the sliding action of your skis.

Work on making each turn <u>around</u> the mogul, and control your speed on the back or downhill side of the bump with the sideslip. Once you make the turn on the backside of the mogul, you can engage the edge of the stance ski to slow down. The run, the steepness, and the type of moguls you are skiing will determine how much edge you want to use.

## Using the Ski Poles

Now that we have the feet and skis under control its time to think about using our ski poles. (See page 192 for a complete review of The Pole Plant.)

- Hold the hands up, in front of your body and slightly out to the sides. All the movements in the pole plant are made with the wrist and elbow.
- Keep the pole touching the mogul as long as possible.
- The pole and hand positions should be held in front of the body where you can see them. This will help maintain balance and stabilize the upper body, letting you use the lower body for turning.
- Make sure you move your free hand forward over the top of the pole after you plant the pole.
- Keep your outside or stance hand up and in your line of sight through the turn.
- As with any turn, avoid dropping the hand after you plant the pole. Dropping the hand after you plant the pole will create a pendulum effect that will throw you off balance and out of control.

I know it can be difficult; concentrate on your feet and you forget about your hands and vice versa. Work on your feet, turns and speed control first, and gradually incorporate the hands to add to your stability and balance.

# Ski the Line

Once I begin to use the Phantom Turn in the moguls I go back to steep, *groomed* blue or black terrain. It is on steeper groomed terrain that I practice skiing the fall-line with the same technique and mental attitude that I would use in the bumps. Moguls are made by skiing down the hill, so it's important that you learn to make turns skiing straight down the fall line. The technique I use here is called "skiing the clothesline."

- From where you are standing on the slope, imagine a clothesline attached to your navel running in a straight line to a fixed point 100 yards down the hill.
- Point your body downhill and begin making turns.
- Keep the upper body stable and one hand on either side of this imaginary line.
- Try to make turns to each side while following the "clothesline" with your upper body. Essentially you are keeping your upper body in the fall line while your lower body makes the turns.
- Use the Phantom Move on each turn.
- When you release the edges and flatten the skis to begin the new turn, do not ski out of the fall line.
- Keep the upper body facing straight down the slope, with your hands on either side of the "clothesline." This takes a tremendous amount of edge control to keep from sliding forward into a traverse.
- You must keep your momentum going straight down the hill, while your skis are turning. If,

when you release the ski edges, you move across the hill, you are doing it incorrectly.
• Make your turns and control your speed in the fall line.

This is a difficult but necessary skill you must master if you want to ski steep bump runs well. That is why you should practice this on a steep, groomed run initially. Once you get the feel for doing this on the flat, go back to the moguls. Now it's time to practice skiing the fall-line in the moguls.

## Where to Turn

The biggest frustration for most skiers is not knowing where to turn. I turn <u>around</u> each mogul, using the downhill side for a controlled sideslip or edge set. Moguls are made by skiing down the hill, not across. On blue runs with easy moguls you don't have to worry if you make a mistake, but on steeper runs with tighter bumps, there is less margin for error.

Find a blue run that is not too steep with moguls that are evenly spaced. Let's go from making one turn as we did before to making three or four turns.

## Finding a Good Line

When you start to think about making more than one turn in the bumps you must think about the path or "line" you will ski. The moguls on a given run are pre-determined and therefore, so are your turns. You must pick the bump where you will make your turn and turn there. There are "good" and "bad" lines when skiing moguls.

A good line has a rhythm and flow that takes you from one mogul to the next and continues the length of the run. Competent mogul skiers who can make quick turns down the fall line usually form these.

A bad line is a series of two or three bumps that leave you no place to go or turn after you reach that third mogul in the series. With a bad line there is no way to establish a rhythm or flow that will give you the feel for putting all the elements together that we've talked about so far.

Finding a good line and developing the ability to ski it takes practice, experience and skill. The more you get in the habit of looking for the right line the easier it becomes.

When looking for a line, you are looking at the moguls that will allow you to flow from one turn to the next.

## Skiing a Good Line

- Rather than turn haphazardly in the bumps, pick your bump and make the turn there.
- To get into this habit you must also practice looking down the hill at least three or four turns.

Courtesy of Keystone Resort; copyright Ben Blankenburg

**Skiing the mogul fields on North Peak at Keystone**

- To work into finding a good line and looking ahead, pick out four moguls that are downhill from you.
- Look and see where you will make your first four turns.
- Keep your skis on the snow and control your speed after each turn. Do this on all four turns.
- Practice this series using only four turns as you work your way down the run.

Limit yourself to just four turns so you can get a feel for keeping both skis on the snow and controlling your speed after each turn. You'll find that once you get the rhythm it's easier to keep going. Now it becomes a matter of consistency. As with any sport you need to train yourself so you can repeat that same feeling of success. Avoid beating yourself up over bad turns. It's more productive to concentrate on the good turns and try to repeat the sensation to develop the muscle memory and body feel.

## Apply All the Steps

Once you start skiing a line, you still need to apply steps one and two, keep your skis on the snow and control your speed after each turn. If you maintain your ski-to-snow contact with the stance leg after each turn you will find it easier to control your speed. When your feet pass the crest and are on the downhill side you must be able to flatten or engage the edge at will. Different terrain and the size and shape of the moguls themselves will determine whether you need to flatten the ski before you engage the edges for more control. This is where experience comes in. If you don't have the ability to control your edges, you will be at the mercy of the hill.

# Keep Your Rhythm

We've worked the first two steps, "Keep your skis on the snow" and "Control your speed", extensively. Now it's time to move on to step three, Keep Your Rhythm. The underlying thought behind Step Three is, once you start turning, keep turning. Outstanding mogul skiers are those who bring the mountain under their control. You must develop the confidence that, when skiing bumps, you are in control, not the mountain. If you don't develop the technique and the attitude to pull it off, you'll always be at the mercy of your terrain.

As I mentioned in the previous chapter, most proficient mogul skiers look for the best "line" or path down the mogul field. This "line" is a path that you choose around the moguls that is pre-determined. The challenge in picking a line is being able to ski the bumps in this path you've chosen. You must pick or "spot" the bump where you want to turn, and make your turn there. It takes

Photo © Bob Winsett, courtesy of Vail Resorts/Keystone

practice to be this precise. The more you do it the better you get.

## Speed Control is Important

Rhythm is closely connected to speed control. Once you start turning you want to keep turning with no pause or hesitation. You must keep your speed the same from beginning to end, not too fast, not too slow. The common mistake is accelerating at the end of the turn until the point where you are picking up speed and out of control. That's why I place so much emphasis on steps one and two. It's easy to go fast and lose control. It takes concentration and effort to maintain balance and speed in steep, difficult conditions.

Let's go back to the four- turn technique.

- Pick out four moguls that are downhill from you.
- Look and see where you will make your first four turns.
- Use the Phantom Turn and keep the stance ski on the snow.
- Control your speed after each turn. Do this on all four turns. You are working on control of both your skis and the terrain.
- Your speed should remain the same after each turn as well as when you finish the four turns.
- If you miss a turn, go too fast, or lose control; stop and start again.
- Practice this series using only four turns as you work your way down the run. Limit yourself to just four turns so you can get a feel for linking the Phantom Turns together.
- The two critical elements are the *ski-to-snow contact of your stance ski* and *control of your speed* after each turn.

Did you make each turn where planned? Did your stance ski stay on the snow the entire time? Did you control your speed after each turn?

Initially, you might make only one good turn out of the four - that's okay! What you are looking to do is increase the consistency of your good turns. Don't beat yourself up if you can't get all four turns at first. If you only made one good turn, try to make it two on your next series of turns. Work toward being able to consistently pick your turns and make them where you planned.

By only making a few turns at a time, you can learn to minimize your mistakes without putting yourself at risk. Most black diamond terrain is unforgiving, so you need to break it down while you learn to become more comfortable on this kind of run. The more comfortable you are, the more confident you become.

## Move Up to Longer Sections

The four-turn technique is the first step in learning how to keep your rhythm in the moguls. Once you feel comfortable making four turns consistently, it's time to ski longer sections. When skiing moguls, it's easier to keep going once you get a feel for the rhythm that comes from your turns.

- Look for a line of moguls that is even and consistent.
- Put yourself in that "line," start turning and maintain your rhythm.
- See if you can get a feel for the rhythm as you go from turn to turn in succession.
- Look down the hill at least three or four turns so you can see where each turn is *before* you get there.
- If necessary, go slower rather than faster to maintain control.

- Do not turn so sharply that you end up skiing into each bump. Make your turn around each bump and use your edge control on the downhill side.

If you look at other proficient mogul skiers you will see a controlled motion that appears effortless. When skiing moguls you want to maintain a constant speed - not too fast, not too slow - and a rhythm that matches your turns.

## A Word On Mogul Skis.

The skis you use for moguls are a matter of personal preference. Pro Mogul skiers traditionally ski an even-flexing slalom ski, 200 to 205cm in length. A conventional or standard ski that is used in moguls should be even-flexing from tip to tail, not too stiff, not too soft. It can either be a slalom or giant slalom cut depending on your preference.

- A ski that is too soft will tend to "wash out" under your foot.

Photo © Bob Winsett, courtesy of Vail Resorts/Breckenridge

**Olympian Donna Weinbrecht in the Breckenridge Freestyle World Cup.**

- A ski that is too stiff will snap or accelerate you from one turn to the next when you release the camber at the end of the turn. The skis will tend to control you and not the other way around.

You want a ski that will allow you to direct the energy from one turn to the next without throwing you off balance or causing you to accelerate down the hill. Many skis that are made for running gates will perform this way and are not recommended for bumps.

I find that the "hourglass" or "modified hourglass" skis are good all-around skis and ideal for moguls. Because of the , they are quick and easy to turn. Most hourglass skis will work in the bumps as long as you use the edge directly under your foot. Because of the ski shape and how you use the edge under your foot you'll get a quick, responsive turn. Avoid putting any weight or pressure forward or on the front of the ski. Unlike a conventional ski, you cannot use the front of an hourglass ski to slow down.

# "Phantomizing" In The Bumps

I enjoy skiing moguls more than any other conditions or terrain on the mountain. Those who know me know I'm not skiing unless I'm in the bumps. Once you begin to feel more comfortable in the moguls you'll find you want to ski them more and more. This is when you are a bona fide mogul skier.

## The Secret to Skiing Moguls

The secret to skiing moguls all day without getting beaten up is to be smooth. We've already covered at length the techniques for keeping the skis on the snow for the control you need. As with anything else you do in life, the more you do something the better you get at it. The same is true with skiing, and with bumps in particular.

## Refine Your Moves

Now that we are feeling more secure with our terrain and using the Phantom Turn, it's time to refine. We know that the Phantom Turn is the quickest, most efficient way to make a turn. Initially, when we first learn the Phantom Move we exaggerate the lift and tilt of the free foot when we do the Phantom Turn. Now, at an advanced stage we begin to think about "Phantomizing" the turn.

- Instead of picking up the free foot, we simply lighten the free foot as we tip to the little toe edge without picking it up. This is all the action we need to initiate the turn.
- When you ski the fall line and use the Phantom Move, you create an oscillation as you go from turn to turn.
- When the skis are to the side, away from the body, you are actually using the hip to create the power or pressure to hold the edge of the ski.
- As your feet and skis pass under your body, absorb the terrain as you balance on the stance ski.
- Do not let your body rise up between your turns.
- The challenge is to keep the skis on the snow, yet maintain a smooth even flow as you go from turn to turn.

## Using Your Hips

- To get the idea of using your hips, stand an arm's length from a wall in your house.
- Put your hand against the wall and move your feet away from the wall so you are leaning on your hand. The further you move your feet

away from the wall the more you have to lower your hips.

- In this position, with your feet away from the wall, imagine you have your skis on.
- The outside leg is your stance leg. It is the platform upon which you stand as you hold your edge and ride the skis through the turn. The skis and feet extend to the side or "laterally" away from your body.
- You can only do this if you lower your hips. Obviously, this is an extreme position but one you can duplicate once on skis.

Phantomizing in the moguls means you are now comfortable skiing in the fall-line. The flexion and extension of the legs will play a critical element in maintaining a smooth, even flow as you make your way from one turn to the next. When you feel comfortable enough to begin Phantomizing, you'll find your balance is strong and secure. Remember to keep your hands up and in front of you. Review the section beginning on page 192 for the correct position of the hands and proper placement of the ski pole.

For most skiers at this level, it is not what you do, but rather what you don't do. In this case, everything begins with the feet and culminates with the upper body and hands. Any extra motion of the upper body will only detract from your turns. So you must work on being as smooth with your upper body as you are with your feet.

# Chapter 12
# Powder Skiing

Photo by Todd Powell, used courtesy of Copper Mountain Resort

John Grugel skiing Resolution Bowl at Copper
Mountain Resort, Colorado

# Powder Skiing For Beginners

Powder snow is one of the greatest experiences you can have in skiing - if you can do it correctly. That means you can make turns, get the skis to come around and establish a rhythm from turn to turn. If you can't get the hang of making a turn in the deep stuff, you spend more energy wallowing around in it than you do skiing. So, what's the best way to handle it?

Photo © Ben Blankenberg, courtesy of Vail Resorts/Keystone

- With accumulations of one or two feet or more, you need to *find a slope that is relatively steep*. The deeper the snow, the more momentum you need to keep going. Otherwise you'll stop after one or two turns. You need sufficient pitch to have enough speed to make your turns.
- In order to ski powder effectively you must *ski in the fall line*. The snow acts as a force that will slow you down and the reason you must ski down the hill.

## Learning to Ski the Fall Line

For many blue and beginning black level skiers, skiing the fall line on a steeper run can be a new sensation. You have to be able to "let yourself go" in order to experience the "flow" of going from one turn to the next. Everything you do must contribute to this flow, or you will end up fighting yourself. Working against yourself will waste your energy and cause you to tire faster. This can be an extremely frustrating way to ski. That's why you must develop the confidence to point your skis down the hill. This way you can find a rhythm with both your body and skis as you go from turn to turn.

## Keep Your Feet Together

Regardless of the depth of the snow, keep your feet close together so your skis "cut" the snow as one. In powder snow, skiing with the feet together is a must. In knee-deep snow or deeper, having the feet together is critical. A narrow stance will increase your balance and enhance your ability to make the turn. Most skiers have a problem with their skis drifting apart. If your feet come apart you will most likely catch your inside ski, which will cause you to lose your balance and fall. And in deep powder snow, it takes too much energy to fall. It is easier to keep your feet together and stay up.

## The Right Terrain for Your Skill Level

If you are a beginner or an intermediate and are not sure about your technique or how to handle powder, I recommend you find the slopes that have been packed out by the Sno-Cat®. The snow on the groomed runs will be soft and consistent so as to give you the feeling of what powder snow is like without worrying about the depth. This will allow you to concentrate on your technique and your turns without the frustration of off-piste conditions.

If you are at the advanced-intermediate to beginning-expert level, and are ready to go "off piste" (off-trail):

- Find a blue or easy black run without moguls.
- Start with your skis pointing straight down the hill.
- If the snow is 12 inches deep or less, stand on both feet, but emphasize your balance and weight on the stance or outside ski as you tip the free foot.
- In deeper snow, initiate with the Phantom Move, but distribute your balance and weight more evenly over both feet.
- Before you can think about turning, you need to build your speed. Otherwise, you will stop after a few turns.
- As your speed builds, begin your turns with an up and down motion of your body. Think of it as "bouncing" from turn to turn. The bouncing motion will give your legs the feeling of flexing and extending under your body. This is rhythm you want to feel not only with your body but your skis as well.

- In the "bounce" or "up" motion, the flexion brings the feet and the skis up to the surface.
- The "down" motion will give an extension of the legs and skis through the turn.
- The knees and ankles should be flexed so that the weight is centered and slightly forward. Up starts the turn, down finishes it.

## Important Points to Remember

In powder there are two important points to remember; the Phantom Turn and your hands. Yes, even in powder snow you still want to use the free foot to begin your turns. However, the deeper the snow, the more you want to evenly distribute your weight and balance evenly over both feet.

In normal skiing situations, you should have the majority of your balance and weight on the stance foot and ski. It usually works out that it's about 60 or 70% on the stance leg and 30 to 40% on the free foot. In deep powder, or if the snow is bottomless, you will want to distribute your balance and weight evenly, 50/50 over both feet. It is critical that your legs remain together throughout the turn.

The key for stability and balance in powder skiing is your use of your hands. Keep both hands up in front of your body with your ski poles out to the sides. The pole plant is made the same way we discussed in the chapter about our use of the poles.

- Dropping one or both of the hands, especially the inside hand, will force the weight back to the heels and create a swinging or pendulum effect with the upper body. This motion will cause you to lose your balance and fall.
- Think instead to hold both hands up and in front of you where you can see them. Advance the outside or stance hand to help maintain balance and drive through the turn.

Avoid dropping the inside hand at all costs. It's primarily the inside hand that will cause problems if you don't hold it up where you can see it when you make a turn.

There is a rhythm and grace that comes with linking turns in deep, soft snow. It takes the right technique combined with the right attitude. With practice and experience you'll find it becoming more enjoyable and less work.

# Advanced Powder Skiing

Powder skiing is the part of skiing that many consider an art form. As a result, there are a great number of devotees who live and breathe to ski powder. It's because the powder ski experience borders on the ethereal that there are many areas and services that cater exclusively to the powder hound. These range from bowl and extreme terrai,n to helicopter skiing and Sno-Cat, tours. In every ski magazine you pick up, there are photos of skiers in snow so deep it's hard to imagine. It's no wonder there is a mystique about skiing powder.

## Common Problems

The there are a number of problems most people have when skiing powder that contribute to a lack of fluidity:

- No flexion and extension with the legs and skis
- Weight on the heels
- Separation of the feet through the turn.

If you have your weight centered on the balls of your feet or through the arches (with the "bouncing" motion) and initiate the turn with the Phantom Move, it's easier to feel the skis working as they were designed. In powder snow it is not as critical to use the edge as it is to use the entire ski surface through your turn. The action of the flexion and extension of your legs will bend the skis underfoot on each turn. This is the action you need to have to be successful in powder. If you don't make your skis work for you, you'll end up fighting yourself as you work your way through the deep stuff.

## DO NOT SIT BACK!

Regardless of what your friends may have told you, this is not the way to ski powder. Those who sit back when they ski usually do so because of movement inside the boot, lack of foot control, or because they believe this the most effective way to bring the skis back to the surface on each turn.

- Sitting back will take the weight off your ski tips so that they float, but relies on the strength of your legs and quadriceps to make the your turn.
- It is an extremely inefficient way to ski as it takes a tremendous amount of strength and energy which will cause you to tire faster.
- Once you are tired you'll find it difficult to make any kind of turn at all.
- Sitting back also demands that you rotate or twist the skis, feet and knees in order to make the skis come around. This twisting action puts a great deal of torque on the lower body which can translate into knee pain and muscle strain.

Instead of sitting back, keep your weight centered so that you are able to use your feet and the tipping action of the Phantom Move to make your turn.

## Up and Down

If you've ever seen film or video footage of people skiing powder, you will notice that they seem to bounce from turn to turn, as if to over-exaggerate the motion needed with each turn. The up is the transition part or the beginning of the new turn. The down is riding the skis through the turn. Depending on the depth of the snow, it may be necessary to have the weight distributed more evenly on both feet on the down motion. It is important to know that *when the skis are in the most flexed position, the*

Photo © T.R. Youngstrom, courtesy Telluride Ski and Gold Company

*Advanced Powder Skiing*

*resistance of your flexed skis against the snow is what slows you down.* This is especially important in bottomless snow. The key is being able to find a rhythm in your up and down that allows you to move gracefully from turn to turn.

## Use Your Hands

Always keep both hands up in front of you when you ski. Use your pole plant to help stabilize your upper body, maintain your balance and set you up for the turn. Make sure you do not drop do not drop your inside hand. If you do everything right with your skis, but fail to keep your hands in front of you when making the turn, you will find yourself floundering more often than not. In powder, it takes more energy to fall down than it does to stand up, so do every thing you can to stay on your feet.

## Powder Cords

If powder is your passion or you find yourself spending much time in deep snow, it might be a good idea to invest in a powder cord or ribbon. The powder cord is to prevent you from losing a ski should you fall. Powder cords are usually 3-5 feet long, are neon or fluorescent in color and attach to your ski brakes. Powder cords work like streamers and make it easier for you to find your ski once your bindings release. (I speak from experience, remembering the time I stepped out of my ski on a steep section of a hill in about four feet of powder. I never found the ski.) The ribbon tucks inside your pant cuffs and will pull out when you fall, helping to find and recover your ski.

## Know Your Equipment

Because you want to ski down the hill, you have to mentally deal with the process of letting go. Letting go **(See page 169)** is an attitude of trust. Trust in yourself, your equipment and your ability. You have to be sure of the fit of your boots and how your skis will perform in the deep stuff.

Your skis should be soft enough to be forgiving, yet still come around on each turn. Many skis that perform on ice or hardpack don't do as well in snow up to your knees. Don't fault your personal, technical ability by confusing it with what your skis can or cannot do in the deep stuff. Some skis simply do not ski well in powder.

## Establish Your Rhythm

One of the problems many have in skiing powder is not being able to ski straight down the hill. This is a must. And if you are skiing in a foot or two of snow you need a slope that is relatively steep. It is because of these two criteria (skiing the fall line, on the steep) that powder skiing represents the ultimate in letting go.

Photo © Byron Hetzler, courtesy of Winter Park Resort

In order to feel a semblance of control (and not like you're hanging on by your toenails), you must establish your rhythm as soon as you begin your movement. If you build your speed before you get your rhythm, you might find yourself going too fast to make a turn. This means you need to over emphasize the up and down motion to get the skis working under your feet. It is the down part, or what I call the "belly" of the turn, where you experience control. This is where the skis are flexing underfoot and turning across the fall line. It is from this action that you create the resistance to slow you down. This is the sensation that draws so many skiers into the realm of the powder experience and makes it effervescent.

Skiing powder can be fun, but it also can be most frustrating. I hope some of these tips will help you the next time you find yourself in powder up to your chest.

# Fat Skis For Powder

If you plan on skiing powder, fat skis are the way to go. Fat skis are a shorter, wider version of a regular ski, and without a doubt make it easier not only to ski deep powder, but crud and junk snow as well. These skis are designed specifically for powder skiing. They are twice as wide as a normal ski and allow you to "float" more easily. A normal slalom or giant slalom ski will tend to sink or "auger" in deep snow, unless they are even flexing and you know how to ski them in powder. Hourglass skis do fairly well in deep snow due to the wide tip and tail, but in extremely deep snow fat skis are the way to go. The benefits of using a fat ski are that they are less likely to sink, easier to turn, and bring you back to the surface after each turn due to the construction and capabilities of the ski.

## Availability

A few years ago, there were only one or two fat skis on the market. Now it seems every company has a fat ski version. I recently had the opportunity to try one of the top selling fat skis on the market, the Volant Chubb. True to Volant, their "Chubb" has a steel cap ski construction (the top layer or "cap" goes from edge to edge, unlike the layered versions of other skis). The benefit of the cap construction is that it makes it easier to put the ski on edge and come around. This was true of the "Chubb" even in knee to waist deep powder. Volant has one of the few fat skis that will turn on the hardpack as well in the powder. (It's probably the reason ski shops can't keep them in stock.)

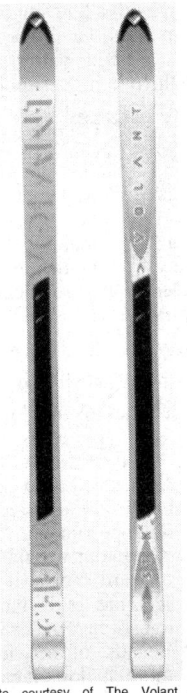

Photo courtesy of The Volant Ski Company, LLC.

Volant Chubb is shown on left.

## Versatility

One of the big complaints about fat skis over the past few years was lack of versatility. Once you got out of the powder onto the hardpack slopes, most fat skis would not perform. This is not so anymore. Now with a blurring of the lines between hourglass shapes and fat skis, every ski company makes skis versatile enough to ski most any condition you find on the hill.

## Advantages

Now, all you critics, put your skepticism aside. Using a fat ski is not "cheater skiing." It simply gives you more energy for more runs. It takes less effort to make a turn. There is less wear and tear on your body, making skiing more enjoyable. (I have many friends, including Warren Miller, who have traded in their regular boards and now only ride fat skis.)

## How to Ski Them

Ski the fat skis like you would a normal pair of skis.

- Use an up and down or bouncing motion to make your turns. This does two things: it gives you a feel for the skis under your feet, and allows you to experience them through a turn - up to start and steer the feet into the turn, and down to finish it.
- Keep your weight centered and slightly forward. You still want to have enough pressure on the balls of your feet so you feel the ski flex under your foot.
- Because of the width of a fat ski you'll float more, making it easier to turn.
- Control your speed at the END of each turn.
- Keep your speed consistent by keeping it the same from one turn to the next.

Fat skis have allowed skiers from the intermediate skill level on up to experience conditions and terrain that were previously inaccessible. Fat skis can be rented at most ski shops and are the way to go when learning how to handle deep snow. If you've lost your joy or enthusiasm for skiing, or simply want to have more fun with less effort, try some fat skis. They're worth the price of the ride and you'll be glad you did.

# Sno-Cat Powder Skiing

Photo courtesy of Steamboat Powder Cats

If you have ever skied at a resort after a fresh snowfall, you know what a rare commodity untracked powder snow is. Usually the snow gets skied up by mid-morning, so unless you were fortunate enough to make the "milk run" (that's when you go up with the patrol before the ski lifts are officially open), are the first one on the lift when the slopes open or get first turns on a secret run, you were probably skiing in somebody else's tracks. Hence, the rarity of a pure powder experience.

I have had the opportunity to go on two Sno-Cat® powder tours. One at Irwin Lodge in Crested Butte, Colorado and the other with Jupiter Jones and the

Steamboat Powder Cats in Steamboat Springs, Colorado. I'd never skied powder by Sno-Cat® before, so this was a chance to see first hand what it was about.

## Benefits

The benefit of using a Sno-Cat® is that you are skiing in untracked powder snow on each run. When was the last time you had six to ten runs or more of unbroken powder snow? Most of the terrain I skied during both trips would be comparable to what you might find in pitch and length at any Colorado ski resort. The obvious difference is that YOU are the one making first tracks in champagne powder snow that is knee to thigh deep. It's an experience like no other.

## How It Works

Sno-Cat® tour operators get their permits from the forest service and offer access to terrain that is otherwise unavailable to the general public. While not cheap, the powder experience can run from as little as $90.00 to $200.00 per day including lunch, which can range from brown bag to four-star fare. (The price may or may not include the rental of fat skis.) I highly recommend using either fat or hourglass skis for your powder cat experience.

## Reasons to Use Fat Skis

What was surprising to me was the effortless and exhilarating feeling fat skis give you. All those skiing with me that day felt the same way when trying fat skis for the first time. Those who were of lesser ability didn't fall as much (if at all), and said it was easier to turn. They said the fat skis took the frustration and draining effort out of learning to ski powder. Those who were more experienced skiers said that, due to ease of turning with the skis, they had more energy to put into their skiing.

In the Irwin Lodge experience, half the skiers in our group were from the East and insisted on using the skis they brought from home. They had stiff slalom skis more suitable for ice or hardpack than deep powder. All these skiers were offered the chance to get fat skis before we left the Lodge, but declined. It was more of a macho thing than anything else. They were all competent technical skiers but once in bottomless powder they were in for a rude awakening. Because their skis were so stiff and had no flex or give, they couldn't make but two or three turns before one would bury a tip and fall.

Those skiing the fat skis had little problem staying up and making turns. The "fat" skiers fell little if at all, so it slowed the group considerably while we waited for those on regular skis. (General rules of safety dictate that you ski together as a group. This means you go as fast as the slowest person in your party.) At any rate, it is advisable to rent your fat

Photo courtesy of Steamboat Powdercats

*Sno-Cat Powder Skiing*     239

skis the night before. This will eliminate any wasted time or lost runs on the morning of your powder experience.

## Safety Considerations

Although skiing in the back country can be risky, the areas accessible to the public for each powder tour have been controlled, ski cut and skier packed. The guides equip each skier with an avalanche beacon as a precautionary measure. Your safety is their first concern, and they take their job very seriously. You generally take a first run together, and split into groups of equal ability after that.

Is a powder tour for you? With the advent of fat and hourglass skis, powder skiing is now accessible to the intermediate skier on up. If you can make a wide track parallel turn on blue slopes, you can handle a powder experience without any problem.

When I first signed up for the Powder Cat Tour, I didn't know what to expect. Now I look forward to going back and repeat the experience. If you have never done a Sno-Cat® powder tour and are a strong intermediate skier or better, do it. It is a great ski experience you'll never forget.

For more information on Steamboat Powder Cats, Inc., call 1-800-288-0543.

Photo courtesy of TLH Heliskiing Ltd.

## "HeliSkiing"

Last winter I had the opportunity to fullfill the
dream of a lifetime - helicopter skiing with TLH
Heliskiing at Tyax Mountain Lodge in British
Columbia. After reading and hearing about such an
experience, I at last had the chance to find out what
it was all about.

## TLH Heliskiing

TLH Heliskiing is located in the Chilcotin Mountains of western Canada, about 125 miles North of Vancouver. With copious amounts of Pacific moisture, the quality and consistency of the snow was similar to the light dry powder we find here in Colorado. The average yearly snowfall is between forty and sixty feet in a season that lasts from December to April.

TLH is considered one of the top five heliskiing operations in Canada. The difference with TLH is the number of groups assigned to each helicopter. A group usually consists of 11 people plus a guide. Unlike other operations that assign four groups per helicopter, TLH only assigns two. So while one group is being dropped off at the top of the mountain the other group is skiing and arriving at the bottom. Both groups depart from and return to the lodge via helicopter. Therefore there are no bus rides and no extended waiting times from one run to the next. You start and finish each day via helicopter.

What this translates into is more skiing, more vertical runs and more powder with less waiting around. The average vertical per group is around 25,000 feet a day. Packages range in length from two to seven days, with the amount of skiing determined by several factors: the skiing ability of your group, the amount you want to ski, the weather and the snow conditions.

## Safety Considerations

I approached the trip to British Columbia with both excitement and apprehension. Excitement over the thought of endless runs with bottomless, untracked powder, apprehension about my safety with helicopters and avalanches in the backcountry. Any fears or concerns I had were put to rest shortly after my arrival.

The pilots that fly the helicopters are carefully selected based on qualifications and their experience flying in the mountains and the helicopter maintenance is provided by an on site team of seasoned engineers.

The ski guides are all international- and Canadian-certified mountain guides, a stringent process that takes between three and six years. They are chosen not only for their guiding skills and qualifications, but for their experience and outgoing personalities as well. They balance exciting and challenging skiing with the safety and enjoyment of the group. These guys are seasoned pros who know their jobs and do them well.

## Bottomless Snow

Heliskiing offers the true essence of skiing. The beauty and serenity of the backcountry combined with abundance of snow in off-piste conditions. This truly was an experience that you can only imagine in your dreams until you experience it firsthand.

Skiing bottomless snow is unique in that there is no base under your feet supporting you. Push your ski pole down and it keeps going. This type of skiing requires a confidence in your ability to turn and control your speed while skiing the fall line.

Although the terrain ranges from easy to extreme, and the groups are divided according to ability, you should be a strong blue-level skier who has some experience in powder snow. The stronger you are and the better shape you are in, the better you'll do in getting around and managing the terrain and conditions.

Ironically, it's not the skiing that takes work but the energy it takes to get up after a fall. Because the snow is so deep, once you fall there is nothing to give any leverage, so you end up wallowing around because the snow is so deep. As a result it takes a tremendous amount of effort and energy to stand up and get back on your feet. But there are ways to make life easier.

The ski of choice at TLH Heliskiing was the Volant Chubb, a ski made right here in our own backyard. Although there were other fat skis available, the "Chubb" was the ski of choice for the guides as well as the guests. A fat ski such as the Chubb is the only way to go in deep bottomless conditions. A fat ski is specifically designed for powder and off-piste conditions and will reduce the amount of energy it takes to make your skis turn. Because of their width (they are twice as wide as a normal slalom ski), fat skis will allow you to float from one turn to the next. The less you work physically, the more energy you have to enjoy your skiing.

For more information on TLH Heliskiing call 1-(800) 667-4854.

# Chapter 13
# Extreme Conditions

Photo courtesy of TLH Heliskiing

# Keys To The Steep

Skiing the steep falls into the same category as skiing moguls. If you can do it, you feel like you're on top of the world; if you can't, you know you're fighting for your life. Skiing steep terrain is really about two areas of technique - making the turn and edge control.

Many people get on the steep stuff and become insecure because they lack know-how or control. They don't know if they can get their skis to come around or, if the skis do come around, they don't know if they can control their speed. With thoughts like these, I'd be insecure too.

## Making the Turn

Let's talk about making the turn. As I have said before (and I'll say it again), *making a turn is the same regardless of the terrain:* the inside leg initiates the turn, and the outside leg acts as the stance or balance leg. This is the Phantom Turn that we talked about on page 102. Remember, it's how you change the angle of your hips that will bring you through your turn.

On extremely steep runs with no bumps, you must begin the turn as early as possible. This means you will use the downhill leg, which becomes the inside ski for the "Lift and Tilt." As soon as you finish a turn, pick up the tail of the downhill ski and tip to the little toe side. It is the downhill ski that becomes the new inside ski when you make the turn. The outside leg is the leg you stand on as you come through the turn. You must be definite when you pick up the inside ski and tilt to the little toe side. Watch any film or videos of extreme skiers and you'll see most use this kind of technique.

That sounds good in theory, but doing it is another story when on the steep. The problem many people have is that of excess movement inside the boot. When you get on a steeper section of hill, this excess movement can give you trouble.

## Movement Inside the Boot

If, when you use the Phantom Move to initiate your turn, your foot slides around inside your boot on your stance leg, your weight will shift to your heels. This weight shift to your heels will cause the skis to squirt out from underneath you like a wet bar of soap, leaving you in the back seat, hanging on for your life. This will generally happen at the most critical part of the turn when you are facing straight down the falline. This is not only scary, it's dangerous. It is also one of the prime reasons that many skiers will not commit to their turn when on a steep run. Ideally, you want to keep the leg pressure forward as you come through the turn. When you go from turn to turn, you must release the energy from the skis into the new turn. If you don't have control of those feet, it's easy to get thrown back on your heels and lose control.

## Using the Upper Body

It is also important to know what to do with the upper body.

- Keep your upper body facing straight down the hill. This means your upper body faces your direction of travel, while your skis and edges help to slow you down.
- Keep both hands and ski poles out in front of the body where you can see them.
- Reach downhill for the pole plant. By reaching down the hill for the pole plant, you put yourself in the proper body position for your next turn.

Essentially, what you are doing when making a turn on steep terrain is going from edge to edge. The moment of truth comes when you make the turn. Here your timing is critical. You want to be as smooth and efficient as possible when going from turn to turn. The more efficient you can be when doing this, the better the turn and the more control you'll have of your skis. On really smooth steep runs, concentrate on tipping the ski to the little toe side. Initially, it might help to over exaggerate the inside ski as you Lift and Tilt to the little toe side. This will give the feel for making the turn and build confidence. It also forces you to balance on the stance leg when you make the turn.

## Phantomize

As you become more confident and comfortable making the turn, Phantomize the process. Initiate the turn by tilting the inside ski to the little toe side *without noticeably picking up the ski*. As the balance shifts to the outside ski, think of extending or lengthening the stance or balance leg. This extension creates a platform of the edge under foot and maintains your ski-to-snow contact.

## Flex and Extend

As the skis pass under the body, flex to absorb the turn and prepare for the new turn. The flexion and extension is an active method of maintaining you ski to snow contact and allows you build your confidence. Flex to draw the legs up under the body and prepare for the new turn. Extend the stance leg through the turn.

## Don't Hesitate

Many people will hesitate slightly as they move toward the fall line and begin to accelerate. This is true especially when it is very steep. This is a mistake that you CANNOT afford to make. Pause or hesitate and you are lost. Timing is critical here. Instead of activating the turn, you lose the moment. As soon as you release the edges from the old turn, you must use your Phantom Move to move you into the new turn. If you don't, you will find yourself in the back seat playing catch-up.

Skiing steep terrain in control is the most exhilarating feeling in the world. Once you master the steep, the world of extreme skiing is yours for the taking.

Photo courtesy of Aspen Skiing Company; Tom Zuccareno, photographer

# Breakable Crust

Of all the conditions found in skiing, breakable crust is not only the most frustrating, but the most difficult. Not long ago, I skied the Mary Jane side of Winter Park Ski Resort. There were three feet of the wettest, heaviest snow I had ever seen. The following day, I skied Copper Bowl at Copper Mountain.

From the time the snow originally fell at Winter Park, to the time I made it to Copper Mountain, the temperature dropped and the wind had picked up. The snow solidified and the wind created a crust on top of the snow that was two inches thick. The result when you skied was a break-through crust that would bury your tips. Once your ski tips submerged below the crust, you were in trouble.

## Recommended Skis

For this kind of condition I recommend a fat or hourglass shape ski. Either ski will help give you more flotation and stability due to its width. If you do not have access to fat or hourglass skis and are skiing on your regular, conventional skis there are a few things you should consider.

## Technique

I have talked about the importance of using an up and down or bouncing motion in powder to help you make your turns. I recommend using the same bouncing technique when you ski breakable crust conditions. The bouncing motion is necessary to enable you to break through the upper crust and keep your balance with your body over your feet. If you do not actively engage this up-and-down motion you break through haphazardly, throwing off your timing and rhythm, and causing you to lose your balance and fall.

It's important to keep your hands up and in front of you. This will help you keep your weight over the balls of your feet and maintain balance and upper body control when making the turn. In breakable crust you must advance the outside hand when you make the turn. This will stabilize your body and pull you through the turn. As with all types of powder skiing *do not drop the inside hand when you advance the outside hand.* You need to keep both hands in front of you where you can see them.

## Other Key Factors

The two key factors to skiing this kind of condition, in addition to your technique, are balance and timing. The snow, because it is inconsistent, will cause you to break through on some turns and not others. When you break through and are not expecting it, it's easy to lose the tip under the snow which will trip you up. A forceful and deliberate up-and-down emphasizes your weight on the down motion and allows you to break through in a balanced controlled manner. Once you can establish this kind of rhythm it is easier to match it with your turns. Here is where the skis work for you. The timing must be such that the skis are flexing on the down motion. You want to use this same technique in light fluffy powder skiing but *it is a must when skiing crust.*

Skiing wind-blown crust challenges even the most seasoned skiers. The ones who do well are those who have the confidence and know-how with their equipment and technique.

# Hard Snow

February and March here in Colorado have a distinct weather pattern. It snows frequently, usually five to seven days between storms. These storms are followed by warm, sunny weather. With the lapse between snowstorms, the skiing is soft for a day or two, but as the sun warms and the snow gets skied up and packed out, the conditions become firm. I wouldn't call it icy as one might experience in the Mid-West or the East. Because we ski at such high elevations in the mountains of Colorado we get spoiled skiing soft, deep snow most of the time, and tend to be biased against hard-pack conditions.

## Prepare Your Equipment

Since most Colorado skiers are not used to these conditions, when we do have them they can be challenging unless you are prepared. First, have your skis tuned and edges sharpened. A good tune will fill in any holes, sharpen the edges and wax the bottoms for a smooth, efficient ride.

## The Importance of a Sharp Edge

A sharp edge is critical if you want to hold or have any control in hard or icy conditions. If you have any doubts about the shape of your edges, take your forefinger and run it lightly the length of your skis. See if you feel any burrs or nicks along the edge, especially under the binding, between your toe and heel. The burrs you will feel are a common occurrence that comes with ski wear. The burrs result from hitting rocks or stones, ice or other debris you might find in the course of a ski run.

If you find these burrs, you need remove them. The best way is with a ski "stone." These stones are available at most ski shops for around ten dollars on up. Carry it in your ski parka and use it frequently. The stone will remove any burrs and give you a smooth, clean edge. An old race coach once told me that a smooth edge is almost as important as a sharp one, and a stone will help in that regard. The stone will act as a "quick fix," but you should know the shape of your ski bottoms and make sure they are in good repair.

## Ski for Speed Control

Once you have a smooth or sharp edge you have to think about using it. Skiing on hard snow is about speed control, and that is where your edge comes into play. It is too easy to be lax or unprepared as you start your run, only to find you are going faster than you want to go or are out of control after two or three turns. You need to *control your speed on each and every turn*.

As with any turn, you want to use the edge under your foot. As soon as you initiate your "Phantom Turn," you will be standing on the big toe edge of the stance ski. If your edge is not sharp, you will have a difficult time having your stance ski "grip" the snow. Once you engage that edge, ride it through the turn. Stand on the whole foot of the stance ski, and flex the knee and ankle slightly forward. The tipping action of the free foot and the pressure from the foot on the stance ski will allow you to feel the edge, and give you a sense of control.

It's not enough to turn or slide the skis sideways. This does not allow the skis to work the way they were intended. If you are not using the edge under your foot it is easy for the turn to become a slide with little or not control. Having been born and raised in the East, where icy conditions prevail, I know you can slide sideways just as fast as going straight down the hill unless you use the edge properly.

## Place Your Turns

It is difficult enough to have the ski hold on hard or icy conditions even with a sharp edge, so it's a good idea to "place" your turns. Get in the habit of looking two or three turns ahead and look where you want to make your turn. Looking ahead will eliminate any surprises and prepare you for what's coming up. Look downhill and spot where you want to turn, preferably where the snow is softest. I am in the habit of picking each and every turn I make. I do not make my turns haphazardly. I look for where the snow is softest or most consistent and then turn there.

Often, skiers fall into the rut of turning where everyone else on the hill turns. That tends to be where the snow is the iciest or most scraped down. Soft snow on a ski run will accumulate. Look for where the snow has been pushed and turn there. More often than not the sides of the run you are skiing will have softer snow than the middle. Most people are not aware that the best snow is usually found here, on the side of the trail. But in skiing to the side of the trail, you must have confidence you won't miss a turn and end up in the trees.

If you can spot where you want to make your turn, you will have an easier time getting the skis to hold. You will feel more confident with your skiing when you use your edges and control your speed on each turn.

# Chapter 14
# Spring Conditions

Photo © Cynthia Hunter, courtesy Steamboat Ski and Resort Corp.

# Spring Skiing

Spring is the time of year most skiers live for. Sunny skies, warm temperatures and perfect snow.

With cold nights and warm days the consistency of the snow can go from hard to soft and back to hard again. All slopes that have a southern exposure (the runs that face directly towards the sun) will have softer, "corn" snow. The runs that remain in the shadows (northern exposure) will have colder and harder snow conditions.

## Effects of Sun on Snow Conditions

After a day of warming, the snow turns hard and freezes as the sun fades. "Corn" snow results from the repeated freezing and thawing in the warmer spring months. The first run or two of the new day can be very firm, so it might be best to look for the slopes that have been groomed the night before. Groomed runs are usually posted at the top or bottom of the main lifts.

If you start out on runs that have a southern exposure or received a lot of sun the day before, and the temperature is still below freezing, you will feel like you are skiing on concrete. Wait until the sun has had a chance to warm the snow. As the sun rises higher in the sky (usually by mid-morning) you will find conditions begin to soften.

Once you are warmed up physically and start feeling comfortable with your turns, look for the runs that face _away_ from the sun or that receive _little or no sun during the course of the day_. Ski slopes that are hidden in the shadows and receive little, if any, sun will have snow that is cold, dry and easier to turn in. A trail that is protected from the sun will give you the most consistent snow for the length of your run.

Photo courtesy of Loveland Ski Area

# Effects of Elevation

It is not uncommon for a resort that has two or three thousand vertical feet to have variable conditions from top to bottom. The bottom of the mountain will tend to be warmer and have spring-like snow. The top of the mountain will have colder, drier snow, especially if there is any kind of breeze blowing at higher altitudes.

My recommendations are:

- Find the runs toward the top of the mountain where the snow is colder and drier for consistency.
- Wait until late morning or early afternoon for those runs that might have the best spring-like conditions.
- Be aware that all of these can change if we have an exceptionally warm, sunny day or if a storm front moves in and the temperature drops, leaving you with a cloudy, overcast day with colder temperatures.

Ski areas with base elevations from seven to eight thousand feet will have softer snow conditions sooner. Resorts like A-Basin and Loveland (both in Colorado), with elevations of ten and twelve thousand feet, are so high that they can have winter-like conditions well into May. It's not uncommon to have storms blow in that drop one or two feet even that late in the year. Be aware that although the snow may be soft on the surface it is probably rock-hard underneath.

In the next two sections we'll talk about how to prepare for spring skiing, and what conditions you are likely to encounter.

# Spring Skiing Preparations

The months of March, April and May bring the high mountains of Colorado an abundance of snow mixed with plenty of sunshine. Great snow, combined with warmer weather, bring people to the Rocky Mountains from all over the world to take advantage of some of the best skiing found anywhere on the planet. But as the sun gets higher in the sky there are some precautions you will want to take.

## Use Sunscreen

First, use an adequate sun block with a sun protection factor (spf) of at least 15. Most Colorado resorts have a base elevation between 6,000 and 10,000 feet, with a summit elevation between 12,000 and 13,000 feet. The sun beating down at these higher elevations can be brutal. Going without any protection is not only foolish, but dangerous. If your skin is not used to the sun at these higher altitudes, you will get seriously burned. If you get fried on the first day of your ski vacation, life will be miserable for the duration of your stay.

All ski shops and grocery stores carry sun protection. Use it generously and apply it often throughout the day. If sunburn is something you want to stay away from altogether, use a total block that will keep you from getting any sun at all. The best time to *put the sun screen on* is *before you leave the house or condo*. It is easy to forget once you get to the hill and think about how great the skiing is going to be. On sunny days you inevitably see people walking around with a mask of zinc oxide. It is a painful reminder to protect yourself *before* you get burned.

Make sure your application includes the forehead all the way back into the hairline (the wind pushes your hair back as you descend the mountain, making this area an easy target) and your ears because they are so sensitive. It is also a good idea to reapply your sun screen at lunchtime if the day is particularly warm.

If you decide to ski in short sleeves or a bathing suit make sure you apply adequate sun screen to _all exposed skin._ One day at high altitude is as intense as three or four days at sea level, not to mention how painful abrasions are if you should fall.

Do not forget your lips. Most lip protection comes with an SPF of 15, but check to make sure before buying. There are also lip protectants that provide total sun block, such as zinc oxide, Labiosan™, etc. Make sure you reapply often. Sunburned lips take a good week to heal.

## Protect Your Eyes

Wear eye protection. I forgot my sunglasses one time when skiing Vail, and burned my eyes so badly I was snow-blind for two days. Because of the sun's intensity at high altitude and when reflecting off the snow, it's a good idea to wear goggles or wraparound sunglasses with maximum UV protection to reduce multi-directional glare. Good sunglasses that provide proper sun protection are the best, and they are worth the expense. Avoid cheap plastic, cosmetic-type glasses. They are a waste of money and can be as harmful as going without sunglasses. At higher altitudes, you need quality sunglasses that will protect your eyes keep them from any serious damage.

These few overlooked tips can be the difference between having a great day or a painful experience on the hill.

# Inconsistent Spring Snow

Spring conditions create some of the best and the worst skiing there is. Wet, heavy spring snow is some of the most difficult to ski due to inconsistencies in the conditions. Even if you are on top of your game with both your equipment and technique, skiing this type of snow presents a challenge to even the most seasoned skiers.

## Off-Piste Conditions

Because of the large amounts of snow the Rocky Mountains can receive in one storm, most slopes on a mountain will not have a chance to get packed out by other skiers. As the slopes get skied up, you'll have areas of tracked and untracked snow, or what I call "off-piste" conditions. These off-piste conditions can be found immediately after a fresh "dump." All the powder has been cut up, but not enough to be completely packed out, leaving a combination of loose and packed-out snow, which makes for inconsistent skiing. The loose snow will slow you down, and the areas that are cut up by other skiers will cause you to go faster. The result is constant acceleration and deceleration from one turn to the next.

## Recommended Technique

In cut-up powder or wet, heavy spring conditions, I recommend skiing much the way you would deep powder. The force of your skis hitting the softer snow will slow you down considerably. This deceleration will have you fighting just to keep your balance, as it constantly throws your weight from back to front.

- Use a more exaggerated "up and down" or bouncing movement with the body. Up with the body to start the turn, down with the hips, knees and ankles flexed forward to finish the turn.
- The Phantom Turn works very effectively in such conditions. As you rise up with your body, Lift and Tilt the inside ski to the little toe side. This forces you to balance on the stance ski as you extend the leg up and through the turn. If you notice your foot sliding back and forth inside the boot, try to buckle the boot slightly tighter around the top of the foot or the ankle to eliminate the movement. The "up and down" movement gives you a better feel for the snow and the terrain, and also gives you a connection between your feet, skis and the inconsistent snow under foot.
- In inconsistent snow, you need to establish your rhythm and not have the hill do it for you. Once you start turning, keep turning, regardless of the size of the turn. When you go up with your body, use the Phantom Move to initiate your new turn. It is not a hop as much as it is an unweighting with your body to get your feet and skis going in a new direction.

The up and down motion you generate from your body creates the energy to allow the skis to flex and bend under your feet. The flexing of the skis allows them to work for you. If you have trouble with your skis coming around, be more precise when you begin the turn, make sure your feet and skis have changed direction before you come down with the

April snowfalls are often the heaviest of the season in Breckenridge, as illustrated by this photo taken in April of last year.

body. Now it is up to you to make each turn as smooth as possible. Knowing how to vary your technique will enable you to adjust to the conditions and master the mountain.

I mentioned in Step Two of the "Six Steps To Effortless Skiing" that advances in boot and ski technology all but eliminate the need for an "up and down" motion. There are exceptions, however, and skiing these spring conditions dictates that you use an "up and down" motion to help your turns. You need to use the body and the rhythm of the body to help you make the turns. Without it you are in a static position with no way to begin each turn. It surprises me the number of people I see skiing down the hill who stand completely static, using little or no rhythm or motion with the body when skiing these conditions. They simply make a turn by thrusting a heel out in a semi-snowplow, or torque the body in the direction of the turn.

## A note about your skis

At this time of the season, it is not a bad idea to take your skis into your local shop to have them tuned and waxed. Have the burs removed from the edges and have the skis sharpened. Fill in any nicks or gouges with p-tex for a smooth base, and finish up with a good coat of wax. The wax is most important, as it reduces the friction between the ski bottom and the snow. Wax also makes it easier to turn. Because there will be more water content in the snow, it is necessary to break any suction the skis might have with the snow.

# Chapter 15

# Something for Everybody

Photo by Craig McNeil

Sean and Moira sharing a ski day.

# Getting the Kids Started

I think one of the greatest gifts you can give your child living here in Colorado, is the gift of skiing. After all, if you live in Colorado, you live in mecca when it comes to the best mountains and the best snow in the world! For many parents how to get the kids started poses a major obstacle. But it's not as bad as you might think. There are low cost ways to involve your children without it being a major financial drain.

## Children's Museum Kid Slope

One of the best places you can take your child to learn to ski is the "Kid Slope" at the Children's Museum. Depending on the ages of your children there are a few factors to consider. If your children are young and have never skied before, start with "Kid Slope." It's one of the best introductions you can give your child to the sport without a lot of brain damage on the part of the parent. They start children from the age of four on up. The cost is $8.00 for a 1 1/2 hour lesson and includes the rental of skis, boots and poles. If the child gets cold, tired or has to use the restroom, the facilities are right there. Weather is never a problem as they use artificial plastic bristle tiles for year round conditions. The Kid Slope is a low cost, non threatening way to see if your child will enjoy skiing and want to continue the sport. Class size averages 4 kids per instructor with three classes a day. Ski school times are 10 a.m., 12:30 p.m. and 3 p.m. everyday except Monday. Reservations are recommended and can be made by calling 303-433-7444, Ext. 123.

## Smaller Resorts

If your child is experienced and has been up on the mountain, there are more options. The smaller ski resorts that populate Colorado (also known as the Gems of the Rockies) are ideal for children and families that want to learn to ski together. The Gems of the Rockies include:

- Arapahoe Basin (west of Loveland Pass)
- Eldora (west of Boulder)
- Loveland (closest resort, west of Denver on I-70)
- Monarch (South of Leadville)
- Powderhorn (on the western slope, east of Grand Junction)
- Silver Creek (10 mins. north of Winter Park)
- Ski Cooper (outside of Leadville)
- Sunlight (outside of Glenwood Springs).

These resorts cater to families, and offer the same famous Colorado snow that you find at the big areas. All are priced lower than the major resorts and offer big discounts. The benefit of a smaller resort is that they offer close-in parking and easy access to the lifts. This is important when you, as a parent, have to lug your ski equipment as well as your child's. I find these areas to be the best if you plan on skiing with or teaching your child yourself. The Gems of the Rockies offer gentle, rolling terrain that is ideal for beginners. Most ski resorts offer free skiing if your child is under the age of five or six. Call to check whether your child qualifies.

Adult and child lift ticket coupons and discount package coupons are available at ski shops and grocery stores in Colorado's front range cities. Also, all the ski areas offer some kind of frequent skier card if you favor skiing one area over another.

# Rent Equipment

A no-cost or low-cost way to get your two to four-year old skiing is to buy or rent a children's ski package and let them walk around the backyard or local park after it snows. Many ski shops rent children's ski equipment for the entire season at a fraction of what it would cost to buy. This can be ideal for parents especially when your children are growing so fast you can't keep up with them. Sliding around and playing on skis after a fresh snowfall goes a long way toward building enjoyment and enthusiasm for the sport. It can also give you a chance to play with the kids and see if they are interested in learning more about the sport.

## Tips on Skiing with Children

If you (Mom and Dad) take the family up to the mountains and intend to ski with your children, the day should be for the kids. If your children are young and do not have much ski experience, I suggest you ski with the children on slopes that are appropriate for them. If you as adults want or need ski time for yourself and lack the expertise or the patience to teach them yourself, put the children in the nursery or in the ski school. If you want to ski with the kids, do it on terrain that is suitable for their ski ability. Do not try to take them on more advanced runs or expect them to keep up with you as parents if they are not technically ready. It will only sour them on the whole ski experience. It's not fair to you or them.

Each of Colorado's ski resorts offers excellent ski programs and instruction ideally suited for children. I've worked at all the Summit County resorts (Keystone, Breckenridge, Copper Mountain and A-Basin), as well as Vail, and am very familiar with the quality of instruction offered at Winter Park. All have great instructors and terrific specialty programs designed for kids.

For more information about Kid Slope at the the Children's Museum, call 303-433-7444, Ext. 123.

Photo © David Lokey, courtesy of Vail Resorts

Children's Ski School at Vail

# Skiing With The Kids

Family skiing, as I mentioned previously, is one of the last great undiscovered joys of this sport. I started my kids skiing when they were old enough to stand up. Actually that's not true; I started them skiing by carrying them in my backpack when they were in diapers. Skiing with my family is one of the most rewarding experiences of my life.

Even though I come from a skiing background and know the ins and outs of getting around a ski area, managing a family even for a day of skiing can be a grueling ordeal. But what if you want to ski as a family? How do you introduce your child to skiing?

With my wife's help we decided what was needed to give our children the kind of ski experience we wanted them to have:

- **Good weather**: Sunny, not too cold
- **Location:** Close enough to the lodge for a rest or hot chocolate.
- **Clothing:** Dress the kids in layers. Start with long underwear top, turtleneck and wool sweater, long underwear bottom and either a ski pant, ski suit or sweat pants underneath water-repellant snow bibs, and ski socks. Top it off with a warm ski jacket.
- **Other Needs:** Pack a separate bag for each child to hold their ski boots, ski hat or headband, goggles or sun glasses for eye protection, neck gaiter, ski mittens or gloves, SPF 15+ lip saver, sun screen, hard candy and water bottle. A ski bag for each child helps to eliminate confusion for you as a parent, and to keep his or her stuff together. The candy in their pockets is for extra energy (give it to them when they're resting, not skiing) and water for the trip home. Skiing dehydrates the body, so water is a must. It could be a long ride back to town and their bodies will <u>need</u> water replacement.
- **Attitude:** The day is for the child, not the parent. If you, the adult, need a ski day, put your child in ski school or childcare. If you choose to ski with your child do it with patience, understanding and the joy of a family adventure. Your child will love you for it, and it will pay off big-time down the road.

# Keep the End in Mind

Think of skiing with your children as an investment. Sometime in the not-too-distant future, you'll be

Photo courtesy of Nordica (Prince Sports Group)

This young skier may already be
able to out ski his parents!

enjoying the sport together. Not too long after that, you parents won't even be able to keep up with your kids!

As parents, it is important to remember that it is the act of skiing together, and not the work it takes to get there which should serve as the goal. When I teach beginners or first time students, I always take time with the entire class to watch skiers coming down the hill. I tell them, "That's what you want and will be doing very soon." This gives them focus and vision greater than the beginner run, and hope that there is life beyond the bunny slope.

It's the same with kids. It's a lot of effort to lug skis, boots, poles and all the other stuff you need, not too mention that you have to park the car and carry their equipment as well as your own to the lift or lodge. It's not just physically exhausting, but frustrating and even discouraging if you don't approach this family experience with a certain know-how and the proper mind-set.

## Allow for the Limitations of Young Children

Most kids under the age of five are good for only a run or two at best. This is the best way to build their stamina without wearing them out. If you push the child too hard or over do with too many runs, you'll end up walking or carrying the child down the hill. It's better to take a break before they need it and avoid wearing yourself out. Grab a hot chocolate or take a potty break, followed by another run and then lunch. If you ski one or two runs after lunch, you're doing well. That's why it's a good idea to stay close to the lodge or warming house. It never fails that after you have the kids dressed, skis on their feet and are ready to ride the lift that they have to go potty. Try to plan ahead, then go with flow as best you can.

## Safe AND Fun

Remember that kids don't know how to handle the cold. It's something you have to teach them. You need to remind them to keep their fingers and hands moving inside their gloves and ski boots to keep the blood circulating. If you feel cold, your young child may feel even colder. They won't know when they're cold and won't be able to tell you, so play it safe and check them after each run for frostbite. If you are in close proximity to the lodge and keep checking, the cold should not present a problem.

The one thing you want when skiing with the kids is to keep it not only safe, but fun. I learned that with my daughter, Moira. She's not interested in what I have to say about technique, only in making as many runs as possible without talking about it. So talk less and ski more. Once children have learned to turn into the hill, control their speed and stop, they can ski most green and blue terrain on the mountain. (I saw a dad with his five-year-old in the Outback at Keystone skiing the double black diamond runs. The kid was able to ski <u>big</u> moguls with total control, all because he knew he was in control.)

Once your child can make a strong turn you can have them follow you down the hill. In this way you can guide or direct where they need to go. It also helps them keep their speed down. If the run or trail you're on is crowded, have the child lead so you can run interference. If you're serious about skiing together as a family, helmets are a good idea for the kids. I have helmets for both of my children. It's just a precaution, but one I highly recommend. It's a fashionable way to insure their safety.

I consider skiing with the kids "family skiing." Whether I get one run or three, it doesn't matter. This day is for them. So if you don't have the time or patience for skiing like this, put your child in the Kid's Ski School. That way you'll all have more fun without the frustration.

## Harness Systems

I should mention that there are a few harness systems sold to enable parents to ski behind their children, while giving the children confidence and control. One is called the "Snow-Poke" and the other "The Ski Starter."

- The "Snow-Poke" is a vest that the child wears with two straps that trail behind.
- "The Ski Starter" has a short velcro strap to attach to the tips (another version of the Edgie Wedgie), and a simple belt for the waist with a strap that attaches to it and is held from behind.

I have used and personally recommend "The Ski Starter." This harness and strap system lets the child ski unassisted, but gives the adult control (and eliminates the back ache you get when you ski with the child between your legs) from behind. Once your child can hold the wedge (using Edgie Wedgies) you can move to the strap. Both strap systems are very effective and take all the work out of skiing with your child. They are recommended for children who weight 25 to 45 pounds, cost around thirty dollars and are available at local ski shops.

# Shape Skis For Kids

I started skiing with my children, Sean and Moira, when they were old enough to stand up. After a fresh snow here in Denver, I would take them out in the yard, strap on the K-Mart specials, build a bump and let them laugh and play while sliding around the backyard. By the time Sean was four (the age at which I recommend you start, but no sooner), I began to take the family up to Loveland Ski Area. Although Moira was half Sean's age, they both enjoyed the snow and would beg me to take them up to the big mountain. Initially I rented kid's skis at one of the local ski shops when I took them to one of the front range resorts. Renting skis for kids is a good way to go until you are sure they want to continue the sport or until they can stay in one size long enough to justify the expense of buying equipment.

When I knew skiing was something they would enjoy and continue to do, I bought them both traditional children's skis at a local garage sale. These were typical kid's skis, approximately 100 centimeters in length, complete with bindings. We continued to use these skis for the next few years as their legs and technique grew stronger. Although they both enjoyed skiing, and the sensation and freedom of flowing downhill, the design and function of traditional children's skis can hold them back, technically speaking. I found myself using "Edgie Wedgies" (an elastic bungie cord, 12" in length, that attaches to the ski tips to help hold them together), and a ski harness to help them find their ski legs, and get them into the flow of moving down the hill.

## My Kids and Hourglass Skis

About mid-way through the '96/97 season I had the opportunity to put both Sean and Moira on hourglass skis designed specifically for children. The hourglass ski for children looks the same as for an adult, wide at the tip and tail, narrow under the foot.

Because of the hourglass design, these skis seem even more suited for children than for adults. If you notice young children between the ages of 4 and 8, you'll see that they have a tendency to be on the inside edges of both skis, especially if they use the "pie" or wedge. With an hourglass ski, once you put the ski on the inside edge, the ski's design causes it to turn. When your child has the sensation of turning, both the skill and confidence level go way up. The turn is where the child will feel the control they need to handle the mountain

A shape or hourglass ski works the same for everyone, regardless of their age or size. The ski

Photo by Craig McNeil

The McNeil family skiing Aspen.

*Something for Everybody*

takes the effort out of learning. Once children know they can turn, control their speed, and stop, they feel secure and confident in their skiing. They will begin to improve dramatically. Steepness and terrain become less intimidating as they make their way down the hill.

I wasn't quite sure what to expect when I got the shape skis for my kids. At the time they were 5 and 7. I got them both skis the same length, 123 centimeters. It was the single best thing I could have done for their skiing. Within the course of a single run, both showed noticeable improvement. Coincidentally, this was also around the same time that I started teaching Primary Movements and the Phantom Turn to both children. With the shape skis and Primary Movements, the technique of both kids literally took off.

Initially, I taught both kids using traditional ski teaching methods, starting both of them from a wedge or snowplow. Although they could both do decent parallel turns, they frequently reverted back to the wedge anytime they felt in trouble.

When I began to teach them Primary Movements on the hourglass skis both the equipment and technique clicked. They found the concept of using the Phantom Turn a bit strange at first, but within a short time, both balance and turning ability were increased. Balance is a skill that must be taught and children adapt very quickly once they begin to use the Phantom Turn. Sean, being older and stronger, was able to adapt more quickly. Within the course of a half day, he was making clean, crisp parallel turns without problem or hesitation. Moira, younger by two years, didn't have the leg strength and stamina of her older brother, so progress was slower. But she, too, took to the Phantom Turn like a fish to water. Because they could see their own progress, a new level of excitement and enthusiasm was introduced. It made my heart soar like a hawk to see my children get so much pleasure out of skiing.

## Boots are Important for Kids, Too

Without a doubt these skis give tremendous confidence to a young skier. It's important to have a ski boot that fits your child's foot properly. Every ski shop I know has ski boots for children in the smallest sizes. A ski boot that is too big will not give your child enough control of the foot and the ski. As it applies to an adult, so too with your child. Control of the foot will help your child put the ski on edge.

A year later, Sean, at the age of eight, could ski most any black diamond run. (His favorites are Outhouse at Winter Park, Ambush at Keystone and "S" lift at Copper Mountain.) Moira, at age six, could manage the steepest groomed blue terrain a mountain has to offer. As her legs and confidence build, she continues to improve each time we ski.

# Chapter 16
# In Closing

Photos by Charlie Winger

Photo by Charlie Winger

## *Avalanche Awareness*

In Colorado, Avalanche Awareness Week is usually the third week in January. Each ski season we read about skiers or boarders who were caught and killed in avalanches they could have avoided. One day while I was skiing Vail's China Bowl in knee-to-waist-deep powder, a skier died while skiing an out-of-bounds area known as the "East Chutes."

### Who Gets Hurt

Most problems do not occur with knowledgeable, experienced, back-country skiers, but with the individual who ducks a rope to get a shot at fresh untracked snow. This is a big mistake that could have serious consequences, including a hefty fine and jail time if you live and get caught.

### Ski Run Preparation

What many skiers may not realize while looking at an out-of-bounds stash of virgin powder is the extent of in-bounds slope preparation that is done to make a trail skiable. The difference between in-bounds and out-of-bounds skiing will be the stability of the snowpack underfoot. All ski areas do preparatory avalanche control within the area boundaries early in the ski season, especially on steep slopes and areas prone to slide. This work is done by members of the area ski patrol who maintain it throughout the season through boot or ski packing, or ski "cutting" a run. Packing or cutting a run stabilizes the snow on steeper trails and reduces the risk of slides throughout the season.

Depending on the resort and the slope, a particular trail that is steep or prone to slide will be prepared in one of the three ways mentioned.

- *Boot packing* a slope is when you have 15 to 20 hearty individuals relatively close together walk across the hill in a back and forth fashion.

Photo © Bob Winsett, courtesy Vail Resorts/Breckenridge

Breckenridge Ski Patrollers perform avalanche control work on nearly 800 acres of above timberline bowls.

- *Boot packing* a slope is when you have 15 to 20 hearty individuals relatively close together walk across the hill in a back and forth fashion.
- *Ski packing* is the same group of skiers side stepping down the hill.
- *Ski cutting* is traversing the hill to break up the snow.

These methods are used to help stabilize and pack the snow so it can maintain and hold additional accumulations.

## High Avalanche Danger

In simple terms, avalanche danger is high when large amounts of new snow build up, or fall on old snow. Wind, temperature and consistency of snow will create unstable snow and prime conditions for an avalanche. With these conditions, most ski areas use explosive charges for releasing unsettled snow. Most avalanche control work is done early each morning prior to opening. If wind or snow conditions necessitate, blasting will be done to minimize the slide risk within area boundaries. Safety of the guest is something the Ski Patrol takes seriously. If there is the slightest possibility that an area is unstable or unsettled, it will remain closed to the public.

## Don't Be Fooled

While all Colorado ski areas are diligent with their in-bounds avalanche control work, don't be fooled. You can get lured into a false sense of security when you ski steep in-bounds slopes covered with deep snow all day without any problem. Then you see an area closed off by a rope that contains untracked snow. Chances are you may be tempted to duck the rope and get some "freshies." Don't do it.

The slopes you have been skiing have been patrolled and controlled since the beginning of the season. Slopes on the other side of those ropes have not. There's a good chance they'll slide and swallow unsuspecting skiers who were foolish enough to go for it. Even slopes with less pitch than you have been skiing that are outside the area boundaries may be prone to slide without the necessary control work.

## Stay In Bounds

If you are not experienced in the back country, stay within the area boundaries. Skiing in the back country demands knowledge, understanding, experience and the right equipment. (That would include a shovel, probe pole and an avalanche beacon device of some sort). If you want to go into the back country, do it with an experienced guide or qualified professional. Never go into a closed area or duck under a rope. If you lose a piece of equipment from the chairlift in such an area, call the patrol. With all the great skiing within ski area boundaries, there is no reason to go looking for trouble. Play it smart, obey the area rules and ski safely.

# It's Not Too Late To Ski

Around about the time that winter turns to spring and people start to think about golf and tennis, spring storms dump the greatest amount of snow in the high country. It's not uncommon to find the most snow and the best skiing in the months of April and May.

## Advantages of Spring Skiing

This is the time when there is more than enough snow, plenty of skiing and NO CROWDS. As a matter of fact, I've talked about how rare it is to catch first tracks or ski untracked powder. Usually after one or two runs the snow gets skied up and it is hard to work on your powder technique. Not when you have spring storms dropping copious amounts of snow in the mountains! It's not unusual to have days where the snow is knee to thigh deep or deeper. Getting untracked snow late in the ski season is generally not a problem.

In late spring most ski areas offer reduced lift tickets that are discounted from 30% to 50% off the regular price. You can still get the best snow that skiing has to offer at a reduced rate.

## Check Your Progress

For those of you who have been with me from the start I have a few questions. How is your skiing now compared to when you first started the season? Did you set any goals for yourself? Did you reach them? To what do you attribute your growth? Did you have an idea or an intention for what you wanted to accomplish each day that you skied? Did you take lessons or work on some specific area in your technique, or did you ski a lot?

Are you skiing better now than at the beginning of the season? Why or why not? In a sport like skiing you have to know where you stand technically in order to progress. The more you understand your limitations, the easier it is for you to move beyond them.

Remember that your initial progress comes from your equipment. Boots are the most important, in that they must fit snugly without hurting your feet. There must be no movement of your foot inside the boot. Skis should be tuned (sharpened edges with smooth bottoms) and poles should allow for a ninety degree bend in the arm.

regardless of your ability, keep your sights set on growth and improvement.

## Improve in the Off Season

As with any sport, the better the shape you are in, the more responsive you are physically, mentally and spiritually. Get involved in an exercise program that will keep you at the top of your game all year long.

Photo © Ben Blankenburg, courtesy of Copper Mountain Resort

Spring "skiing" at Copper Mountain, Colorado.

spiritually. Get involved in an exercise program that will keep you at the top of your game all year long.

Whether you are pleased or not with your skiing, now is the time to do something about it. If you can get your equipment right, and become aware of your technique, you are on your way to becoming a better skier. Make up your mind that you will be the very best you can be. Until next season, happy skiing. ◆

# Cold Weather Safety and First Aid

# First Aid Priorities

This section is meant as a general guide only and is not a definitive First Aid reference. If you do not know First Aid, GET HELP from someone knows First Aid! **>>> Get the Ski Patrol <<<**

*1. Make sure that it's safe to help the victim.*

*2. Remove your own skis. Stand them up in an X, 10-15 feet above the victim on the hill to warn oncoming traffic of the problem.*

*3. Do NOT move the victim unless you absolutely know what you're doing!* You can kill or permanently disable someone with a back or neck injury by moving them.

*4. Check for life-threatening conditions:*
  * Unconsciousness - See A. below.
  * No breathing - See B. below.
  * No pulse - See C. below.
  * Heavy bleeding - See D. Below.

**A. CHECK FOR UNCONSCIOUSNESS**
  * **Ask "Are you OK?"** Tap the victim on one shoulder if it is safe to do so.
  * **If no response**, get the Ski Patrol or call an ambulance before doing anything else.
  * **If the victim is conscious**, ask permission to give first aid before continuing.

**B. CHECK FOR BREATHING**
  * **Look** to see if his chest is rising and falling, **listen** for breathing sounds, and **feel** for air coming from the victim's mouth and/or nose for about 5 seconds. **If you find no sign of breathing, give the victim a couple of breaths immediately.**

## C. CHECK FOR PULSE

- Place your fingertips at the left side of the victim's neck on the carotid artery. If the victim is an infant, check at the inside of the arm between the shoulder and the elbow.
- If there is no pulse, administer CPR.

## D. CHECK FOR BLEEDING

Bleeding may not be obvious, especially in the dark. If you suspect that someone is bleeding but cannot see, feel around (gently) for moist, sticky areas. Look for other signs of serious blood loss such as:

- Cool, damp skin or profuse sweating.
- Pale
- Fast, weak pulse (>60-80 bpm in an adult)
- Thirst
- Blurred vision
- Faintness or giddiness, talkative, restless
- Shallow breathing with yawning or sighing

### Signs of Internal Bleeding:

- Bruises or wounds to the chest
- Signs of fractured ribs
- Tender, swollen, bruised or rigid abdomen
- Vomiting blood
- Excessive thirst
- Rectal or vaginal bleeding
- Impaired breathing or irregular pulse
- Skin feels damp and cool

If any of these signs are present, **get assistance** from the ski patrol **immediately**, monitor the victim carefully and be ready to give CPR. Make sure none of the victim's clothes are impeding his breathing or circulation. If it is possible to remove the person's skis without any chance of further injuring him or her, remove them. Comfort the person while you wait for the ski patrol. Treat for shock.

# Frostbite

If a person has frostbite, be alert for signs of hypothermia as well.

## Symptoms:

- *Superficial frostbite:* Skin has white or gray patches and feels firm, but not hard. Once frostbite sets in, it is not painful. No tissue loss will occur if it is treated properly.
- *Deep frostbite* may involve an entire finger or toe or other body part. The skin feels hard and cold; affected tissue looks white or gray. Skin does not rebound when pressed. No pulse can be felt in the affected area.

## Treatment:

- It is best not to rewarm the tissue in the field, unless there is no alternative.
  - The risk of damage due to improper warming is greater than the risk of delaying treatment
  - tissue that is thawed and then refreezes nearly always dies. Frostbitten tissue must be handled extremely gently.

## DO NOT:

- rub the frozen tissue,
- apply ice or snow,
- use cold water or high temperatures to try to thaw the frozen part;
- give the victim alcohol or tobacco, or
- break any blister which may form.
- If possible, get the patient to a hospital while protecting the frozen area from further damage.
- Warmed tissue is extremely painful. Get advice from a physician for pain relief. Pain after rewarming usually indicates that treatment has been successful.

- Keep rewarmed extremities above heart level if possible.

If feet have been frostbitten and rewarmed, do not allow the patient to walk on them unless his/her life (or yours) depends on it.

# Hypothermia

**Mild:**
- **Symptoms:** Shivering, loss of coordination, complains of being cold.
- **Treatment:**
  - Move victim to someplace warm and dry.
  - Add more clothing or replace wet clothing with dry.
  - Cover the person's head and/or neck.
  - Put a barrier between the person and the ground.
  - Cover the person with a space blanket or other vapor barrier.
  - Offer warm nonalcoholic liquids or food.
  - Encourage the person to move around to generate more heat.
  - Apply heat packs to head, neck, underarms, sides of chest, or groin; insulate heavily to prevent further heat loss.
  - Warm shower or bath if available and victim is alert.
  - As a last resort, have someone who is NOT hypothermic get into a sleeping bag with the victim. This method may endanger the rescuer. Two people who are hypothermic should not do this.

## Moderate:

- **Symptoms:** Listless, confused, does not recognize problem; shivers uncontrollably, uncoordinated, speech slurred.
- **First Aid:** Same treatment as above, but cover the person rather than moving him. Do not allow victim to exercise or move, treat very gently. Check for other injuries, including frostbite. (Page 290)

## Severe:

- **Symptoms:** Unconsciousness, slow pulse and respiration, no shivering, physical collapse, unresponsive to pain or words.
- **First Aid:** *Life-threatening - call for professional care.* If pulse and respiration are present, treat as above, but don't give oral fluids unless completely conscious. Do not put the person in a warm shower or bath, and be careful to handle the person very gently. Do not rub hands or feet.
- If pulse and respiration are not present, take the above measures to rewarm the person, start CPR, and get to a medical facility ASAP.

# Wind Chill Temperature Chart

| Air Temp | Wind Speed | | | | | | | | |
|---|---|---|---|---|---|---|---|---|---|
| | 5 | 10 | 15 | 20 | 25 | 30 | 35 | 40 | 45 |
| 45 | 43 | 34 | 29 | 25 | 23 | 21 | 19 | 18 | 17 |
| 40 | 37 | 28 | 22 | 18 | 15 | 13 | 11 | 10 | 9 |
| 35 | 32 | 22 | 16 | 11 | 8 | 6 | 4 | 3 | 2 |
| 30 | 27 | 16 | 9 | 4 | 1 | -3 | -5 | -6 | -7 |
| 25 | 22 | 10 | 2 | -3 | -7 | -11 | -13 | -14 | -15 |
| 20 | 16 | 4 | -5 | -11 | -15 | -18 | -20 | -22 | -23 |
| 15 | 11 | -3 | -12 | -18 | -22 | -26 | -28 | -30 | -31 |
| 10 | 6 | -9 | -19 | -25 | -30 | -33 | -36 | -38 | -39 |
| 5 | 1 | -15 | -25 | -32 | -37 | -41 | -44 | -46 | -47 |
| 0 | -5 | -22 | -32 | -39 | -45 | -49 | -52 | -54 | -55 |
| -5 | -10 | -28 | -39 | -47 | -52 | -56 | -59 | -61 | -63 |
| -10 | -16 | -34 | -45 | -54 | -60 | -64 | -67 | -69 | -71 |
| -15 | -21 | -40 | -52 | -61 | -67 | -72 | -75 | -77 | -79 |
| -20 | -26 | -46 | -59 | -68 | -74 | -79 | -83 | -85 | -87 |
| -25 | -31 | -52 | -66 | -75 | -82 | -87 | -91 | -93 | -101 |
| -30 | -37 | -59 | -72 | -82 | -89 | -95 | -98 | -101 | -103 |
| -35 | -42 | -65 | -79 | -89 | -97 | -102 | -106 | -114 | -122 |
| -40 | -47 | -71 | -86 | -96 | -104 | -110 | -114 | -117 | -124 |
| -45 | -53 | -77 | -93 | -104 | -112 | -117 | -122 | -124 | -127 |

Find the outside air temperature in the left column, then read across the row to the wind speed.

| Wind Chill | Possible Effects |
|---|---|
| 30°F or higher | Generally unpleasant |
| 30° to 15 °F | Unpleasant |
| 14° to 0 °F | Very unpleasant |
| -01 ° to -20 °F | Frostbite possible |
| -21° to -60 °F | Frostbite likely; outdoor activity dangerous |
| -61° or lower | Exposed flesh freezes within 30 seconds. |

# Altitude Sickness

Those who live at sea level, and fly directly from that altitude to a high-altitude ski resort (higher than 8000 feet), may have difficulty adjusting to the lower levels of oxygen in the air.

**Symptoms:**
- Headache
- Shortness of breath
- Loss of appetite, nausea or vomiting
- Fatigue

**Treatment:**
- A person suffering these symptoms should head to lower ground.
- If you are out on the ski slopes and don't feel you can ski down safely, ski patrols often have oxygen available.
- Stay well-hydrated and avoid caffeine and alcohol.
- Don't overexert yourself for the first day or two at high altitude.

Altitude sickness (also known as AMS, acute mountain sickness) usually goes away within a few days as the body acclimates. If it does not go away, or if the person develops a cough or seems to have fluid in the lungs, see a doctor, since serious cases can be life threatening.

Symptoms can be prevented by heading to higher altitudes gradually - say, spending the night at 5,000 to 7,000 feet on your way to the slopes. Some prescription drugs are now available that may help prevent or reduce the severity of altitude sickness.

# Ice Thickness - Safety
## Safe Loads for Clear Solid Ice

| Thickness of Ice | Load or Activity |
|------------------|------------------|
| 3 inches | Cross Country Skiers |
| 4 inches | 1 person ice fishing |
| 5 inches | 1 snowmobile |
| 6 inches | 1 ice boat |
| 7 inches | Group activities |
| 8 inches | 1 car or truck |
| 9 inches | Several vehicles |

**Ice thickness may vary within a small area**
- New (black) ice is stronger than old (milky) ice
- Ice closer to shore is weaker than ice farther out
- Obstructions i.e., rocks, logs and plants, weaken ice
- Underground springs weaken ice
- Waterfowl and schools of fish prevent ice formation
- Water currents weaken ice
- Covered by snow and/or water weakens the ice.

**Survival equipment for each person**
- Ice awls
- Life Jacket
- 25 feet of rope
- Whistle

*Because ice strength is influenced by so many factors, this information should be used only as a general guide. If you're not sure - stay off the ice.*

# Cold Water Survival Times

| Water Temperature | Exhaustion | Death |
|---|---|---|
| 80° F (27°C) | indefinite | indefinite |
| 70-80° (21-27°C) | 3-12 hrs | 3 hrs - indefinite |
| 60-70° (16-21°C) | 2-7 hrs | 2-40 hrs |
| 50-60° (10-16°C) | 1-2 hrs | 1-6 hrs |
| 40-50° (4-10°C) | 30-60 min | 1-3 hrs |
| 32.5-40° (0-4°C) | 15-30 min | 30-90 min |
| 32.5° (0°C) | <15 min | 15 - 45 min |

# Ski Areas
# of the
# United States

Photo © Jack Affleck, courtesy of Vail Resorts/Vail

# Alabama

## *Alpenglow*

Location:
Alabama

| | | | |
|---|---|---|---|
| Base Elevation (ft)...........2500 | Summit (ft) .....................3900 |
| Vertical Drop (ft)............1400 | Skiable Acres...................600 |
| Avg Snowfall (in).............250 | Number of Lifts....................4 |
| Runs:...Green 20% Blue 20% | Black 60% DoubleBlack- |
| Date Open ......Mid November | Date Close.....Late March |
| Hours................10 a.m.-9 p.m. | Night Skiing? ..................Yes |
| Tickets: Adult Full ............$22 | Adult Half.....................$15 |
| Tickets: Adult Night.........$12 | Jr Full..........................$15 |
| Tickets: Jr Half................$12 | Jr Night.......................$10 |
| Main.................907-428-1208 | |
| Fax .................907-562-4277 | |
| Snow Report .....907-249-9292 | |

## *Cloudmont Ski Resort*

Location: 50 Miles from Chattanooga
RTE 1 Box 435, Mentone, Alabama 35984

| | |
|---|---|
| Base Elevation (ft)...........1650 | Summit (ft) .....................1800 |
| Vertical Drop (ft)..............150 | Skiable Acres .................2 tra |
| Avg Snowfall (in)................12 | Number of Lifts....................2 |
| Runs:...Green 50% Blue 50% | Black-        DoubleBlack- |
| Date Open .........December 15 | Date Close.................March 15 |
| Hours..............10 a.m.-10 p.m. | Night Skiing? ..................Yes |
| Tickets: Adult Weekday ....$16 | Adult Weekend.................$18 |
| Tickets: Child Weekday ....$13 | Child Weekend.................$16 |
| Tickets: Night Ski..............$15 | |
| Main.................205-634-4344 | Snow Report .....205-634-3891 |

# Alaska

## *Alyeska Resort*

Location: 40 Miles from Anchorage
PO Box 249, Girdwood, Alabama 99587

| | |
|---|---|
| Base Elevation (ft)............250 | Summit (ft) .....................3939 |
| Vertical Drop (ft)............3689 | Skiable Acres...................786 |
| Avg Snowfall (in).............550 | Number of Lifts....................7 |
| Runs:...Green 12% Blue 71% | Black 17% DoubleBlack- |
| Date Open ......Mid November | Date Close...............Mid April |
| Hours...10:30 a.m. -5:30 p.m. | Night Skiing? ..................Yes |
| Tickets: Adult Full ............$39 | Adult Half.....................$21 |
| Tickets: Child................$17 | Night Ski .....................$16 |
| Main.................907-754-1111 | Toll Free ..........800-880-3880 |
| Snow Report .....907-754-7669 | |

### *Eaglecrest Ski Area*

Location: 12 Miles North of Juneau
155 S Seward St, Juneau, Alabama 99801
Web Site: www.juneau.lib.ak.us/eaglecrest/eaglcrst.htm

| | | | |
|---|---|---|---|
| Base Elevation (ft)..........1200 | Summit (ft) ......................2600 |
| Vertical Drop (ft)............1400 | Skiable Acres....................640 |
| Avg Snowfall (in)............200 | Number of Lifts....................3 |
| Runs      Green 20%  Blue 40% | Black 40%   DoubleBlack - |
| Date Open ...........December 1 | Date Close......................April |
| Hours...................9 a.m-4 p.m. | Night Skiing? ....................Yes |
| Tickets: Adult Full ............$25 | Adult Half.........................$20 |
| Tickets: Youth & 0ver 60..$17 | Child ................................$12 |
| Tickets: Child Night............$8 | |
| Main..................907-790-2000 | |
| Snow Report .....907-586-5330 | |

Photo © Bob Winsett, courtesy of Vail Resorts/Breckenridge

*Alaska*

## Hilltop Ski Area

Location: Anchorage
7015 Abbott Rd, Anchorage, Alabama 99516

| | | | |
|---|---|---|---|
| Base Elevation (ft) | 2606 | Summit (ft) | 2900 |
| Vertical Drop (ft) | 294 | Skiable Acres | 25 |
| Avg Snowfall (in) | 40" | Number of Lifts | 2 |
| Runs:...Green 50% Blue 50% | | Black- DoubleBlack 0% | |
| Date Open | November 15 | Date Close | April 15 |
| Hours | | Night Skiing? | Yes |
| Tickets: Adult Full | $18 | Jr/Sr | $16 |
| Tickets: Under 6 | $10 | | |
| Main | 907-346-1446 | | |
| Fax | 907-346-3391 | | |
| Snow Report | 907-346-2167 | | |

## Moose Mountain Ski Resort

Location: 20 Miutes from Fairbanks
Fairbanks, Alabama 99515
Web Site: www.ptialaska.net/~moosemtn/

| | | | |
|---|---|---|---|
| Base Elevation (ft) | 670 | Summit (ft) | 1930 |
| Vertical Drop (ft) | 1260 | Skiable Acres | 500 |
| Avg Snowfall (in) | 72" | Number of Lifts | bus |
| Runs:...Green 20% Blue 40% | | Black 40% DoubleBlack- | |
| Date Open | November | Date Close | April |
| Hours | 10 a.m.-5 p.m. | Night Skiing? | No |
| Tickets: Adult Weekday | $20 | Adult Weekend | $23 |
| Tickets: 13-17 weekday | $15 | 13-17 weekend | $18 |
| Tickets: 7-12 Weekend | $12 | Over 70, under 6 | $0 |
| Main | 907-479-8362 | | |

*10 buses available for uphill transportation*

# Arizona

## Arizona Snowbowl

Location: 30 Minutes from Flagstaff
Flagstaff, Arizona 86001
Web Site: www.snowbowl.com

| | | | |
|---|---|---|---|
| Base Elevation (ft) | 9200 | Summit (ft) | 11500 |
| Vertical Drop (ft) | 2300 | Skiable Acres | 31 tr |
| Avg Snowfall (in) | 250 | Number of Lifts | 5 |
| Runs:...Green 30% Blue 40% | | Black 30% DoubleBlack- | |
| Date Open | Mid December | Date Close | Easter |
| Hours | 9 a.m.-4 p.m. | Night Skiing? | No |
| Tickets: Adult Full | $33 | Adult Half | $20 |
| Tickets: Jr Full (8-12) | $18 | Jr Half | $13 |
| Tickets: 65-69 | $13 | Over 70, under 7 | $0 |
| Main | 520-779-1951 | | |

Fax ..................520-779-3019
Snow Report .....520-779-4577

## Mt Lemmon Ski Valley

Location: 26 Miles Northeast of Tucson
Mt Lemmon, Arizona 85619

| | | | |
|---|---|---|---|
| Base Elevation (ft)...........8130 | Summit (ft) ......................9000 |
| Vertical Drop (ft)...............870 | Skiable Acres.......................80 |
| Avg Snowfall (in)..............200 | Number of Lifts.....................3 |
| Runs:...Green 20%  Blue 45% | Black 35%  DoubleBlack- |
| Date Open........Mid December | Date Close ......................April |
| Hours.................9 a.m.-4 p.m. | Night Skiing?......................No |
| Tickets: Adult Full ...........$25 | Adult Half...........................$20 |
| Tickets: Child Full, <12.......$10 | Child Half...........................$10 |
| Main.................520-576-1321 | |
| Fax ..................520-885-0033 | |
| Snow Report .....602-576-1400 | |

## Sunrise Ski Resort

Location: 210 miles from Phoenix, Tucson 235 miles
PO Box 217, McNary, Arizona 85930

| | | | |
|---|---|---|---|
| Base Elevation (ft)...........9300 | Summit (ft) ....................11000 |
| Vertical Drop (ft)............1700 | Skiable Acres...................800 |
| Avg Snowfall (in)..............250 | Number of Lifts.................12 |
| Runs:...Green 40%  Blue 40% | Black 20%  DoubleBlack- |
| Date Open ............December 8 | Date Close ...............Mid April |
| Hours.................9 a.m.-4 p.m. | Night Skiing? ....................Yes |
| Tickets: Adult Full ...........$29 | Adult Half...........................$23 |
| Tickets: Jr Full.................$16 | Jr Half..................................$11 |
| Tickets: Senior 62-69 ........$10 | Over 70 ................................$0 |
| Main.................502-735-7676 | |
| Lodging.............800-554-6835 | Fax ...................520-735-7315 |
| Snow Report .....800-772-7669 | |

## Williams Ski Area

Location: 4 Miles off I-40 Via Williams
Box 953, Williams, Arizona 86046

| | | | |
|---|---|---|---|
| Base Elevation (ft)...........7550 | Summit (ft) ......................8150 |
| Vertical Drop (ft)...............600 | Skiable Acres.......................37 |
| Avg Snowfall (in)..............150 | Number of Lifts.....................2 |
| Runs:...Green 20%  Blue 65% | Black 15%  DoubleBlack- |
| Date Open........Mid December | Date Close ......................Easter |
| Hours........9:30 a.m.-4:30 p.m. | Night Skiing?......................No |
| Tickets: Adult Wkday .......$16 | Adult Wkend .....................$21 |
| Tickets: Under 12, 65+, wkdy.. | $13 |
| Under 12, 65+, wkend............... | $16 |
| Main.................520-635-9330 | |

# California

### *Alpine Meadows Ski Area*

Location: 6 miles from Tahoe City, 50 from Reno on I-80
Tahoe City, California 96145

| | | | |
|---|---|---|---|
| Base Elevation (ft) | 6840 | Summit (ft) | 8637 |
| Vertical Drop (ft) | 1797 | Skiable Acres | 2000 |
| Avg Snowfall (in) | 425 | Number of Lifts | 12 |
| Runs:...Green 25% Blue 40% | | Black 35% DoubleBlack- | |
| Date Open | Mid November | Date Close | May |
| Hours | 9 a.m.-4 p.m. | Night Skiing? | No |
| Tickets: Adult Full | $46 | Adult Half | $32 |
| Tickets: Child | $10 | Senior 65-69 | $32 |
| Tickets: Over 70 | $6 | | |
| Main | 916-583-4232 | Toll Free | 800-441-4423 |
| Lodging | 800-824-6348 | | |
| Snow Report | 916-581-8374 | | |

### *Badger Pass Ski Area*

Location: 84 Miles from Fresno on Hwy 41
Yosemite National Park, Yosemite, California 95389

| | | | |
|---|---|---|---|
| Base Elevation (ft) | 7200 | Summit (ft) | 8000 |
| Vertical Drop (ft) | 800 | Skiable Acres | 9 tra |
| Avg Snowfall (in) | 300 | Number of Lifts | 5 |
| Runs:...Green 35% Blue 50% | | Black 15% DoubleBlack- | |
| Date Open | Mid November | Date Close | Mid April |
| Hours | 9 a.m. -4:30 p.m. | Night Skiing? | No |
| Tickets: Adult Wkday | $22 | Adult Wkend | $28 |
| Tickets: Ages 7-12 | $13 | 7-12 Half | $9 |
| Tickets: Over 65 | $0 | | |
| Main | 209-372-1000 | | |
| Snow Report | 209-372-1000 | Road Report | 209-372-8430 |

### *Bear Mountain Ski Resort*

Location: 32 miles from San Bernardino
PO Box 6812, Big Bear Lake, California 92315-6812

| | | | |
|---|---|---|---|
| Base Elevation (ft) | 7140 | Summit (ft) | 8805 |
| Vertical Drop (ft) | 1665 | Skiable Acres | 695 |
| Avg Snowfall (in) | 140 | Number of Lifts | 11 |
| Runs:...Green 25% Blue 50% | | Black 25% DoubleBlack- | |
| Date Open | Early November | Date Close | Late April |
| Hours | 8 a.m. -4 p.m. | Night Skiing? | No |
| Tickets: Adult Full | $38 | Adult Half | $24 |
| Tickets: Child Full | $21 | Child Half | $16 |
| Tickets: Under 6 | $0 | | |
| Main | 909-585-2519 | | |
| Lodging | 909-866-7000 | Snow Report | 909-585-2519 |

## Bear Valley Ski Area

Location: 104 Miles East of Stockton on Hwy 4
Bear Valley, California 95223
Web Site: www.bearvalley.com

| | | | |
|---|---|---|---|
| Base Elevation (ft) | 6600 | Summit (ft) | 8500 |
| Vertical Drop (ft) | 1900 | Skiable Acres | 1280 |
| Avg Snowfall (in) | 360 | Number of Lifts | 11 |
| Runs:..Green 30% Blue 40% | | Black 30% DoubleBlack- | |
| Date Open | Mid November | Date Close | Mid April |
| Hours | 9 a.m. to 4 p.m. | Night Skiing? | No |
| Tickets: Adult Full | $33 | | |
| Tickets: Age 7-12, Full | $13 | Adult Half | $25 |
| Tickets: Over 65, under 6 | $0 | Age 7-12, Half | $10 |
| Main | 209-753-2301 | | |
| Lodging | 800-794-3866 | | |
| Snow Report | 209-753-2308 | | |

## Big Air Winter Park

Location: 85 Miles from Los Angeles
Green Valley Lake, California 92341

| | | | |
|---|---|---|---|
| Base Elevation (ft) | 7000 | Summit (ft) | 7500 |
| Vertical Drop (ft) | 500 | Skiable Acres | 40 |
| Avg Snowfall (in) | 150 | Number of Lifts | 3 |
| Runs:..Green 25% Blue 50% | | Black 25% DoubleBlack- | |
| Date Open | 1st snow | Date Close | Easter |
| Hours | 8 a.m.-4 p.m. | Night Skiing? | No |
| Tickets: Adult Wkday | $19 | Adult Wkend | $27 |
| Tickets: Adult Half | $20 | Child Wkday | $14 |
| Tickets: Child Wkend | $20 | Child Half | $15 |
| Main | 909-867-2338 | Fax | 90-867-7626 |

*Under 6/Over 65 Free. Open Fri. to Mon. only*

## Boreal Ski Area

Location: 40m from Reno, 90m from Sacramento
Truckee, California 96160

| | | | |
|---|---|---|---|
| Base Elevation (ft) | 7200 | Summit (ft) | 7700 |
| Vertical Drop (ft) | 500 | Skiable Acres | 380 |
| Avg Snowfall (in) | 400 | Number of Lifts | 9 |
| Runs:..Green- Blue 30% | | Black 55% DoubleBlack 15% | |
| Date Open | Early November | Date Close | Late April |
| Hours | 9 a.m.-9 p.m. | Night Skiing? | Yes |
| Tickets: Adult Full | $28 | Adult night | $19 |
| Tickets: Ages 5-12 | $10 | Over 60, Full | $14 |
| Tickets: Over 60, Night | $10 | Over 70, under 4 | $0 |
| Main | 530-426-3666 | | |
| Lodging | 530-426-3666 | | |

## _Dodge Ridge_

Location: 40 Miles from Reno, 10 Miles from Truckee
PO Box 1188, Pinecrest, California 95365

| | |
|---|---|
| Base Elevation (ft)..........6600 | Summit (ft) .....................8200 |
| Vertical Drop (ft).............1600 | Skiable Acres...................815 |
| Avg Snowfall (in).............400 | Number of Lifts.................12 |
| Runs:...Green 20% Blue 40% | Black 40% DoubleBlack- |
| Date Open.........Thanksgiving | Date Close .....................Easter |
| Hours.................9 a.m.-4 p.m. | Night Skiing?.....................No |
| Tickets: Adult Full ...........$34 | Adult Half...........................$26 |
| Tickets: Ages 13-17 Full ...$28 | Ages 7-12 Full ..................$16 |
| Tickets: Over 62 ...............$10 | |
| Main.................209-965-3474 | |
| Lodging.............800-446-1333 | |
| Snow Report .....209-965-4444 | |

## _Donner Ski Ranch_

Location: 10 Miles from Truckee, 40 Miles from Reno
PO Box 66, Old Hwy 40, Norden, California 95724

| | |
|---|---|
| Base Elevation (ft)..........7031 | Summit (ft) .....................7751 |
| Vertical Drop (ft).............720 | Skiable Acres...................400 |
| Avg Snowfall (in).............396 | Number of Lifts.................6 |
| Runs:...Green 25% Blue 50% | Black 25% DoubleBlack- |
| Date Open.........November 24 | Date Close.....................April 16 |
| Hours.............8:30 a.m.-4 p.m. | Night Skiing?.....................No |
| Tickets: Adult Fri-Mon. ....$20 | Adult Tues-Thurs. .............$10 |
| Tickets: Adult Half...........$16 | Ages 6-12, Full .................$10 |
| Tickets: Ages 60-69, Full ..$10 | |
| Main.................530-426-3635 | |
| Lodging.............530-426-3622 | |

Photo by Ken Missbrenner, courtesy of Aspen Skiing Company,

## Granlibakken Ski Resort

Location: 45 Miles from Reno, I-80 To Hwy 89 South
Tahoe City, California 95730

| | | | |
|---|---|---|---|
| Base Elevation (ft)...........6330 | Summit (ft) .....................6610 |
| Vertical Drop (ft)..............280 | Skiable Acres.....................10 |
| Avg Snowfall (in)..............200 | Number of Lifts...................2 |
| Runs:...Green 50% Blue 50% | Black- DoubleBlack- |
| Date Open ..........December 15 | Date Close..................April 15 |
| Hours.................9 a.m.-4 p.m. | Night Skiing?.....................No |
| Tickets: Adult Full ............$15 | Adult Half...........................$10 |
| Tickets: Child Full..............$8 | Child Half............................$6 |
| Main...................530-583-4242 | |
| Lodging.............800-543-3221 | |

## Heavenly/Lake Tahoe

Location: 58 Miles from Reno on Hwy 50
P.O. Box 2180, Stateline, California 89449
Web Site: www.skiheavenly.com

| | | | |
|---|---|---|---|
| Base Elevation (ft)...........6540 | Summit (ft) ...................10040 |
| Vertical Drop (ft).............3500 | Skiable Acres................4800 |
| Avg Snowfall (in)..............340 | Number of Lifts...................26 |
| Runs:...Green 20% Blue 47% | Black 33% DoubleBlack- |
| Date Open .......Mid November | Date Close .....................April |
| Hours.................8:30am-4 p.m. | Night Skiing?.....................No |
| Tickets: Ages 16-64, Full ...$49 | Ages 16-64, Half ..............$33 |
| Tickets: Ages 13-15, Full ...$34 | Ages 13-15, Half ..............$26 |
| Tickets: Ages 4-12, Full ....$22 | Over 65, Full .....................$22 |
| Main...................702-586-7000 | Toll Free ........800-2HEAVEN |
| Lodging.........800-243-2836 | Fax ....................702-588-5517 |
| Snow Report .....916-541-7544 | |

*NEW:$3.5 million in improvements, 6 pass Hi speed chair, 3 trails*

## June Mountain

Location: 20m N of Mammoth, LA 320m on Hwy 395
P.O. Box 24, Mammoth Lakes, California 93546

| | | | |
|---|---|---|---|
| Base Elevation (ft)...........7545 | Summit (ft) ...................10135 |
| Vertical Drop (ft).............2590 | Skiable Acres.....................500 |
| Avg Snowfall (in)..............250 | Number of Lifts...................8 |
| Runs:...Green 35% Blue 45% | Black 20% DoubleBlack- |
| Date Open..........Thanksgiving | Date Close .....................Easter |
| Hours.................8:30 a.m.-4 p.m. | Night Skiing?.....................No |
| Tickets: Adult Full ............$37 | Adult Half...........................$27 |
| Tickets: Ages 13-18, Full ...$27 | Ages 13-18, Half ..............$25 |
| Tickets: Over 65, Child .....$20 | Under 6................................$0 |
| Main...................760-648-7733 | Lodging.............800-462-5589 |
| Snow Report .....760-934-2224 | |

## Kirkwood Ski Resort

Location: 30 Miles from S Lake Tahoe, 70 Miles from Reno
P.O. Box 1, Kirkwood, California 95646
Web Site: www.skikirkwood.com

| | |
|---|---|
| Base Elevation (ft)............7800 | Summit (ft) ....................9800 |
| Vertical Drop (ft)............2000 | Skiable Acres................2000 |
| Avg Snowfall (in)............450 | Number of Lifts.................13 |
| Runs:...Green 15% Blue 50% | Black 35% DoubleBlack- |
| Date Open ......Mid November | Date Close..............Late April |
| Hours........8:30 a.m.-4:30 p.m. | Night Skiing?.......................No |
| Tickets: Adult Full ............$41 | Adult Half..........................$30 |
| Tickets: Ages 13-24, Full..$31 | Ages 13-24, Half ............$20 |
| Tickets: Over 60, Full........$20 | Ages 6-12 ...........................$5 |
| Main.................209-258-6000 | |
| Fax ..................209-258-8899 | |
| Snow Report .....209-258-3000 | |

## Mammoth Mountain Ski Area

Location: 300 Miles from L.A., Hwy 395 To Rt 203
P.O. Box 24, Mammoth Lakes, California 93546
Web Site: www.mammoth-mtn.com

| | |
|---|---|
| Base Elevation (ft)...........7953 | Summit (ft) ...................11053 |
| Vertical Drop (ft)............3100 | Skiable Acres................3500 |
| Avg Snowfall (in)............353 | Number of Lifts.................29 |
| Runs:...Green 30% Blue 40% | Black 30% DoubleBlack- |
| Date Open ............November | Date Close........................June |
| Hours............8:30 a.m.-4 p.m. | Night Skiing? .....................Yes |
| Tickets: Adult Full ............$47 | Adult Half..........................$37 |
| Tickets: Ages 13-15, Full..$34 | Ages 7-12, Full ...............$23 |
| Tickets: Over 65 ...............$23 | Under 6 ................................$0 |
| Main.................619-934-2571 | Toll Free ...888-4MAMMOTH |
| Lodging............800-462-5571 | Fax ...............760-934-0603 |
| Snow Report .888-SNOWRPT | Road Report...800-427-ROAD |

*NEW:3 hi speed quads, terrain park & halfpipe, & night skiing. Night skiing Fri-Sun, 4-9 p.m., $20.00*

## Mountain High Resort

Location: 35 Miles North of Ontario Airport
Wrightwood, California 92397
Web Site: www.mtnhigh.com

| | |
|---|---|
| Base Elevation (ft)...........6600 | Summit (ft) ....................8200 |
| Vertical Drop (ft)............1600 | Skiable Acres.................220 |
| Avg Snowfall (in)............120 | Number of Lifts.................12 |
| Runs:...Green 25% Blue 50% | Black 25% DoubleBlack- |
| Date Open ......Mid November | Date Close..........Mid April |
| Hours..............8 a.m.-10 p.m. | Night Skiing? .....................Yes |
| Tickets: Adult Full ............$39 | Adult Half..........................$27 |

| Tickets: Ages 10-13, Full ..$17 | Ages 14-59, Full...............$29 |
| Tickets: Over 60...............$25 | Under 10 w/ adult..............$0 |
| Main...................760-249-5808 | |
| Lodging.........619-249-5787 | |
| Snow Report .....714-972-9242 | |

## *Mt Shasta Ski Park*

Location: 250m from San Francisco, 60m from Redding
104 Siskiyou Ave, Mt Shasta, California 96067

| Base Elevation (ft)...........5500 | Summit (ft) ......................6900 |
| Vertical Drop (ft).............1400 | Skiable Acres...................425 |
| Avg Snowfall (in).............250 | Number of Lifts..................4 |
| Runs:...Green 20%  Blue 55% | Black 25%   DoubleBlack- |
| Date Open.............November | Date Close ...............Mid April |
| Hours................9 a.m.-10 p.m. | Night Skiing? ....................Yes |
| Tickets: Adult Full.............$29 | Jr Full..............................$17 |
| Tickets: Adult Half............$21 | Jr Half.............................$14 |
| Tickets: Under 7 .................$3 | |
| Main..................916-926-8610 | |
| Fax ...................916-926-8607 | |
| Snow Report .....916-926-8686 | |

## *Mt Waterman*

Location: 43 Miles from Los Angeles
La Canada, California 91011

| Base Elevation (ft)...........7000 | Summit (ft) ......................8000 |
| Vertical Drop (ft).............1000 | Skiable Acres...................250 |
| Avg Snowfall (in).............130 | Number of Lifts..................3 |
| Runs:...Green 20%  Blue 20% | Black 60%   DoubleBlack- |
| Date Open.............November | Date Close .......................May |
| Hours.............8 a.m.-4:30 p.m. | Night Skiing?......................No |
| Tickets: Adult Full............$32 | Adult Half.......................$20 |
| Tickets: Child (6-12) .........$12 | Over 65............................$5 |
| Tickets: Under 5 .................$0 | |
| Main..................626-440-1041 | |
| Fax ...................626-969-1413 | |
| Snow Report .....626-790-2002 | |

## *Mt. Baldy Ski Area*

Location: 16 Miles from Upland, East on I-10
P.O. Box 459, Mt. Baldy, California 91759

| Base Elevation (ft)...........6500 | Summit (ft) ......................8600 |
| Vertical Drop (ft).............2100 | Skiable Acres...................100 |
| Avg Snowfall (in).............150 | Number of Lifts..................4 |
| Runs:...Green 20%  Blue 40% | Black 20%   DoubleBlack 20% |
| Date Open .......Mid November | Date Close ...............Mid April |
| Hours.............8 a.m.-4:30 p.m. | Night Skiing?......................No |
| Tickets: Adult Full ............$35 | Adult Half.......................$24 |

| Tickets: Under 13, Full......$21 | Under 13, Half.................$14 |
| Tickets: Over 65, Full........$18 | Over 65, Half....................$12 |
| Main.................909-931-4458 | Lodging.............909-946-9643 |
| Fax...................909-931-7681 | Snow Report .....909-981-3344 |

## Northstar At Tahoe Ski Area

Location: 40 miles from Reno, 6 miles from Truckee
PO Box 129, Truckee, California 95734
Web Site: www.skinorthstar.com

| Base Elevation (ft)...........6330 | Summit (ft) ......................8610 |
| Vertical Drop (ft).............2280 | Skiable Acres...................2420 |
| Avg Snowfall (in)..............300 | Number of Lifts..................12 |
| Runs:...Green 25% Blue 50% | Black 25% DoubleBlack- |
| Date Open..........November 22 | Date Close ...............Mid April |
| Hours............8:30 a.m.-4 p.m. | Night Skiing?........................No |
| Tickets: Adult Full ...........$46 | Adult Half.........................$31 |
| Tickets: Ages 5-12 ...........$10 | Ages 13-22, Full...............$38 |
| Tickets: Ages 60-69 .........$23 | Over 70 ...............................$5 |
| Main.................530-562-1010 | |
| Lodging.............800-466-6784 | |
| Snow Report .....530-562-1330 | |

*NEW:200 acres of off-piste terrain*

*Northstar is a corporation owned by George Gillette (formerly of Vail)*

## Plumas-Eureka Ski Bowl     (Unverified data)

Location: 30 Miles East of Quincy on Hwy 70
Quincy, California 95971

| Base Elevation (ft)...........5550 | Summit (ft) ......................6200 |
| Vertical Drop (ft)..............650 | Skiable Acres........................... |
| Avg Snowfall (in).................. | Number of Lifts....................3 |
| Runs:...Green-      Blue- | Black-      DoubleBlack- |
| Date Open .........December 15 | Date Close ..................March 31 |
| Hours...........10 a.m.-4:30 p.m. | Night Skiing?........................No |
| Tickets: Adult Full ...........$16 | Adult Half.........................$12 |
| Tickets: Child Full............$12 | Child Half........................$10 |
| Main.................530-836-2317 | |

## Sierra At Tahoe

Location: 12 miles from S Lake Tahoe, 90m from Sacrmnto
Twin Bridges, California 95735

| Base Elevation (ft)...........6640 | Summit (ft) ......................8852 |
| Vertical Drop (ft).............2212 | Skiable Acres...................2000 |
| Avg Snowfall (in)..............450 | Number of Lifts..................10 |
| Runs:...Green 25% Blue 50% | Black 25% DoubleBlack- |
| Date Open...............November | Date Close ......................April |
| Hours.................9 a.m.-4 p.m. | Night Skiing?........................No |

| Tickets: Adult Full | $37 | Adult Half | $25 |
| Tickets: Ages 6-12, Full | $17 | Teen, Full | $27 |
| Tickets: Over 60, Full | $17 | | |
| Main | 916-659-7453 | | |
| Lodging | 800-at-Tahoe | | |
| Snow Report | 916-659-7475 | | |

## Sierra Summit Mt Resort

Location: 67 Miles from Fresno
on Huntington Lake, Box 236, Lakeshore, California 93634

| Base Elevation (ft) | 7030 | Summit (ft) | 8709 |
| Vertical Drop (ft) | 1679 | Skiable Acres | 400 |
| Avg Snowfall (in) | 120 | Number of Lifts | 8 |
| Runs:...Green 11% | Blue 61% | Black 28% | DoubleBlack |
| Date Open | November | Date Close | April |
| Hours | 9 a.m.-4 p.m. | Night Skiing? | No |
| Tickets: Adult Holiday | $35 | Child Holiday | $15 |
| Tickets: Adult MidWk | $25 | Child Midwk | $10 |
| Tickets: Over 65 | $0 | | |
| Main | 209-233-2500 | | |
| Lodging | 209-233-1200 | | |
| Snow Report | 209-233-3330 | | |

## Ski Homewood

Location: 6 Miles from Tahoe City, 140 from Sacramento
Homewood, California 91641

| Base Elevation (ft) | 6230 | Summit (ft) | 7880 |
| Vertical Drop (ft) | 1650 | Skiable Acres | 1260 |
| Avg Snowfall (in) | 560 | Number of Lifts | 8 |
| Runs:...Green 8% | Blue 50% | Black 35% | DoubleBlack 7% |
| Date Open | Thanksgiving | Date Close | Easter |
| Hours | 9 a.m.-4 p.m. | Night Skiing? | No |
| Tickets: Adult Full | $35 | Adult Half | $26 |
| Tickets: Ages 9-13 | $11 | Over 60 | $12 |
| Main | 916-525-2992 | | |
| Lodging | 916-525-6728 | | |
| Snow Report | 916-525-2900 | | |

## Snow Crest At Kratka Ridge

Location: 35 Miles N.E. of La Canada
Angeles Winter Development, Inc, Star Route, La Canada,
California 9101

| Base Elevation (ft) | 6900 | Summit (ft) | 7650 |
| Vertical Drop (ft) | 750 | Skiable Acres | 56 |
| Avg Snowfall (in) | 60" | Number of Lifts | 3 |
| Runs:...Green 30% | Blue 30% | Black 40% | DoubleBlack |
| Date Open | Mid December | Date Close | Mid April |
| Hours | 8 a.m.-4:30 p.m. | Night Skiing? | No |

| Tickets: Adult Full | $28 | Adult Half | $18 |
|---|---|---|---|
| Tickets: Ages 12-16, Full | $15 | Ages 12-16, Half | $10 |
| Tickets: Under 12 w adult | $0 | Over 65 | $5 |
| Main | 626-440-9749 | | |
| Lodging | 626-440-9749 | | |
| Snow Report | 818-583-9477 | | |

## *Snow Summit Mountain Resort*

Location: 100 miles from L.A.
Big Bear Lake, California 92315

| Base Elevation (ft) | 7000 | Summit (ft) | 8200 |
|---|---|---|---|
| Vertical Drop (ft) | 1200 | Skiable Acres | 230 |
| Avg Snowfall (in) | 75 | Number of Lifts | 12 |
| Runs:...Green 10% Blue 65% | | Black 25% DoubleBlack | |
| Date Open | Mid November | Date Close | Mid April |
| Hours | 7:30 a.m.-9:30 p.m. | Night Skiing? | Yes |
| Tickets: Adult Full | $32 | Adult Half | $26 |
| Tickets: Ages 7-12, Full | $10 | Under 6, w/ parent | $0 |
| Main | 909-866-5766 | | |
| Lodging | 909-866-7000 | | |
| Snow Report | 909-866-4621 | | |

## *Snow Valley Mountain Sports Park*

Location: 85 Miles from Downtown L.A.
PO Box 2337, Running Springs, California 92382

| Base Elevation (ft) | 6800 | Summit (ft) | 7898 |
|---|---|---|---|
| Vertical Drop (ft) | 1098 | Skiable Acres | 235 |
| Avg Snowfall (in) | 132 | Number of Lifts | 14 |
| Runs:...Green 30% Blue 35% | | Black 35% DoubleBlack | |
| Date Open | Thanksgiving | Date Close | Mid April |
| Hours | 8 a.m.-9 p.m. | Night Skiing? | Yes |
| Tickets: Adult Full | $34 | Ages 7-12 | $30 |
| Tickets: Over 55 | $30 | Night Ski | $25 |
| Tickets: Over 70, under 6 | $0 | | |
| Main | 909-867-2751 | Lodging | 800-UP-ABOVE |
| Snow Report | 909-867-5151 | | |

## *Soda Springs*

Location: 45 Miles West of Reno
Soda Springs, California 96160

| Base Elevation (ft) | 6700 | Summit (ft) | 7352 |
|---|---|---|---|
| Vertical Drop (ft) | 652 | Skiable Acres | 200 |
| Avg Snowfall (in) | 400 | Number of Lifts | 2 |
| Runs:...Green 30% Blue 50% | | Black 20% DoubleBlack | |
| Date Open | Mid November | Date Close | April |
| Hours | 9 a.m.-4:30 p.m. | Night Skiing? | No |
| Tickets: Adult Full | $15 | Over 70, under 7 | $0 |
| Main | 530-426-3666 | | |

## Squaw Valley USA

Location: 6 miles from Tahoe City, 45 miles from Reno
Squaw Valley, California 96146
Web Site: www.squaw.com

| | |
|---|---|
| Base Elevation (ft)...........6200 | Summit (ft)......................9050 |
| Vertical Drop (ft).............2850 | Skiable Acres...............4000+ |
| Avg Snowfall (in)..............450 | Number of Lifts....................30 |
| Runs:...Green 25% Blue 45% | Black 30% DoubleBlack- |
| Date Open .......Mid November | Date Close........................June |
| Hours...................9 a.m.-9 p.m. | Night Skiing? ...................Yes |
| Tickets: Adult Full ............$48 | Adult Half..........................$32 |
| Tickets: Ages 13-15, Full ..$24 | Over 65 ..............................$24 |
| Tickets: 12 & under.............$5 | Night, adult.......................$20 |
| Main...................916-583-6895 | Toll Free ...........800-545-4350 |
| Lodging.............916-583-5585 | Fax ...................916-581-7106 |
| Snow Report .....916-583-6955 | |

## Sugar Bowl Resort

Location: 41 Miles from Reno
Norden, California 95724

| | |
|---|---|
| Base Elevation (ft)...........6883 | Summit (ft) ......................8383 |
| Vertical Drop (ft).............1500 | Skiable Acres...................1500 |
| Avg Snowfall (in)..............500 | Number of Lifts....................12 |
| Runs:...Green 17% Blue 43% | Black 40% DoubleBlack- |
| Date Open..............November | Date Close.........................May |
| Hours...................9 a.m.-4 p.m. | Night Skiing?......................No |
| Tickets: Adult Full ............$42 | Adult Half..........................$27 |
| Tickets: Ages 13-21, Full ..$35 | Ages 6-12 ...........................$10 |
| Tickets: Seniors, 60 -69 ....$20 | 70+, Under 5........................$0 |
| Main...................916-426-9000 | Snow Report .....916-426-1111 |

## Tahoe Donner

Location: 6 Miles from Truckee, 35 Miles from Reno
Truckee, California 96161

| | |
|---|---|
| Base Elevation (ft)...........6750 | Summit (ft) ......................7350 |
| Vertical Drop (ft).............600 | Skiable Acres.....................120 |
| Avg Snowfall (in)..............300 | Number of Lifts.....................3 |
| Runs:...Green 35% Blue 65% | Black-       DoubleBlack- |
| Date Open.........Thanksgiving | Date Close......................Easter |
| Hours...................9 a.m.-4 p.m. | Night Skiing?......................No |
| Tickets: Adult Full ............$26 | Adult Half..........................$15 |
| Tickets: Ages 7-12, 55-69 ..$12 | 7-12, 55-69 Half ..................$7 |
| Tickets: Over 70, under 6....$0 | |
| Main...................530-587-9444 | Snow Report .....530-587-9494 |
| Road Report......800-427-7623 | |

Photo © Ken Redding, courtesy of Vail Resorts/Beaver Creek

**Beaver Creek Resort**

# Colorado

### *Arapahoe Basin*

Location: 68 Miles West of Denver
P.O. 8787, Arapahoe Basin, Colorado 80435
Web Site: www.arapahoebasin.com

| | | | |
|---|---|---|---|
| Base Elevation (ft)........10800 | Summit (ft) ....................13050 |
| Vertical Drop (ft)............2250 | Skiable Acres....................490 |
| Avg Snowfall (in)............367 | Number of Lifts....................5 |
| Runs:...Green 15%  Blue 45% | Black 20%  DoubleBlack 20% |
| Date Open ......Mid November | Date Close...............Late June |
| Hours.............8:30 a.m.-4 p.m. | Night Skiing?....................No |
| Tickets: Adult Full ............$40 | Adult Half.........................$30 |
| Tickets: Kids 6-14 .............$12 | 60-69 yrs............................$30 |
| Tickets: 5 & under/70+ ......$0 | |
| Main.................970-468-0718 | Toll Free .....888-ARAPAHOE |
| Fax ..................970-496-4546 | |
| Snow Report ..888-ARAPAHOE | Road Report......303-639-1111 |

*NEW:Free skiing on beginner lift, Free child ticket with full
price adult*

*Excellent spring conditions, longest ski season in Colorado (into June or July), great steep skiing, but also 60% green and blue skiing. Single base ski area, free parking, easy access, close to lifts, great family skiing.*

## Aspen Highlands

Location: 220 Southwest of Denver, I-70 to Hwy 82
C/O Aspen Skiing Co, P.O. Box 1248, Aspen, Colorado 81612
Web Site: www.skiaspen.com

| | |
|---|---|
| Base Elevation (ft)............8040 | Summit (ft) ....................11675 |
| Vertical Drop (ft)............3635 | Skiable Acres....................619 |
| Avg Snowfall (in)..............300 | Number of Lifts ..................8 |
| Runs:...Green 20% Blue 33% | Black 17% DoubleBlack 30% |
| Date Open..........November 22 | Date Close....................April 7 |
| Hours................9 a.m.-4 p.m. | Night Skiing?....................No |
| Tickets: Adult Full ..........$59 | Ages 7-12 ........................$35 |
| Tickets: Ages 13-27 ..........$39 | Under 6 ..............................$0 |
| Tickets: Over 70 ..................$0 | |
| Main................970-925-1220 | Toll Free ..........800-525-6200 |
| Lodging............800-262-7736 | Fax ..................970-920-0771 |
| Snow Report .....970-925-1221 | Road Report......970-920-5454 |

**NEW: 2 new high speed quads**

*Extremely steep terrain in Highlands Bowl area "Y" zones, most spectacular views of all four Aspen Mountains. Free skiing for those over age 70.*

## Aspen Mountain

Location: 220 Miles SW of Denver, via I-70 then Hwy 82
C/O Aspen Skiing Co, PO Box 1248, Aspen, Colorado 81612
Web Site: www.skiaspen.com

| | |
|---|---|
| Base Elevation (ft)............7945 | Summit (ft) ....................11212 |
| Vertical Drop (ft)............3267 | Skiable Acres....................675 |
| Avg Snowfall (in)..............300 | Number of Lifts ..................8 |
| Runs:...Green 0%% Blue 35% | Black 35% DoubleBlack 30% |
| Date Open..........November 22 | Date Close....................April 14 |
| Hours................9 a.m.-3:30pm | Night Skiing?....................No |
| Tickets: Adult....................$59 | Ages 7-12 ........................$35 |
| Tickets: Ages 13-27 ..........$39 | Under 6 ..............................$0 |
| Tickets: Over 70 ..................$0 | |
| Main................970-925-1220 | Toll Free ..........800-525-6200 |
| Lodging............800-262-7736 | Fax ..................970-920-0771 |
| Snow Report .....970-925-1221 | Road Report......970-920-5454 |

**NEW: High speed double chair**

*Known as the "athletes" mountain (due to intermediate and advanced runs, with no beginner terrain). Great powder skiing via snowcat. The place to see and be seen. Great social atmosphere and mega celebrities. No snowboarding allowed.*

## Beaver Creek Resort

Location: 15 minutes west of vail on I-70
P.O. Box 7, Vail, Colorado 81658
Web Site: www.snow.com

| | |
|---|---|
| Base Elevation (ft)............7400 | Summit (ft) ..................11450 |
| Vertical Drop (ft)............4050 | Skiable Acres..................1625 |
| Avg Snowfall (in).............331 | Number of Lifts ..................14 |
| Runs:...Green 34% Blue 39% | Black 27% DoubleBlack 0% |
| Date Open..........November 21 | Date Close ..................April 14 |
| Hours..........8:30 a.m.-3:30pm | Night Skiing?..................No |
| Tickets: Adult Full ..........$54 | Ages 5-12 ..................$35 |
| Tickets: Seniors 65-69.......$45 | |
| Tickets: Over 70 ..............$0 | Under 4 ..................$0 |
| Main..................970-949-5750 | |
| Lodging.............800-622-3131 | Fax ..................970-845-5728 |
| Snow Report .....800-404-3535 | Road Report......303-639-1111 |

*NEW: 1 new high speed quad, completion of Beaver Creek Village*

*Known for award winning mountain design with diverse terrain, no lift lines.*

## Berthoud Pass

Location: 65m from Denver, I-70 to Hwy 40, Exit 232
P.O. Box 3314, Winter Park, Colorado 80482
Web Site: www.berthoudpass.com

| | |
|---|---|
| Base Elevation (ft)........11307 | Summit (ft) ..................12045 |
| Vertical Drop (ft)............738 | Skiable Acres..................1000 |
| Avg Snowfall (in).............475 | Number of Lifts ..................2 |
| Runs:...Green 15% Blue 20% | Black 35% DoubleBlack 30% |
| Date Open..............November | Date Close ..................June |
| Hours..................9 a.m.-4 p.m. | Night Skiing?..................No |
| Tickets: Adult Full ..........$20 | Adult Half..................$15 |
| Tickets: Ages 6-12 ..........$7 | Over 70, under 5:..............$0 |
| Main..................303-569-0100 | Toll Free........800-SKI-BERT |
| Fax ..................303-569-3472 | |
| Snow Report...800-SKI-BERT | |

*NEW:Opening of the "Divide Lift," on the west face*

*Reasonable rates, great for the family. Great food at Pauly's Pub. Specializing in Berthoud Discount Sports.*

## Breckenridge Ski Area

Location: 105 Miles West of Denver, I-70 to Hwy 9
PO Box 1058, Breckenridge, Colorado 80424
Web Site: www.snow.com

| | |
|---|---|
| Base Elevation (ft)..........9600 | Summit (ft) ..................12998 |
| Vertical Drop (ft)............3398 | Skiable Acres..................2031 |

| | |
|---|---|
| Avg Snowfall (in)..............300 | Number of Lifts...................19 |
| Runs:...Green 14% Blue 26% | Black 60% DoubleBlack 0% |
| Date Open..........November 17 | Date Close................April 14 |
| Hours...............9 a.m.-3:45 p.m. | Night Skiing?....................No |
| Tickets: Adult Full ...........$47 | Ages 5-12 ..........................$17 |
| Tickets: Seniors 65-69.........$0 | |
| Tickets: Over 70 ...............$0 | Under 4..............................$0 |
| Main..................970-453-5000 | Toll Free ...........800-789-7669 |
| Lodging............800-427-8308 | Fax...................970-453-3213 |
| Snow Report ......800-404-3535 | Road Report......303-639-1111 |

*NEW:2 hi speed quads, 159 acres of snowmaking, Peak 8 base remodelled.*

*Renowned for advanced skiing terrain and above timberline bowls. Known for nightlife, restaurants and bars. Steeped in mining history. Multi-day tickets good at Keystone, A-Basin, Vail and Beaver Creek.*

## Buttermilk Mountain

Location: 220 sw of Denver, I-70 to Hwy 82
C/O Aspen Skiing Company, PO Box 1248,
Aspen, Colorado 81612
Web Site: www.snow.com

| | |
|---|---|
| Base Elevation (ft)...........7870 | Summit (ft) ......................9900 |
| Vertical Drop (ft)............2030 | Skiable Acres....................410 |
| Avg Snowfall (in)..............250 | Number of Lifts....................7 |
| Runs:...Green 35% Blue 39% | Black 26% DoubleBlack 0%% |
| Date Open..........November 22 | Date Close................April 14 |
| Hours.................9 a.m.-4 p.m. | Night Skiing?....................No |
| Tickets: Adult Full ...........$59 | Ages 7-12 ..........................$35 |
| Tickets: Ages 13-27 ..........$39 | Under 6..............................$0 |
| Tickets: Over 70 .................$0 | |
| Main..................303-925-1220 | Toll Free ...........800-525-6200 |
| Lodging.............800-262-7736 | |
| Snow Report .....888-282-4272 | |

*NEW:On-mountain dining, mongolian BBQ @ "Clubhouse"*

*Premiere learning mountain in North America, mild and gently rolling terrain, great children's ski school.*

## Copper Mountain

Location: 70 West of Denver on I-70
PO Box 3001, Copper Mountain, Colorado 80443
Web Site: www.ski-copper.com or www.ride-copper.com

| | |
|---|---|
| Base Elevation (ft)..........9712 | Summit (ft) ....................12313 |
| Vertical Drop (ft).............2601 | Skiable Acres..................2433 |
| Avg Snowfall (in).............280 | Number of Lifts.................20 |
| Runs:...Green 21% Blue 25% | Black 36% DoubleBlack 18% |
| Date Open..........November 16 | Date Close ..............Mid April |

| Hours...............9 a.m.-4 p.m. | Night Skiing?...................No |
|---|---|
| Tickets: Adult Full ...........$47 | Child Full...........................$12 |
| Tickets: Senior 60-69 ......$28 | Under 5 ...............................$0 |
| Tickets: Over 70 .................$0 | |
| Main...............970-968-2882 | |
| Lodging..........800-458-8386 | Fax ................970-968-6267 |
| Snow Report .....800-789-7609 | Road Report......303-639-1111 |

*NEW:Terrain park and halfpipe, tubing hill, 2 restaurant coffee shop and cafe.*

*"Where the skiers ski,"* Copper is being redeveloped, village and on-hill renovations costing over $400 million.

## Crested Butte

Location: 28m N of Gunnison, Colorado Spgs 196m
Crested Butte Mountain Resort Inc, Box A,
Mt Crested Butte, Colorado 81225
Web Site: www.crestedbutteresort.com

| Base Elevation (ft)..........9375 | Summit (ft) ...................12162 |
|---|---|
| Vertical Drop (ft).............2787 | Skiable Acres................1160 |
| Avg Snowfall (in)............300 | Number of Lifts...............14 |
| Runs:...Green 12% Blue 29% | Black 11% DoubleBlack 47% |
| Date Open..........November 20 | Date Close................April 18 |
| Hours.................9 a.m.-4 p.m. | Night Skiing?...................No |
| Tickets: Adult Full ...........$47 | Adult Half.....................$35 |
| Tickets: Age 65-69............$-50 | Over 70 ...............................$0 |
| Tickets: 11/20/98 to 12/19/98$0 | 4/5/99 to 4/18/99 ..............$0 |
| Main................970-349-2333 | Toll Free ..........800-544-8448 |
| Lodging..........800-544-8448 | Fax ................970-349-2250 |
| Snow Report .....970-349-2323 | Road Report......970-249-9363 |

*NEW:$20 million in improvements, upgrades on trails, signage and warming houses*

*Home of the U.S. Extreme Skiing & Snowboarding Championships, the ESPN Winter X Games & the finest adventure skiing in the Rocky Mountains. Crested Butte is known among skiers as the place where anyone can find the right challenge. Author's first home in 1972.*

## Cuchara Mountain Resort

Location: 5 mins from Cuchara, 185m S of Denver on I-25
946 Panadero, Cuchara, Colorado 81055
Web Site: www.cuchara.com

| Base Elevation (ft)..........9248 | Summit (ft) ...................10810 |
|---|---|
| Vertical Drop (ft)............1562 | Skiable Acres ................230+ |
| Avg Snowfall (in)............250 | Number of Lifts...................4 |
| Runs:...Green 40% Blue 40% | Black 20% DoubleBlack- |
| Date Open........Mid December | Date Close.......Early April |
| Hours.................9 a.m.-4 p.m. | Night Skiing?...................No |

| Tickets: Adult Full | $31 | Adult Half | $21 |
|---|---|---|---|
| Tickets: 7-12 Full | $21 | | |
| Tickets: | $0 | Under 6/Over 65 | $0 |
| Main | 719-742-3163 | Toll Free | 888-282-4272 |
| Lodging | 719-742-5179 | Fax | 719-742-3164 |
| Snow Report | 888-282-4272 | Road Report | 888-282-4272 |

**NEW:Tubing hill, Half pipe, (w/ 2 surface lifts) 30% increase rental shop**

*No pass to cross to reach Cuchara from Denver, affordable for families*

## Eldora Mountain Resort

Location: 21m W of Boulder, 45m from Denver
PO Box 1697, Nederland, Colorado 80466
Web Site: www.eldora.com

| Base Elevation (ft) | 9200 | Summit (ft) | 10600 |
|---|---|---|---|
| Vertical Drop (ft) | 1400 | Skiable Acres | 495 |
| Avg Snowfall (in) | 300 | Number of Lifts | 10 |
| Runs:...Green 20% Blue 50% | | Black 30% DoubleBlack- | |
| Date Open | Mid November | Date Close | Mid April |
| Hours | 9 a.m.-4 p.m. | Night Skiing? | No |
| Tickets: Adult Full | $35 | Adult Half | $28 |
| Tickets: 7-12/Over 65 | $16 | 5 & under/70+ | $0 |
| Main | 303-440-8700 | | |

Photo courtesy of Copper Mountain Resort; Todd Powell, photographer

### Copper Mountain Resort

| Lodging............303-440-8700 | Fax ..................303-440-8797 |
| Snow Report .....303-440-8700 | Road Report......303-639-1111 |

*NEW:2nd quad chair, increased free parking*

Closest area to metro Denver. No I-70 traffic hassles.

## *Howelsen Hill Ski Area*

Location: In dwntwn Steamboat/Denver 157m Gran Junc 201m
Steamboat Springs, Colorado 80477

| Base Elevation (ft)..........6696 | Summit (ft) ....................7136 |
| Vertical Drop (ft)..............440 | Skiable Acres...................... |
| Avg Snowfall (in)............... | Number of Lifts ....................3 |
| Runs:...Green-      Blue- | Black-       DoubleBlack- |
| Date Open ............December 3 | Date Close..............April 2 |
| Hours..................noon-10 p.m. | Night Skiing? ..................Yes |
| Tickets: Adult Wkday ........$2 | Child Wkday ...................$2 |
| Tickets: Adult Wkend ......$10 | Child Wkend ...................$5 |
| Main.................970-879-4700 | |

## *Keystone Mountain*

Location: 90 miles west of Denver, I-70 to Hwy 6
Keystone Resort, PO Box 38, Keystone, Colorado 80435
Web Site: www.snow.com

| Base Elevation (ft)........9300 | Summit (ft) ..................11640 |
| Vertical Drop (ft).............2340 | Skiable Acres..................1755 |
| Avg Snowfall (in)............230 | Number of Lifts ...............20 |
| Runs:...Green 32%  Blue 55% | Black 13%  DoubleBlack- |
| Date Open..........Late October | Date Close..............Late April |
| Hours..............8:30 a.m.-10 p.m. | Night Skiing? ..................Yes |
| Tickets: Adult Full .........$47 | Ages 5-12 ......................$17 |
| Tickets: Seniors 65-69......$30 | |
| Tickets: Over 70 .............$0 | Under 4 ............................$0 |
| Main.............303-468-2316 | Toll Free ..........800-235-3391 |
| Lodging............800-235-3391 | Fax ................970-496-4105 |
| Snow Report .....303-468-4111 | Road Report......303-639-1111 |

*NEW: 1 quad, triple chair, 2 beginner runs, 1 on-mountain*

One of the top areas for snow grooming, consistently high
quality guest service.

## *Loveland Ski Area*

Location: 60 miles west of Denver on I-70
PO Box 899, Georgetown, Colorado 80444
Web Site: www.skiloveland.com

| Base Elevation (ft).........10800 | Summit (ft) ..................13010 |
| Vertical Drop (ft)............2210 | Skiable Acres..................1360 |
| Avg Snowfall (in)..............400 | Number of Lifts ...............10 |
| Runs:...Green 22%  Blue 55% | Black 23%  DoubleBlack- |

| | |
|---|---|
| Date Open ..........Mid October | Date Close ...............Mid May |
| Hours.................9 a.m.-4 p.m. | Night Skiing?.....................No |
| Tickets: Adult Full ...........$35 | Kids 6-14 .........................$17 |
| Tickets: Seniors 60-69......$26 | Over 70 w/$25 pass ............$0 |
| Tickets: Under 5 .................$0 | |
| Main..................303-571-5580 | Toll Free ..........800-736-3754 |
| Lodging............800-225-5683 | Fax ...................303-571-5580 |
| Snow Report .....303-571-5554 | Road Report......303-639-1111 |

*NEW: Rental Shop, The "Ridge," 400 acres of off-piste terrain*

*Known for great snow, good variety of terrain at a great value. Outstanding early (Oct.) and late season (May) skiing.*

## Monarch Ski Resort

Location: 45m from Gunnison, Salida 20m, Colorado Spgs 130m
#1 Powder Place, Monarch, Colorado 81227

| | |
|---|---|
| Base Elevation (ft)........10790 | Summit (ft) ...................11900 |
| Vertical Drop (ft)............1110 | Skiable Acres....................670 |
| Avg Snowfall (in)..............350 | Number of Lifts....................4 |
| Runs:...Green 21% Blue 37% | Black 42%  DoubleBlack 0% |
| Date Open.........November 21 | Date Close................April 7 |
| Hours.................9 a.m.-4 p.m. | Night Skiing?.....................No |
| Tickets: Adult Full ...........$32 | Kids .................................$18 |
| Tickets: Seniors 62-69......$18 | Over 70 ..............................$0 |
| Main..................888-996-7669 | Toll Free ..........888-996-7669 |
| Lodging............800-332-3668 | Fax ...................719-539-7652 |

*NEW: Terrain park for skiers & boarders. Restaurant and bar improvements.*

*Great family resort & learn to ski area, outstanding terrain for advanced & experts, "all natural powder all the time," over 350"/year. Great Divide snowcat tours.*

## Powderhorn Ski Resort

Location: 35m from Grand Junction, Exit 49 off I-70
PO Box 370, Mesa, Colorado 81643
Web Site: www.powderhorn.com

| | |
|---|---|
| Base Elevation (ft)...........8200 | Summit (ft) .....................9850 |
| Vertical Drop (ft)............1650 | Skiable Acres....................510 |
| Avg Snowfall (in)..............220 | Number of Lifts....................4 |
| Runs:...Green 20% Blue 60% | Black 20%  DoubleBlack- |
| Date Open.........December | Date Close................April |
| Hours.................9 a.m.-4 p.m. | Night Skiing?.....................No |
| Tickets: Adult Full ...........$31 | Adult Half.........................$23 |
| Tickets: 7-18/55-69 Full....$23 | 7-18/55-69 Half ...............$16 |
| Tickets: Over 70 .................$0 | |
| Main..................970-268-5700 | Lodging............800-241-6997 |
| Fax ...................970-268-5351 | Snow Report .....970-268-5700 |

## Purgatory

Location: Southwest Colorado, 25m N of Durango
PO Box 666, Durango, Colorado 81302
Web Site: www.ski-purg.com

| | | |
|---|---|---|
| Base Elevation (ft)..........8793 | Summit (ft) ....................10822 | |
| Vertical Drop (ft)............2029 | Skiable Acres..................1200 | |
| Avg Snowfall (in) ..............20' | Number of Lifts................11 | |
| Runs:...Green 23% Blue 51% | Black 26% DoubleBlack 0% | |
| Date Open..........Thanksgiving | Date Close ..............Mid April | |
| Hours................9 a.m.-4 p.m. | Night Skiing?......................No | |
| Tickets: Adult Full ...........$40 | Kids 6-12 ........................$18 | |
| Tickets: Senior 62-69 ........$22 | Under 5 ..............................$0 | |
| Tickets: Over 70 ..................$0 | | |
| Main ..................970-247-9000 | Lodging..............800-525-0892 | |
| Fax ...................970-385-2131 | Snow Report .....970-247-9000 | |

*NEW:Tubing hill, snowboard park, base restaurant, on-mountain test center.*

*Consistently scores for best weather rating in North America. Lodging in Durango is cheaper in winter. Gentle rollercoaster type terrain.*

## Silver Creek Ski Area

Location: 78 m NW of Denver, I70 to US 40, 2m S of Granby.
PO Box 1110, Granby, Colorado 80446
Web Site: www.silvercreek-resort.com

| | | |
|---|---|---|
| Base Elevation (ft)..........8202 | Summit (ft) ....................9202 | |
| Vertical Drop (ft)............1000 | Skiable Acres..................251 | |
| Avg Snowfall (in)..............180 | Number of Lifts....................5 | |
| Runs:...Green 30% Blue 50% | Black 20% DoubleBlack- | |
| Date Open..........November 26 | Date Close ..............April 12 | |
| Hours.................9 a.m.-4 p.m. | Night Skiing?......................No | |
| Tickets: Adult 18-61..........$32 | Ages 13-17 ......................$28 | |
| Tickets: Ages 6-12 ...........$15 | Seniors 62-69....................$18 | |
| Main .................970-887-3384 | | |
| Lodging..............800-887-3384 | Fax ....................970-887-3849 | |
| Snow Report .....800-754-7458 | Road Report......800-754-7458 | |

*NEW:Tubing hill, ticket scan system, women's ski rental (Elan parabolic)*

*Closest area to Denver to offer Harald Harb's Primary Movement Teaching System. Family ski area, great for beginners, great learning terrain. All runs lead to central base area, making it hard to lose other members in your party.*

## Ski Cooper

Location: 10m N of Leadville on Hwy 24/Denver 120m
PO Box 896, Leadville, Colorado 80461

Web Site: www.skicooper.com

| | |
|---|---|
| Base Elevation (ft)....10500 | Summit (ft) ..................11700 |
| Vertical Drop (ft)............1200 | Skiable Acres....................365 |
| Avg Snowfall (in)............260 | Number of Lifts....................4 |
| Runs:...Green 30% Blue 40% | Black 30% DoubleBlack- |
| Date Open.........November 22 | Date Close................April 12 |
| Hours.............9 a.m.-4 p.m. | Night Skiing?.....................No |
| Tickets: 13-59 Full .........$25 | 13-59 Half ...................$20 |
| Tickets: 6-12 Full ............$15 | 6-12 Half .........................$12 |
| Tickets: 60-69................$16 | Under 5/Over 70................$0 |
| Main.............719-486-3684 | |
| Lodging............800-748-2057 | Fax ..................719-486-3685 |
| Snow Report .....719-486-2277 | |

## Snowmass Ski Area

Location: 220 miles southwest of Denver, I-70 to Hwy 82
Aspen Skiing Company, PO Box 1248, Aspen, Colorado 81612
Web Site: www.skiaspen.com

| | |
|---|---|
| Base Elevation (ft)..........8104 | Summit (ft) ..................12510 |
| Vertical Drop (ft)............4406 | Skiable Acres................2655 |
| Avg Snowfall (in).............300 | Number of Lifts.................20 |
| Runs:...Green 10% Blue 52% | Black 18% DoubleBlack 20% |
| Date Open.........November 22 | Date Close................April 19 |
| Hours .............8:30-3:30 p.m. | Night Skiing?.....................No |
| Tickets: Adult ................$59 | Ages 7-12 ....................$35 |
| Tickets: Ages 13-27 .........$39 | Under 6........................$0 |
| Tickets: Over 70 .................$0 | |
| Main.................303-925-1220 | Toll Free ..........800-525-6200 |
| Lodging............800-262-7736 | Fax ................970-920-0771 |
| Snow Report .....970-925-1221 | Road Report......970-920-5454 |

### NEW: Cirque lift, halfpipe & yurt terrain park

*Biggest of Aspen's four mountains, larger than the other 3 combined. Outstanding family facilities, 90% ski-in/ski-out accomodations. Day care facilities from 6 weeks old and up.*

## Steamboat

Location: 157 miles NW of Denver, I-70 to Hwy 9 to US 40
Steamboat Ski Corporation, 2305 Mt Werner Cir, Steamboat, Colorado 8048
Web Site: www.steamboat-ski.com

| | |
|---|---|
| Base Elevation (ft)..........6900 | Summit (ft) ..................10568 |
| Vertical Drop (ft)............3668 | Skiable Acres................2939 |
| Avg Snowfall (in).............335 | Number of Lifts.................21 |
| Runs:...Green 13% Blue 56% | Black 31% DoubleBlack 0% |
| Date Open.........November 22 | Date Close................April 12 |
| Hours.............8:30 a.m.-4 p.m. | Night Skiing?.....................No |
| Tickets: Adult Full ...........$48 | Adult Half........................$39 |
| Tickets: 12 & under..........$28 | Adult after 2:15p.m. ..........$26 |

| Tickets: Seniors 65-69.......$29 | Over 70 .................................$0 |
|---|---|
| Main................303-879-6111 | |
| Lodging............800-922-2722 | Fax ...................970-879-7844 |
| Snow Report .....970-879-7300 | Road Report.....303-639-1234 |

**NEW:"Thunder Head Express" quad, 260 acre expansion, added snowmaking.**

*Best tree skiing & riding in the world. Western town with a western flair & down home hospitality. Great family and kids programs, consistently one of the top ski schools in the country.*

## Sunlight Mountain Resort

Location: 150 miles W of Denver on I-70
10901 Road 117, Glenwood Springs, Colorado 81601
Web Site: www.sunlightmtn.com

| Base Elevation (ft).........7885 | Summit (ft) ....................9895 |
|---|---|
| Vertical Drop (ft).............2010 | Skiable Acres....................460 |
| Avg Snowfall (in)..............260 | Number of Lifts ..................4 |
| Runs:...Green 20% Blue 55% | Black 20% DoubleBlack 5%% |
| Date Open.........November 26 | Date Close................April 12 |
| Hours.................9 a.m.-4 p.m. | Night Skiing?.........................No |
| Tickets: Adult Full ...........$28 | Adult Half...........................$25 |
| Tickets: 12 & under, Full day$19 | 12 & under, 1/2 day..........$17 |
| Tickets: Senior 60-69 .........$19 | Over 70 .................................$0 |
| Main.............800-445-7931 | Toll Free ........800-445-7931 |
| Lodging............800-445-7931 | Fax ..................970-945-4437 |
| Snow Report .....800-445-7931 | |

**NEW: 2 advanced runs, refurbish base area, added parking, more snowmaking.**

*Family-oriented and affordable skiing, one of the steepest runs in the state, good varied terrain for skiers of all abilities, varied intermediate terrain makes up 55% of mountain. Close to world's largest outdoor hot springs pool.*

## Telluride Ski Resort

Location: 65 miles south of Montrose
Telluride Ski Resort, Inc., PO Box 11155,
Telluride, Colorado 81435
Web Site: www.telski.com

| Base Elevation (ft)...........8725 | Summit (ft) ..................12247 |
|---|---|
| Vertical Drop (ft)............3522 | Skiable Acres.................1050 |
| Avg Snowfall (in)..............300 | Number of Lifts ................13 |
| Runs:...Green 21% Blue 47% | Black 20% DoubleBlack 12% |
| Date Open.........November 21 | Date Close................April 7 |
| Hours.................9 a.m.-4 p.m. | Night Skiing?.........................No |
| Tickets: Adult Full ...........$49 | Adult Half...........................$39 |
| Tickets: Child Full ...........$17 | Senior 65-69 .....................$25 |
| Tickets: Over 70 ................$0 | Under 5 .................................$0 |

| Main...............970-728-7533 | Toll Free..........800-801-4832 |
|---|---|
| Lodging...........888-355-8743 | Fax..................970-728-6364 |
| Snow Report.....970-728-7425 | Road Report......970-249-9363 |

***NEW:Terrain Park, snowboard camps, Mountain Village Activity Center.***

*Nation's 1st Integrated Bio-mechanic Learning Program, (Harald Harb's Primary Movement Teaching System.) Small town, friendly locals, gorgeous scenery, renowned for steeps, but also great for beginners and families. Peaks Spa has best massage anywhere!*

## Vail

Location: 100 miles west of Denver on I-70
Vail Associates, PO Box 7, Vail, Colorado 81658
Web Site: www.snow.com

| | | | |
|---|---|---|---|
| Base Elevation (ft)........8120 | Summit (ft)...................11450 |
| Vertical Drop (ft)............3330 | Skiable Acres.................4644 |
| Avg Snowfall (in)............341 | Number of Lifts...................30 |
| Runs:...Green 40% Blue 32% | Black 28% DoubleBlack 0% |
| Date Open.........November 21 | Date Close.................April 14 |
| Hours............8:30-3:30pm | Night Skiing?.....................No |
| Tickets: Adult Full...........$54 | Ages 12 & under..............$35 |
| Tickets: Seniors 65-69.......$45 | |
| Tickets: Over 70...............$0 | Under 4...............................$0 |
| Main.................970-476-5601 | Lodging...........800-404-3535 |
| Road Report.....303-639-1111 | |

***NEW:2 halfpipes, 2 tubing lanes, expanded Adventure Ridge Ice Rink.***

*Legendary back bowls w/ outstanding snow, huge amount of terrain with something for everyone. You could ski here for a week and never ski the same run twice. Both the village and Lionshead areas are accessible from anywhere on the mountain.*

Photo© Ken Redding, courtesy Vail Resorts/Beaver Creek

## Winter Park/Mary Jane

Location: 67 miles west of Denver, I-70 to hwy 40
Winter Park Resort, PO Box 36, Winter Park, Colorado 80482
Web Site: www.skiwinterpark.com

| | | |
|---|---|---|
| Base Elevation (ft) | 9000 | Summit (ft) | 12060 |
| Vertical Drop (ft) | 3060 | Skiable Acres | 2581 |
| Avg Snowfall (in) | 370 | Number of Lifts | 20 |
| Runs:...Green 12% Blue 30% | | Black 17% DoubleBlack 41% |
| Date Open | November 8 | Date Close | April 19 |
| Hours | 8:30 a.m.-4 p.m. | Night Skiing? | No |
| Tickets: Adult Full | $46 | 1/2 day a.m. or p.m | $29 |
| Tickets: Ages 6-13 | $15 | Seniors 62-69 | $22 |
| Tickets: Over 70 | $0 | Under 5 | $0 |
| Main | 970-726-5514 | Lodging | 800-729-5813 |
| Fax | 303-892-5823 | Snow Report | 303-572-7669 |

*NEW: Vasquez Cirque*

*Where more Coloradoans have learned to ski than anywhere else. Closest major resort to Denver. Gets the most snow of any major Colorado resort. Has a reputation for friendliness.*

## Wolf Creek

Location: 23m from Pagosa Springs, Albuquerque 225m
Box 1036, Pagosa Springs, Colorado 81147
Web Site: www.wolfcreekski.com; e mail: wolfcreekski@wo

| | | |
|---|---|---|
| Base Elevation (ft) | 10300 | Summit (ft) | 11904 |
| Vertical Drop (ft) | 1604 | Skiable Acres | 1000 |
| Avg Snowfall (in) | 465 | Number of Lifts | 5 |
| Runs:...Green 20% Blue 35% | | Black 25% DoubleBlack 20% |
| Date Open | Late November | Date Close | Mid April |
| Hours | 9 a.m.-4 p.m. | Night Skiing? | No |
| Tickets: Adult Full | $34 | Adult Half | $25 |
| Tickets: Under 12/65+ Full $22 | | Under 12/65+ Half | $16 |
| Tickets: Under 5 | $5 | | |
| Main | 970-264-5639 | Lodging | 970-264-5639 |
| Snow Report .800-SKI-WOLF | | | |

# Connecticut

## Mohawk Mountain Ski Area

Location: 38 Miles N. of Danbury, 48m from New Haven
PO Box 27, Cornwall, Connecticut 06753
Web Site: www.mohawkmountain.com

| | | |
|---|---|---|
| Base Elevation (ft) | 960 | Summit (ft) | 1600 |
| Vertical Drop (ft) | 640 | Skiable Acres | 107 |
| Avg Snowfall (in) | 92 | Number of Lifts | 5 |
| Runs:...Green 20% Blue 60% | | Black 20% DoubleBlack- |
| Date Open | Thanksgiving | Date Close | April |

| Hours..........8:30 a.m.-10 p.m. | Night Skiing?....................Yes |
| Tickets: Adult Full ............$25 | Adult Half.........................$20 |
| Tickets: Jr/Sr, Full.............$20 | Jr/Sr, Half.........................$15 |
| Tickets: Jr/Sr Half, Night..$15 | Under 5.............................$10 |
| Main.................203-672-6100 | |
| Fax ...................203-672-0117 | |
| Snow Report .....800-895-5222 | |

## *Mt. Southington*

Location: 17m from Hartford on I-84, 30m from New Haven
Southington, Connecticut 06489

| Base Elevation (ft)..............100 | Summit (ft) ........................525 |
| Vertical Drop (ft)..............425 | Skiable Acres.......................55 |
| Avg Snowfall (in)..............50" | Number of Lifts.....................7 |
| Runs:...Green 30% Blue 50% | Black 20%  DoubleBlack- |
| Date Open.........Thanksgiving | Date Close .............Mid March |
| Hours.............9 a.m.-10:30pm | Night Skiing? ...................Yes |
| Tickets: Adult wkdy.........$24 | Adult wkend ......................$28 |
| Tickets: Jr wkday ............$20 | Jr wkend ...........................$22 |
| Tickets: Night ..................$18 | Under 6..............................$6 |
| Main.................860-628-0954 | Toll Free ..........800-982-6828 |
| Fax ..................860-621-1833 | |

*Author's hometown ski resort. Spent the greater majority of his
youth skiing here. Began teaching skiing here at age 14.
Achieved PSIA full certificate status at age 18. Moved to
Colorado at age 19.*

## *Powder Ridge Ski Area*

Location: 7m from Meridan, 20m from Hartford
Middlefield, Connecticut 06455

| Base Elevation (ft)..............250 | Summit (ft) ........................750 |
| Vertical Drop (ft)..............500 | Skiable Acres.......................90 |
| Avg Snowfall (in) ..............50" | Number of Lifts.....................5 |
| Runs:...Green 30% Blue 50% | Black 20%  DoubleBlack- |
| Date Open.........November 15 | Date Close..............April 1 |
| Hours.................9 a.m.-1pm | Night Skiing? ...................Yes |
| Tickets: Adult wkdy.........$25 | Adult wkend ......................$30 |
| Tickets: Under 12, wkdy ...$20 | Under 12, wkend ...............$23 |
| Tickets: Night ..................$18 | |
| Main.................860-349-3454 | Toll Free ..........800-622-3321 |

## *Ski Sundown*

Location: 2m NE of New Hartford on Rt 219
PO Box 298, New Hartford, Connecticut 06057

| Base Elevation (ft)..............450 | Summit (ft) ......................1075 |
| Vertical Drop (ft)..............625 | Skiable Acres.......................65 |
| Avg Snowfall (in)..............60 | Number of Lifts.....................4 |
| Runs:...Green 40% Blue 40% | Black 20% DoubleBlack 0% |

| Date Open | December 1 | Date Close | April 1 |
|---|---|---|---|
| Hours | 9 a.m.-10 p.m. | Night Skiing? | Yes |
| Tickets: Adult Full | $32 | Adult Half | $28 |
| Tickets: Ages 6-14, Full | $28 | Ages 6-14, Half | $24 |
| Tickets: Over 65 | $18 | Night | $22 |
| Main | 860-379-9851 | | |
| Snow Report | 860-379-7669 | | |

## _Woodbury Ski Area_

Location: 4m from Woodbury, 17m from Waterbury
Rte 47, Woodbury, Connecticut 06798

| Base Elevation (ft) | 550 | Summit (ft) | 850 |
|---|---|---|---|
| Vertical Drop (ft) | 300 | Skiable Acres | 150 |
| Avg Snowfall (in) | 75" | Number of Lifts | 4 |
| Runs:...Green 33% | Blue 33% | Black 33% | DoubleBlack- |
| Date Open | December 1 | Date Close | March 15 |
| Hours | 9 a.m.-10 p.m. | Night Skiing? | Yes |
| Tickets: Adult Full | $20 | Adult Half | $17 |
| Tickets: Night Ski | $15 | Child Wkdy | $17 |
| Tickets: Child Half | $15 | Child Wkend | $20 |
| Main | 203-263-2203 | | |

# Georgia

## _Sky Valley Ski Resort_

Location: 50m from Ashville, NC
PO Box 1, Dillard, Georgia 30537

| Base Elevation (ft) | 3115 | Summit (ft) | 3325 |
|---|---|---|---|
| Vertical Drop (ft) | 210 | Skiable Acres | 22 |
| Avg Snowfall (in) | 15" | Number of Lifts | 2 |
| Runs:...Green 33% | Blue 34% | Black 33% | DoubleBlack- |
| Date Open | December 15 | Date Close | Mid March |
| Hours | 9 a.m.-10 p.m. | Night Skiing? | Yes |
| Tickets: Adult Wkdy | $152 | Adult Wkend | $20 |
| Tickets: Jr/Sr Wkdy | $12 | Jr/Sr Wkend | $15 |
| Tickets: Night Adult | $15 | Night Jr/Sr | $12 |
| Main | 706-746-5302 | Fax | 706-746-5198 |
| Snow Report | 800-437-2416 | | |

# Idaho

## _Bald Mountain_    (_Unverified data_)

Location: 42m E of Orofino, 6m N of Pierce on Hwy 11
P.O. Box 1126, Orofino, Idaho 83544

| Base Elevation (ft) | | Summit (ft) | 684 |
|---|---|---|---|
| Vertical Drop (ft) | 684 | Skiable Acres | |
| Avg Snowfall (in) | | Number of Lifts | 2 |
| Runs:...Green- | Blue- | Black- | DoubleBlack- |

| Date Open.............................. | Date Close .............................. |
|---|---|
| Hours..................................... | Night Skiing?......................No |
| Main..................208-464-2311 | |

## *Bogus Basin*

Location: 16m from Boise on I-84
2405 Bogus Basin Road, Boise, Idaho 83702
Web Site: http://skibogus.com

| | |
|---|---|
| Base Elevation (ft)...........5800 | Summit (ft) .......................7600 |
| Vertical Drop (ft)............1800 | Skiable Acres..................2600 |
| Avg Snowfall (in)..............250 | Number of Lifts....................8 |
| Runs:...Green 22% Blue 45% | Black 33% DoubleBlack- |
| Date Open..........Thanksgiving | Date Close................Mid April |
| Hours...........10 a.m.-10 p.m. | Night Skiing? ....................Yes |
| Tickets: Adult Full .............$31 | Adult Half..........................$26 |
| Tickets: Child Full..............$22 | Child Night .........................$17 |
| Tickets: Adult Night...........$20 | Over 65 Full ......................$22 |
| Main..................208-332-5100 | Toll Free ..........800-367-4397 |
| Lodging............800-367-4397 | Fax ..................208-332-5102 |
| Snow Report .....208-342-2100 | |

## *Brundage Mountain Ski Area*

Location: 100m from Boise on Hwy 55
PO Box 1062, McCall, Idaho 83638
Web Site: www.brundage.com

| | |
|---|---|
| Base Elevation (ft)...........5840 | Summit (ft) .......................7640 |
| Vertical Drop (ft)............1800 | Skiable Acres..................1300 |
| Avg Snowfall (in)..............300 | Number of Lifts....................5 |
| Runs:...Green 13% Blue 48% | Black 34% DoubleBlack 5% |
| Date Open..........Thanksgiving | Date Close................April 15 |
| Hours.................9 a.m.-4 p.m. | Night Skiing?......................No |
| Tickets: Adult Full .............$29 | Adult Half..........................$24 |
| Tickets: Ages 13-18, Over 65$24 | Ages 13-18,65+, Half........$19 |
| Tickets: Ages 7-12, Full ....$17 | Ages 7-12, Half .................$14 |
| Main..................208-634-4151 | Toll Free ..........800-888-7544 |
| Fax ..................208-634-4153 | |
| Snow Report .....888-255-7669 | |

*NEW:hi speed quad*

## *Cottonwood Butte*

Location: 19m N of Grangeville,65m S. of Lewiston, US-95
P.O. Box 162, Cottonwood, Idaho 83522

| | |
|---|---|
| Base Elevation (ft)...........4780 | Summit (ft) .......................5125 |
| Vertical Drop (ft)..............845 | Skiable Acres..................260 |
| Avg Snowfall (in) .............45" | Number of Lifts....................2 |
| Runs:...Green 28% Blue 29% | Black 43% DoubleBlack- |
| Date Open .....Christmas Week | Date Close .........Mid February |
| Hours...............10 a.m.-4 p.m. | Night Skiing? ....................Yes |

Tickets: Wkend/Holidays ..$10  Halfday ............................$8
Tickets: Wednesday ...........$8
Main.................208-962-3624
*Night skiing on Wed. only.*

## *Kelly Canyon Ski Area*   *(Unverified data)*

Location: 25m NE of Idaho Falls on Hwy 26
P.O. Box 367, Ririe, Idaho 83443

| | | |
|---|---|---|
| Base Elevation (ft)...........5600 | Summit (ft) .....................6600 |
| Vertical Drop (ft).............1000 | Skiable Acres..................... |
| Avg Snowfall (in).............. | Number of Lifts ....................4 |
| Runs:...Green- Blue- | Black- DoubleBlack- |
| Date Open ..............December | Date Close......................April |
| Hours................10 a.m.-4 p.m. | Night Skiing? ...................Yes |
| Tickets: Unknown ..............$0 | |
| Main.................208-423-6221 | |

## *Lookout Pass Ski Area*

Location: 12m E of Wallace on Hwy 90
P.O. Box 108, Wallace, Idaho 83873
Web Site: www.skilookout.com

| | | |
|---|---|---|
| Base Elevation (ft)...........4800 | Summit (ft) .....................5650 |
| Vertical Drop (ft)..............850 | Skiable Acres..................100 |
| Avg Snowfall (in).............400 | Number of Lifts ....................2 |
| Runs:...Green 25%  Blue 50% | Black 25%  DoubleBlack- |
| Date Open..........November 20 | Date Close.................April 30 |
| Hours................9 a.m.- 4 p.m. | Night Skiing?....................No |
| Tickets: Adult Full ...........$19 | Adult Half..........................$14 |
| Tickets: Ages 7-18, 65+ ....$14 | Ages 7-18, 65+ ...............$11 |
| Main.................208-744-1392 | |
| Fax.................208-744-7219 | |
| Snow Report .....208-744-1301 | |

*Open Thurs.-Sun., & all holiday season.*

## *Magic Mountain Ski Area*

Location: 28m S of Hansen on I-84, Exit 182
3367 N. 3600 E., Kimberly, Idaho 83341

| | | |
|---|---|---|
| Base Elevation (ft)...........6500 | Summit (ft) .....................7200 |
| Vertical Drop (ft).............700 | Skiable Acres..................120 |
| Avg Snowfall (in).............180 | Number of Lifts ....................3 |
| Runs:...Green 30%  Blue 35% | Black 35%  DoubleBlack- |
| Date Open......Early December | Date Close.........Early April |
| Hours.................9 a.m.-4 p.m. | Night Skiing?....................No |
| Tickets: Wkday ...................$9 | Wkend ............................$14 |
| Tickets: Half ......................$11 | |
| Main.................208-423-6221 | Toll Free ..........800-255-8946 |

*Open Fri.-Sun.*

## Pebble Creek Ski Resort

Location: 15m from Pocatello on I-15
Box 370, Inkom, Idaho 83245

| | |
|---|---|
| Base Elevation (ft)..........6300 | Summit (ft) ....................8300 |
| Vertical Drop (ft)...........2000 | Skiable Acres...................600 |
| Avg Snowfall (in)............250 | Number of Lifts...................3 |
| Runs:...Green 20%  Blue 20% | Black 30%  DoubleBlack 30% |
| Date Open........Mid December | Date Close.................April |
| Hours............9:30a.m.-4p.m. | Night Skiing? ...................Yes |
| Tickets: Adult Full ...........$23 | Adult Half.........................$18 |
| Tickets: Ages 12 under, Full$14 | Ages 12 under, Half |
| $11 | |
| Tickets: Teen, 65+, Full ...$19 | Night................................$7 |
| Main.................208-775-4452 | |
| Fax.................208-775-4453 | |
| Snow Report .....208-775-4451 | |

## Pomerelle Mountain Resort

Location: 190m from Salt Lake City on I-84
P.O. Box 158, Albion, Idaho 83311

| | |
|---|---|
| Base Elevation (ft)..........8000 | Summit (ft) ....................9000 |
| Vertical Drop (ft)...........1000 | Skiable Acres...................200 |
| Avg Snowfall (in)............500 | Number of Lifts...................3 |
| Runs:...Green 30%  Blue 50% | Black 20%  DoubleBlack- |
| Date Open .......Mid November | Date Close.................April |
| Hours............9:30a.m.-10p.m. | Night Skiing? ...................Yes |
| Tickets: Wkdy ...................$15 | Wkend ...............................$20 |
| Tickets: Half ...................$15 | Night................................$10 |
| Main.................208-638-5599 | Snow Report .....208-638-5555 |

## Schweitzer Mountain Resort

Location: 86m NE of Spokane on I-90-Hwy 95
PO Box 815, Sandpoint, Idaho 83864
Web Site: www.schweitzer.com

| | |
|---|---|
| Base Elevation (ft)..........3910 | Summit (ft) ....................6389 |
| Vertical Drop (ft)...........2479 | Skiable Acres.................2350 |
| Avg Snowfall (in)............300 | Number of Lifts...................6 |
| Runs:...Green 20%  Blue 40% | Black 35%  DoubleBlack 5% |
| Date Open .......Late November | Date Close.............Mid April |
| Hours.................9 a.m.-9 p.m. | Night Skiing? ...................Yes |
| Tickets: Adult Full ...........$34 | Adult half.........................$27 |
| Tickets: Ages 7-12, Full ....$20 | Ages13-17, 65+, Full........$27 |
| Tickets:Ages 13-17,65+ half .$22 | Night................................$15 |
| Main.................509-467-5011 | Toll Free ...........800-831-8810 |
| Lodging.............208-263-2161 | Fax ....................208-263-0775 |
| Snow Report .....800-831-8810 | |

*NEW:hi speed chair*

## _Silver Mountain Ski & Summer Resort_

Location: 36m from Coeur D' Alene, 1/4 from I-90
610 Bunker Avenue, Kellogg, Idaho 83837
Web Site: www.silvermt.com

| | |
|---|---|
| Base Elevation (ft)..........4000 | Summit (ft) .....................6300 |
| Vertical Drop (ft)...........2300 | Skiable Acres................1500 |
| Avg Snowfall (in).............300 | Number of Lifts .................7 |
| Runs:...Green 15% Blue 45% | Black 40% DoubleBlack- |
| Date Open ......Mid November | Date Close .............Mid April |
| Hours............8:30 a.m.-4 p.m. | Night Skiing? ...................Yes |
| Tickets: Adult Full .........$29 | Adult Half......................$23 |
| Tickets: Ages 7-17, Full ...$20 | Ages 7-17, Half ...............$18 |
| Tickets: Over 65, Full........$23 | Over 65, Half....................$21 |
| Main.................208-783-1111 | |
| Lodging.........800-667-7765 | Fax ..................208-783-9201 |
| Snow Report .....800-204-6428 | |

_No half days prices mid-week_

## _Snowhaven_

Location: 7m S of Grangeville
225 W. North, Grangeville, Idaho 83530

| | |
|---|---|
| Base Elevation (ft)..........3400 | Summit (ft) .....................3800 |
| Vertical Drop (ft)..............400 | Skiable Acres.................2 Tra |
| Avg Snowfall (in).............360 | Number of Lifts ..................1 |
| Runs:...Green 50% Blue 50% | Black-        DoubleBlack- |
| Date Open..........Thanksgiving | Date Close.............Late March |
| Hours............10 a.m.-4 p.m. | Night Skiing? .....................Yes |
| Tickets: Full......................$10 | Half......................................$8 |
| Main.................208-983-2851 | |

Photo courtesy of Crested Butte Mountain Resort; Tom Stillo, photographer

**Crested Butte Mountain Resort**

Fax ....................208-983-2336
Snow Report .....208-983-2299

## *Soldier Mountain Resort*

Location: 11m N of Fairfield, from Boise, I-84 To Rt 20
P.O. Box 510, Fairfield, Idaho 83327

| | |
|---|---|
| Base Elevation (ft)..........5740 | Summit (ft) .....................7150 |
| Vertical Drop (ft)............1410 | Skiable Acres....................670 |
| Avg Snowfall (in)..............195 | Number of Lifts....................4 |
| Runs:...Green 25% Blue 60% | Black 15% DoubleBlack- |
| Date Open.......Late November | Date Close .............Early April |
| Hours.................9:30-4 p.m. | Night Skiing?.....................No |
| Tickets: Adult...................$20 | Child ................................$15 |
| Tickets: Seniors ...............$10 | 6 & Under ...........................$0 |
| Main.................208-764-2327 | |
| Fax ..................208-764-2368 | |
| Snow Report .....208-764-2526 | |

*Open Wed - Sun, & holidays*

## *Sun Valley*

Location: 150m from Boise, I-84E to Rt 20
P.O. Box 2420, Sun Valley, Idaho 83353
Web Site: www.sunvalley.com e-mail:sunval@micron.net

| | |
|---|---|
| Base Elevation (ft)..........5750 | Summit (ft) .....................9140 |
| Vertical Drop (ft)............3390 | Skiable Acres..................2054 |
| Avg Snowfall (in)..............220 | Number of Lifts..................17 |
| Runs:...Green 36% Blue 42% | Black 22% DoubleBlack- |
| Date Open..........Thanksgiving | Date Close ..................May 1 |
| Hours.................9 a.m.-4 p.m. | Night Skiing?.....................No |
| Tickets: Adult Full ...........$52 | Adult Half..........................$37 |
| Tickets: Ages 12 under, Full$29 | Ages 12 under, Half ..........$21 |
| Main.................208-622-4111 | Toll Free ...........800-634-3347 |
| Lodging.............800-786-8259 | Fax ...................208-622-3700 |
| Snow Report .....800-635-4150 | |

# Illinois

## *Chestnut Mountain Resort*

Location: 135m from Chicago on NW Tollway, SE from US 20
8700 W Chestnut Rd, Galena, Illinois 61036
Web Site: www.chestnutmtn.com

| | |
|---|---|
| Base Elevation (ft).........2900 | Summit (ft) .....................5400 |
| Vertical Drop (ft)............2200 | Skiable Acres....................100 |
| Avg Snowfall (in)...............40 | Number of Lifts....................8 |
| Runs:...Green 30% Blue 40% | Black 30% DoubleBlack- |
| Date Open..........Thanksgiving | Date Close .............Mid March |
| Hours...........8:30 a.m.-10 p.m. | Night Skiing? ...................Yes |
| Tickets: Adult Wkdy .........$23 | Adult Wkend ......................$30 |

| Tickets: 6-12 Wkdy | $17 | 6-12 Wkend | $22 |
| Tickets: Over 70, under 6 | $0 | Adult Night | $20 |
| Main | 815-777-1320 | Toll Free | 800-397-1320 |
| Fax | 815-777-1068 | | |
| Snow Report | 800-798-0098 | | |

## Four Lakes Village

Location: Closest Area To Chicago, 15m W on I-88
5800 Forest View Road, Lisle, Illinois 60532

| Base Elevation (ft) | 600 | Summit (ft) | 700 |
| Vertical Drop (ft) | 100 | Skiable Acres | 9 |
| Avg Snowfall (in) | 30" | Number of Lifts | 6 |
| Runs:...Green 30% Blue 70% | | Black- DoubleBlack- | |
| Date Open | December | Date Close | February |
| Hours | 10 a.m.-7pm | Night Skiing? | Yes |
| Tickets: All Lifts | $12 | | |
| Main | 630-964-2551 | | |
| Fax | 630-852-7091 | | |
| Snow Report | 630-964-2550 | | |

## Ski Snowstar

Location: 15 Mins from Quad Cities Thru Andalusia
9500 - 126th St West, Taylor Ridge, Illinois 61284
Web Site: www.skisnowstar.com

| Base Elevation (ft) | 120 | Summit (ft) | 400 |
| Vertical Drop (ft) | 260 | Skiable Acres | 25 |
| Avg Snowfall (in) | 28" | Number of Lifts | 2 |
| Runs:...Green 20% Blue 40% | | Black 40% DoubleBlack- | |
| Date Open | December | Date Close | Mid March |
| Hours | 9 a.m.-9 p.m. | Night Skiing? | Yes |
| Tickets: Adult Wkdy | $19 | Adult Wkend | $23 |
| Tickets: Jr/Sr Wkdy | $16 | Jr/Sr Wkend | $19 |
| Tickets: Wkdy Night | $12 | Wkend | $17 |
| Main | 309-798-2666 | Toll Free | 800-383-4002 |
| Fax | 309-798-2080 | | |
| Snow Report | 309-798-2113 | | |

## Villa Olivia Ski Area

Location: 45 Mins from Chicago
Bartlett, Illinois 60103
Web Site: www.skiolivia.com

| Base Elevation (ft) | | Summit (ft) | |
| Vertical Drop (ft) | 180 | Skiable Acres | 15 |
| Avg Snowfall (in) | 25" | Number of Lifts | 10 |
| Runs:...Green 40% Blue 50% | | Black 10% DoubleBlack- | |
| Date Open | Early December | Date Close | Mid March |
| Hours | 9 a.m.-10 p.m. | Night Skiing? | Yes |
| Tickets: Adult Wkday | $16 | Adult Wkend | $21 |

Tickets: Child Wkday........$13     Child Wkend ....................$18
Tickets: Adult Night..........$16     Child Night......................$13
Main.................630-289-1000
Fax ...................630-289-2934
Snow Report .709-289-SNOW

# Indiana

## *Perfect North Slopes*

Location: 25m from Cincinnati on I-275
19640 State Route 1, Lawrenceburg, Indiana 47025
Web Site: www.perfectnorth.com

| | | |
|---|---|---|
| Base Elevation (ft).............400 | Summit (ft) ........................800 |
| Vertical Drop (ft)...............400 | Skiable Acres....................70 |
| Avg Snowfall (in)..............25" | Number of Lifts..................13 |
| Runs:...Green 25%  Blue 50% | Black 25%   DoubleBlack- |
| Date Open......Early December | Date Close ............Mid March |
| Hours............10 a.m.-10 p.m. | Night Skiing? ...................Yes |
| Tickets: Adult Wkdy .........$25 | Adult Wkend ....................$30 |
| Tickets: Child, 60+ Wkdy .$20 | Child, 60+, Wkend ...........$25 |
| Tickets: Adult Night..........$25 | Child, 60+ Night..............$20 |
| Main.................812-537-3754 | |
| Fax ...................812-537-3352 | |
| Snow Report .....812-537-3754 | |

## *Ski Paoli Peaks*

Location: 1.5m from Paoli, 80m from Indianapolis, US 37
PO Box 67, Paoli, Indiana 47454

| | | |
|---|---|---|
| Base Elevation (ft).............600 | Summit (ft) ........................900 |
| Vertical Drop (ft)...............300 | Skiable Acres....................65 |
| Avg Snowfall (in)...............19 | Number of Lifts....................8 |
| Runs:...Green 15%  Blue 75% | Black 10%  DoubleBlack- |
| Date Open ..............December | Date Close.....................March |
| Hours.............10 a.m.-10 p.m. | Night Skiing? ...................Yes |
| Tickets: Adult Wkdy ........$28 | Adult Twilight...................$28 |
| Tickets: Adult Night..........$16 | 7-12 Wkdy......................$10 |
| Tickets: 7-12 Wkend ........$15 | Over 70, under 7.................$0 |
| Main.................812-723-4696 | Snow Report .....816-723-4698 |

## *Ski World*

Location: 4mi from Nashville on Hwy 46, Bloomington 12m
Rt. 46 West, Nashville, Indiana 47448

| | | |
|---|---|---|
| Base Elevation (ft).............600 | Summit (ft) ........................950 |
| Vertical Drop (ft)...............350 | Skiable Acres....................100 |
| Avg Snowfall (in) ..............40" | Number of Lifts....................5 |
| Runs:...Green 25%  Blue 25% | Black 25%  DoubleBlack 25% |
| Date Open ..............December | Date Close.....................March |
| Hours................9 a.m.-10 p.m. | Night Skiing? ...................Yes |

Tickets: Adult Wkday .......$16
Tickets: Night Wkday .....$12
Tickets: Over 70, under 7 ....$0
Main.................812-988-6638
Fax ...................812-988-6694

Adult Wkend ....................$25
Night Wkend ....................$14

Lodging............818-988-6647
Snow Report ....812-988-6693

# Iowa

## *Crescent Hills*

Location: 7m N of Council Bluffs
Crescent, Iowa 51526

| | | |
|---|---|---|
| Base Elevation (ft)...........1200 | Summit (ft) ......................1500 |
| Vertical Drop (ft)...............300 | Skiable Acres....................50 |
| Avg Snowfall (in) .............30' | Number of Lifts...................2 |
| Runs:...Green 33% Blue 34% | Black 33% DoubleBlack- |
| Date Open ...........December 1 | Date Close................March 15 |
| Hours................9 a.m.-9:30p | Night Skiing? ..................Yes |
| Tickets: Adult Wkday .....$22 | Adult Wkend ...................$26 |
| Tickets: Over 13, Wkdy ....$18 | Over 13, Wkend ...............$22 |
| Tickets: Child Wkend .....$22 | Adult Night.....................$19 |
| Main.................712-545-3850 | |
| Fax ...................712-545-3915 | |

## *Nor-Ski Runs*

Location: 70m from Waterloo, 60m from Rochchester, Mn
Decorah, Iowa 52101

| | | |
|---|---|---|
| Base Elevation (ft)................ | Summit (ft) ...................... |
| Vertical Drop (ft)...............250 | Skiable Acres .................5 Tra |
| Avg Snowfall (in) .............10" | Number of Lifts..................3 |
| Runs:...Green 45% Blue 45% | Black 10% DoubleBlack- |
| Date Open........Mid December | Date Close ............Mid March |
| Hours................11am-9 p.m. | Night Skiing? ..................Yes |
| Tickets: Adult Daily ..........$6 | Adult Night.......................$5 |
| Tickets: Child Daily ...........$5 | Child Night.......................$4 |
| Main.................319-382-4158 | |

## *Riverside Hills*

Location:
Iowa

| | | |
|---|---|---|
| Base Elevation (ft)................ | Summit (ft) ...................... |
| Vertical Drop (ft)...............190 | Skiable Acres....................40 |
| Avg Snowfall (in) .............60" | Number of Lifts..................3 |
| Runs:...Green 20% Blue 40% | Black 40% DoubleBlack- |
| Date Open......Early December | Date Close ............Mid March |
| Hours.............................Varied | Night Skiing? ..................Yes |
| Tickets: Adult Wkdy ........$10 | Adult Wkend ...................$12 |
| Tickets: Adult Night..........$8 | Jr Wkdy ...........................$8 |
| Tickets: Jr Wkend.............$10 | Jr Night.............................$6 |

Main................712-362-5376
Snow Report.....800-286-5376

*Open Wed- Fri. 3:30 to 9pm; Sat. 10 a.m. to 9pm; Sun. 12 p.m. to 9pm*

## Seven Oaks Recreation Park

Location: 3.5m W of Boone, 5m E of Ogden on Hwy 30
Boone, IOWA

| | | |
|---|---|---|
| Base Elevation (ft)...........1000 | Summit (ft)......................1240 |
| Vertical Drop (ft)..............275 | Skiable Acres.....................30 |
| Avg Snowfall (in)................30 | Number of Lifts....................3 |
| Runs:...Green 20%  Blue 40% | Black 40%  DoubleBlack- |
| Date Open......Early December | Date Close ............Mid March |
| Hours ............................Varied | Night Skiing? ...................Yes |
| Tickets: Adult Wkdy .........$10 | Adult Wkend ....................$18 |
| Tickets: Jr Full.....................$6 | |
| Main................515-432-9457 | |

*Mon. - Fri. 12 p.m. to 9:30pm; Wkend 10 a.m. to 9:30pm*

## Sleepy Hollow Sports Park

Location:
Iowa

| | | |
|---|---|---|
| Base Elevation (ft).................. | Summit (ft) ............................ |
| Vertical Drop (ft).................... | Skiable Acres.................6 Tra |
| Avg Snowfall (in).................... | Number of Lifts....................3 |
| Runs:...Green-      Blue- | Black-      DoubleBlack- |
| Date Open......Early December | Date Close ............Mid March |
| Hours ............................Varied | Night Skiing? ...................Yes |
| Tickets: Wkday .................$12 | Wkend ..............................$14 |

Photo courtesy of Dynastar

Tickets: Night ..................$10

| Main ................515-262-4100 | |
| Lodging ............515-262-4100 | Fax ..................515-263-9114 |

## *Sundown Mountain*

Location: 3.5m from Dubuque on Hwy 20
17017 Asbury Road, Dubuque, Iowa 52002

| Base Elevation (ft)............584 | Summit (ft) ....................1059 |
| Vertical Drop (ft)............475 | Skiable Acres...................45 |
| Avg Snowfall (in)..............48 | Number of Lifts...................6 |
| Runs:...Green 30% Blue 60% | Black 10% DoubleBlack- |
| Date Open....Thanksgiving | Date Close ......St Patricks Day |
| Hours...............9 a.m.-10 p.m. | Night Skiing? ...................Yes |
| Tickets: Adult Full ...........$24 | Adult Half .....................$19 |
| Tickets: Child Full ...........$20 | Child Half .....................$15 |
| Tickets: Night Adult..........$17 | Night Child .....................$14 |
| Main ...............319-556-6676 | Toll Free ...........800-397-6676 |
| Snow Report .....888-786-3696 | |

## *Sunset Ski Area     (Unverified data)*

Location: 1m E of Cherokee on E Main
Cherokee, Iowa 51012

| Base Elevation (ft)................ | Summit (ft) ........................ |
| Vertical Drop (ft)................0 | Skiable Acres...................... |
| Avg Snowfall (in).................. | Number of Lifts...................4 |
| Runs:...Green-   Blue- | Black-   DoubleBlack- |
| Date Open......................... | Date Close........................ |
| Hours...............10 a.m.-9 p.m. | Night Skiing? ...................Yes |
| Tickets: Adult Wkday ........$11 | Adult Wkend .....................$12 |
| Tickets: Child Wkday ........$4 | Child Wkend .....................$5 |
| Tickets: Night Adult..........$10 | Night Child .....................$8 |
| Main .................712-225-4190 | |

# Maine

## *Big Rock Ski Area*

Location: 15m from Presque Isle, 25m from Houlton
Mars Hill, Maine 04758

| Base Elevation (ft)............770 | Summit (ft) ....................1750 |
| Vertical Drop (ft)............980 | Skiable Acres...................70 |
| Avg Snowfall (in)............100 | Number of Lifts...................4 |
| Runs:...Green 30% Blue 40% | Black 30% DoubleBlack- |
| Date Open ...............December | Date Close..............March |
| Hours...............9 a.m.-4 p.m. | Night Skiing? ...................Yes |
| Tickets: Adult Wkday ........$18 | Adult Wkend ...................$20 |
| Tickets: Jr Wkday .............$14 | Jr Wkend ......................$16 |
| Tickets: Over 65 Wkend ...$10 | Night Adult......................$12 |
| Main .................207-425-6711 | |

Fax ...................207-429-8188

## *Big Squaw Mountain*

Location:
Maine

| | |
|---|---|
| Base Elevation (ft)...........1450 | Summit (ft) ....................3200 |
| Vertical Drop (ft)............1750 | Skiable Acres...............400 |
| Avg Snowfall (in)..............175 | Number of Lifts....................4 |
| Runs:...Green 33%  Blue 33% | Black 34%  DoubleBlack- |
| Date Open .......Late December | Date Close ............Mid April |
| Hours.................9 a.m.-4 p.m. | Night Skiing?......................No |
| Tickets: Adult Wkday .......$15 | Adult Wkend ...................$20 |
| Tickets: Child Full............$15 | |
| Main.................207-695-1000 | |
| Fax ..................207-695-2273 | |
| Snow Report ....207-695-2272 | |

## *Black Mountain Of Maine     (Unverified data)*

Location: 4m from Rumford, 40m from Auburn & Lewiston
Rumford, Maine 04276

| | |
|---|---|
| Base Elevation (ft)................. | Summit (ft) ............................ |
| Vertical Drop (ft)................475 | Skiable Acres.......................... |
| Avg Snowfall (in)................. | Number of Lifts ....................2 |
| Runs:...Green 20%  Blue 40% | Black 40%  DoubleBlack- |
| Date Open ..............December | Date Close ....................March |
| Hours................................. | Night Skiing? ..................Yes |
| Tickets: Adult Day ...........$16 | Adult Night......................$11 |
| Tickets: Jr Day ..............$12 | Jr Night .............................$9 |
| Tickets: Over 65..............$-50 | |
| Main.................207-364-8977 | |

## *Camden Snow Bowl*

Location: 3m from Camden on Rt 1
Camden, Maine 04843
Web Site: www.midcoast.com/-snowbowl

| | |
|---|---|
| Base Elevation (ft).............100 | Summit (ft) ....................1000 |
| Vertical Drop (ft)..............900 | Skiable Acres.....................40 |
| Avg Snowfall (in)..............50" | Number of Lifts ...................3 |
| Runs:...Green 10%  Blue 80% | Black 10%  DoubleBlack- |
| Date Open........Mid December | Date Close ...........Mid March |
| Hours.................9 a.m.-9 p.m. | Night Skiing?.....................Yes |
| Tickets: Adult Wkdy ........$14 | Adult Wkend ...................$20 |
| Tickets: Under 12.............$12 | Night..................................$10 |
| Main.................207-236-3438 | Lodging............207-236-4404 |
| Fax ..................207-236-0490 | Snow Report .....207-236-4418 |

## *Eaton Mountain Ski Area*

Location: 5m E of Skowhegan, 22m from Waterville
Skowhegan, Maine 04976

| | | | |
|---|---|---|---|
| Base Elevation (ft)...........1680 | Summit (ft) .....................2200 |
| Vertical Drop (ft)..............520 | Skiable Acres.................130 |
| Avg Snowfall (in)...............72 | Number of Lifts ...................2 |
| Runs:...Green 20%  Blue 40% | Black 40%  DoubleBlack- |
| Date Open......Late November | Date Close ..............Mid April |
| Hours...............9 a.m.-10 p.m. | Night Skiing? .......................Yes |
| Tickets: Adult Wkdy ........$14 | Adult Wkend ....................$16 |
| Tickets: Child ...................$11 | Adult Night ......................$12 |
| Tickets: Child Night ...........$8 | Under 6 ................................$0 |
| Main.................207-474-2666 | |

## *Hermon Mountain*

Location: 3m from Bangor off Rt 2
Hermon, Maine 04974

| | |
|---|---|
| Base Elevation (ft)........... | Summit (ft) ..................... |
| Vertical Drop (ft)..............350 | Skiable Acres.......................75 |
| Avg Snowfall (in)............90" | Number of Lifts ...................2 |
| Runs:...Green 40%  Blue 30% | Black 30%  DoubleBlack- |
| Date Open ..............December | Date Close ....................March |
| Hours...............9 a.m.-10 p.m. | Night Skiing? ....................Yes |
| Tickets: Adult Full ...........$18 | Adult Half/Night ............$11 |
| Tickets: Jr Full...................$13 | Jr Half ..................................$9 |
| Tickets: Over 70 ..................$0 | |
| Main.................207-848-5192 | |
| Fax ...................207-848-5746 | |
| Snow Report .....207-848-5192 | |

## *Lost Valley Ski Area*

Location: 3/4 Hour Drive from Portland
Auburn, Maine 04210
Web Site: www.lostvalleyski.com

| | |
|---|---|
| Base Elevation (ft)............255 | Summit (ft) .....................495 |
| Vertical Drop (ft)..............240 | Skiable Acres.......................45 |
| Avg Snowfall (in)...............50 | Number of Lifts ...................3 |
| Runs:...Green 40%  Blue 30% | Black 30%  DoubleBlack- |
| Date Open ..............December | Date Close ..........Mid March |
| Hours...................9 a.m.-11pm | Night Skiing? ....................Yes |
| Tickets: Adult Wkdy ........$18 | Adult Wkend ....................$30 |
| Tickets: 6-12 Wkdy ..........$16 | 6-12 Wkend ......................$19 |
| Tickets: Adult Wkend Night$20 | 6-12 Wkend Night............$19 |
| Main.................207-784-1561 | |
| Lodging.............207-784-1561 | |
| Snow Report .....207-784-1561 | |

## _Mt. Jefferson_

Location: Maine

| | |
|---|---|
| Base Elevation (ft)................ | Summit (ft)............................ |
| Vertical Drop (ft)..............432 | Skiable Acres.......................12 |
| Avg Snowfall (in)..............75 | Number of Lifts....................3 |
| Runs:...Green 33% Blue 34% | Black 33% DoubleBlack- |
| Date Open ......Late December | Date Close............Late March |
| Hours ............................Varied | Night Skiing? ....................Yes |
| Tickets: Adult Wkdy ........$12 | Adult Wkend ......................$15 |
| Tickets: Adult Night..........$10 | Jr. Wkdy ..............................$7 |
| Tickets: Jr Wkend..............$10 | Jr Night ................................$7 |
| Main..................207-738-2377 | |
| Fax ...................207-738-2377 | |

## _Saddleback Ski Area_

Location: 7m from Rangeley, 4.5 Hrs from Boston
PO 490, Rangeley, Maine 04970

| | |
|---|---|
| Base Elevation (ft)..........2286 | Summit (ft)......................4116 |
| Vertical Drop (ft)............1830 | Skiable Acres.....................100 |
| Avg Snowfall (in)..............200 | Number of Lifts....................5 |
| Runs:...Green 33% Blue 33% | Black 34% DoubleBlack- |
| Date Open..............November | Date Close.......................April |
| Hours....................9 a.m.-4 p.m. | Night Skiing?....................No |
| Tickets: Wkdy, All ages ....$24 | Adult Wkend ......................$38 |
| Tickets: Sr/Jr Wkend.........$18 | Under 6/70+.........................$0 |
| Main..................207-864-5671 | |
| Fax ...................207-864-5878 | |

## _Shawnee Peak_

Location: 6m from Bridgton, 45m from Portland
Box 734, RR #1, Bridgton, Maine 04009
Web Site: www.shawneepeak.com

| | |
|---|---|
| Base Elevation (ft)..............649 | Summit (ft)......................1949 |
| Vertical Drop (ft)............1300 | Skiable Acres.....................225 |
| Avg Snowfall (in)..............125 | Number of Lifts....................5 |
| Runs:...Green 25% Blue 50% | Black 25% DoubleBlack- |
| Date Open ..............December | Date Close............Late March |
| Hours..........8:30 a.m.-10 p.m. | Night Skiing? ....................Yes |
| Tickets: Adult Wkdy ........$26 | Adult wkend ......................$35 |
| Tickets: Adult Night..........$21 | 7-12, Over 65 Wkdy .........$17 |
| Tickets: 7-12/65+ Wkend..$21 | 7-12, Over 65 Night .........$19 |
| Main..................207-647-8444 | |
| Lodging.............207-647-8444 | |
| Snow Report .....207-647-8444 | |

## Ski Mt Abram

Location: 10 Mins from Bethel, 65m from Portland
Locke Mills, Maine 04255
Web Site: www.neoutdoors.com/mtabram

| | |
|---|---|
| Base Elevation (ft)............970 | Summit (ft) ................2000 |
| Vertical Drop (ft)............1030 | Skiable Acres..................170 |
| Avg Snowfall (in)..............115 | Number of Lifts..................5 |
| Runs:...Green 28% Blue 48% | Black 24% DoubleBlack |
| Date Open.........Thanksgiving | Date Close ............Early April |
| Hours................8:30 a.m.-4 p.m. | Night Skiing?.....................No |
| Tickets: Adult Wkdy .........$20 | Adult Wkend ...................$30 |
| Tickets: Teen Wkdy .........$18 | Teen Wkend ...................$24 |
| Tickets: Jr/Sr Wkdy.........$15 | Sr Wkend ........................$24 |
| Main.................207-875-5003 | |
| Fax ...................207-875-5006 | |
| Snow Report .....207-875-5003 | |

## Sugarloaf/USA

Location: 7m from Carrabassett, 16m from Portland
RR1, Box 5000, Carrabassett Valley, Maine 04947-9799
Web Site: www.sugarloaf.com

| | |
|---|---|
| Base Elevation (ft)..........1400 | Summit (ft) ................4237 |
| Vertical Drop (ft)............2837 | Skiable Acres.......................... |
| Avg Snowfall (in)..............168 | Number of Lifts..................14 |
| Runs:...Green 33% Blue 35% | Black 32% DoubleBlack- |
| Date Open .....Early November | Date Close ....................April |
| Hours.................9 a.m.-4 p.m. | Night Skiing?.....................No |
| Tickets: Adult Wkdy .......$34 | Adult Wkend ...................$38 |
| Tickets: 13-18 Wkdy .......$27 | 13-18 Wkend ...................$31 |
| Tickets: 6-12, 65+ .........$21 | Under 5 ............................$0 |
| Main .................207-237-2000 | Lodging ........800-THE-LOAF |
| Fax ...................207-237-2718 | Snow Report ...207-237-2000 |

**NEW:20% increased snowmaking, 4 groomers, Halfpipe grinder**

*Among the top 50 resorts in North America.*

## Sunday River Ski Resort

Location: 6m from Bethel, 75m from Portland
PO Box 450, Bethel, Maine 04217
Web Site: www.sundayriver.com

| | |
|---|---|
| Base Elevation (ft)............800 | Summit (ft) ................3140 |
| Vertical Drop (ft)............2340 | Skiable Acres..................654 |
| Avg Snowfall (in)..............155 | Number of Lifts..................17 |
| Runs:...Green 25% Blue 35% | Black 40% DoubleBlack- |
| Date Open ..........Mid October | Date Close ......................May |
| Hours.................9 a.m.-4 p.m. | Night Skiing?.....................No |
| Tickets: Adult Wkdy .........$43 | Adult Wkend ...................$46 |

Tickets: 6-12, 65+ Wkdy...$22
Tickets: 65+ Wkend .........$23
Main.................207-824-3000
Snow Report .....207-824-5200

6-12 Wkend ......................$29

Lodging ............800-543-2SKI

## *Titcomb Mountain*

Location: Maine

| | |
|---|---|
| Base Elevation (ft)............380 | Summit (ft) ........................720 |
| Vertical Drop (ft)...............340 | Skiable Acres......................45 |
| Avg Snowfall (in).............110 | Number of Lifts ...................2 |
| Runs:...Green 30%  Blue 40% | Black 30%  DoubleBlack- |
| Date Open........Mid December | Date Close............Late March |
| Hours ...........................Varied | Night Skiing? ...................Yes |
| Tickets: Full.....................$12 | Half.......................................$8 |
| Tickets: Under 5/70+.........$0 | |
| Main.................207-778-9031 | Fax ..................207-778-9031 |

# Maryland

## *Wisp Ski Resort*

Location: 3 hours from Washington DC on I-270
McHenry, Maryland 21541
Web Site: www.gcnet.wisp

| | |
|---|---|
| Base Elevation (ft)....2470 | Summit (ft) ....................3080 |
| Vertical Drop (ft)..............610 | Skiable Acres......................80 |
| Avg Snowfall (in)..........90" | Number of Lifts ...................7 |
| Runs:...Green 20%  Blue 50% | Black 30%  DoubleBlack- |
| Date Open .....Early November | Date Close....................March |

Photo © Ben Blankenburg, courtesy of Vail Resorts/Keystone

Skier enjoys fresh powder at Keystone Resort

Hours.................8:30-10 p.m.
Tickets: Adult Full ...........$42
Tickets: Child Full............$29
Tickets: Over 65 ..............$21
Main.................301-387-4911
Lodging............301-387-4911
Snow Report .....301-387-4911

Night Skiing? ....................Yes
Adult Wkday ....................$35
Child Wkday ....................$24
Night................................$21

Fax ...................301-387-4797

# Massachusetts

## *Berkshire East Ski Area*

Location: 77m M from Hartford, CT. 17m W of Greenfield
Charlemont, Massachusetts 01339

Base Elevation (ft)............660
Vertical Drop (ft).............1180
Avg Snowfall (in)............110
Runs:...Green 30%  Blue 35%
Date Open ..............December
Hours.........9:30 a.m.-10 p.m.
Tickets: Adult Wkdy .......$25
Tickets: Adult Night........$15
Tickets: Child Wkend.......$25
Main.................413-339-6617
Fax ...................413-339-8454
Snow Report .....413-339-6617

Summit (ft) .....................1840
Skiable Acres....................400
Number of Lifts .................4
Black 35%  DoubleBlack-
Date Close ....................March
Night Skiing? ..................Yes
Adult Wkend ..................$32
Child Wkdy ....................$20
Child Night .....................$12

## *Blandford Ski Area*

Location: Located off Mass Trnpk Exit 3 & Rt 20
PO Box 158, Second Division Rd,
Blandford, Massachusetts 01008

Base Elevation (ft)..........1035
Vertical Drop (ft).............465
Avg Snowfall (in) ............50"
Runs:...Green 20%  Blue 70%
Date Open........Mid December
Hours.............9:30am-10 p.m.
Tickets: All Skiers Wkdy ..$10
Tickets: All Skiers Wkend $20
Main.................413-848-2860
Fax ...................413-568-4341

Summit (ft) .....................1500
Skiable Acres....................158
Number of Lifts .................5
Black 10%  DoubleBlack-
Date Close....................Late March
Night Skiing? ..................Yes
All Skiers Half.................$15

Toll Free........800-SKI-TYME
Snow Report .800-SKI-TYME

## *Blue Hills Ski Area*

Location: 10m S of Boston
4001 Washington St, Canton, Massachusetts 02021
Web Site: www.gis.net/~slopes

Base Elevation (ft)............635
Vertical Drop (ft).............325
Avg Snowfall (in) ............40"

Summit (ft) .....................1280
Skiable Acres ................8 tra
Number of Lifts ....................4

| | | |
|---|---|---|
| Runs:...Green 20% Blue 60% | Black 10% DoubleBlack 10% | |
| Date Open .............December | Date Close.....................March | |
| Hours..............9:30am-10 p.m. | Night Skiing? ....................Yes | |
| Tickets: Adult Wkdy .........$17 | Adult Wkend .....................$22 | |
| Tickets: Adult Night..........$17 | Child/ 65+ Wkdy..............$14 | |
| Tickets: Child/ 65+ Wkend $19 | Child/ 65+ Night .............$14 | |
| Main.................781-828-7490 | | |
| Fax ...................781-828-7615 | | |
| Snow Report .....781-828-5070 | | |

## Bousquet Ski Area

Location: 2.5m S of Pittsfield on Rts 7 & 20
Pittsfield, Massachusetts 01201

| | | |
|---|---|---|
| Base Elevation (ft)...........1125 | Summit (ft) ......................1875 | |
| Vertical Drop (ft)..............750 | Skiable Acres....................200 | |
| Avg Snowfall (in) ..............83" | Number of Lifts.....................5 | |
| Runs:...Green-     Blue 34% | Black 33% DoubleBlack 33% | |
| Date Open..........Thanksgiving | Date Close ............Early April | |
| Hours................9 a.m.-10 p.m. | Night Skiing? ....................Yes | |
| Tickets: Adult Day ...........$15 | Adult Night.........................$10 | |
| Tickets: Over 65 Day .........$7 | Over 65 Night......................$5 | |
| Tickets: Over 70, Under 5...$0 | | |
| Main.................413-442-8316 | | |
| Lodging.............413-443-9186 | Fax ...................413-445-4534 | |
| Snow Report .....413-442-2436 | | |

## Bradford Ski Area

Location: 31m from Boston
Po Box 99, Bradford, Massachusetts 01835
Web Site: www.skibradford.com

| | | |
|---|---|---|
| Base Elevation (ft).............175 | Summit (ft) ........................325 | |
| Vertical Drop (ft)..............250 | Skiable Acres......................48 | |
| Avg Snowfall (in) ..............40" | Number of Lifts.....................8 | |
| Runs:...Green 60% Blue 20% | Black 20% DoubleBlack- | |
| Date Open..............December | Date Close............March 15 | |
| Hours...........8:30 a.m.-10 p.m. | Night Skiing? ....................Yes | |
| Tickets: Full Wkend..........$25 | Half Wkend .....................$22 | |
| Tickets: Full Wkdy............$18 | Half Wkdy ........................$14 | |
| Tickets: Night....................$17 | | |
| Main.................978-373-0071 | | |
| Fax .................978-373-5091 | | |

## Brodie Mountain

Location: 5m from Lanesboro, 10m from Pittsfield
US Rt7, New Ashford, Massachusetts 01237

| | | |
|---|---|---|
| Base Elevation (ft)...........1450 | Summit (ft) .....................2700 | |
| Vertical Drop (ft)............1250 | Skiable Acres....................250 | |
| Avg Snowfall (in)...............85 | Number of Lifts.....................6 | |

Runs:...Green 18%  Blue 50%  Black 32%  DoubleBlack-
Date Open..............November
Hours..................9 a.m.-11pm
Date Close......................April
Night Skiing?......................Yes
Tickets: Adult Wkdy.........$24
Tickets: 7-12/65+ Wkdy......$20
Adult Wkend......................$38
7-12/65+ Wkend................$30
Tickets: Night, All ages.....$10
Under 6 ..............................$10
Main...............413-443-4752
Lodging............413-443-4752
Snow Report .....413-443-4751

## *Butternut Ski Area*

Location: 55m from Hartford, 2m from Great Barrington
Great Barrington, Massachusetts 01230
Base Elevation (ft)..............800
Summit (ft) ......................1800
Vertical Drop (ft)............1000
Skiable Acres....................110
Avg Snowfall (in)............70
Number of Lifts................8
Runs:...Green 15%  Blue 60%  Black 25%  DoubleBlack-
Date Open ...........December 1
Date Close................March 30
Hours..................9 a.m.-4 p.m.
Night Skiing?......................No
Tickets: Adult Wkdy ........$30
Adult Wkend......................$38
Tickets: 7-13, 65-69 Wkdy$20
7-13, 65-69 Wkend............$25
Tickets: Under 6 .................$6
Over 70 ................................$7
Main..................413-528-2000
Snow Report .800-438-SNOW

## *Jericho Ski Area*

Location: 27m from Boston, off Rt 20 & 85
Marlboro, Massachusetts 01752
Base Elevation (ft)..............900
Summit (ft) ......................1075
Vertical Drop (ft)..............175
Skiable Acres......................19
Avg Snowfall (in)............42
Number of Lifts................2
Runs:...Green 50%  Blue 50%  Black-  DoubleBlack-
Date Open ..............December
Date Close..................March
Hours ......................Varied
Night Skiing? ......................Yes
Tickets: Adult Wkdy/Night.$8
Adult Wkend......................$10
Tickets: Child Wkdy/Night.$5
Child Wkend ........................$6
Main..................508-460-3718
Fax ...................508-624-6940
Snow Report .....508-340-3718

## *Jiminy Peak*

Location: 45mins from Albany, I-90 E to exit 8
Hancock, Massachusetts 01237
Base Elevation (ft)............1250
Summit (ft) ......................2390
Vertical Drop (ft)............1140
Skiable Acres....................175
Avg Snowfall (in)............98
Number of Lifts................8
Runs:...Green 21%  Blue 50%  Black 29%  DoubleBlack-
Date Open..............November
Date Close......................April

| Hours.............9 a.m.-10:30pm | Night Skiing?.................Yes |
|---|---|
| Tickets: Adult Wkdy.........$29 | Adult wkend....................$39 |
| Tickets: Over 62 Wkdy.....$25 | Over 62 Wkend.................$28 |
| Tickets: Night, all ages......$21 | |
| Main.................413-738-5500 | Snow Report......888-4-JIMINY |

Photo courtesy of Nordica (Prince Sports Group)

## Mt Tom Ski Area

Location: 2m from Holyoke, 40mins from Hartford on I-91
Route 5, PO Box 1158, Holyoke, Massachusetts 01041

| | | | |
|---|---|---|---|
| Base Elevation (ft)............700 | Summit (ft) ....................1380 |
| Vertical Drop (ft)............680 | Skiable Acres....................85 |
| Avg Snowfall (in)..............50 | Number of Lifts....................5 |
| Runs:...Green 20% Blue 60% | Black 20% DoubleBlack |
| Date Open .............December | |
| Hours...............9 a.m.-10 p.m. | Night Skiing? ...................Yes |
| Tickets: Adult Wkdy ........$25 | Adult Wkend ..................$29 |
| Tickets: Adult 3-10 p.m. ...$25 | Under 12/Over 65Wkdy ....$21 |
| Tickets:Under 12/65+Wknd$25 | Little Jr .........................$10 |
| Main................413-536-0516 | |
| Snow Report .....508-528-8160 | |

## Nashoba Valley Ski Area

Location: 25m W of Boston on Rt 2
Towers Rd, Westford, Massachusetts 01886

| | | | |
|---|---|---|---|
| Base Elevation (ft)............200 | Summit (ft) ....................440 |
| Vertical Drop (ft)............240 | Skiable Acres....................53 |
| Avg Snowfall (in) .............50" | Number of Lifts....................9 |
| Runs:...Green 20% Blue 50% | Black 30% DoubleBlack- |
| Date Open ....................November | Date Close ....................April |
| Hours..........8:30 a.m.-10 p.m. | Night Skiing? ...................Yes |
| Tickets: Adult Wkdy ........$20 | Adult Wkend ..................$29 |
| Tickets: Adult Night..........$18 | Under 12 Wkend ..............$27 |
| Tickets: Under 12, Wkdy ..$18 | |
| Main................978-692-3033 | Toll Free........800-400-SNOW |
| Fax..................978-692-0448 | |
| Snow Report .978-400-SNOW | |

## Otis Ridge

Location: 30m from Springfield on Rt 23
Otis, Massachusetts 01253

| | | | |
|---|---|---|---|
| Base Elevation (ft)..........1300 | Summit (ft) ....................1700 |
| Vertical Drop (ft)............400 | Skiable Acres....................65 |
| Avg Snowfall (in)..............100 | Number of Lifts....................5 |
| Runs:...Green 30% Blue 40% | Black 30% DoubleBlack- |
| Date Open .............December | Date Close ....................April |
| Hours...............9:30am-10 p.m. | Night Skiing? ...................Yes |
| Tickets: Adult/Jr Wkdy .....$15 | Adult/Jr Wkend ..............$20 |
| Tickets: Adult/Jr Night......$10 | Over 65 Wkdy ....................$7 |
| Tickets: Over 65 Wkend ...$10 | Over 65 Night ....................$5 |
| Main................413-269-4444 | |

### Ski Ward

Location: 5m from Worcester, 30m from Boston
Shrewsbury, Massachusetts 01545

| | |
|---|---|
| Base Elevation (ft)............210 | Summit (ft) ......................410 |
| Vertical Drop (ft)............200 | Skiable Acres ..................5 tra |
| Avg Snowfall (in)............ | Number of Lifts....................3 |
| Runs:...Green 40%  Blue 60% | Black-        DoubleBlack- |
| Date Open......Late November | Date Close............Early March |
| Hours..............10 a.m.-10 p.m. | Night Skiing? ...................Yes |
| Tickets: NA .........................$0 | |
| Main................508-842-6346 | |
| Fax ...................508-842-9368 | |

*Open Fri, Sat & Sun only. Rates vary*

### Wachusett Mountain

Location: 14m from Worcester, 52m from Boston
Wachusett Mountain Ski Resort, 499 Mountain Road,
Princeton, Massachusetts 01541

| | |
|---|---|
| Base Elevation (ft)............990 | Summit (ft) ......................2006 |
| Vertical Drop (ft)............1016 | Skiable Acres....................105 |
| Avg Snowfall (in)............100 | Number of Lifts....................5 |
| Runs:...Green 30%  Blue 40% | Black 30%  DoubleBlack- |
| Date Open......Late November | Date Close............Late March |
| Hours..............9 a.m.-10 p.m. | Night Skiing? ...................Yes |
| Tickets: Adult Wkdy ........$29 | Adult Wkend ....................$35 |
| Tickets: Adult Night........$24 | Jr/Sr Wkdy ......................$24 |
| Tickets: Jr/Sr Wkend........$27 | Jr/Sr Night ......................$22 |
| Main................978-464-2300 | Lodging.............978-874-2000 |
| Fax ...................978-464-5462 | Snow Report.....800-SKI-1234 |

# Michigan

### Al Quaal Recreation

Location: Municipal Slope run by the City
Ishpeming, Michigan 49849

| | |
|---|---|
| Base Elevation (ft)................. | Summit (ft) ......................... |
| Vertical Drop (ft)................70 | Skiable Acres......................20 |
| Avg Snowfall (in)............160 | Number of Lifts....................2 |
| Runs:...Green 50%  Blue 50% | Black-        DoubleBlack- |
| Date Open .......Late December | Date Close ............Mid March |
| Hours....................Select times | Night Skiing?.....................No |
| Tickets: All Skiers ............$3 | ...........................................$0 |
| Main................906-486-6181 | |
| Fax ...................906-486-1108 | |
| Snow Report .....906-486-6181 | |

## Alpine Valley

Location: 10m from Pontiac
White Lake, Michigan 48383

| | | |
|---|---|---|
| Base Elevation (ft) | 910 | Summit (ft) .................1210 |
| Vertical Drop (ft) | 300 | Skiable Acres .................25 Sl |
| Avg Snowfall (in) | 50 | Number of Lifts .................18 |
| Runs:...Green 39% Blue 26% | | Black 35% DoubleBlack- |
| Date Open | November | Date Close .............Mid March |
| Hours | 10 a.m.-11pm | Night Skiing? .................Yes |
| Tickets: Adult Wkday | $18 | Adult Wkend .................$24 |
| Tickets: Under 6, wkdy | $13 | Under 6, wkend .................$18 |
| Tickets: Over 65 | $13 | Night wkend .................$19 |
| Main | 313-887-4183 | |
| Snow Report | 313-887-4183 | |

## Apple Mt. Resort

Location: 8m from Saginaw, 4.5m from Freeland
Freeland, Michigan 49849

| | | |
|---|---|---|
| Base Elevation (ft) | 600 | Summit (ft) .................800 |
| Vertical Drop (ft) | 200 | Skiable Acres .................45 |
| Avg Snowfall (in) | 20" | Number of Lifts .................10 |
| Runs:...Green 40% Blue 40% | | Black 20% DoubleBlack- |
| Date Open | December 1 | Date Close .................March |
| Hours | 10 a.m.-10 p.m. | Night Skiing? .................Yes |
| Tickets: Adult Full | $12 | Over 65, under 6 .................$7 |
| Tickets: Adult Night | $12 | 65+, under 6, Night .................$7 |
| Main | 517-781-0170 | |
| Fax | 517-781-7727 | |
| Snow Report | 517-781-0170 | |

## Big Powderhorn Mountain

Location: Located off US 2, Ironwood & Bessemer
N 11375 Powderhorn Road, Bessemer, Michigan 49911
Web Site: www.bigpowderhorn.net

| | | |
|---|---|---|
| Base Elevation (ft) | 1200 | Summit (ft) .................1800 |
| Vertical Drop (ft) | 600 | Skiable Acres .................250 |
| Avg Snowfall (in) | 214 | Number of Lifts .................10 |
| Runs:...Green 35% Blue 35% | | Black 30% DoubleBlack- |
| Date Open | Thanksgiving | Date Close .................Easter |
| Hours | 9 a.m.-4 p.m. | Night Skiing? .................No |
| Tickets: Adult Full | $28 | Adult Half .................$23 |
| Tickets: Jr Full | $22 | Jr Half .................$17 |
| Tickets: Over 65 | $14 | |
| Main | 906-932-4838 | Toll Free .................800-222-3131 |
| Lodging | 906-932-3100 | |
| Snow Report | 800-272-7000 | |

## Bittersweet Ski Area

Location: 13m NW of Kalamazoo, US 131 To M-89
600 River Rd, Otsego, Michigan 49078
Web Site: www.skibittersweet.com

| | |
|---|---|
| Base Elevation (ft) ........................... | Summit (ft) ........................... |
| Vertical Drop (ft) ..............350 | Skiable Acres ........................30 |
| Avg Snowfall (in) ..............85" | Number of Lifts ..............12 |
| Runs:...Green 40%  Blue 40% | Black 20%  DoubleBlack- |
| Date Open ......Mid November | Date Close ............Mid March |
| Hours............10 a.m.-10:30pm | Night Skiing? ....................Yes |
| Tickets: Adult Wkday.......$19 | Adult Wkend ....................$24 |
| Tickets: Child Wkday.......$12 | Child Wkend ....................$19 |
| Tickets: Night ..................$19 | |
| Main................616-694-2032 | Fax ..................616-694-6860 |
| Snow Report .....616-694-2032 | |

## Blackjack Ski Resort

Location: 6m NE of Ironwood, MI & Hurley WI
Blackjack Road, Bessemer, Michigan 49911

| | |
|---|---|
| Base Elevation (ft) ..........1200 | Summit (ft) ....................1650 |
| Vertical Drop (ft) ..............450 | Skiable Acres ..................20 tr |
| Avg Snowfall (in) ..............180 | Number of Lifts ..............6 |
| Runs:...Green 20%  Blue 40% | Black 40%  DoubleBlack- |
| Date Open.......Late November | Date Close ............Early April |
| Hours.................9 a.m.-4 p.m. | Night Skiing?.....................No |
| Tickets: Adult wkdy .........$18 | Adult wkend ....................$20 |
| Tickets: Child wkdy .........$10 | Child wkend ....................$12 |
| Tickets: Junior wkdy .........$14 | Junior wkend ..................$16 |
| Main................906-229-5115 | Toll Free ..........800-848-1125 |
| Lodging............906-229-5157 | Snow Report .....800-272-7000 |

## Boyne Highlands

Location: 10m from Petoskey, 5m from Harbor Springs
Harbor Springs, Michigan 49740
Web Site: www.boyne.com

| | |
|---|---|
| Base Elevation (ft) ............745 | Summit (ft) ....................1290 |
| Vertical Drop (ft) ..............545 | Skiable Acres ..................44 tr |
| Avg Snowfall (in) ..............150 | Number of Lifts ..............10 |
| Runs:...Green 40%  Blue 28% | Black 30%  DoubleBlack 2%% |
| Date Open.........Thanksgiving | Date Close ....................Easter |
| Hours.................9 a.m.-4:30 p.m. | Night Skiing? ...................Yes |
| Tickets: Adult (20+), wknd $38 | Ages 13-19, wknd...........$32 |
| Tickets: Ages 9-12, wkend$25 | Seniors 65+, wkend.........$25 |
| Tickets: Under age 8 ..........$0 | |
| Main................616-526-3000 | Toll Free ......800-GO-BOYNE |
| Lodging .......800-GO-BOYNE | Snow Report800-GO-BOYNE |

*NEW:3 lifts, added snowmaking*

## *Boyne Mountain*

Location: 15m from Petoskey on US 131
Boyne Falls, Michigan 49713

Base Elevation (ft)............720
Vertical Drop (ft)...............500
Avg Snowfall (in).............145

Summit (ft) ......................1220
Skiable Acres......................41 tr
Number of Lifts....................10

Photo courtesy of TLH Heliskiing

### Skiers make first tracks in fresh powder snow

Runs:...Green 30%  Blue 41%
Date Open..........Thanksgiving
Hours.............9 a.m.-4:30 p.m.
Tickets: 20+ wkdy.............$32
Tickets: Ages 13-19, wkend $32
Tickets: 65+, wkend ..........$25
Main..................616-549-6000
Lodging...........800-GO-BOYNE
Snow Report ...800-GO-BOYNE

Black 26%  DoubleBlack 3%%
Date Close .....................Easter
Night Skiing? ...................Yes
20+ wkend.......................$38
Ages 9-12, wkend..............$25
Under 8 ...............................$0
Toll Free .........800-GO-BOYNE
Fax ...................616-549-6094

## *Caberfae Peaks Ski Resort*

Location: 12m from Cadillac on M55, 100m from Grand Rapid
Caberfae Road, Cadillac, Michigan 49601

Base Elevation (ft)..........1060
Vertical Drop (ft)..............509
Avg Snowfall (in).............125
Runs:...Green 26%  Blue 43%

Summit (ft) ......................1569
Skiable Acres....................161
Number of Lifts....................6
Black 31%  DoubleBlack-

| | | | |
|---|---|---|---|
| Date Open...............November | Date Close......................April |
| Hours..............10 a.m.-10 p.m. | Night Skiing?....................Yes |
| Tickets: Adult wkdy.........$24 | Adult wkend.....................$29 |
| Tickets: Junior wkdy.........$17 | Junior wkend....................$29 |
| Tickets: Under 6...................$0 | |
| Main...................616-862-3000 | |
| Lodging............616-862-3333 | |
| Snow Report.....800-968-7544 | |

## Cannonsburg Ski Area

Location: 10 Minutes from Grand Rapids on Rt 131
PO Box 14, 6800 Cannonsburg Road,
Cannonsburg, Michigan 49317

| | |
|---|---|
| Base Elevation (ft)................... | Summit (ft).............................. |
| Vertical Drop (ft)...............250 | Skiable Acres....................100 |
| Avg Snowfall (in)..............100 | Number of Lifts..................12 |
| Runs:...Green 35% Blue 50% | Black 15%  DoubleBlack- |
| Date Open.......Late November | Date Close.............Mid March |
| Hours..............10 a.m.-10 p.m. | Night Skiing?....................Yes |
| Tickets: Adult Wkdy.........$18 | Adult Wkend.....................$28 |
| Tickets: Adult Night.........$17 | Jr Wkdy...........................$14 |
| Tickets: Jr Wkend..............$20 | Under 6/70+........................$0 |
| Main...................616-874-6711 | |
| Fax...................616-874-6677 | |
| Snow Report.....616-874-6711 | |

## Crystal Mountain Resort

Location: 28m from Traverse City, 2.5m from Thompsonville
M 115, Thompsonville, Michigan 49683

| | |
|---|---|
| Base Elevation (ft)........757 | Summit (ft)....................1132 |
| Vertical Drop (ft)...............375 | Skiable Acres...............1500 |
| Avg Snowfall (in)..............150 | Number of Lifts...................7 |
| Runs:...Green 25%  Blue 50% | Black 25%  DoubleBlack- |
| Date Open.........Thanksgiving | Date Close.............April 7 |
| Hours...............9 a.m.-10 p.m. | Night Skiing?....................Yes |
| Tickets: Adult wkdy.........$28 | Adult wkend.....................$37 |
| Tickets: Ages 7-12, wkend$23 | Ages 13-18, wkend..........$30 |
| Tickets: Adult night..........$20 | Over 65 is 50% off..............$0 |
| Main...................616-378-2000 | Toll Free...........800-968-7686 |
| Snow Report.....800-968-7754 | |

## Gladstone Sports Park

Location: 2m from center of Gladstone
Gladstone, Michigan 49837

| | |
|---|---|
| Base Elevation (ft)................... | Summit (ft).............................. |
| Vertical Drop (ft)...............130 | Skiable Acres......................30 |
| Avg Snowfall (in)..............20" | Number of Lifts.....................5 |
| Runs:...Green 60%  Blue 40% | Black-         DoubleBlack- |

Date Open..........Thanksgiving  
Hours .................5:30-9:30pm  
Tickets: Adult Full ...............$7  
Main..................906-428-9222  
Fax ....................906-428-3122  
Snow Report .....906-428-9130  

Date Close ............Mid March  
Night Skiing? ...................Yes  
Student................................$5  

## *Hanson Hills Recreation Area*

Location: 3m West of Grayling, M-72 To M-93  
Grayling, Michigan 49738  

| | | |
|---|---|---|
| Base Elevation (ft).................. | Summit (ft) ......................... | |
| Vertical Drop (ft)..............225 | Skiable Acres....................125 | |
| Avg Snowfall (in) ..............60" | Number of Lifts....................5 | |
| Runs:...Green 50% Blue 50% | Black- DoubleBlack- | |
| Date Open......Early December | Date Close.............Late March | |
| Hours..................11am-9 p.m. | Night Skiing? ...................Yes | |
| Tickets: Adult Wkdy ..........$8 | Adult Wkend ...................$11 | |
| Tickets: Adult Night............$9 | Child Wkdy ........................$7 | |
| Tickets: Child Wkend.......$10 | Child Night .........................$8 | |
| Main..................517-348-9266 | | |
| Fax ....................517-348-1393 | | |
| Snow Report .....517-348-9266 | | |

## *Hickory Hills       (Unverified data)*

Location: 1.5m west of Traverse City  
Traverse City, Michigan 49684  

| | | |
|---|---|---|
| Base Elevation (ft).............302 | Summit (ft) ......................540 | |
| Vertical Drop (ft)..............238 | Skiable Acres...................... | |
| Avg Snowfall (in).................. | Number of Lifts....................5 | |
| Runs:...Green- Blue- | Black- DoubleBlack- | |
| Date Open........Mid December | Date Close ............Mid March | |
| Hours..................11am-9 p.m. | Night Skiing? ...................Yes | |
| Tickets: Adult Wkday .........$6 | Adult Wkend .....................$7 | |
| Tickets: Adult Night............$6 | Child Wkday ......................$5 | |
| Tickets: Child Wkend..........$6 | | |
| Main..................616-947-8566 | | |

## *Indianhead Mt & Bear Creek Resort*

Location: 1.5m from Wakefield on Rt 2, 110m from Duluth  
Wakefield, Michigan 49968  

| | | |
|---|---|---|
| Base Elevation (ft)...........1297 | Summit (ft) ....................1935 | |
| Vertical Drop (ft)..............638 | Skiable Acres....................160 | |
| Avg Snowfall (in)..............211 | Number of Lifts....................9 | |
| Runs:...Green 21% Blue 37% | Black 42% DoubleBlack- | |
| Date Open...............November | Date Close...........................April | |
| Hours..................9 a.m.-4 p.m. | Night Skiing?......................No | |
| Tickets: Adult Wkday .......$24 | Adult Wkend ...................$28 | |
| Tickets: Child Wkday.......$15 | Child Wkend ....................$17 | |

Tickets: Over 65 Wkdy .....$12    Over 65 Wkend ..................$14
Main.................906-229-5181    Toll Free .........800-3-INDIAN
Lodging.............906-229-5184
Snow Report .....800-272-7000

## Marquette Mountain

Location: Located within city limits of Marquette
PO Box 487, County Rd 553, Marquette, Michigan 49855

| | |
|---|---|
| Base Elevation (ft)...........1200 | Summit (ft) ......................1800 |
| Vertical Drop (ft)..............600 | Skiable Acres....................140 |
| Avg Snowfall (in)..............200 | Number of Lifts ...................5 |
| Runs:...Green 15% Blue 50% | Black 35% DoubleBlack- |
| Date Open ............December 1 | Date Close.......................April 1 |
| Hours..............9 a.m.-9:30pm | Night Skiing? ....................Yes |
| Tickets: Adult Wkends......$27 | Child WKends ..................$22 |
| Tickets: Adult Wkdays......$22 | Child Wkdays ..................$17 |
| Tickets: Adult Night..........$15 | |
| Main.................906-225-1155 | Toll Free........800-944-SNOW |
| Lodging.............906-226-6591 | Fax ...................906-225-0416 |
| Snow Report .....906-225-1155 | |

## Mio Mountain Ski Area

Location: 1.5m W of Mio, 180m from Detroit
1282 Mountain Drive, Mio, Michigan 48647

| | |
|---|---|
| Base Elevation (ft).................. | Summit (ft) ........................ |
| Vertical Drop (ft)..............250 | Skiable Acres....................40 |
| Avg Snowfall (in).................. | Number of Lifts ...................5 |
| Runs:...Green 40% Blue 40% | Black 20% DoubleBlack 0% |
| Date Open........Mid December | Date Close ............Mid March |
| Hours...............10 p.m.-4 p.m. | Night Skiing? ....................Yes |
| Tickets: Adult Wkend .........$9 | Thurs Night ........................$6 |
| Tickets: Fri/Sat Nite ...........$7 | |
| Main.................517-826-5569 | |
| Fax .................517-826-5569 | |
| Snow Report .....517-826-5569 | |

*Thurs-Sat hours: 7-10 p.m.*

## Missaukee Mountain     *(Unverified data)*

Location: Michigan

| | |
|---|---|
| Base Elevation (ft).................. | Summit (ft) .............................. |
| Vertical Drop (ft)..............220 | Skiable Acres....................15 |
| Avg Snowfall (in) .............90" | Number of Lifts ...................2 |
| Runs:...Green- | Black- DoubleBlack- |
| Date Open .......Late December | Date Close ............Mid March |
| Hours....................11am-6pm | Night Skiing? ....................Yes |
| Tickets: Wkend ..................$6 | |
| Main.................616-839-7575 | |
| Snow Report .....616-839-7575 | |

Photo courtesy of Winter Park Resort, © 1997, Byron Hetzler

*Sat & Sun / Christmas Vacation only.*

## *Mont Ripley*

Location: 1m from Hancock/Houghton, 180m from Detroit
1400 Townsend Dr., Houghton, Michigan 49931
Web Site: www.aux.mtu.auedu/ski/

| | | | |
|---|---|---|---|
| Base Elevation (ft)............700 | Summit (ft) ..................1120 |
| Vertical Drop (ft)...............420 | Skiable Acres ..................10 tr |
| Avg Snowfall (in)............275 | Number of Lifts...................2 |
| Runs:...Green 10%  Blue 10% | Black 80%  DoubleBlack |
| Date Open ..............December | Date Close............Late March |
| Hours ..............12:30pm-5:10 | Night Skiing?.....................No |
| Tickets: Adult Full ..........$16 | Student Full ....................$14 |
| Tickets: Adult Half...........$10 | Student Half......................$8 |
| Main.................906-487-2340 | |
| Fax ...................906-487-3314 | |

## *Mott Mountain*     *(Unverified data)*

Location: Michigan

| | | | |
|---|---|---|---|
| Base Elevation (ft).................. | Summit (ft) ............................ |
| Vertical Drop (ft)................... | Skiable Acres........................ |
| Avg Snowfall (in)................... | Number of Lifts..................... |
| Runs:...Green-    Blue- | Black-    DoubleBlack- |
| Date Open............................. | Date Close ............................ |
| Hours ................................... | Night Skiing?.....................No |
| Tickets: ...............................$0 | .............................................$0 |
| Main.................517-588-2945 | |

## Mt Brighton Ski Area

Location: 1.5m from Brighton, Detroit/Lansing/Flint 50m
Brighton, Michigan 48116

| | | | |
|---|---|---|---|
| Base Elevation (ft) | 1100 | Summit (ft) | 1330 |
| Vertical Drop (ft) | 230 | Skiable Acres | 130 |
| Avg Snowfall (in) | 60 | Number of Lifts | 17 |
| Runs:...Green 30% Blue 40% | | Black 30% DoubleBlack- | |
| Date Open | Mid November | Date Close | Mid March |
| Hours | 10 a.m.-11pm | Night Skiing? | Yes |
| Tickets: Weekdays | $18 | Weekends | $23 |
| Tickets: Halfday | $20 | Night | $20 |
| Tickets: Over 65 | $0 | Under 5 w/ adult | $0 |
| Main | 810-229-9581 | | |
| Lodging | 810-229-9581 | | |
| Snow Report | 810-229-9581 | | |

## Mt Holly Ski Area

Location: 15m from Flint on I-75, 50m from Detroit
13536 S Dixie Hwy, Holly, Michigan 48442

| | | | |
|---|---|---|---|
| Base Elevation (ft) | | Summit (ft) | |
| Vertical Drop (ft) | 350 | Skiable Acres | 18 Tr |
| Avg Snowfall (in) | 42" | Number of Lifts | 13 |
| Runs:...Green 22% Blue 39% | | Black 39% DoubleBlack- | |
| Date Open | December | Date Close | March 15 |
| Hours | 10 a.m.-11pm | Night Skiing? | Yes |
| Tickets: Adult Wkdy | $14 | Adult Wkend | $18 |
| Tickets: Adult Night | $14 | Student | $8 |
| Tickets: Over 65 | $-10 | | |
| Main | 810-834-8260 | Toll Free | 800-582-7256 |
| Lodging | 313-634-8269 | Fax | 810-634-0808 |

## Mt Zion Ski Area

Location: 250m from Minn/St Paul on I-35N & US-2 E
Ironwood, Michigan 49938

| | | | |
|---|---|---|---|
| Base Elevation (ft) | 1200 | Summit (ft) | 1502 |
| Vertical Drop (ft) | 302 | Skiable Acres | 20 |
| Avg Snowfall (in) | 200 | Number of Lifts | 2 |
| Runs:...Green 25% Blue 50% | | Black 25% DoubleBlack- | |
| Date Open | Mid December | Date Close | Mid March |
| Hours | 9 a.m.-9 p.m. | Night Skiing? | Yes |
| Tickets: Daily | $9 | Hfday | $7 |
| Tickets: Night | $7 | Over 62 | $0 |
| Main | 906-932-3718 | | |
| Fax | 906-932-0868 | | |
| Snow Report | 906-932-5059 | | |

*Open 2-7 p.m. Tues -Fri; Sat. 9-4 p.m.; Sun. 12-4 p.m.*

## Mt. McSauba

Location: Michigan

| | |
|---|---|
| Base Elevation (ft).................. | Summit (ft) ............................ |
| Vertical Drop (ft)...............140 | Skiable Acres.......................20 |
| Avg Snowfall (in)................130 | Number of Lifts.....................3 |
| Runs:...Green 20% Blue 80% | Black- DoubleBlack- |
| Date Open ......Late December | Date Close .............Mid March |
| Hours .............................varied | Night Skiing? ...................Yes |
| Tickets: All .........................$7 | |
| Main................616-547-3267 | |

*Mon, Wed, Thurs: 5-9pm; Sat,10 a.m.-4 p.m.; Sun, 11am-4 p.m.*

## Mulligan's Hollow Ski Bowl

Location: Located off Harbour Ave in Grand Haven
Grand Haven, Michigan 49417

| | |
|---|---|
| Base Elevation (ft)............570 | Summit (ft) ......................700 |
| Vertical Drop (ft)..............130 | Skiable Acres......................10 |
| Avg Snowfall (in)..............60" | Number of Lifts.....................3 |
| Runs:...Green 50% Blue 50% | Black- DoubleBlack- |
| Date Open ......Late December | Date Close............Late March |
| Hours .............................varied | Night Skiing? ...................Yes |
| Tickets: Adult Wkdy ........$10 | Adult Wkend .................$12 |
| Tickets: YMCA Wkdy ........$8 | YMAC Wkend .................$10 |
| Main................616-842-7051 | |
| Fax ..................248-625-3017 | |
| Snow Report .....616-842-0634 | |

*Mon-Wed, 5-9pm; Fri, 4-9pm; Sat, 1-9pm; Sun, 1-6pm*

## Nubs Nob

Location: 5m from Harbor Spgs, 200m from Detroit
4021 Nubs Nob Road, Harbor Springs, Michigan 49740

| | |
|---|---|
| Base Elevation (ft)............911 | Summit (ft) ....................1338 |
| Vertical Drop (ft)..............427 | Skiable Acres...................241 |
| Avg Snowfall (in)..............130 | Number of Lifts.....................8 |
| Runs:...Green 30% Blue 50% | Black 20% DoubleBlack- |
| Date Open..........Thanksgiving | Date Close ...................Easter |
| Hours ...............9 a.m.-4:30 p.m. | Night Skiing? ...................Yes |
| Tickets: Adult Wkday ......$30 | Adult Wkend .................$39 |
| Tickets: Child Wkdy ........$20 | Child Wkend .................$27 |
| Tickets: 60-69 ...................$12 | Night...............................$12 |
| Main................616-526-2131 | Toll Free ..........800-845-2828 |
| Lodging............616-347-4150 | |
| Snow Report ..800-SKI-NUBS | |

## *Pando*

Location: 5m from Rockford, 20 Mins NE of Grand Rapids
Rockford, Michigan 49341

| | |
|---|---|
| Base Elevation (ft)..................125 | Summit (ft) ............................ |
| Vertical Drop (ft)...............125 | Skiable Acres.......................40 |
| Avg Snowfall (in)..............90 | Number of Lifts....................4 |
| Runs:...Green 33% Blue 34% | Black 33% DoubleBlack- |
| Date Open........Mid December | Date Close ............Mid March |
| Hours ............................varied | Night Skiing? ...................Yes |
| Tickets: Adult Wkdy ........$10 | Adult Wkend ...................$15 |
| Tickets: Night ................$12 | Jr Wkdy .............................$8 |
| Tickets: Jr Wkend............$12 | Jr night .............................$9 |
| Main.................616-874-8343 | |

*Weekdays, 5-10 p.m.; Sat, 10-10 p.m.; Sun, 10 a.m.-8pm*

## *Petoskey Winter Sports Park*

Location: 30m S of I-75 & Mackinaw Bridge off US-31
1100 Winter Park Land, Petoskey, Michigan 49770

| | |
|---|---|
| Base Elevation (ft)............740 | Summit (ft) ..........................890 |
| Vertical Drop (ft)..............150 | Skiable Acres ...................1 tra |
| Avg Snowfall (in)..............150 | Number of Lifts....................1 |
| Runs:...Green-      Blue 10% | Black-      DoubleBlack- |
| Date Open .............Christmas | Date Close ....................March |
| Hours.................Noon-9 p.m. | Night Skiing? ...................Yes |
| Tickets: Free ......................$0 | |
| Main.................616-347-2500 | |
| Fax ...................616-348-0350 | |
| Snow Report .....616-347-1252 | |

## *Pine Knob Ski Resort*

Location: 8m from Pontiac on I-75 N
7777 Pine Knob Road, PO Box 130, Clarkston, Michigan 48016

| | |
|---|---|
| Base Elevation (ft)...........1000 | Summit (ft) .......................1300 |
| Vertical Drop (ft)..............300 | Skiable Acres.......................85 |
| Avg Snowfall (in)................... | Number of Lifts....................10 |
| Runs:...Green 30% Blue 35% | Black 30% DoubleBlack 5% |
| Date Open.......Late November | Date Close ............Mid March |
| Hours................10 a.m.-11pm | Night Skiing? ...................Yes |
| Tickets: Wkdy/Night.........$19 | Wkend/Night ....................$24 |
| Main.................313-625-0800 | |
| Fax ...................248-625-3017 | |
| Snow Report .....800-642-7669 | |

## Pine Mountain

Location: 2.5m from Iron Mtn, 100m from Green Bay, WI
Iron Mountain, Michigan 49801

| | | | |
|---|---|---|---|
| Base Elevation (ft)............700 | Summit (ft) ..................1150 |
| Vertical Drop (ft)............450 | Skiable Acres...............100 |
| Avg Snowfall (in)............80 | Number of Lifts...............4 |
| Runs:..Green 30% Blue 40% | Black 30% DoubleBlack- |
| Date Open.........Thanksgiving | Date Close..................April |
| Hours........9:30 a.m.-4:30 p.m. | Night Skiing?...................No |
| Tickets: Adult Wkdy ......$18 | Adult Wkend ................$24 |
| Tickets: Junior Wkdy ......$15 | Junior Wkend ..............$18 |
| Tickets: 65-69 Wkend ......$18 | 7-10 Wkend ................$12 |
| Main ..............906-774-2747 | Toll Free ..........800-321-6298 |
| Lodging...........906-774-2747 | |

## Porcupine Mountains

Location: 9m from White Pine, Rts 64 & 107, Duluth 180m
599 M-107, Ontonagon, Michigan 49953

| | |
|---|---|
| Base Elevation (ft)............727 | Summit (ft) ..................1368 |
| Vertical Drop (ft)............641 | Skiable Acres...............100 |
| Avg Snowfall (in)............200 | Number of Lifts...............4 |
| Runs:..Green 21% Blue 50% | Black 29% DoubleBlack- |
| Date Open.........Mid December | Date Close.......Early April |
| Hours..........9:30am-5pm | Night Skiing?...................No |
| Tickets: Adult Wkdy ......$20 | Adult Wkend ................$25 |
| Tickets: Jr/Sr Wkdy..........$15 | Jr/Sr Wkend ................$20 |
| Main..............906-885-5275 | Lodging...........906-932-4850 |
| Fax...............906-885-5798 | Snow Report .....800-272-7000 |

## Shanty Creek

Location: 1.5m from Bellaire, 38m from Traverse City
Bellaire, Michigan 49615
Web Site: www.shantycreek.com

| | |
|---|---|
| Base Elevation (ft)............675 | Summit (ft) ..................1125 |
| Vertical Drop (ft)............450 | Skiable Acres................41 Tr |
| Avg Snowfall (in)............200 | Number of Lifts...............9 |
| Runs:..Green 29% Blue 47% | Black 24% DoubleBlack- |
| Date Open.........Thanksgiving | Date Close.......Mid April |
| Hours..........9 a.m.-10 p.m. | Night Skiing? ...................Yes |
| Tickets: Adult Wkdy ........$26 | Adult Wkend ................$36 |
| Tickets: 6-12 Wkend ........$22 | 13-17,55-69 Wkend......$29 |
| Tickets: Night ..............$10 | Over 70, Under 5 ...........$0 |
| Main..............616-533-8621 | Snow Report .....800-678-4111 |

## Ski Brule Mtn/Ski Homestead

Location: 6m SW of Iron River, between MI-189 & M-73
Iron River, Michigan 49935

| | |
|---|---|
| Base Elevation (ft)...........1440 | Summit (ft) ..................1861 |

Photo © Ben Blankenburg, courtesy of Copper Mountain Resort

| | |
|---|---|
| Vertical Drop (ft)..............421 | Skiable Acres...................145 |
| Avg Snowfall (in).............130 | Number of Lifts.................11 |
| Runs:...Green 30%  Blue 40% | Black 30%  DoubleBlack- |
| Date Open..........November 15 | Date Close.................April 15 |
| Hours................9 a.m.-9 p.m. | Night Skiing? ...................Yes |
| Tickets: Adult Wkday .......$21 | Adult Wkend ....................$27 |
| Tickets: Junior Wkday ......$17 | Junior Wkend ...................$21 |
| Tickets: Over 65 Wkend ...$24 | Under 9 ..............................$0 |

Main................906-265-4957
Lodging........800-DO-BRULE    Snow Report 800-DO-BRULE

## Skyline Ski Area

Location: 6m from Grayling, 100m from Saginaw
Grayling, Michigan 49738

| | |
|---|---|
| Base Elevation (ft)..........1305 | Summit (ft) ......................1515 |
| Vertical Drop (ft)..............210 | Skiable Acres....................40 |
| Avg Snowfall (in) .............62" | Number of Lifts.................10 |
| Runs:...Green 15%  Blue 75% | Black 10%  DoubleBlack- |
| Date Open........Mid December | Date Close ............Early April |
| Hours.............10 a.m.-10 p.m. | Night Skiing? ...................Yes |
| Tickets: Adult Wkday ......$19 | Adult Wkend ....................$23 |
| Tickets: Jr Wkdy .............$14 | Jr Wkend .........................$18 |
| Tickets: Night Skiing ........$10 | Under 8 ..............................$0 |
| Main................517-275-5445 | |

## Snowsnake Mountain

Location: 9m N of Clare on US 27
3407 E Mannsiding Road, Harrison, Michigan 48625

| | |
|---|---|
| Base Elevation (ft).................. | Summit (ft) ...................... |
| Vertical Drop (ft)..............210 | Skiable Acres....................40 |
| Avg Snowfall (in).................. | Number of Lifts...................6 |
| Runs:...Green 30%  Blue 50% | Black 20%  DoubleBlack- |
| Date Open........Mid December | Date Close ............Mid March |
| Hours .........................varied | Night Skiing? ...................Yes |
| Tickets: Wkdy ..................$10 | Wkend .............................$14 |
| Tickets: Night .................$11 | Over 70, Under 5 .................$0 |
| Main................517-539-6583 | Fax ...................517-539-2246 |
| Snow Report .....517-539-6583 | |

*Sat & Sun, 10 a.m.-10 p.m.; Weekdays, 10 a.m.-9pm*

## Sugar Loaf Resort

Location: 18m from Traverse City, 72 W to 651 N
Cedar, Michigan 49621
Web Site: www.theloaf.com

| | |
|---|---|
| Base Elevation (ft)............550 | Summit (ft) ......................1050 |
| Vertical Drop (ft)..............500 | Skiable Acres....................80 |
| Avg Snowfall (in)..............180 | Number of Lifts...................9 |
| Runs:...Green 33%  Blue 34% | Black 33%  DoubleBlack- |
| Date Open......Late November | Date Close ............Mid March |
| Hours.................9 a.m.-10 p.m. | Night Skiing? ...................Yes |
| Tickets: Adult Wkday ......$27 | Adult Wkend ....................$35 |
| Tickets: 9-17 Wkdy ..........$24 | 9-17 Wkend .....................$30 |
| Tickets: Adult Night..........$17 | Over 65, Under 8 .................$0 |
| Main................616-228-5461 | Toll Free ..........800-968-0576 |
| Lodging............616-228-5461 | Fax ...................616-228-6545 |
| Snow Report .....616-228-1553 | |

## Swiss Valley Ski Lodge

Location: 12m from Three Rivers, 21m from Elkhart
Jones, Michigan 49061

| | |
|---|---|
| Base Elevation (ft).............975 | Summit (ft) ....................1200 |
| Vertical Drop (ft)..............225 | Skiable Acres.......................60 |
| Avg Snowfall (in) .............60" | Number of Lifts.....................7 |
| Runs:...Green 20% Blue 60% | Black 20% DoubleBlack- |
| Date Open........Mid December | Date Close ............Mid March |
| Hours.............9 a.m.-10 p.m. | Night Skiing? ..................Yes |
| Tickets: Adult Wkdy ........$18 | Adult Wkend ...................$24 |
| Tickets: 6-9 Wkdy ............$13 | 6-9 Wkend .......................$18 |
| Tickets: Adult Night..........$15 | Under 5 ...............................$0 |
| Main.................616-244-5635 | |
| Fax ...................616-244-5839 | |
| Snow Report .....616-244-8016 | |

## The Homestead Resort

Location: 21m West of Traverse City
Glen Arbor, Michigan 49636

| | |
|---|---|
| Base Elevation (ft).............500 | Summit (ft) ....................875 |
| Vertical Drop (ft)..............375 | Skiable Acres.......................16 |
| Avg Snowfall (in) .............150 | Number of Lifts.....................4 |
| Runs:...Green 25% Blue 55% | Black 20% DoubleBlack- |
| Date Open .........December 14 | Date Close...............March 10 |
| Hours.............9 a.m.-9 p.m. | Night Skiing? ..................Yes |
| Tickets: Adult Full ...........$24 | Adult Half..........................$14 |
| Tickets: Adult Night..........$14 | Under 5 ...............................$0 |
| Tickets: Over 65, Full........$15 | |
| Main.................616-334-5000 | |
| Fax ...................616-334-5120 | |
| Snow Report .....616-334-5555 | |

*Open weekends only.*

## Timber Ridge Ski Area

Location: 15m from Kalamazoo, 160m from Chicago
07500 23 1/2 St, Gobles, Michigan 49055

| | |
|---|---|
| Base Elevation (ft)................... | Summit (ft) ............................ |
| Vertical Drop (ft)..............240 | Skiable Acres.......................60 |
| Avg Snowfall (in) .............60" | Number of Lifts.....................9 |
| Runs:...Green 20% Blue 70% | Black 10% DoubleBlack- |
| Date Open........Mid December | Date Close ............Mid March |
| Hours.............10 a.m.-10 p.m. | Night Skiing? ..................Yes |
| Tickets: Adult Wkdy ........$19 | Adult Wkend ...................$24 |
| Tickets: 6-9 Wkdy ............$15 | 6-9 Wkend .......................$18 |
| Tickets: Sr/Sat ..................$20 | Under 5 ...............................$0 |
| Main.................616-694-9449 | Toll Free ..........800-253-2920 |
| Fax ...................616-694-6004 | Snow Report .....800-285-6525 |

### Treetops Sylvan Resort

Location: 3m E of Gaylord, 3.5 Hrs from Detroit
Gaylord, Michigan 49735

| | |
|---|---|
| Base Elevation (ft)..........1120 | Summit (ft) .....................1345 |
| Vertical Drop (ft)...............225 | Skiable Acres....................80 |
| Avg Snowfall (in).............153 | Number of Lifts...................7 |
| Runs:...Green 20% Blue 60% | Black 20% DoubleBlack |
| Date Open........Mid December | Date Close ...........Mid March |
| Hours................9 a.m.-9 p.m. | Night Skiing? ...................Yes |
| Tickets: Adult Wkdy ........$19 | Adult Wkend ..................$27 |
| Tickets: Under 18 Wkdy ...$16 | Under 18 Wkend ............$23 |
| Tickets: Adult Night..........$16 | Under 18 Night................$16 |
| Main.................517-732-6711 | Toll Free ..........888-873-3867 |
| Fax ..................517-732-9858 | Snow Report .....800-444-6711 |

# Minnesota

### Afton Alps

Location: 4m from Afton, 20m from St. Paul
Hastings, Minnesota 55033

| | |
|---|---|
| Base Elevation (ft)................. | Summit (ft) ....................... |
| Vertical Drop (ft)...............350 | Skiable Acres...................250 |
| Avg Snowfall (in).............55 | Number of Lifts...................21 |
| Runs:...Green 20% Blue 60% | Black 20% DoubleBlack |
| Date Open .....Early November | Date Close ...........Early April |
| Hours................9 a.m.-10 p.m. | Night Skiing? ...................Yes |
| Tickets: Adult Wkdy ........$20 | Adult Wkend ..................$25 |
| Tickets: Under 12 Wkdy ...$14 | Under 12 Wkend ............$19 |
| Tickets: 13-17 Wkdy ........$17 | 13-17 Wkend ................$22 |
| Main.................612-436-5245 | Toll Free ..........800-436-5245 |
| Fax ..................612-436-8584 | Snow Report .....800-328-1328 |

*Night ski rates: Adult-$16, Under 12-$13, 13-17 $16*

### Andres Tower Hills Ski Area

Location: 15m W of Alexandria off Hwy 27, 95m from Fargo
Rte 3 Box 258, Alexandria, Minnesota 56308

| | |
|---|---|
| Base Elevation (ft)................. | Summit (ft) ....................... |
| Vertical Drop (ft)...............275 | Skiable Acres...................30 |
| Avg Snowfall (in).............55 | Number of Lifts...................6 |
| Runs:...Green 30% Blue 40% | Black 30% DoubleBlack |
| Date Open .....Early November | Date Close ...........Late March |
| Hours................10 a.m.-9 p.m. | Night Skiing? ...................Yes |
| Tickets: Adult Wkdy ........$16 | Adult Wkend ..................$22 |
| Tickets: Adult Night..........$16 | Child Wkdy ..................$12 |
| Tickets: Child Wkend.......$16 | Child Night ..................$12 |
| Main.................320-965-2455 | |
| Lodging..............320-965-2455 | Fax ..................320-965-2278 |

## *Buck Hill Ski Area*

Location: 10m from Minn/St Paul on I-35 W
Burnsville, Minnesota 55337

| | |
|---|---|
| Base Elevation (ft)............919 | Summit (ft) .....................1225 |
| Vertical Drop (ft)............306 | Skiable Acres....................45 |
| Avg Snowfall (in)..............42 | Number of Lifts.....................9 |
| Runs:...Green 40%  Blue 45% | Black 15%  DoubleBlack- |
| Date Open .......Mid November | Date Close ............Early April |
| Hours...............10 a.m.-10 p.m. | Night Skiing? ...................Yes |
| Tickets: Adult Wkday .......$17 | Adult Wkend ...................$25 |
| Tickets: Adult Night........$17 | Child Wkday ...................$15 |
| Tickets: Chile Wkend.......$20 | Child Night......................$15 |
| Main.................612-435-7174 | Lodging............612-435-7174 |
| Fax ..................612-435-7511 | Snow Report .....612-435-7187 |

## *Buena Vista Ski Area*

Location: 12m N of Bemidji on #15
PO Box 1308, Bemidji, Minnesota 56601

| | |
|---|---|
| Base Elevation (ft)..........1280 | Summit (ft) .....................1510 |
| Vertical Drop (ft)..............230 | Skiable Acres....................30 |
| Avg Snowfall (in)..............78 | Number of Lifts.....................5 |
| Runs:...Green 20%  Blue 55% | Black 25%  DoubleBlack- |
| Date Open.......Late November | Date Close ............Mid March |
| Hours...............10 a.m.-9 p.m. | Night Skiing? ...................Yes |
| Tickets: Adult Wkend ......$24 | Adult Wkdy ....................$15 |
| Tickets: Adult Night.........$13 | Jr Wkend ........................$14 |
| Tickets: Jr Wkdy ...........$11 | Sr Wkend ........................$12 |
| Main.................218-243-2231 | Fax ..................218-243-2544 |
| Snow Report .....800-777-7958 | |

## *Chester Bowl Park*

Location: In Duluth off Skyline Dr
1801 E Skyline Drive, Duluth, Minnesota 55812

| | |
|---|---|
| Base Elevation (ft)............700 | Summit (ft) ......................875 |
| Vertical Drop (ft)..............175 | Skiable Acres.....................6 |
| Avg Snowfall (in)..............100 | Number of Lifts.....................1 |
| Runs:...Green 40%  Blue 60% | Black-  DoubleBlack- |
| Date Open........Mid December | Date Close ............Mid March |
| Hours...............4:30-8:30pm | Night Skiing? ...................Yes |
| Tickets: All rates .................$3 | |
| Main.................218-724-9832 | Fax ..................218-724-2458 |
| Snow Report .....218-724-9832 | |

## *Coffee Mill Ski Area*

Location: In Wabasha, 30m from Winona
Rt 2 Box 5, Hwy 60, Wabasha, Minnesota 55981

| | |
|---|---|
| Base Elevation (ft)............725 | Summit (ft) .....................1150 |

| | |
|---|---|
| Vertical Drop (ft)............425 | Skiable Acres..................28 |
| Avg Snowfall (in) ............40" | Number of Lifts..................3 |
| Runs:...Green 30% Blue 40% | Black 30% DoubleBlack- |
| Date Open ..............December | Date Close..................March |
| Hours.............10 a.m.-10 p.m. | Night Skiing?..................Yes |
| Tickets: Adult Wkend ......$23 | Adult Wkdy ..................$14 |
| Tickets: Nights ................$14 | Jr Wkend ..................$19 |
| Tickets: Jr Wkdy .............$14 | |
| Main................612-565-2777 | Snow Report .....612-565-2777 |

## *Detroit Mountain Ski Area* *(Unverified data)*

Location: 2.5m E of Detroit Lakes, 196m from Minn/St Paul
Detroit Lakes, Minnesota 55801

| | |
|---|---|
| Base Elevation (ft)............... | Summit (ft)..................... |
| Vertical Drop (ft)..................0 | Skiable Acres.................. |
| Avg Snowfall (in)............... | Number of Lifts..................3 |
| Runs:...Green- Blue- | Black- DoubleBlack- |
| Date Open ..............December | Date Close..................March |
| Hours...............9:30am-9 p.m. | Night Skiing?..................Yes |
| Tickets: Adult....................$13 | Jr....................................$12 |
| Tickets: Child ....................$9 | |
| Main................218-847-1661 | |

## *Giants Ridge Resort*

Location: 6m from Biwabik
Po Box 190, Biwabik, Minnesota 55708
Web Site: www.GiantsRidge.com

| | |
|---|---|
| Base Elevation (ft)..........1472 | Summit (ft) .....................1972 |
| Vertical Drop (ft)..............500 | Skiable Acres..................200 |
| Avg Snowfall (in)...............85 | Number of Lifts..................6 |
| Runs:...Green 31% Blue 44% | Black 25% DoubleBlack- |
| Date Open..........Thanksgiving | Date Close......................April |
| Hours..................9 a.m.-9 p.m. | Night Skiing?..................Yes |
| Tickets: Adult Wkdy ........$30 | Adult Wkend ..................$35 |
| Tickets: Adult Night........$16 | 6-12 Wkdy ..................$15 |
| Tickets: Child Wkend......$20 | Child Night ..................$10 |
| Main................218-865-4143 | Fax ..................218-865-4733 |
| Snow Report .800-688-SNOW | |

## *Hole In The Mountain* *(Unverified data)*

Location: Minnesota

| | |
|---|---|
| Base Elevation (ft)............... | Summit (ft) ..................... |
| Vertical Drop (ft)............... | Skiable Acres.................. |
| Avg Snowfall (in)............... | Number of Lifts............... |
| Runs:...Green- Blue- | Black- DoubleBlack- |
| Date Open............... | Date Close ............... |
| Hours ............... | Night Skiing?..................No |
| Main................507-368-9350 | |

## _Hyland Ski & Snowboard Area_

Location: 1m from Bloomington, 12m from Minneapolis
Bloomington, Minnesota 55438

| | |
|---|---|
| Base Elevation (ft).............900 | Summit (ft) ......................1075 |
| Vertical Drop (ft).............175 | Skiable Acres......................35 |
| Avg Snowfall (in)................55 | Number of Lifts......................6 |
| Runs:...Green 40%  Blue 40% | Black 20%   DoubleBlack- |
| Date Open.......Late November | Date Close .............Mid March |
| Hours........10 a.m.-10 p.m. | Night Skiing? ....................Yes |
| Tickets: Adult Wkday .......$19 | Adult Wkend ....................$22 |
| Tickets: Child Wkday........$17 | Child Wkend ....................$19 |
| Tickets: Adult Wkend Night$19 | Over 65 Wkend ................$11 |
| Main..................612-835-4250 | Fax ...................612-835-1180 |
| Snow Report .....612-835-4250 | |

## _Lutsen Mountains_

Location: 90m from Duluth on Hwy 61
Box 128, Lutsen, Minnesota 55612
Web Site: www.Lutsen.com

| | |
|---|---|
| Base Elevation (ft).............600 | Summit (ft) ......................1688 |
| Vertical Drop (ft).............1088 | Skiable Acres....................385 |
| Avg Snowfall (in).............114 | Number of Lifts......................8 |
| Runs:...Green 18%  Blue 51% | Black 22%   DoubleBlack 9% |
| Date Open........November | Date Close......................April |
| Hours........9:30 a.m.-4:30 p.m. | Night Skiing?.....................No |
| Tickets: Adult Full ............$37 | Adult Half..........................$32 |
| Tickets: Child Full.............$27 | Child Half.........................$22 |

Photo courtesy of Aspen Skiing Co.

Tickets: Over 65 ...............$32
Main ....................218-663-7281      Lodging.........800-360-ROOM
Fax ....................218-663-7109      Snow Report .800-260-SNOW

## *Mount Frontenac Ski Area*

Location: 6m from Lake City, 1hr from Minn/St Paul
PO Box 119, Frontenac, Minnesota 55026

| | |
|---|---|
| Base Elevation (ft)............500 | Summit (ft) .......................920 |
| Vertical Drop (ft)............420 | Skiable Acres....................80 |
| Avg Snowfall (in)...............70 | Number of Lifts...................5 |
| Runs:...Green 20%  Blue 50% | Black 20%  DoubleBlack 10% |
| Date Open .............December | Date Close .....................March |
| Hours................9 a.m.-10 p.m. | Night Skiing? ....................Yes |
| Tickets: Adult Full ...........$21 | Adult Half/Night .............$13 |
| Tickets: Student ..............$17 | Child Full..........................$19 |
| Tickets: Child Night .........$10 | |
| Main ..................612-388-5826 | |
| Fax ...................612-388-5826 | |
| Snow Report .....800-488-5826 | |

## *Mount Kato Ski Area*

Location: In Mankato
Route One, Mankato, Minnesota 56001

| | |
|---|---|
| Base Elevation (ft) ............. | Summit (ft) ...................... |
| Vertical Drop (ft)...............240 | Skiable Acres....................55 |
| Avg Snowfall (in)...............50 | Number of Lifts...................8 |
| Runs:...Green 24%  Blue 59% | Black 17%  DoubleBlack..... |
| Date Open.........Thanksgiving | Date Close.......................April |
| Hours................9 a.m.-10 p.m. | Night Skiing? ....................Yes |
| Tickets: Adult Wkdy .........$19 | Adult Wkend ....................$23 |
| Tickets: Jr Wkdy ..............$16 | Jr Wkend ..........................$21 |
| Tickets: Under 12 Wkdy ....$13 | Under 12 Wkend ..............$18 |
| Main ..................507-625-3363 | Lodging...........507-345-1234 |
| Fax ...................507-625-2168 | Snow Report .....800-668-5286 |

## *Powder Ridge Ski Area*

Location: 2m from Kimball, 15m from St Cloud
PO Box 339, Kimball, Minnesota 55353

| | |
|---|---|
| Base Elevation (ft) ............. | Summit (ft) ...................... |
| Vertical Drop (ft)...............310 | Skiable Acres....................60 |
| Avg Snowfall (in)...............45 | Number of Lifts...................6 |
| Runs:...Green 40%  Blue 40% | Black 20%  DoubleBlack 0% |
| Date Open .......Mid November | Date Close ............Mid March |
| Hours................9 a.m.-10 p.m. | Night Skiing? ....................Yes |
| Tickets: Adult Wkdy .........$14 | Adult Wkend ....................$22 |
| Tickets: Adult Night.........$14 | Child Wkdy ......................$12 |
| Tickets: Child Wkend........$16 | Child Night.......................$12 |
| Main ..................320-398-7200 | Toll Free ..........800-348-7734 |

Fax ....................320-398-2565

## *Quadna Mountain Ski Center*

Location: 18m S of Grand Rapids
Hill City, Minnesota 55748

| | |
|---|---|
| Base Elevation (ft)...........1300 | Summit (ft) ......................1650 |
| Vertical Drop (ft)...............350 | Skiable Acres ...................16 tr |
| Avg Snowfall (in)...............100 | Number of Lifts.....................4 |
| Runs:..Green 33% Blue 47% | Black 20%  DoubleBlack- |
| Date Open.......Late November | Date Close .............Mid March |
| Hours...........9 a.m.-4:30 p.m. | Night Skiing?.......................No |
| Tickets: Adult Wkday ......$15 | Adult Wkend ....................$23 |
| Tickets: Jr Wkday.............$12 | Jr Wkend ...........................$17 |
| Tickets: Child Wkday........$10 | Child Wkend ....................$15 |
| Main..................218-697-8444 | Toll Free ...........800-422-6649 |
| Fax ...................218-697-8400 | Snow Report .....800-422-6649 |

## *Spirit Mountain*

Location: 5 Min from Downtown Duluth
Duluth, Minnesota 55810

| | |
|---|---|
| Base Elevation (ft)............620 | Summit (ft) ......................1320 |
| Vertical Drop (ft)...............700 | Skiable Acres......................175 |
| Avg Snowfall (in)................92 | Number of Lifts.....................8 |
| Runs:..Green 32% Blue 32% | Black 36%  DoubleBlack- |
| Date Open .......Mid November | Date Close ...............Mid April |
| Hours................10 a.m.-9 p.m. | Night Skiing? ....................Yes |
| Tickets: Adult wkday .......$31 | Adult Wkend ....................$35 |
| Tickets: 13-18 Wkdy ........$26 | 13-18 Wkend ....................$31 |
| Tickets: 7-12, 65+ Wkend.$23 | Adult Night........................$17 |
| Main..................218-628-2891 | Toll Free ...........800-642-6377 |
| Fax ...................218-624-0213 | Snow Report .....218-628-2891 |

## *Welch Village Ski Area*

Location: 15m from Minn/St Paul
Box 123, Welch, Minnesota 55089

| | |
|---|---|
| Base Elevation (ft)............725 | Summit (ft) ......................1050 |
| Vertical Drop (ft)...............325 | Skiable Acres.....................125 |
| Avg Snowfall (in)................50 | Number of Lifts.....................9 |
| Runs:..Green 31% Blue 50% | Black 19%  DoubleBlack- |
| Date Open .......Mid November | Date Close.............Late March |
| Hours................9 a.m.-10 p.m. | Night Skiing? ....................Yes |
| Tickets: Adult Wkends.....$29 | Adult Wkday ....................$24 |
| Tickets: Adult night..........$24 | Child Wkends ...................$23 |
| Tickets: Child Wkdays......$19 | |
| Main..................612-222-7079 | Toll Free ...........800-421-0699 |
| Lodging.............612-258-4567 | Fax ...................612-222-2813 |
| Snow Report .....612-222-7079 | |

### _Wild Mountain Ski Area_

Location: 7m from Taylor Falls, 50m from Minn/St Paul
Taylors Falls, Minnesota 55084

| | | |
|---|---|---|
| Base Elevation (ft)............813 | Summit (ft) ....................1113 |
| Vertical Drop (ft)...............300 | Skiable Acres...................100 |
| Avg Snowfall (in).................50 | Number of Lifts.....................6 |
| Runs:...Green 33% Blue 34% | Black 33% DoubleBlack- |
| Date Open .....Early November | Date Close............Late March |
| Hours.............10 a.m.-10 p.m. | Night Skiing? ....................Yes |
| Tickets: Adult Wkdy .......$20 | Adult Wkend .................$26 |
| Tickets: 6-12 Wkdy .........$15 | 6-12 Wkend .................$19 |
| Tickets: 13-17 Wkdy ........$16 | 13-17 Wkend ................$21 |
| Main.................651-465-6315 | Toll Free ..........800-447-4958 |
| Lodging............612-465-6315 | Fax ..................651-465-0506 |
| Snow Report .....651-257-3550 | |

_Night Ski: Adult $15.50, 6-12,65+ $12.50, 13-17 $15.50_

# Montana

### _Bear Paw Ski Bowl._

Location: 28m S of Havre
2110 Heritage Dr, Havre, Montana 59501

| | |
|---|---|
| Base Elevation (ft)..........8100 | Summit (ft) ....................9000 |
| Vertical Drop (ft)..............900 | Skiable Acres...................80 |
| Avg Snowfall (in)..............100 | Number of Lifts.....................1 |
| Runs:...Green 25% Blue 25% | Black 50% DoubleBlack- |
| Date Open.....Mid December | Date Close ..............Mid April |
| Hours..............10 a.m.-4 p.m. | Night Skiing?.......................No |
| Tickets: Adult Full ...........$15 | Adult Half...........................$10 |
| Tickets: Child ...................$10 | Under 8 ..............................$0 |
| Main.................406-265-8404 | |

### _Big Sky Ski And Summer Resort_

Location: 45m from Bozeman on US 191
PO Box 1, Big Sky, Montana 59716
Web Site: www.bigskyresort.com

| | |
|---|---|
| Base Elevation (ft)..........6970 | Summit (ft) ..................11150 |
| Vertical Drop (ft)............4180 | Skiable Acres.................3500 |
| Avg Snowfall (in)............400 | Number of Lifts.................15 |
| Runs:...Green 10% Blue 47% | Black 43% DoubleBlack- |
| Date Open .......Mid November | Date Close ..............Mid April |
| Hours..............9 a.m.-4 p.m. | Night Skiing?.......................No |
| Tickets: Adult Full ...........$46 | Child Full..........................$40 |
| Tickets: Seniors 70+ ........$-50 | Mon & Tues Half ...........$40 |
| Tickets: Under 10 w adult ...$0 | |
| Main.................406-995-5000 | Toll Free ..........800-548-4486 |
| Lodging............800-548-4486 | Snow Report .....406-995-5900 |

Photo courtesy of Crested Butte Mountain Resort, Tom Stillo Photographer

## *Bridger Bowl*

Location: 16m from NE of Bozeman
15795 Bridger Canyon Road, Bozeman, Montana 59715

| | |
|---|---|
| Base Elevation (ft)..........6100 | Summit (ft) ......................8100 |
| Vertical Drop (ft).............2000 | Skiable Acres...................1200 |
| Avg Snowfall (in).............300 | Number of Lifts....................7 |
| Runs:...Green 25% Blue 35% | Black 40% DoubleBlack- |
| Date Open........Mid December | Date Close ...............Mid April |
| Hours.................9 a.m.-4 p.m. | Night Skiing?.....................No |
| Tickets: Adult Full ...........$29 | Adult Half.........................$25 |
| Tickets: Under 12 .............$12 | Over 65 .............................$20 |
| Main.................406-587-2111 | Toll Free ...........800-223-9609 |
| Lodging............406-587-2111 | |
| Snow Report .....406-586-2389 | |

## *Discovery Basin Ski Area*

Location: 20m from Anaconda, 95m from Missoula on I-90
1500 Fairmont Rd, Anaconda, Montana 59711

| | |
|---|---|
| Base Elevation (ft)..........6850 | Summit (ft) ......................8150 |
| Vertical Drop (ft).............1300 | Skiable Acres...................360 |
| Avg Snowfall (in).............200 | Number of Lifts....................4 |
| Runs:...Green 33% Blue 33% | Black 34% DoubleBlack- |
| Date Open.........Thanksgiving | Date Close ....................Easter |
| Hours.............9:30 a.m.-4 p.m. | Night Skiing?.....................No |
| Tickets: Adult Full ...........$22 | Adult Half.........................$17 |
| Tickets: 6-12/65+ .............$11 | Under 5 ................................$0 |
| Main.................406-563-2184 | Snow Report .888-678-SNOW |

## Great Divide Ski Area

Location: 1.5m from Marysville, 22m NW of Helena
PO Box SKI, Marysville, Montana 59640

| | | | |
|---|---|---|---|
| Base Elevation (ft)..........5880 | Summit (ft) ....................7210 |
| Vertical Drop (ft)............1330 | Skiable Acres................700 |
| Avg Snowfall (in)..............150 | Number of Lifts...................3 |
| Runs:...Green 15%  Blue 35% | Black 35%  DoubleBlack 15% |
| Date Open .......Mid November | Date Close............Early April |
| Hours.................9 a.m.-9 p.m. | Night Skiing? ....................Yes |
| Tickets: Adult Full ...........$20 | Adult Half...........................$15 |
| Tickets: Jr/Sr Full .............$15 | Jr/Sr Half ...........................$10 |
| Tickets: Night ...................$10 | |
| Main.................406-449-3746 | |
| Fax ...................406-443-0540 | |
| Snow Report .....406-449-3746 | |

## Lost Trail Powder Mountain

Location: 90m S of Missoula, 30m from Danby
PO Box 191, Darby, Montana 59829

| | |
|---|---|
| Base Elevation (ft)..........6600 | Summit (ft) ....................7700 |
| Vertical Drop (ft)............1100 | Skiable Acres................500 |
| Avg Snowfall (in)..............300 | Number of Lifts...................4 |
| Runs:...Green 20%  Blue 60% | Black 20%  DoubleBlack- |
| Date Open ...........December | Date Close....................April |
| Hours.................9:30am-4 p.m. | Night Skiing?......................No |
| Tickets: Adult Full ...........$18 | Adult Half...........................$14 |
| Tickets: Child Full .............$9 | Child Half .............................$6 |
| Tickets: Sr Full .................$12 | Sr Half ................................$10 |
| Main.................406-821-3211 | |
| Snow Report .....406-821-3211 | |

## Marshall Mountain

Location: 7m from Missoula, E on Hwy 200
5250 Marshall Canyon Road, Misoula, Montana 59802

| | |
|---|---|
| Base Elevation (ft)..........3900 | Summit (ft) ....................5400 |
| Vertical Drop (ft)............1500 | Skiable Acres................130 |
| Avg Snowfall (in)..............175 | Number of Lifts...................3 |
| Runs:...Green 25%  Blue 55% | Black 20%  DoubleBlack- |
| Date Open ...........December | Date Close...................March |
| Hours.............9:30am-9:30pm | Night Skiing? ....................Yes |
| Tickets: Adult Full ...........$19 | Adult Half...........................$15 |
| Tickets: Adult Night ...........$9 | Jr/Sr Full ............................$15 |
| Tickets: Jr/Sr Half ...........$12 | Jr/Sr Night ...........................$8 |
| Main.................406-258-6000 | |
| Fax ...................406-258-2900 | |

*Open Wed 4:30-9:30; Thur & Fri, 9:30 a.m. 9:30 pm; Sat, Sun & holidays, 9:30 a.m. -4:30 pm*

## Maverick Mountain

Location: 38m NW of Dillon, 98m SW of Butte
Box 475, Polaris, Montana 59746

| | | | |
|---|---|---|---|
| Base Elevation (ft) | 6800 | Summit (ft) | 8920 |
| Vertical Drop (ft) | 2120 | Skiable Acres | 180 |
| Avg Snowfall (in) | 140 | Number of Lifts | 2 |
| Runs:...Green 20% Blue 35% | | Black 35% DoubleBlack 10% | |
| Date Open | December | Date Close | April |
| Hours | 9 a.m.-4 p.m. | Night Skiing? | No |
| Tickets: Adult/Jr/65+ Wkdy | $9 | Adult Wkend | $18 |
| Tickets: Jr Wkend | $11 | Over 65 Wkend | $15 |
| Tickets: Adult/65+ Half | $10 | Jr Half | $6 |
| Main | 406-834-3454 | | |
| Fax | 406-834-3540 | | |

## Montana Snowbowl

Location: 12m from Missoula on I-90
1700 Snowbowl Road, Missoula, Montana 59802

| | | | |
|---|---|---|---|
| Base Elevation (ft) | 5000 | Summit (ft) | 7600 |
| Vertical Drop (ft) | 2600 | Skiable Acres | 1200 |
| Avg Snowfall (in) | 300 | Number of Lifts | 4 |
| Runs:...Green 10% Blue 40% | | Black 40% DoubleBlack 10% | |
| Date Open | Late November | Date Close | Mid April |
| Hours | 9:30 a.m.-9:30pm | Night Skiing? | Yes |
| Tickets: Adult Full | $26 | Adult Half | $23 |
| Tickets: Child | $13 | Jr/Sr | $23 |
| Tickets: Night | $5 | | |
| Main | 406-549-9777 | | |
| Snow Report | 406-549-9696 | | |

## Red Lodge Mountain Resort

Location: 60m SW of Billings, I-90 To US 212
PO Box 750, Red Lodge, Montana 59068

| | | | |
|---|---|---|---|
| Base Elevation (ft) | 7016 | Summit (ft) | 9416 |
| Vertical Drop (ft) | 2400 | Skiable Acres | 1600 |
| Avg Snowfall (in) | 250 | Number of Lifts | 8 |
| Runs:...Green 15% Blue 55% | | Black 30% DoubleBlack- | |
| Date Open | Mid November | Date Close | Mid April |
| Hours | 9 a.m.-4 p.m. | Night Skiing? | No |
| Tickets: Adult Full | $32 | Adult Half | $26 |
| Tickets: Jr Full | $26 | Jr Half | $20 |
| Tickets: Sr Full | $22 | Child | $12 |
| Main | 406-446-2610 | | |
| Lodging | 800-444-8977 | Fax | 406-446-3604 |
| Snow Report | 406-446-2610 | | |

## Showdown Ski Area

Location: 8m from Neihart, 30m from Great Falls
Ski Lift Inc., PO Box 92, Neihart, Montana 59465

| | |
|---|---|
| Base Elevation (ft)..........6800 | Summit (ft) .....................8200 |
| Vertical Drop (ft).............1400 | Skiable Acres...................640 |
| Avg Snowfall (in)..............240 | Number of Lifts....................4 |
| Runs:...Green 30% Blue 40% | Black 30% DoubleBlack- |
| Date Open.......Late November | Date Close .............Early April |
| Hours............9:30 a.m.-4 p.m. | Night Skiing?........................No |
| Tickets: Adult Wkdy ........$18 | Adult Wkend .....................$25 |
| Tickets: Adult Half............$18 | Jr Full..............................$13 |
| Tickets: Over 70 ...............$13 | Under 6..............................$0 |
| Main.................406-236-5522 | Toll Free ..........800-433-0022 |
| Lodging.........800-433-0022 | |
| Snow Report .....406-771-1300 | |

## The Big Mountain

Location: 8m from Whitefish, 137m from Missoula/Hwy 93 N
PO Box 1400, Whitefish, Montana 59937
Web Site: www.bigmtn.com

| | |
|---|---|
| Base Elevation (ft)..........4700 | Summit (ft) .....................7000 |
| Vertical Drop (ft).............2300 | Skiable Acres...................3000 |
| Avg Snowfall (in)..............300 | Number of Lifts....................11 |
| Runs:...Green 25% Blue 55% | Black 20% DoubleBlack- |
| Date Open..........Thanksgiving | Date Close ...............Mid April |
| Hours............9:30am-10 p.m. | Night Skiing? ....................Yes |
| Tickets: Adult Full ............$40 | Adult Half.........................$30 |
| Tickets: Age 7-18, 62+ Full.$27 | Age7-18, 62+ Half............$20 |
| Tickets: Night ....................$12 | |
| Main.................406-862-1900 | |
| Lodging.........800-858-5439 | |
| Snow Report ...406-862-7669 | |

## Turner Mountain

Location: 22m NW of Libby
Libby, Montana 59923

| | |
|---|---|
| Base Elevation (ft)..........3842 | Summit (ft) .....................5952 |
| Vertical Drop (ft).............2110 | Skiable Acres...................1000 |
| Avg Snowfall (in)..............375 | Number of Lifts....................2 |
| Runs:...Green 10% Blue 30% | Black 30% DoubleBlack 30% |
| Date Open .......Late December | Date Close .............March 20 |
| Hours............9:30 a.m.-4 p.m. | Night Skiing?........................No |
| Tickets: Adult Full ............$16 | Adult Half.........................$12 |
| Tickets: Child Full.............$13 | Child Half.........................$10 |
| Tickets: Under 6 .................$0 | |
| Main.................406-293-4317 | |

# Nevada

## *Diamond Peak Ski Resort*

Location: 2 miles from Incline Village, 35m from Reno
Incline Village, Nevada 89451

| | |
|---|---|
| Base Elevation (ft)..........6700 | Summit (ft) .....................8540 |
| Vertical Drop (ft)............1840 | Skiable Acres....................755 |
| Avg Snowfall (in).............300 | Number of Lifts ....................6 |
| Runs:...Green 18% Blue 46% | Black 36% DoubleBlack- |
| Date Open..........Thanksgiving | Date Close ..............Mid April |
| Hours...................9 a.m.-4:30 | Night Skiing?.....................No |
| Tickets: Adult Full ...........$38 | Adult Half .......................$29 |
| Tickets: Ages 13-19, Full...$29 | Ages 60-69, Full .............$18 |
| Tickets: Ages 6-12, Full ....$14 | Over 70, under 6.................$0 |
| Main.................702-832-1177 | |
| Lodging .......800-GO-TAHOE | |
| Snow Report .....702-831-3211 | |

## *Las Vegas Ski & Snowboard Resort*

Location: 47 Miles from Las Vegas, US 95 To NV 156
Lee Canyon Ski Area, Las Vegas, Nevada 89129

| | |
|---|---|
| Base Elevation (ft)..........8510 | Summit (ft) .....................9510 |
| Vertical Drop (ft)............1000 | Skiable Acres......................40 |
| Avg Snowfall (in).............120 | Number of Lifts ....................3 |
| Runs:...Green 20% Blue 60% | Black 20% DoubleBlack- |
| Date Open..........Thanksgiving | Date Close ....................Easter |
| Hours...............9 a.m.-10 p.m. | Night Skiing? ...................Yes |
| Tickets: Adult Full ...........$27 | Adult Half .......................$22 |
| Tickets: Adult Night..........$27 | Jr/Sr Full .........................$20 |
| Tickets: Jr/Sr Half .............$15 | Jr/Sr Night .......................$20 |
| Main.................702-385-2754 | |
| Fax ...................702-892-0093 | |
| Snow Report .....702-593-9500 | |

## *Mt Rose Ski Area*

Location: 22 SW of Reno on Rt. 431
Reno, Nevada 89511

| | |
|---|---|
| Base Elevation (ft)..........8260 | Summit (ft) .....................9700 |
| Vertical Drop (ft)............1440 | Skiable Acres....................900 |
| Avg Snowfall (in).............450 | Number of Lifts ....................5 |
| Runs:...Green 30% Blue 35% | Black 35% DoubleBlack- |
| Date Open .......Mid November | Date Close..............Late April |
| Hours...................9 a.m.-4 p.m. | Night Skiing?.....................No |
| Tickets: Adult Full ...........$38 | Adult Half .......................$26 |
| Tickets: Ages 6-12, Full....$14 | Ages 6-12, Half ................$8 |
| Tickets: Over 60 ...............$19 | Over 70, under 5.................$0 |
| Main.................702-849-0704 | Toll Free .........800-SKI ROSE |

# New Hampshire

## *Attitash Bear Peak*

Location: 8m from N Conway on Rt 302, 150m to Boston
Bartlett, New Hampshire 03812

| | |
|---|---|
| Base Elevation (ft)............600 | Summit (ft) ......................2350 |
| Vertical Drop (ft).............1750 | Skiable Acres....................273 |
| Avg Snowfall (in)...............130 | Number of Lifts.................11 |
| Runs:...Green 20% Blue 48% | Black 32% DoubleBlack- |
| Date Open .....Early November | Date Close..............Late April |
| Hours.................9 a.m.-4 p.m. | Night Skiing?......................No |
| Tickets: Adult Wkdy ........$37 | Adult Wkend .....................$44 |
| Tickets: 6-12 Wkdy ..........$23 | 6-12 Wkend ......................$27 |
| Tickets:13-17/65+Wkdy....$25 | Under 6 ...............................$0 |
| Main.................603-374-2368 | Lodging.........800-223-SNOW |
| Snow Report .....603-374-0946 | |

## *Black Mountain*

Location: 1.5m from Jackson on Rt 16B, 3hrs from Boston
Route 16B, Jackson, New Hampshire 03846
Web Site: www.blackmt.com

| | |
|---|---|
| Base Elevation (ft)..........1300 | Summit (ft) ......................2400 |
| Vertical Drop (ft).............1100 | Skiable Acres....................101 |
| Avg Snowfall (in).............120 | Number of Lifts...................4 |
| Runs:...Green 33% Blue 33% | Black 34% DoubleBlack- |
| Date Open ..............December | Date Close................March |
| Hours.................9 a.m.-4 p.m. | Night Skiing?......................No |
| Tickets: Adult Wkdy ........$19 | Adult Wkend ....................$32 |

Photo Courtesy Nordica (Prince Sports Group)

| Tickets: 6-17/65+ Wkdy....$15 | 6-17/65+ Wkend...............$20 |
| Main.................603-383-4490 | |

## *Bretton Woods Ski Resort*

Location: 30 Mins from N Conway, 2hrs from Manchester
Bretton Woods, New Hampshire 03575

| | |
|---|---|
| Base Elevation (ft)............1600 | Summit (ft)......................3100 |
| Vertical Drop (ft)............1500 | Skiable Acres...................30 tr |
| Avg Snowfall (in)..............160 | Number of Lifts.....................5 |
| Runs:...Green 30% Blue 43% | Black 27% DoubleBlack- |
| Date Open.........November 24 | Date Close.................April 14 |
| Hours.................9 a.m.-10 p.m. | Night Skiing? ....................Yes |
| Tickets: Adult Wkdy ........$31 | Adult Wkend ....................$38 |
| Tickets: Child Wkdy ........$15 | Child/62+ Wkend .............$25 |
| Tickets: 62+ Wkdy ...........$22 | Night All............................$12 |
| Main.................603-278-5000 | Toll Free ...........800-232-2972 |
| Lodging............603-278-1000 | |
| Snow Report .....603-278-5051 | |

## *Cannon Mountain*

Location: 4m S of Franconia, 75m from Concord
Franconia, New Hampshire 03580

| | |
|---|---|
| Base Elevation (ft)...........2034 | Summit (ft) ......................4180 |
| Vertical Drop (ft)............2146 | Skiable Acres...................163 |
| Avg Snowfall (in)..............150 | Number of Lifts.....................6 |
| Runs:...Green 19% Blue 52% | Black 29% DoubleBlack- |
| Date Open...........November 6 | Date Close ....................May 1 |
| Hours.................9 a.m.-4 p.m. | Night Skiing? ....................No |
| Tickets: Adult Wkdy ........$28 | Adult Wkend ....................$37 |
| Tickets: 6-17 Wkdy ..........$19 | 6-12 Wkend .....................$27 |
| Tickets: 13-17 Wkend ......$32 | Under 5 w/ Parent..............$0 |
| Main.................603-823-5563 | Toll Free ........800-WE SKI 93 |
| Lodging............603-823-5661 | |
| Snow Report .....800-552-1234 | |

## *Cranmore*

Location: 1m from N Conway, 140m from Boston
North Conway, New Hampshire 03860

| | |
|---|---|
| Base Elevation (ft)............547 | Summit (ft) ......................1714 |
| Vertical Drop (ft)............1167 | Skiable Acres...................185 |
| Avg Snowfall (in)..............100 | Number of Lifts.....................7 |
| Runs:...Green 30% Blue 40% | Black 30% DoubleBlack- |
| Date Open.........November 25 | Date Close ......................April |
| Hours.................9 a.m.-10 p.m. | Night Skiing? ...................Yes |
| Tickets: Adult Wkdy ........$32 | Adult Wkend ....................$39 |
| Tickets: Teen Wkdy ..........$24 | Teen Wkend ....................$30 |
| Tickets: Adult Night.........$20 | Teen Night........................$15 |
| Main.................603-356-5544 | Lodging............800-543-9206 |

Fax ...................603-356-8526    Snow Report .....603-356-7070

*Under 12,$10; Over 65, $15*

## *Dartmouth Skiway*

Location: 20m from White Rvr Junct, 2.5 Hrs from Boston
Hanover, New Hampshire 03755

Base Elevation (ft)............975     Summit (ft) ......................1943
Vertical Drop (ft)..............968    Skiable Acres.....................104
Avg Snowfall (in) ............60"     Number of Lifts .....................3
Runs:...Green 25%  Blue 50%    Black 25%   DoubleBlack-
Date Open......Early December    Date Close ............Early April
Hours..................9 a.m.-4 p.m.   Night Skiing? .......................No
Tickets: Adult Wkdy ...$21     Adult Wkend ....................$28
Tickets: Under 14 Wkdy ...$16    Under 14 Wkend ..............$21
Tickets: Over 65 Wkdy ....$13    Over 65 Wkend .................$23
Main...................603-795-2143
Fax ...................603-795-2421
Snow Report .....603-795-2143

## *Gunstock Ski Area*

Location: 90m from Boston, 120m from Providence
Po Box 1307, Gilford, New Hampshire 03247

Base Elevation (ft)............900     Summit (ft) ......................2300
Vertical Drop (ft)............1400    Skiable Acres.....................185
Avg Snowfall (in)............100     Number of Lifts .....................7
Runs:...Green 16%  Blue 60%    Black 24%   DoubleBlack-
Date Open...............November    Date Close ......................April 1
Hours................9 a.m.-10 p.m.   Night Skiing? .......................No
Tickets: Adult Wkend ......$39    Adult Wkday ....................$28
Tickets: 7-12/65-69 Wkend$24    7-12/65-69 Wkday.........$20
Tickets: Adult Night.........$19    7-12/65-69 Night ...........$15
Main...................603-293-4341    Toll Free .....800-GUNSTOCK
Lodging.............800-531-2347    Snow Report .....603-293-4345

*Under 6 w/ parent, Free*

## *King Pine Ski Area*

Location: 9m from Conway, 60m from Portsmouth
Rte 153, E. Madison, New Hampshire 03849

Base Elevation (ft)............500     Summit (ft) ......................850
Vertical Drop (ft)..............350    Skiable Acres.....................60
Avg Snowfall (in)............120     Number of Lifts .....................4
Runs:...Green 50%  Blue 31%    Black 19%   DoubleBlack-
Date Open ...............December    Date Close ....................March
Hours..................9 a.m.-9:30pm   Night Skiing? ......................Yes
Tickets: Adult Wkendl ......$28    Adult Wkdy ....................$19
Tickets: Adult Night.........$13    Jr Wkend ...........................$18
Tickets: Jr Wkdy ............$12    Sr Wkend.........................$12

Main................603-367-8896 | Lodging.............800-FREE SKI
Fax ..................603-367-8664 | Snow Report .....800-367-8897

*Over 70/ Under 5, Free*

## Loon Mountain

Location: 2m from Lincoln, Concord 66m, Boston 130m
Lincoln, New Hampshire 03251
Web Site: www.loonmtn.com

| | | |
|---|---|---|
| Base Elevation (ft)............950 | Summit (ft)....................3050 |
| Vertical Drop (ft)............2100 | Skiable Acres...................250 |
| Avg Snowfall (in)............118 | Number of Lifts.................7 |
| Runs:..Green 20% Blue 64% | Black 16% DoubleBlack- |
| Date Open .....Early November | Date Close ............Early May |
| Hours................9 a.m.-4 p.m. | Night Skiing?....................No |
| Tickets: Adult Wkday .......$38 | Adult Wkend .................$45 |
| Tickets: 6-12 Wkdy .......$25 | 6-12 Wkend ...................$28 |
| Tickets: 13-21/70+ Wkdy..$32 | 13-21/70+ Wkend............$40 |
| Main..........603-745-8111 | Toll Free ...........800-WESKI93 |
| Lodging...........800-227-4191 | |
| Snow Report .....603-745-8100 | |

## McIntyre Ski Area  (Unverified data)

Location: 18m from Concord on I-93N, Boston 50m on I-93S
Manchester, New Hampshire 03104

| | |
|---|---|
| Base Elevation (ft)................. | Summit (ft) .................... |
| Vertical Drop (ft)................0 | Skiable Acres................... |
| Avg Snowfall (in).................. | Number of Lifts .............3 |
| Runs:..Green-    Blue- | Black-    DoubleBlack- |
| Date Open ...............December | Date Close ..........Mid March |
| Hours .................................. | Night Skiing? ................Yes |
| Tickets: Adult Wkdy/Nt .....$10 | Adult Wkend ..................$15 |
| Tickets: Under 14 Wkdy .....$7 | Under 14 Wkend/Night....$10 |
| Main.................603-624-6571 | |

## Mt Sunapee Ski Area

Location: Located in Mt Sunapee State Park
Mt Sunapee, New Hampshire 03255

| | |
|---|---|
| Base Elevation (ft)............1230 | Summit (ft) ....................2743 |
| Vertical Drop (ft)............1513 | Skiable Acres....................210 |
| Avg Snowfall (in).............100 | Number of Lifts.................7 |
| Runs:..Green 20% Blue 70% | Black 10% DoubleBlack- |
| Date Open .............December | Date Close ..........March/April |
| Hours.................8am-4 p.m. | Night Skiing?....................No |
| Tickets: Adult Wkdy ........$28 | Adult Wkend .................$37 |
| Tickets: 7-17/65+ Wkdy...$19 | 13-17 Wkend ..................$32 |
| Tickets: 7-12/65+ Wkend..$27 | Main.................603-763-2356 |
| Toll Free ...........800-552-1234 | Snow Report .....603-763-4020 |

## *Pats Peak Ski Area*

Location: 3m from Henniker, 18m from Concord
PO Box 656, Henniker, New Hampshire 03242

| | |
|---|---|
| Base Elevation (ft)............690 | Summit (ft) .....................1400 |
| Vertical Drop (ft)............710 | Skiable Acres................19 tr |
| Avg Snowfall (in)..............100 | Number of Lifts.....................7 |
| Runs:........Green 38% Blue 30% | Black 32% DoubleBlack- |
| Date Open........Mid December | Date Close............Late March |
| Hours.................9 a.m.-9 p.m. | Night Skiing? ...................Yes |
| Tickets: Adult Wkdy ........$25 | Adult Wkend ....................$34 |
| Tickets: Child/64+ Wkdy ..$19 | Child/64+ Wkend ............$26 |
| Tickets: Adult Night.........$19 | Child/64+ Night ..............$15 |
| Main..................603-428-3245 | |
| Lodging..............603-428-3245 | |
| Snow Report ...888 PATS PEAK | |

## *Ragged Mountain*

Location: 10m from Bristol, Concord 35m, Boston 2 Hrs
PO Box 106-E, Danbury, New Hampshire 03230
Web Site: www.ragged-mt.com

| | |
|---|---|
| Base Elevation (ft)...........1000 | Summit (ft) .....................2250 |
| Vertical Drop (ft)............1250 | Skiable Acres....................150 |
| Avg Snowfall (in)..............100 | Number of Lifts.....................6 |
| Runs:...Green 30% Blue 40% | Black 30% DoubleBlack- |
| Date Open..........Thanksgiving | Date Close ............Early April |
| Hours.................9 a.m.-4 p.m. | Night Skiing?.....................No |
| Tickets: Adult/Jr Wdy ......$15 | Adult Wkend ....................$30 |
| Tickets: Adult Half...........$25 | Jr Wkend ..........................$25 |
| Tickets: Jr Half.................$20 | |
| Main..................603-768-3475 | Lodging............800-400-3911 |
| Fax ....................603-768-3929 | Snow Report .....603-768-3971 |

## *Snow Hill*

Location: 37m N of Concord, Exit 13 off I-89
PO Box 53, Grantham, New Hampshire 13753

| | |
|---|---|
| Base Elevation (ft)...........1100 | Summit (ft) .....................1343 |
| Vertical Drop (ft)..............243 | Skiable Acres......................25 |
| Avg Snowfall (in).............85" | Number of Lifts.....................1 |
| Runs:...Green 33% Blue 34% | Black 33% DoubleBlack 0% |
| Date Open ..............December | Date Close ....................March |
| Hours.................9 a.m.-4 p.m. | Night Skiing?.....................No |
| Tickets: Adult Full ...........$14 | Adult Half .........................$8 |
| Tickets: Child Full............$10 | Child Half .........................$6 |
| Main..................603-863-6772 | Lodging............603-863-6772 |
| Fax ....................603-863-4714 | Snow Report ....603-863-4500 |

## *Temple Mountain*

Location: 4m from Peterborough, Nashua 23m, Boston 63m
Rte 101, Box 368, Peterborough, New Hampshire 03458

| | | | |
|---|---|---|---|
| Base Elevation (ft)...........1486 | Summit (ft).....................2084 |
| Vertical Drop (ft)...............598 | Skiable Acres........................45 |
| Avg Snowfall (in)..............85" | Number of Lifts.......................6 |
| Runs:...Green 40% Blue 40% | Black 20%  DoubleBlack- |
| Date Open ..............December | Date Close.......................April |
| Hours................9 a.m.-10 p.m. | Night Skiing?....................Yes |
| Tickets: Wkdy All............$20 | Adult Wkend ....................$30 |
| Tickets: Adult Night..........$18 | 7-12/65-69 Wkend............$25 |
| Tickets: 7-12/65-69 Night .$16 | Under 6..............................$6 |
| Main.................603-924-6949 | Fax ..................603-924-7371 |

Photo © Ben Blankenburg, courtesy Copper Mountain Resort

## *Tenney Mountain Ski Resort*

Location: 6m from Plymouth
RR #4, Box 1300, Plymouth, New Hampshire 03264

| | |
|---|---|
| Base Elevation (ft)............750 | Summit (ft).....................2150 |
| Vertical Drop (ft)............1400 | Skiable Acres........................97 |
| Avg Snowfall (in)..............140 | Number of Lifts.......................4 |
| Runs:...Green-12% Blue-58% | Black-30%  DoubleBlack- |
| Date Open......Early December | Date Close.......................April |
| Hours................9 a.m.-4 p.m. | Night Skiing?.....................No |
| Tickets: Wkdy All ............$17 | Adult Wkend ....................$32 |
| Tickets: Jr/65-69 ..............$19 | Adult Wkend Half ............$23 |
| Tickets: Adult Wkdy Half .$17 | |
| Main.................603-536-4125 | Lodging.............888-TENNEY2 |
| Snow Report .....888-TENNEY2 | |

## The Balsams/Wilderness

Location: 10m W of Colebrook on Rt 26, 220m from Boston
Dixville Notch, New Hampshire 03576

| | | |
|---|---|---|
| Base Elevation (ft)...........1754 | Summit (ft) .....................2760 |
| Vertical Drop (ft)...........1006 | Skiable Acres....................88 |
| Avg Snowfall (in).............225 | Number of Lifts..................4 |
| Runs:...Green 25%  Blue 50% | Black 25%  DoubleBlack |
| Date Open........Mid December | Date Close.........Late March |
| Hours.............9 a.m.-4 p.m. | Night Skiing?...................No |
| Tickets: Adult Wkend ......$25 | Adult Wkday .................$20 |
| Tickets: Child Wkend ......$18 | Child Wkday .................$15 |
| Tickets: Over 70 ...............$0 | |
| Main.................603-255-3951 | Toll Free ..........800-255-0600 |
| Fax..................603-255-4221 | Snow Report .....603-255-3951 |

## Waterville Valley Resort

Location: 20m from Plymouth, Manchester 80m
Waterville Valley, New Hampshire 03458
Web Site: www.waterville.com

| | | |
|---|---|---|
| Base Elevation (ft)...........1984 | Summit (ft) .....................4004 |
| Vertical Drop (ft).............2020 | Skiable Acres..................255 |
| Avg Snowfall (in)..............140 | Number of Lifts................11 |
| Runs:...Green 20%  Blue 60% | Black 20%  DoubleBlack |
| Date Open...............November | Date Close...............May 1 |
| Hours.............9 a.m.-4 p.m. | Night Skiing?...................No |
| Tickets: Adult Wkdy ........$37 | Adult Wkend ................$43 |
| Tickets:Teen/Student Wkdy $34 | Teen/Student Wkend.........$39 |
| Tickets: Over 65 Wknd ....$29 | 6-12 All .........................$10 |
| Main.................603-236-8311 | Lodging............800-468-2553 |
| Snow Report .....603-236-4144 | |

*Under 5, Free*

## Wildcat Mountain

Location: 8m from Jackson, N Conway 12m, Boston 150m
Jackson, New Hampshire 03846

| | | |
|---|---|---|
| Base Elevation (ft)..........1950 | Summit (ft) .....................4050 |
| Vertical Drop (ft).............2100 | Skiable Acres..................130 |
| Avg Snowfall (in)..............174 | Number of Lifts................7 |
| Runs:...Green 20%  Blue 45% | Black 35%  DoubleBlack |
| Date Open ......Mid November | Date Close.............Late April |
| Hours.................9 a.m.-4 p.m. | Night Skiing?...................No |
| Tickets: Adult Wkdy ........$27 | Adult Wkend ................$39 |
| Tickets: Jr Wkdy .............$20 | Jr Wkend ......................$23 |
| Tickets: Sr ........................$9 | |
| Main.................603-466-3326 | Toll Free ..........888-754-9453 |
| Fax ..................603-466-5813 | |

# New Jersey

## Belle Mountain Ski Area      (Unverified data)

Location: 25m from Philadelphia on Rt 29
Lambertville, New Jersey 08530

| | |
|---|---|
| Base Elevation (ft) .................... | Summit (ft) .................................... |
| Vertical Drop (ft) ...................0 | Skiable Acres ........................20 |
| Avg Snowfall (in) ................... | Number of Lifts ......................4 |
| Runs:...Green-     Blue- | Black-     DoubleBlack- |
| Date Open ..............December | Date Close ...................March |
| Hours...............9 a.m.-10 p.m. | Night Skiing? ....................Yes |
| Tickets: Adult Wkdy/Nt ...$13 | Adult Wkend ...................$18 |
| Tickets: Child Wkdy/Nt ...$12 | Child Wkend ...................$16 |
| Main.................609-397-0043 | |

## Campgaw Mountain Ski Center

Location: 18m from New York City off Rt 17
200 Campgaw Road, Mahwah, New Jersey 07430

| | |
|---|---|
| Base Elevation (ft)............450 | Summit (ft) ........................720 |
| Vertical Drop (ft)...............270 | Skiable Acres .................8 tra |
| Avg Snowfall (in) .............45" | Number of Lifts ..................5 |
| Runs:...Green 50% Blue 38% | Black 12% DoubleBlack- |
| Date Open........Mid December | Date Close ...........Mid March |
| Hours...............9 a.m.-10 p.m. | Night Skiing? ....................Yes |
| Tickets: Adult Wkdy ........$15 | Adult Wkend ...................$21 |
| Tickets: Adult Night..........$13 | Under 12 Wkdy .............$13 |
| Tickets: Under 12 Wkend .$19 | Under 12 Night ..............$12 |
| Main.................201-327-7800 | Snow Report .....201-327-7800 |

## Craigmeur Ski Area

Location: 38m from New York City on I-80
Newfoundland, New Jersey 07435

| | |
|---|---|
| Base Elevation (ft)...........1000 | Summit (ft) ......................1250 |
| Vertical Drop (ft)...............250 | Skiable Acres ......................30 |
| Avg Snowfall (in) .............50" | Number of Lifts ..................3 |
| Runs:...Green 75%  Blue 25% | Black-     DoubleBlack- |
| Date Open ..............December | Date Close ............End March |
| Hours...............9 a.m.-10 p.m. | Night Skiing? ....................Yes |
| Tickets: Adult Full ...........$29 | Adult Night ...................$22 |
| Tickets: 7-12 Full ............$25 | 7-12 Night ....................$22 |
| Tickets: Over 65 Full.........$15 | Over 65 Night...................$12 |
| Main.................201-697-4500 | |
| Fax ...................201-697-2282 | |
| Snow Report .....201-697-4500 | |

## Hidden Valley Ski Resort

Location: 49m from New York City Via The Lincoln Tunnel

PO Box 433, Breakneck Road, Vernon, New Jersey 07462

| | | | |
|---|---|---|---|
| Base Elevation (ft) | 815 | Summit (ft) | 1435 |
| Vertical Drop (ft) | 620 | Skiable Acres | 36 |
| Avg Snowfall (in) | 70 | Number of Lifts | 3 |
| Runs:...Green 10% Blue 40% | | Black 50% DoubleBlack- | |
| Date Open | December | Date Close | March |
| Hours | 9 a.m.-10 p.m. | Night Skiing? | Yes |
| Tickets: Adult Wkday | $30 | Adult Wkend | $36 |
| Tickets: Jr Wkday | $25 | Jr Wkend | $30 |
| Tickets: Adult Night | $25 | Jr Night | $20 |
| Main | 973-764-6161 | | |
| Fax | 973-764-3313 | | |
| Snow Report | 973-764-4200 | | |

### *Vernon Valley/Great Gorge Ski Area*

Location: 45m from Newark, 48m from New York City
Rte 94, Vernon, New Jersey 07462

| | | | |
|---|---|---|---|
| Base Elevation (ft) | 440 | Summit (ft) | 1480 |
| Vertical Drop (ft) | 1040 | Skiable Acres | 52 tr |
| Avg Snowfall (in) | 89 | Number of Lifts | 17 |
| Runs:...Green 25% Blue 45% | | Black 30% DoubleBlack- | |
| Date Open | Thanksgiving | Date Close | April |
| Hours | 9 a.m.-11pm | Night Skiing? | Yes |
| Tickets: Adult Full | $38 | Adult Night | $28 |
| Tickets: Child Full | $27 | Child Night | $19 |
| Tickets: Over 65, Day/Night | $7 | | |
| Main | 201-827-2000 | | |
| Lodging | 201-827-2222 | | |
| Snow Report | 201-827-2000 | | |

# New Mexico

### *Angel Fire*

Location: 26m from Taos
PO Box B, Angel Fire, New Mexico 87710
Web Site: www.angelfireresort.com

| | | | |
|---|---|---|---|
| Base Elevation (ft) | 8600 | Summit (ft) | 10650 |
| Vertical Drop (ft) | 2050 | Skiable Acres | 206 |
| Avg Snowfall (in) | 220 | Number of Lifts | 6 |
| Runs:...Green 33% Blue 51% | | Black 16% DoubleBlack- | |
| Date Open | Late November | Date Close | Late March |
| Hours | 9 a.m.-4 p.m. | Night Skiing? | No |
| Tickets: Adult Full | $36 | Adult Half | $27 |
| Tickets: Child Full | $21 | Child Half | $19 |
| Tickets: Over 65 | $0 | | |
| Main | 505-377-6401 | Toll Free | 800-633-7463 |
| Lodging | 800-633-7463 | Fax | 505-377-4200 |

## Pajarito Mountain

Location: 39m from Santa Fe on Rt 4, 2hrs to Albuquerque
Los Alamos, New Mexico 87544
Web Site: www.losalamos.org/ski.html

| | | |
|---|---|---|
| Base Elevation (ft)..........9200 | Summit (ft) ....................10441 | |
| Vertical Drop (ft).............1241 | Skiable Acres....................280 | |
| Avg Snowfall (in)..............140 | Number of Lifts .....................6 | |
| Runs:...Green 20% Blue 50% | Black 30% DoubleBlack- | |
| Date Open........Mid December | Date Close......................April | |
| Hours ................Varied Times | Night Skiing?......................No | |
| Tickets: Adult Full .........$32 | Adult Half ........................$23 | |
| Tickets: Child/Sr Full ........$21 | Child/Sr Half ....................$16 | |
| Tickets: Over 75 ................$0 | | |
| Main..................505-662-5725 | | |
| Lodging.............505-662-7669 | | |
| Snow Report .....888-662-8105 | | |

## Red River Ski Area

Location: Red River at base, 37m from Taos
PO Box 900, Red River, New Mexico 87558
Web Site: www.taoswebb.com/nmusa/redriver

| | | |
|---|---|---|
| Base Elevation (ft)..........8750 | Summit (ft) ....................10350 | |
| Vertical Drop (ft).............1600 | Skiable Acres....................213 | |
| Avg Snowfall (in)..............214 | Number of Lifts .....................7 | |
| Runs:...Green 32% Blue 38% | Black 30% DoubleBlack- | |
| Date Open..............November | Date Close......................March | |
| Hours.................9 a.m.-4 p.m. | Night Skiing?......................No | |
| Tickets: Adult Full ............$37 | Adult Half ........................$27 | |
| Tickets: Child/60+ Full .....$23 | Child/60+ Half ................$16 | |
| Main..................505-754-2223 | Lodging.............800-331-7669 | |
| Fax ...................505-754-6184 | Snow Report .....505-754-2220 | |

## Sandia Peak

Location: 30 mins from Albuquerque, E on I-40 to Hwy 14; take
Cedar Crest exit, then 6 miles to rightt turn on Crest Road, then 8
miles up moutain.
#10 Tramway Loop NE, Albuquerque, New Mexico 87122
Web Site: www.rt66.com/-visual/sandia/race1.htm

| | | |
|---|---|---|
| Base Elevation (ft)..........8678 | Summit (ft) ....................10378 | |
| Vertical Drop (ft).............1700 | Skiable Acres....................198 | |
| Avg Snowfall (in)..............125 | Number of Lifts .....................7 | |
| Runs:...Green 35% Blue 55% | Black 10% DoubleBlack- | |
| Date Open .............December | Date Close......................March | |
| Hours.................9 a.m.-4 p.m. | Night Skiing?......................No | |
| Tickets: Adult Full .........$32 | Adult Half ........................$22 | |
| Tickets: Under 12/62+ Full $22 | Under 12/62+ Half ............$14 | |
| Tickets: Over 71/under 48" .$0 | | |
| Main..................505-242-9133 | Lodging.............800-473-1000 | |

Fax .................505-856-6355     Snow Report .....505-857-8977

## *Santa Fe Ski Area*

Location: 16m from Santa Fe on Rt 475
1210 Luisa, Suite #10, Santa Fe, New Mexico 87505
Web Site: www.skisantafe.com

| | | |
|---|---|---|
| Base Elevation (ft)........10350 | Summit (ft) ...................12000 |
| Vertical Drop (ft)............1650 | Skiable Acres....................150 |
| Avg Snowfall (in)............225 | Number of Lifts ....................7 |
| Runs:...Green 20%  Blue 40% | Black 40%  DoubleBlack- |
| Date Open..........Thanksgiving | Date Close ...................April 5 |
| Hours................9 a.m.-4 p.m. | Night Skiing?......................No |
| Tickets: Adult Full ...........$39 | Adult Half ........................$26 |
| Tickets: Child/62+............$24 | Over 72/Under 46" ............$0 |
| Main...................505-982-4429 | Lodging ...........800-776-SNOW |
| Fax ...................505-986-0645 | Snow Report ....505-983-9155 |

## *Sipapu Ski Area*

Location: 25m SE of Taos, 65m from Santa Fe
Route Box 29, Vadito, New Mexico 87579
Web Site: www.sipapunm.com/paradise

| | | |
|---|---|---|
| Base Elevation (ft)..........8200 | Summit (ft) .....................9065 |
| Vertical Drop (ft)..............865 | Skiable Acres......................37 |
| Avg Snowfall (in).............100 | Number of Lifts ....................3 |
| Runs:...Green 20%  Blue 50% | Black 30%  DoubleBlack- |
| Date Open.......Mid December | Date Close...........Late March |
| Hours................9 a.m.-4 p.m. | Night Skiing?......................No |
| Tickets: Adult Wkdy.........$28 | Adult Wkend ....................$28 |
| Tickets: Adult Half ...........$20 | Under 13 Full ...................$21 |
| Tickets: Under 13 Half......$16 | Over 70/Under 5 ................$0 |
| Main...................505-587-2240 | Lodging............505-587-2240 |
| Fax ...................505-587-1038 | Snow Report ....505-587-2240 |

## *Ski Apache*

Location: 12m from Ruidoso
PO Box 220, Ruidoso, New Mexico 88345
Web Site: www.fort.lookingglass.net/skiapach/

| | | |
|---|---|---|
| Base Elevation (ft)..........9600 | Summit (ft) ...................11500 |
| Vertical Drop (ft)............1900 | Skiable Acres....................750 |
| Avg Snowfall (in).............185 | Number of Lifts ..................11 |
| Runs:...Green 20%  Blue 35% | Black 45%  DoubleBlack- |
| Date Open..........Thanksgiving | Date Close ...................Easter |
| Hours................8:45am-4 p.m. | Night Skiing?......................No |
| Tickets: Adult Full ...........$39 | Adult Half ........................$29 |
| Tickets: 6-12 Full .............$24 | 6-12 Half ..........................$20 |
| Main...................505-336-4356 | Lodging............800-253-2255 |
| Fax ...................505-336-8327 | Snow Report ....505-257-9001 |

## *Taos Ski Valley*

Location: 147m from Albuquerque, 228m from Denver
Ski Valley Station, Taos Ski Valley, New Mexico 87525
Web Site: http://taoswebb.com/nmusa/skitaos

| | |
|---|---|
| Base Elevation (ft)..........9207 | Summit (ft)...................11819 |
| Vertical Drop (ft)............2612 | Skiable Acres..................1000 |
| Avg Snowfall (in)...........320 | Number of Lifts...............11 |
| Runs:...Green 24%  Blue 25% | Black 51%  DoubleBlack- |
| Date Open..............November | Date Close.......................April |
| Hours.................9 a.m.-4 p.m. | Night Skiing?....................No |
| Tickets: Adult Full...........$40 | Adult Half.......................$27 |
| Tickets: Junior Full...........$20 | Junior Half.....................$21 |
| Tickets: Under 12 Full......$25 | Over 70............................$0 |
| Main.............505-776-2291 | Toll Free..........800-776-1111 |
| Lodging............505-776-2233 | Fax ...................505-776-8596 |
| Snow Report.....505-776-2916 | |

# New York

## *Belleayre Mountain*

Location: 38m from Kingston, Oneonta 60m, NY City 137m
PO Box 313, Highmount, New York 12441
Web Site: www.belleayre.com

| | |
|---|---|
| Base Elevation (ft)..........2025 | Summit (ft) ....................3429 |
| Vertical Drop (ft)............1404 | Skiable Acres....................133 |
| Avg Snowfall (in)...........110 | Number of Lifts................9 |
| Runs:...Green 23%  Blue 54% | Black 23%  DoubleBlack- |
| Date Open..............November | Date Close.......................April |
| Hours.................9 a.m.-4 p.m. | Night Skiing?....................No |
| Tickets: Adult Wkdy ........$28 | Adult Wkend ...................$37 |
| Tickets: 11-17/62+ Wkdy..$25 | 11-17/62+ Wkend ...........$29 |
| Tickets: 6-10 Wkdy ..........$20 | 6-10 Wkend .....................$24 |
| Main...........914-254-5600 | |
| Snow Report.....800-942-6904 | |

## *Big Birch Ski Area (Unverified data)*

Location: 10m from Brewster on Rt 22, Ny City 65m
Patterson, New York 12563

| | |
|---|---|
| Base Elevation (ft)..........820 | Summit (ft) ....................1320 |
| Vertical Drop (ft)..............500 | Skiable Acres............................ |
| Avg Snowfall (in)............. | Number of Lifts.................5 |
| Runs:...Green-        Blue- | Black-        DoubleBlack 0% |
| Date Open ............December 1 | Date Close................March 31 |
| Hours................10 a.m.-10 p.m. | Night Skiing? ...................Yes |
| Tickets: Adult Wkday ......$25 | 28 ...................................$25 |
| Tickets: Junior Wkday ......$20 | Junior Wkend ..................$23 |
| Tickets: Night ...................$20 | Under 5 .............................$0 |

Main.................914-878-3181
Lodging.............914-279-8011
Snow Report .....914-878-6242

## *Big Tupper Ski Area*

Location: 3m S of Tupper Lake, 1hr W of Syracuse on Rt 3
Box 897, Tupper Lake, New York 12986

| | | | |
|---|---|---|---|
| Base Elevation (ft)..........2000 | Summit (ft) ......................3136 |
| Vertical Drop (ft).............1136 | Skiable Acres....................105 |
| Avg Snowfall (in).............128 | Number of Lifts.....................5 |
| Runs:...Green 30%  Blue 45% | Black 25%  DoubleBlack- |
| Date Open.............November | Date Close............................April |
| Hours.................9 a.m.-4 p.m. | Night Skiing? ...................Yes |
| Tickets: Adult Wkdy ........$25 | Adult Wkend ....................$30 |
| Tickets: Student Wkdy .....$20 | Student Wkend ..................$25 |
| Tickets: Under 8/70+.........$0 | |
| Main.................518-359-7902 | Toll Free ..........800-824-4754 |
| Lodging.............800-824-4754 | |

## *Brantling Ski Slopes*

Location: 40m E of Rochester off Rt 88
Sodus, New York 14551

| | | | |
|---|---|---|---|
| Base Elevation (ft).............600 | Summit (ft) ........................850 |
| Vertical Drop (ft).............250 | Skiable Acres......................36 |
| Avg Snowfall (in)............100 | Number of Lifts.....................6 |
| Runs:...Green 30%  Blue 40% | Black 30%  DoubleBlack- |
| Date Open ..........December 1 | Date Close............March 10 |
| Hours.................Until 10 p.m. | Night Skiing? ...................Yes |
| Tickets: Adult 8 Hrs .........$19 | Adult 4 Hrs ......................$16 |
| Tickets: Child 8 Hrs .........$15 | Child 4 Hrs ......................$14 |
| Tickets: Adult Night..........$15 | Child Night ......................$12 |
| Main.................315-331-2365 | |

## *Bristol Mountain Ski Area*

Location: 12m from Canandaigua, Rochester 35m
Canandaigua, New York 14424

| | | | |
|---|---|---|---|
| Base Elevation (ft)..........1000 | Summit (ft) ......................2200 |
| Vertical Drop (ft).............1200 | Skiable Acres....................163 |
| Avg Snowfall (in).............110 | Number of Lifts.....................5 |
| Runs:...Green 14%  Blue 67% | Black 19%  DoubleBlack- |
| Date Open .......Mid November | Date Close............................April |
| Hours.................9 a.m.-10 p.m. | Night Skiing? ...................Yes |
| Tickets: Adult 8 Hrs .........$34 | Adult 4 Hrs ......................$32 |
| Tickets: 8-12/65+, 8 Hrs ...$27 | 8-12/65+, 4 Hrs ..............$25 |
| Tickets: Adult Night..........$23 | 8-12/65+ Night ................$18 |
| Main.................716-374-6000 | Snow Report .....716-234-5000 |

## Catamount Ski Area

Location: 3m E of Hillsdale; Egremont, MA 3m W
Route 23, Hillsdale, New York 12529

| | | |
|---|---|---|
| Base Elevation (ft)...........1000 | Summit (ft) .....................2000 | |
| Vertical Drop (ft)............1000 | Skiable Acres....................100 | |
| Avg Snowfall (in) .............75" | Number of Lifts ....................6 | |
| Runs:...Green 30%  Blue 40% | Black 50%  DoubleBlack- | |
| Date Open ............December 1 | Date Close....................April 1 | |
| Hours...............9 a.m.-10 p.m. | Night Skiing? ....................Yes | |
| Tickets: Adult Wkdy ........$25 | Adult Wkend ...................$39 | |
| Tickets: 7-13/62+, Wkdy...$20 | 7-13/62+, Wkend...............$25 | |
| Tickets: Adult Night..........$20 | 7-13/62+, Night ...............$15 | |
| Main.................518-325-3200 | | |
| Snow Report .....800-342-1840 | | |

## Cockaigne Ski Area

Location: 18m from Jamestown, Buffalo 60m
Cherry Creek, New York 14723

| | | |
|---|---|---|
| Base Elevation (ft)...........1592 | Summit (ft) .....................2022 | |
| Vertical Drop (ft)..............430 | Skiable Acres....................100 | |
| Avg Snowfall (in) ............300 | Number of Lifts ....................4 | |
| Runs:...Green 25%  Blue 60% | Black 15%  DoubleBlack- | |
| Date Open .......Mid November | Date Close ................Mid April | |
| Hours.............10 a.m.-10 p.m. | Night Skiing? ....................Yes | |
| Tickets: Adult Wkdy ........$17 | Adult Wkend ...................$26 | |
| Tickets: Child Wkdy ........$15 | Child Wkend ...................$22 | |
| Tickets: Adult Night..........$18 | Child Night .......................$16 | |
| Main.................716-287-3223 | | |
| Fax ..................716-287-3404 | | |
| Snow Report .....716-287-3545 | | |

## Dry Hill Ski Area

Location: on Brookside Dr, 4m off I-81 Exit 44
Watertown, New York 13601

| | | |
|---|---|---|
| Base Elevation (ft).............650 | Summit (ft) .......................950 | |
| Vertical Drop (ft)..............300 | Skiable Acres......................38 | |
| Avg Snowfall (in)..............125 | Number of Lifts ....................3 | |
| Runs:...Green 33%  Blue 34% | Black 33%  DoubleBlack- | |
| Date Open........Mid December | Date Close....Late March | |
| Hours ................Varied Hours | Night Skiing? ....................Yes | |
| Tickets: Adult Wkend ......$16 | Adult Wkdy ....................$10 | |
| Tickets: Jr Wkend ............$14 | Jr Wkdy ...........................$9 | |
| Tickets: Adult Night..........$10 | Child Night ........................$9 | |
| Main.................315-782-8584 | Toll Free ...........800-329-8584 | |
| Snow Report .....315-782-0796 | | |

## Four Seasons Ski Center

Location: 1m from Fayetteville, Syracuse 8m
Fayetteville, New York 13066

| | | |
|---|---|---|
| Base Elevation (ft)............450 | Summit (ft) ......................550 | |
| Vertical Drop (ft)..............100 | Skiable Acres....................12 | |
| Avg Snowfall (in)..............125 | Number of Lifts..................2 | |
| Runs:...Green 40% Blue 40% | Black 20% DoubleBlack- | |
| Date Open .............December 1 | Date Close................March 15 | |
| Hours...........10 a.m.-4:30 p.m. | Night Skiing?....................No | |
| Tickets: Adult Wkend ......$14 | Adult Half......................$12 | |
| Tickets: Child Wkend ......$10 | Child Half......................$10 | |
| Main.................315-637-9023 | | |
| Fax ...................315-637-8178 | | |

## Frost Ridge Ski Area

Location: 3m from LeRoy, Rochester 19m E
Le Roy, New York 14482

| | | |
|---|---|---|
| Base Elevation (ft)............640 | Summit (ft) ......................790 | |
| Vertical Drop (ft)..............150 | Skiable Acres....................5 | |
| Avg Snowfall (in)..............86" | Number of Lifts..................3 | |
| Runs:...Green 14% Blue 57% | Black 29% DoubleBlack- | |
| Date Open..............November | Date Close......................April | |
| Hours...........9 a.m.-4:30 p.m. | Night Skiing?....................No | |
| Tickets: Adult Wkend ........$7 | Adult Half........................$5 | |
| Tickets: Child Wkend.........$5 | Child Half........................$4 | |
| Main.................716-768-4883 | | |
| Snow Report .....716-768-4883 | | |

## Gore Mountain Ski Area

Location: 2m from N Creek, Glen Falls 40 Mins, NYC 4 Hrs
North Creek, New York 12853

| | | |
|---|---|---|
| Base Elevation (ft)..........1500 | Summit (ft) ....................3600 | |
| Vertical Drop (ft)............2100 | Skiable Acres .................44 tr | |
| Avg Snowfall (in)..............135 | Number of Lifts..................9 | |
| Runs:...Green 10% Blue 70% | Black 20% DoubleBlack- | |
| Date Open .......Mid November | Date Close..........Mid April | |
| Hours................9 a.m.-4:15pm | Night Skiing?....................No | |
| Tickets: Adult Wkend ......$36 | Adult Wkdy ....................$25 | |
| Tickets: 7-12/65+ .............$20 | Under 6/70+.....................$0 | |
| Main.................518-251-2411 | Toll Free ..........800-342-1234 | |
| Lodging..........800-880-GORE | | |
| Snow Report .....518-251-2523 | | |

## Greek Peak Ski Resort

Location: 8m from Cortland, Ithaca 18m, Syracuse 36m
2000 NYS Rte 392, Cortland, New York 13045
Web Site: www.sanyips.com/greekpeak

| | |
|---|---|
| Base Elevation (ft)..........1200 | Summit (ft) .....................2100 |
| Vertical Drop (ft).............900 | Skiable Acres ..................28 tr |
| Avg Snowfall (in)..............116 | Number of Lifts ....................8 |
| Runs:...Green 24%  Blue 41% | Black 35%  DoubleBlack- |
| Date Open........November | Date Close.........................April |
| Hours..........9:30 a.m.-10 p.m. | Night Skiing? ....................Yes |
| Tickets: Adult Full ...........$40 | Adult Half........................$37 |
| Tickets: 7-12 Full ............$30 | 7-12 Half .........................$28 |
| Tickets: Over 65 Full........$39 | Over 65 Half.....................$36 |
| Main..............607-835-6111 | Toll Free ...........800-955-2754 |
| Lodging ...........800-955-2SKI | |
| Snow Report .....800-365-7669 | |

*Adult/7-12, Night $20; Over 65 Night, 19; Under 6 w/ Adult, Free*

## Hickory Ski Center

Location: New York

| | |
|---|---|
| Base Elevation (ft).............700 | Summit (ft) ....................1900 |
| Vertical Drop (ft)............1200 | Skiable Acres......................70 |
| Avg Snowfall (in)..............100 | Number of Lifts....................3 |
| Runs:...Green 30%  Blue 20% | Black 50%  DoubleBlack- |
| Date Open .......Late December | Date Close.............Late March |
| Hours...................9 a.m.-4 p.m. | Night Skiing?.....................No |
| Tickets: Adult Full ...........$20 | Adult Half.........................$15 |
| Tickets: Jr/Sr Full ............$15 | Jr/Sr Half .........................$12 |
| Tickets: ...............................$0 | ..............................................$0 |
| Main..................518-623-2825 | |

## Highmount Ski Center          *(Unverified data)*

Location: 36m from Kingston, NYC 125m
Highmount, New York 12441

| | |
|---|---|
| Base Elevation (ft)............2100 | Summit (ft) ....................3150 |
| Vertical Drop (ft)............1050 | Skiable Acres............................ |
| Avg Snowfall (in)................... | Number of Lifts ....................5 |
| Runs:...Green-    Blue- | Black-    DoubleBlack- |
| Date Open ..............December | Date Close.........................April |
| Hours.................9 a.m.-4 p.m. | Night Skiing?.....................No |
| Tickets: Adult Wkend ......$25 | Adult Half........................$18 |
| Tickets: 10-15/65+ Wkend$20 | 10-15/65+ Half ...............$14 |
| Tickets: 6-9 Wkend ..........$15 | 6-9 Half ...........................$10 |
| Main..................914-254-5265 | |
| Snow Report .....800-255-7669 | |

### _Holiday Mountain Ski Area_

Location: 4m from Monticello on Rt 17, NYC 80m
PO Box 629, Monticello, New York 12701

| | | | |
|---|---|---|---|
| Base Elevation (ft) | 900 | Summit (ft) | 1300 |
| Vertical Drop (ft) | 400 | Skiable Acres | 15 sl |
| Avg Snowfall (in) | 90 | Number of Lifts | 7 |
| Runs:...Green 30% Blue 40% | | Black 30% DoubleBlack- | |
| Date Open | December | Date Close | March |
| Hours | 9 a.m.-10 p.m. | Night Skiing? | Yes |
| Tickets: Adult/Child Wkdy | $16 | Adult Wknd | 25 |
| Tickets: Child Wkend | $20 | Night | $10 |
| Main | 914-796-3161 | Fax | 914-796-1201 |
| Snow Report | 914-796-3161 | | |

### _Holiday Valley Resort_

Location: 1m from Ellicottville, Buffalo 40m on Rt 219 S
Ellicottville, New York 14731
Web Site: www.holidayvalley.com

| | | | |
|---|---|---|---|
| Base Elevation (ft) | 1500 | Summit (ft) | 2250 |
| Vertical Drop (ft) | 750 | Skiable Acres | 266 |
| Avg Snowfall (in) | 180 | Number of Lifts | 12 |
| Runs:...Green 33% Blue 33% | | Black 34% DoubleBlack- | |
| Date Open | November | Date Close | April |
| Hours | 9:30 a.m.10:30pm | Night Skiing? | Yes |
| Tickets: Adult Wkdy | $31 | Adult Wkend | $34 |
| Tickets: 6-11 Wkdy | $21 | 6-11 Wkend | $24 |
| Tickets: Adult Night | $21 | 6-11 Night | $15 |
| Main | 716-699-2345 | Fax | 716-699-5204 |
| Snow Report | 716-699-2644 | | |

_Over 70, $23; Under 5, Free_

Photo courtesy of Nordica (Prince Sports Group)

## Hunt Hollow Ski Area          (Unverified data)

Location: 4m from Naples, Rochester 40m on Cty Rd 36
7532 County Road 36, Naples, New York 14512

| | |
|---|---|
| Base Elevation (ft)..........1105 | Summit (ft) .....................1920 |
| Vertical Drop (ft)..............815 | Skiable Acres.....................90 |
| Avg Snowfall (in).......... | Number of Lifts ...................2 |
| Runs:...Green-     Blue- | Black-     DoubleBlack- |
| Date Open..........November 24 | Date Close.......................April 1 |
| Hours........9:30 a.m.-10 p.m. | Night Skiing? ...................Yes |
| Tickets: Adult Full ...........$40 | Adult Half.........................$37 |
| Tickets: Junior Full...........$30 | Junior Half........................$28 |
| Tickets: Over 65 Full.........$39 | Over 65 Half.....................$36 |
| Main.................716-374-5428 | |
| Snow Report .....716-381-8270 | |

*Night, $20; Under 6 w/ Adult, Free*

## Hunter Mountain Ski Bowl

Location: 20m from Catskill, NYC 120m
Hunter, New York 12442

| | |
|---|---|
| Base Elevation (ft)..........1600 | Summit (ft) .....................3200 |
| Vertical Drop (ft)..............1600 | Skiable Acres.....................230 |
| Avg Snowfall (in).............125 | Number of Lifts ...................12 |
| Runs:...Green 30% Blue 30% | Black 40% DoubleBlack- |
| Date Open...............November | Date Close.......................April |
| Hours................9 a.m.-4 p.m. | Night Skiing?...................No |
| Tickets: Adult Wkdy .........$36 | Adult Wkend .....................$43 |
| Tickets: 13-18 Wkdy .........$32 | 13-18 Wkend....................$38 |
| Tickets: 7-12/65+ Wkdy.....$22 | 7-12/65+ Wkend...............$28 |
| Main.................518-263-4223 | Toll Free ...........800-775-4641 |
| Lodging.............518-263-3707 | |
| Snow Report ...800-FOR-SNOW | |

## Kissing Bridge

Location: 25m from Buffalo on NY Thruway & Rt 219
Glenwood, New York 14069

| | |
|---|---|
| Base Elevation (ft)..........1200 | Summit (ft) .....................1750 |
| Vertical Drop (ft)..............550 | Skiable Acres.....................700 |
| Avg Snowfall (in).............185 | Number of Lifts ...................10 |
| Runs:...Green 30% Blue 50% | Black 20% DoubleBlack- |
| Date Open .............December | Date Close.......................April |
| Hours.............9 a.m.-10:30pm | Night Skiing? ...................Yes |
| Tickets: Adult 8 Hrs .........$28 | Adult 6 Hrs .....................$24 |
| Tickets: Adult 4 Hrs .........$20 | Jr 8 Hrs ............................$18 |
| Tickets: Jr 4 Hrs ...............$14 | Night.................................$20 |
| Main.................716-592-4963 | |
| Lodging.............716-592-4963 | |
| Snow Report .....716-592-4961 | |

## Labrador Mountain

Location: 25m S of Syracuse on I-81 S
R 91, PO Box 105, Truxton, New York 13158

| | | | |
|---|---|---|---|
| Base Elevation (ft)...........1190 | Summit (ft) .....................1890 |
| Vertical Drop (ft)..............700 | Skiable Acres.....................200 |
| Avg Snowfall (in)..............110 | Number of Lifts.....................4 |
| Runs:...Green 27% Blue 27% | Black 46%  DoubleBlack- |
| Date Open......Early December | Date Close.............Late March |
| Hours................9 a.m.-10 p.m. | Night Skiing? .....................Yes |
| Tickets: Adult 9 Hrs .........$27 | Adult/6-12 4 Hrs................$25 |
| Tickets: 6-12 9 Hrs.............$25 | Over 65 9 Hrs ....................$22 |
| Tickets: Over 65 4 Hrs .......$20 | Adult/6-12 Night .............$12 |
| Main.................607-842-6204 | |
| Fax.............607-842-6306 | |
| Snow Report ....800-446-9559 | |

## Maple Ski Ridge

Location: 4m W of Schenectady off Rt 159
2387 Mariaville Rd, Schenectady, New York 12306

| | |
|---|---|
| Base Elevation (ft).............528 | Summit (ft) .......................968 |
| Vertical Drop (ft)..............450 | Skiable Acres.......................55 |
| Avg Snowfall (in) .............80" | Number of Lifts.....................4 |
| Runs:...Green 50% Blue 40% | Black 10%  DoubleBlack- |
| Date Open......Early December | Date Close.........Mid March |
| Hours................9 a.m.-10 p.m. | Night Skiing? .....................Yes |
| Tickets: Daily ....................$20 | Half.....................................$17 |
| Tickets: Night ....................$12 | |
| Main.................518-381-4700 | |
| Fax.............518-381-4700 | |
| Snow Report .....518-377-5172 | |

*Open Sat & Sun, holidays and school vacations; Night Skiing,*
*Tues - Sat 6:30 til 10 p.m.*

## McCauley Mountain

Location: 2.5m from Old Forge, Utica 50m, Rome 50m
Old Forge, New York 13420

| | |
|---|---|
| Base Elevation (ft)...........1720 | Summit (ft) .....................2200 |
| Vertical Drop (ft)..............480 | Skiable Acres.......................70 |
| Avg Snowfall (in)..............225 | Number of Lifts.....................5 |
| Runs:...Green 33% Blue 34% | Black 33%  DoubleBlack- |
| Date Open .............December | Date Close......................March |
| Hours........9:30 a.m.4:30 p.m. | Night Skiing?.......................No |
| Tickets: Adult Wkdy ........$18 | Adult Wkend ....................$22 |
| Tickets: Child ....................$15 | Under 4/70+.........................$0 |
| Main.................315-369-3225 | |
| Fax .................315-369-6942 | |
| Snow Report .....315-369-6983 | |

## Mt. Peter Ski Area

Location: 2m from Greenwood Lake, NYC 50m
PO Box 1167, Warwick, New York 10990

| | |
|---|---|
| Base Elevation (ft)............600 | Summit (ft).....................1050 |
| Vertical Drop (ft)..............450 | Skiable Acres.......................77 |
| Avg Snowfall (in)..............40 | Number of Lifts....................4 |
| Runs:...Green 34% Blue 33% | Black 33% DoubleBlack- |
| Date Open.......End November | Date Close....................April 7 |
| Hours.......8:30 a.m.-10 p.m. | Night Skiing? .......................Yes |
| Tickets: Adult Wkdy.........$15 | Adult Wkend.....................$20 |
| Tickets: Night..................$12 | Under 4/65+........................$7 |
| Main.................914-986-4940 | Lodging...........914-986-4992 |
| Fax ..................914-986-4996 | Snow Report .....914-986-4992 |

## Oak Mountain Ski Center

Location: 1hr from Albany, Schenectady & Troy
PO Box 399, Speculator, New York 12164

| | |
|---|---|
| Base Elevation (ft)...........1600 | Summit (ft).....................2250 |
| Vertical Drop (ft)..............650 | Skiable Acres..................13 tr |
| Avg Snowfall (in)..............140 | Number of Lifts....................3 |
| Runs:...Green 40% Blue 40% | Black 20% DoubleBlack 0% |
| Date Open.......Mid December | Date Close..............Mid April |
| Hours..................9 a.m.-4 p.m. | Night Skiing?......................No |
| Tickets: Adult Full.........$14 | Adult Half...........................$12 |
| Tickets: Child/65+ Full .....$10 | Child/65+ Half....................$8 |
| Main.................518-548-7311 | |

## Orange County Ski Area

Location: 10m from Middleton, 60m from NYC on Rt 416
211 RT 416, Montgomery, New York 12549

| | |
|---|---|
| Base Elevation (ft)............407 | Summit (ft).....................538 |
| Vertical Drop (ft)..............131 | Skiable Acres.......................5 |
| Avg Snowfall (in)..............10" | Number of Lifts....................1 |
| Runs:...Green 10% Blue- | Black- DoubleBlack- |
| Date Open.........December 21 | Date Close..................March 1 |
| Hours..............9:30 -4:30 p.m. | Night Skiing?......................No |
| Tickets: Adult/Child..........$10 | |
| Main.................914-457-4949 | |

*Open Wkends & School Holidays*

## Peek'n Peak

Location: 14m from Erie, PA on I-90, Buffalo 90m
Clymer, New York 14724

| | |
|---|---|
| Base Elevation (ft)...........1400 | Summit (ft).....................1800 |
| Vertical Drop (ft)..............400 | Skiable Acres..................27 tr |
| Avg Snowfall (in)..............200 | Number of Lifts....................9 |
| Runs:...Green 20% Blue 70% | Black 10% DoubleBlack- |

| | |
|---|---|
| Date Open .......Mid November | Date Close .....................April |
| Hours ...........9:30 a.m.10 p.m. | Night Skiing? ...................Yes |
| Tickets: Adult Wkdy ........$28 | Adult wkend ....................$32 |
| Tickets: Child Wkdy ........$16 | Child Wkend ....................$22 |
| Tickets: Over 65 ..............$21 | Adult Wkend Night ..........$26 |
| Main.................716-355-4141 | Toll Free ..........800-367-9691 |
| Lodging............716-355-4141 | Snow Report .....716-355-4141 |

Photo © Cynthia Hunter, courtesy of Steamboat Ski and Resort Corp.

## Nelson Carmichael skiing Steamboat

*Ski Areas of the United States*

## *Rocking Horse Ranch*

Location: 75m N of NYC off Rt 87
600 Rt 44-55, Highland, New York 12528
Web Site: www.rhranch.com

| | |
|---|---|
| Base Elevation (ft)..........1030 | Summit (ft) ......................1180 |
| Vertical Drop (ft)..............150 | Skiable Acres.......................10 |
| Avg Snowfall (in) ..............30" | Number of Lifts.....................2 |
| Runs:...Green 10% Blue- | Black- DoubleBlack- |
| Date Open........Mid December | Date Close .............Mid March |
| Hours................10 a.m.-4 p.m. | Night Skiing?.....................No |
| Main..................914-691-2927 | Lodging............800-647-2624 |
| Fax ...................914-691-6434 | Snow Report .....914-691-2927 |

*Package price available which includes skiing*

## *Royal Mountain*

Location: NW of Johnstown on Rt 10
Johnstown, New York 12032

| | |
|---|---|
| Base Elevation (ft)..........1250 | Summit (ft) ......................1800 |
| Vertical Drop (ft)..............550 | Skiable Acres.......................30 |
| Avg Snowfall (in) ..............90" | Number of Lifts.....................3 |
| Runs:...Green 33% Blue34% | Black 33% DoubleBlack- |
| Date Open .............Sat/Sun/Hol | Date Close - |
| Hours ......................................... | Night Skiing?.....................No |
| Tickets: Adult Full ............$20 | Adult Half.........................$16 |
| Tickets: Child Full..............$20 | Child Half.........................$10 |
| Tickets: Over 70.................$10 | |
| Main..................518-835-6445 | |

## *Scotch Valley Resort*

Location: 3m from Stamford on Rt 10/Albany 64m, NYC 146m
Stamford, New York 12167

| | |
|---|---|
| Base Elevation (ft)..........2050 | Summit (ft) ......................2900 |
| Vertical Drop (ft)..............850 | Skiable Acres..................20 sl |
| Avg Snowfall (in) ..............120 | Number of Lifts.....................3 |
| Runs:...Green 10% Blue 75% | Black 15% DoubleBlack- |
| Date Open..........Thanksgiving | Date Close ....................Easter |
| Hours ..................9 a.m.-9 p.m. | Night Skiing? ...................Yes |
| Tickets: Adult Wkdy ........$15 | Adult Wkend ....................$29 |
| Tickets: Jr/60+ Wkdy........$10 | Jr/60+ Wend ....................$24 |
| Tickets: Under 5 with Adult or 70+..............................................$0 | |
| Main..................607-652-2470 | |
| Lodging............888-640-3660 | |
| Snow Report .....888-640-7669 | |

## Shu-Maker Mountain

Location: off Rt 167 In Little Falls
PO Box 553, Cheese Factory Rd, Little Falls, New York 13365

| | |
|---|---|
| Base Elevation (ft)............500 | Summit (ft) .....................1250 |
| Vertical Drop (ft)..............750 | Skiable Acres....................90 |
| Avg Snowfall (in)..............125 | Number of Lifts ...................4 |
| Runs:...Green 27%  Blue 59% | Black 14%  DoubleBlack- |
| Date Open ..............December | Date Close ...................March |
| Hours ...............Varied Hours | Night Skiing? ....................Yes |
| Tickets: Adult Wkend ......$23 | Adult Half..........................$20 |
| Tickets: Child/62+ Wkend $19 | Child/62+ Half................$16 |
| Tickets: Night.....................$16 | |
| Main.................315-823-4470 | Toll Free ..........800-689-0969 |
| Fax ..................315-823-0837 | Snow Report .....315-823-1110 |

## Ski Plattekill

Location: NY Thruway from NYC To Exit 19
Box 205, Roxburg, New York 12474

| | |
|---|---|
| Base Elevation (ft)...........2150 | Summit (ft) .....................3500 |
| Vertical Drop (ft)..............1350 | Skiable Acres....................76 |
| Avg Snowfall (in)..............160 | Number of Lifts ...................3 |
| Runs:...Green 20%  Blue 40% | Black 20%  DoubleBlack 20% |
| Date Open ..............December | Date Close ...........Early April |
| Hours ...............9 a.m.-4:15pm | Night Skiing?.....................No |
| Tickets: Adult Wkend ......$34 | Adult Wkday ..................$24 |
| Tickets: Child Wkend.......$24 | Child Wkday ..................$19 |
| Tickets: Student Wkend ...$28 | Student Wkday ..................$19 |
| Main.................607-326-3500 | Toll Free.........800-NEED-2-SKI |
| Fax ..................607-326-3034 | |
| Snow Report ..800-NEED-2-SKI | |

## Ski Tamarack

Location: 19m S of Buffalo on Rt 240
7556 Lower E Hill Rd, Colden, New York 14033

| | |
|---|---|
| Base Elevation (ft)...........1000 | Summit (ft) .....................1500 |
| Vertical Drop (ft)..............500 | Skiable Acres....................100 |
| Avg Snowfall (in).............180 | Number of Lifts ...................3 |
| Runs:...Green 13%  Blue 47% | Black 40%  DoubleBlack- |
| Date Open .........December 15 | Date Close ...............March 20 |
| Hours ...............9 a.m.-10 p.m. | Night Skiing? ....................Yes |
| Tickets: Adult Wkdy ........$18 | Adult Wkend ..................$22 |
| Tickets: 12-16 Wkdy........$16 | 12-16 Wkend ..................$20 |
| Tickets: Over 65.............$-25 | Night...............................$10 |
| Main.................716-941-6821 | |
| Fax ..................716-941-5889 | |
| Snow Report .....716-941-5654 | |

## Ski Valley Club     (Unverified data)

Location: 40m from Rochester, Rt 64S To Rt 34W
6586 County Rd 33, Naples, New York 14512

| | |
|---|---|
| Base Elevation (ft)...........1500 | Summit (ft) ......................2200 |
| Vertical Drop (ft)..............700 | Skiable Acres.....................63 |
| Avg Snowfall (in).................... | Number of Lifts .......................3 |
| Runs:...Green-     Blue- | Black-     DoubleBlack- |
| Date Open........Mid December | Date Close .............End March |
| Hours.................10 a.m.-10 p.m. | Night Skiing? ....................Yes |
| Tickets: Adult Wkdy .........$18 | Adult Wkend ....................$29 |
| Tickets: Under 12 Wkdy ...$14 | Under 12 Wkend ..............$24 |
| Tickets: Adult Night.........$20 | Under 12 Night.................$17 |
| Main..................716-374-5157 | Snow Report .....716-924-2180 |

## Ski Windham

Location: 57m from Albany, NYC 118m
Clarence D Lane Road, Windham, New York 12496

| | |
|---|---|
| Base Elevation (ft)...........1500 | Summit (ft) ......................3100 |
| Vertical Drop (ft).............1600 | Skiable Acres....................234 |
| Avg Snowfall (in)..............110 | Number of Lifts .......................7 |
| Runs:..Green 30% Blue 45% | Black 25% DoubleBlack- |
| Date Open .......Mid November | Date Close ...............Mid April |
| Hours.................9 a.m.-4 p.m. | Night Skiing?......................No |
| Tickets: Adult Wkdy .........$32 | Adult Wkend ....................$41 |
| Tickets: Adult Half...........$27 | 7-12 Wkdy ........................$28 |
| Tickets: 7-12 Wkend .........$34 | 7-12 Half ..........................$25 |
| Main..................518-734-4300 | Toll Free.....800-SKIWINDHAM |
| Lodging ............800-729-SKIW | Fax ...................518-734-5732 |
| Snow Report .....800-729-4766 | |

## Snow Ridge Ski Area

Location: 1m from Turin, Watertown 40m, Syracuse 75m
Box B, Turin, New York 13473

| | |
|---|---|
| Base Elevation (ft)...........1350 | Summit (ft) ......................1850 |
| Vertical Drop (ft)..............500 | Skiable Acres....................130 |
| Avg Snowfall (in)..............225 | Number of Lifts .......................7 |
| Runs:...Green 20% Blue 60% | Black 20% DoubleBlack- |
| Date Open.........Thanksgiving | Date Close.......................April |
| Hours..............10 a.m.-10 p.m. | Night Skiing? ...................Yes |
| Tickets: Adult Wkdy .........$17 | Adult Wkend ....................$25 |
| Tickets: Under 12 Wkdy ...$14 | Under 12 Wkend ..............$21 |
| Tickets: 65+ Wkdy ...........$15 | 65+ Wkend .......................$25 |
| Main..................315-348-8456 | Lodging............315-348-8456 |
| Snow Report .....800-962-8419 | |

## *Song Mountain*

Location: 10m from Cortland on I-81, Syracuse 30m
Tully, New York 13159

| | |
|---|---|
| Base Elevation (ft)..........1200 | Summit (ft) ....................1900 |
| Vertical Drop (ft)..............700 | Skiable Acres..................100 |
| Avg Snowfall (in)..............125 | Number of Lifts.................5 |
| Runs:...Green 58%  Blue 29% | Black 13%  DoubleBlack- |
| Date Open........Mid December | Date Close............Late March |
| Hours...............10 a.m.-10:30pm | Night Skiing? ...................Yes |
| Tickets: Adult Wkdy ........$22 | Adult Wkend ....................$27 |
| Tickets: Jr Wkdy ..............$22 | Jr Wkend .........................$19 |
| Tickets: Night All..............$15 | |
| Main.................315-696-5711 | Fax ..................315-696-5718 |
| Snow Report ....315-696-5712 | |

## *Sterling Forest Ski Center*

Location: 6m from Tuxedo, NYC 40m on I-87
Turin, New York 13473

| | |
|---|---|
| Base Elevation (ft).............950 | Summit (ft) ....................1350 |
| Vertical Drop (ft)..............400 | Skiable Acres....................35 |
| Avg Snowfall (in)................36 | Number of Lifts.................4 |
| Runs:...Green 20%  Blue 70% | Black 10%  DoubleBlack- |
| Date Open .........December 16 | Date Close............March 17 |
| Hours..............10 a.m.-10 p.m. | Night Skiing? ...................Yes |
| Tickets: Adult Wkdy ........$20 | Adult Wkend ....................$32 |
| Tickets: Jr Wkdy ..............$15 | Jr Wkend .........................$24 |
| Tickets: Under 8 Wkend ...$13 | Over 55 Wkend ................$15 |
| Main.................914-351-2163 | Lodging............914-357-4800 |
| Snow Report ....914-351-4788 | |

## *Swain Ski & Snowboard Center*

Location: In Swain Town Limits, Rochester 50m
Swain, New York 14884
Web Site: www.swain.com

| | |
|---|---|
| Base Elevation (ft)..........1300 | Summit (ft) ....................1950 |
| Vertical Drop (ft)..............650 | Skiable Acres..............18 tr |
| Avg Snowfall (in)..............150 | Number of Lifts.................4 |
| Runs:...Green 40%  Blue 45% | Black 15%  DoubleBlack- |
| Date Open.........Thanksgiving | Date Close......................April |
| Hours...............9 a.m.-10 p.m. | Night Skiing? ...................Yes |
| Tickets: Adult 8 Hrs ..........$34 | Adult 4 Hrs ......................$32 |
| Tickets: Under 12/55+,8hrs$26 | Under 12/55+, 4 hrs..........$24 |
| Tickets: 4-10 p.m...............$24 | |
| Main.................607-545-6511 | |
| Lodging............607-545-6511 | |
| Snow Report .716-234-SNOW | |

## *Titus Mountain*  (*Unverified data*)

Location: 15 Mins from Malone
Malone, New York 12953

| | |
|---|---|
| Base Elevation (ft)................. | Summit (ft)............................ |
| Vertical Drop (ft)..................0 | Skiable Acres....................120 |
| Avg Snowfall (in)................. | Number of Lifts....................8 |
| Runs:...Green-     Blue 80% | Black-      DoubleBlack- |
| Date Open ..........December 15 | Date Close....................April 15 |
| Hours...............9 a.m.-10 p.m. | Night Skiing? ...................Yes |
| Tickets: Adult Wkdy ........$15 | Adult Wkend ...................$19 |
| Tickets: Child Wkdy ........$11 | Child Wkend ...................$15 |
| Tickets: Over 65 Wkdy .......$8 | Over 65 Wkend ...............$19 |
| Main.................518-483-3740 | Toll Free ...........800-848-8766 |

## *Toggenburg Ski Center*

Location: 20m from Syracuse, Rt 81 S To 481 E
Toggenburg Road, Fabius, New York 13063

| | |
|---|---|
| Base Elevation (ft)...........1550 | Summit (ft)........................2200 |
| Vertical Drop (ft)..............650 | Skiable Acres......................80 |
| Avg Snowfall (in)..............160 | Number of Lifts....................6 |
| Runs:...Green 25%  Blue 50% | Black 25%  DoubleBlack- |
| Date Open......Early December | Date Close .............Early April |
| Hours...............9 a.m.-10 p.m. | Night Skiing? ...................Yes |
| Tickets: Adult 9 Hrs .........$28 | Adult 4 Hrs ........................$26 |
| Tickets: Jr 9 Hrs ...............$24 | Jr 4 Hrs .............................$22 |
| Tickets: Night...................$20 | |
| Main.................315-683-5842 | Fax ....................315-683-5543 |
| Snow Report .....315-446-6666 | |

Photo courtesy of Telluride Ski and Golf Company, Grafton M. Smith, photographer
Skiing Prospect Bowl at Telluride, Colorado

## Villa Roma Ski Area

Location: 90m from NY on NY Thruway. Monticello 1/2 Hr
340 Villa Roma Rd, Callicoon, New York 12723

| | | |
|---|---|---|
| Base Elevation (ft)..........1250 | Summit (ft) .....................1500 | |
| Vertical Drop (ft)...............250 | Skiable Acres ...................7 tra | |
| Avg Snowfall (in) .............50" | Number of Lifts ....................3 | |
| Runs:...Green 45%  Blue 45% | Black 10%  DoubleBlack- | |
| Date Open ......Late December | Date Close .............Mid March | |
| Hours ..............................varied | Night Skiing? ....................Yes | |
| Tickets: Wkdy Full............$13 | Wkend Full .......................$19 | |
| Tickets: Night ...................$9 | | |
| Main.................914-887-4880 | Toll Free ..........800-727-8455 | |
| Lodging............800-727-8455 | Fax ...................914-887-4824 | |
| Snow Report .....914-887-4880 | | |

## West Mountain Ski Area

Location: 5m from Glens Falls, Boston/Montreal 3.5-4 Hrs
Glens Falls, New York 12804

| | | |
|---|---|---|
| Base Elevation (ft).............460 | Summit (ft) .....................1470 | |
| Vertical Drop (ft).............1010 | Skiable Acres ...................22 tr | |
| Avg Snowfall (in) .............85 | Number of Lifts ....................6 | |
| Runs:...Green 25%  Blue 60% | Black 15%  DoubleBlack- | |
| Date Open ..................December | Date Close ...........................April | |
| Hours..........9:30 a.m.10:30pm | Night Skiing? ....................Yes | |
| Tickets: 13-64, 8 Hr Wkdy$25 | 13-64, 4 Hr Wkdy ..........$20 | |
| Tickets: 13-64, 8 Hr Wkend $32 | 13-64, 4 Hr Wkend ..........$27 | |
| Tickets: -13/65-Wkdy .........$20 | -13/65-69 Wkend..............$25 | |
| Main.................518-793-6606 | | |
| Snow Report .....518-793-6606 | | |

## Whiteface Mt Ski Center

Location: 8m from Lake Placid, Montreal 2 Hrs, NYC 4 Hrs
Wilmington, New York 12997
Web Site: www.orda.org

| | | |
|---|---|---|
| Base Elevation (ft)..........1220 | Summit (ft) .....................4436 | |
| Vertical Drop (ft)..........3216 | Skiable Acres ...................170 | |
| Avg Snowfall (in).............110 | Number of Lifts .................10 | |
| Runs:...Green 27%  Blue 37% | Black 36%  DoubleBlack- | |
| Date Open ......Mid November | Date Close .............Mid April | |
| Hours..........8:30 a.m.-4:15pm | Night Skiing? .....................No | |
| Tickets: 13-69 Full ............$39 | 7-12 Full ..........................$19 | |
| Tickets: 65-69 Full ..........$25 | Over 70/Under 5................$0 | |
| Main.................518-946-2223 | Toll Free ........800-2-PLACID | |
| Lodging............800-447-5227 | | |
| Snow Report .....800-462-6236 | | |

### Willard Mountain Ski Area

Location: 35 Mins from Albany, Troy, Saratoga on Rt 40
Greenwich, New York 12834

| | |
|---|---|
| Base Elevation (ft)............910 | Summit (ft) ......................1415 |
| Vertical Drop (ft)............505 | Skiable Acres......................85 |
| Avg Snowfall (in) ............80" | Number of Lifts....................3 |
| Runs:...Green 30% Blue 40% | Black 30% DoubleBlack- |
| Date Open .........December 15 | Date Close...................April 1 |
| Hours ................Varied Hours | Night Skiing? ...................Yes |
| Tickets: Adult Full ...........$20 | Adult Half/Night ..............$16 |
| Tickets: Child Full...........$16 | Child Half/Night...............$12 |
| Main.................518-692-7337 | Fax ....................518-692-9287 |

### Woods Valley Ski Area

Location: 7m N of Rome, Rt 46 Near Westerville
PO Box 215, Drop Hill Rd, Rte 46, Westernville, New York
13486

| | |
|---|---|
| Base Elevation (ft)............900 | Summit (ft) ......................1400 |
| Vertical Drop (ft)............500 | Skiable Acres......................25 |
| Avg Snowfall (in)............180 | Number of Lifts....................3 |
| Runs:...Green 20% Blue 60% | Black 20% DoubleBlack- |
| Date Open .........December 10 | Date Close...................April 1 |
| Hours......................Tues-Sun | Night Skiing? ...................Yes |
| Tickets: Adult Wkdy ........$14 | Adult Wkend ....................$17 |
| Tickets: Child Wkdy ........$11 | Child Wkend ....................$14 |
| Tickets: Night .................$13 | Under 5 ..............................$0 |
| Main.................315-827-4721 | Fax ....................315-827-4249 |
| Snow Report .....315-827-4206 | |

# North Carolina

### Appalachian Ski Mountain

Location: 2m off US 221 & 321, Between Boone & Blowng Rk
Blowing Rock, North Carolina 28605

| | |
|---|---|
| Base Elevation (ft)..........3635 | Summit (ft) ......................4000 |
| Vertical Drop (ft)............365 | Skiable Acres..................9 slo |
| Avg Snowfall (in)..............59 | Number of Lifts....................5 |
| Runs:...Green 22% Blue 45% | Black 33% DoubleBlack- |
| Date Open .......Mid November | Date Close....................March |
| Hours................9 a.m.-10 p.m. | Night Skiing? ...................Yes |
| Tickets: Adult Wkdy ........$20 | Adult/Student Wkend........$30 |
| Tickets: Adult Night ........$16 | Child Wkdy ......................$12 |
| Tickets: Child Wkend........$19 | Student Wkdy ..................$18 |
| Main.................704-295-7828 | Toll Free ..........800-322-2373 |
| Lodging............800-322-2373 | Fax ....................704-295-3277 |
| Snow Report .....704-295-7820 | |

Photo courtesy of Crested Butte Mountain Resort; Tom Stillo Phtotgrapher

Kim Reichelm skiing Crested Butte

## *Cataloochee Ski Area*

Location: 4m from Maggie Valley, 40m from Asheville
Maggie Valley, North Carolina 28751
Base Elevation (ft)...........4660    Summit (ft) .....................5400

| | |
|---|---|
| Vertical Drop (ft)...............740 | Skiable Acres......................15 |
| Avg Snowfall (in) .............48" | Number of Lifts.....................3 |
| Runs:...Green 25% Blue 50% | Black 25% DoubleBlack- |
| Date Open ...........December 7 | Date Close............Mid March |
| Hours...............9 a.m.-10 p.m. | Night Skiing? ....................Yes |
| Tickets: Adult Wkday ......$20 | Adult Wkend ....................$33 |
| Tickets: Child Wkday.......$13 | Child Wkend ....................$18 |
| Tickets: Adult Night..........$18 | Child Night ......................$14 |
| Main.................704-926-0285 | Toll Free ..........800-768-0285 |
| Fax ..................704-926-0354 | Snow Report .....800-768-3588 |

## *Hawknest Golf & Ski Resort*

Location: 90m from Winston/Salem on US 421 & NC 105
Seven Devils, North Carolina 28604
Web Site: www.Hawknest-Resort.com

| | |
|---|---|
| Base Elevation (ft)...........4130 | Summit (ft) ......................4819 |
| Vertical Drop (ft)...............689 | Skiable Acres .................12 ru |
| Avg Snowfall (in) .............90% | Number of Lifts.....................4 |
| Runs:...Green 30% Blue 40% | Black 30% DoubleBlack- |
| Date Open ..............December | Date Close....................March |
| Hours...............9 a.m.-10 p.m. | Night Skiing? ....................Yes |
| Tickets: Adult Wkday ......$23 | Adult Wkend ....................$31 |
| Tickets: Jr/Sr Wkday.........$15 | Jr/Sr Wkend ....................$23 |
| Tickets: Adult Night..........$18 | Jr/Sr Night ......................$12 |
| Main.................704-963-6561 | Toll Free .........800-822-HAWK |
| Snow Report .....704-963-6563 | |

## *Sapphire Valley*

Location: 4m from Cashiers on Rt 64, 60m from Asheville
Sapphire, North Carolina 28771

| | |
|---|---|
| Base Elevation (ft)...........4375 | Summit (ft) ......................4800 |
| Vertical Drop (ft)...............425 | Skiable Acres......................20 |
| Avg Snowfall (in) .............30" | Number of Lifts.....................3 |
| Runs:...Green 25% Blue 50% | Black 25% DoubleBlack- |
| Date Open.......Mid December | Date Close..........Early March |
| Hours...............9 a.m.-10 p.m. | Night Skiing? ....................Yes |
| Tickets: Adult Wkday ......$16 | Adult Wkend ....................$20 |
| Tickets: Adult Night..........$12 | Child Wkdy ......................$13 |
| Tickets: Child Wkend........$21 | |
| Main.................704-743-1164 | Fax ..................704-743-5516 |
| Snow Report .....704-743-1162 | |

## *Scaly Mountain*

Location: 7m from Dillard on Hwy 246
Scaly Mountain, North Carolina 28775

| | |
|---|---|
| Base Elevation (ft)...........3800 | Summit (ft) ......................4025 |
| Vertical Drop (ft)...............225 | Skiable Acres..................3 slo |
| Avg Snowfall (in)................... | Number of Lifts.....................2 |

| Runs:...Green 1% | Blue 2% | Black- | DoubleBlack- |
| Date Open........................... | | Date Close .......................... |

Hours................9 a.m.-10 p.m.
Night Skiing? ...................Yes
Tickets: Adult Wkday ......$15
Over65/Jr Wkday .........$10
Tickets: Adult Wkend ......$25
Over 65/Jr Wkend ..........$15
Tickets: Night.................$10
Main.............704-526-3737
Toll Free........800-929-SNOW
Lodging.............404-746-5348

## *Ski Beech Mountain*

Location: 4m from Banner Elk, 21m from Boone
PO Box 1118, Banner Elk, North Carolina 28604
Web Site: www.skibeech.com

| | | | |
|---|---|---|---|
| Base Elevation (ft)..........4675 | Summit (ft) .....................5505 |
| Vertical Drop (ft)...............830 | Skiable Acres....................14 tr |
| Avg Snowfall (in)................70 | Number of Lifts......................9 |
| Runs:...Green 30% Blue 40% | Black 30% DoubleBlack- |
| Date Open .......Mid November | Date Close........................March |
| Hours............8:30 a.m.-10 p.m. | Night Skiing? ...................Yes |
| Tickets: Adult Day ............$33 | Adult Night........................$18 |
| Tickets: Jr/Sr Day ............$25 | Jr/Sr Night .......................$16 |
| Main............704-387-2011 | Snow Report .....800-438-2093 |

## *Sugar Mountain Resort*

Location: 3m from Banner Elk, 100m from Charlotte
Banner Elk, North Carolina 28604
Web Site: www.aminews.com/sugarmt/

| | | | |
|---|---|---|---|
| Base Elevation (ft)..........4100 | Summit (ft) .....................5300 |
| Vertical Drop (ft)............1200 | Skiable Acres....................115 |
| Avg Snowfall (in)................78 | Number of Lifts......................8 |
| Runs:...Green 40% Blue 50% | Black 10% DoubleBlack- |
| Date Open .......Mid November | Date Close ............Mid March |
| Hours................9 a.m.-10 p.m. | Night Skiing? ...................Yes |
| Tickets: Adult Wkday ......$28 | Adult Wkend ....................$43 |
| Tickets: Child Wkday........$22 | Child Wkend ....................$32 |
| Tickets: Adult Night..........$22 | Child Night ......................$18 |
| Main............704-898-4521 | Lodging.............800-438-4555 |
| Snow Report ....800-SUGARMT | |

## *Wolf Laurel Slopes*

Location: 32m from Asheville
PO Box 750, Mars Hill, North Carolina 28754

| | | | |
|---|---|---|---|
| Base Elevation (ft)..........3950 | Summit (ft) .....................4600 |
| Vertical Drop (ft)..............650 | Skiable Acres....................54 |
| Avg Snowfall (in)................50 | Number of Lifts......................3 |
| Runs:...Green 12% Blue 44% | Black 32% DoubleBlack 12% |
| Date Open......Late November | Date Close ..........Mid March |
| Hours................9 a.m.-10 p.m. | Night Skiing? ...................Yes |

| Tickets: Adult Wkdy | $20 | Adult Wkend | $28 |
| Tickets: Adult Night | $18 | Under 9 Wkdy | $10 |
| Tickets: Under 9 Wkend | $14 | Under 9 Night | $9 |
| Main | 704-689-4111 | Toll Free | 800-THE-WOLF |
| FAX | 704-689-9819 | | |

# North Dakota

## *Bears Den Mt*

Location: 20m NW of Lisbon, 80m SW of Fargo
Ft Ransom, North Dakota 58033

| Base Elevation (ft) | 900 | Summit (ft) | 1190 |
| Vertical Drop (ft) | 290 | Skiable Acres | 30 |
| Avg Snowfall (in) | 35" | Number of Lifts | 4 |
| Runs:...Green 25%  Blue 50% | | Black 25%   DoubleBlack- | |
| Date Open | Late November | Date Close | Mid March |
| Hours | Wed-Sun | Night Skiing? | Yes |
| Tickets: Adult Wkdy | $12 | Adult Wkend | $14 |
| Tickets: 6-11/65+ Wkdy | $8 | 6-11/65+ Wkend | $10 |
| Tickets: Under 6 | $0 | | |
| Main | 701-973-2711 | | |

## *Bottineau Winter Park*

Location: 15m from The Canadian Border, off Rt 5 & 14
Bottineau, North Dakota 58318

| Base Elevation (ft) | 1880 | Summit (ft) | 2080 |
| Vertical Drop (ft) | 200 | Skiable Acres | 50 |
| Avg Snowfall (in) | 35" | Number of Lifts | 5 |
| Runs:...Green 40%  Blue 40% | | Black 20%   DoubleBlack- | |
| Date Open | Mid November | Date Close | Late March |
| Hours | Varied Hours | Night Skiing? | Yes |
| Tickets: Adult Wkday | $12 | Adult Wkend | $15 |
| Tickets: Adult Night | $8 | 6-13 Wkday | $9 |
| Tickets: 6-13 Wkend | $11 | Over 65 Wkend | $13 |
| Main | 701-263-4556 | Toll Free | 800-305-8079 |
| Fax | 701-263-4446 | | |

## *Frostfire Mountain*

Location: 6m W of Walhalla on Hwy 55, 100m from Grand Forks
Walhalla, North Dakota 58282

| Base Elevation (ft) | 1000 | Summit (ft) | 1350 |
| Vertical Drop (ft) | 350 | Skiable Acres | 25 |
| Avg Snowfall (in) | 35" | Number of Lifts | 3 |
| Runs:...Green 25%  Blue 25% | | Black 50%   DoubleBlack- | |
| Date Open | November | Date Close | Mid March |
| Hours | 9:30 a.m.-4:30 p.m. | Night Skiing? | No |
| Tickets: Adult Full | $19 | Child Full | $9 |
| Main | 701-549-3600 | | |

Fax ....................701-549-3602

## *Huff Hills*          *(Unverified data)*

Location: North Dakota

| | |
|---|---|
| Base Elevation (ft)................. | Summit (ft) ............................ |
| Vertical Drop (ft).................... | Skiable Acres........................ |
| Avg Snowfall (in).................... | Number of Lifts ..................... |
| Runs:...Green-    Blue- | Black-      DoubleBlack- |
| Date Open............................. | Date Close ............................ |
| Hours ................................... | Night Skiing?.....................No |
| Main..................701-663-6421 | |

## *Skyline Skiway*     *(Unverified data)*

Location: 10m from Devils Lake
Devils Lake, North Dakota 58301

| | |
|---|---|
| Base Elevation (ft)..........1430 | Summit (ft) .....................1740 |
| Vertical Drop (ft)...............310 | Skiable Acres......................20 |
| Avg Snowfall (in)............... | Number of Lifts ....................2 |
| Runs:...Green-    Blue- | Black-    DoubleBlack- |
| Date Open.......Mid December | Date Close ...........Early March |
| Hours.....................Sat & Sun | Night Skiing?.....................No |
| Tickets: Adult Full ...........$12 | Child Full............................$8 |
| Main..................701-766-4035 | |
| Snow Report .....701-662-5618 | |

# Ohio

## *Alpine Valley Ski Area*

Location: 18m from Cleveland, 10m E of I271
Chesterland, Ohio 44026

| | |
|---|---|
| Base Elevation (ft)..........1260 | Summit (ft) .....................1500 |
| Vertical Drop (ft)...............230 | Skiable Acres......................72 |
| Avg Snowfall (in)............120 | Number of Lifts ....................7 |
| Runs:...Green 33% Blue 34% | Black 33% DoubleBlack- |
| Date Open........Mid December | Date Close ............Mid March |
| Hours...................9 a.m.-11pm | Night Skiing? ...................Yes |
| Tickets: Adult Wkdy .........$21 | Adult Wkend .....................$32 |
| Tickets: Under 12 Wkdy ...$19 | Under 12 Wkend ..............$29 |
| Tickets: Over 65 .................$0 | |
| Main..................440-285-2211 | |
| Fax ...................440-285-4844 | |
| Snow Report .....440-729-9775 | |

## *Boston Mills/Brandywine Ski Resorts*

Location: 10m from Akron, 15m from Cleveland
Penninsula, Ohio 44264

| | |
|---|---|
| Base Elevation (ft)............420 | Summit (ft) .......................660 |

| | |
|---|---|
| Vertical Drop (ft)...............240 | Skiable Acres....................100 |
| Avg Snowfall (in)...............54 | Number of Lifts................17 |
| Runs:...Green 20%  Blue 40% | Black 40%  DoubleBlack- |
| Date Open...............December | Date Close....................March |
| Hours...............9:30 a.m.11pm | Night Skiing? ....................Yes |
| Tickets: Wkdy/ 4 hrs .......$16 | Wkdy/ 8 hrs ......................$21 |
| Tickets: Wkend/ 4 hrs .......$20 | Wkend/ 8 hrs ...................$25 |
| Main..................216-467-2242 | |
| Fax.................216-657-2660 | |
| Snow Report .....216-656-4489 | |

## *Clear Fork Ski Area*

Location: 20m from Mansfield
Butler, Ohio 44822

| | |
|---|---|
| Base Elevation (ft)...........2100 | Summit (ft) .....................2400 |
| Vertical Drop (ft)...............300 | Skiable Acres....................60 |
| Avg Snowfall (in)...............75 | Number of Lifts................6 |
| Runs:...Green 29%  Blue 42% | Black 29%  DoubleBlack- |
| Date Open ...............December | Date Close....................March |
| Hours..............10 a.m.-10 p.m. | Night Skiing? ....................Yes |
| Tickets: Adult Wkday/Night$20 | Adult Wkend |
| $30 | |
| Tickets: Child Wkday........$10 | Child Wkend/Night ...........$15 |
| Main..................419-883-2000 | |
| Fax.................419-883-2225 | |
| Snow Report .....800-237-5673 | |

## *Mad River Mountain*

Location: 6m from Bellefontaine, 40m from Columbus
Bellefontaine, Ohio 43311

| | |
|---|---|
| Base Elevation (ft)...........1160 | Summit (ft) .....................1460 |
| Vertical Drop (ft)...............300 | Skiable Acres....................120 |
| Avg Snowfall (in)...............30 | Number of Lifts................4 |
| Runs:...Green 22%  Blue 34% | Black 44%  DoubleBlack- |
| Date Open......Early December | Date Close....................March |
| Hours............9:30 a.m.10 p.m. | Night Skiing? ....................Yes |
| Tickets: Adult Wkday .......$15 | Adult Wkend ..................$25 |
| Tickets: Child/65+ Wkday $14 | Child/65+ Wkend ............$20 |
| Tickets: Adult Night..........$13 | Child/65+ Night ..............$14 |
| Main..................937-599-1015 | Fax ...................937-599-4225 |
| Snow Report .....800-231-7669 | |

## *Snow Trails Ski Area*

Location: 5m from Mansfield, Cleveland/Columbus 55-65m
Mansfield, Ohio 44903
Web Site: www.snowtrails.com

| | |
|---|---|
| Base Elevation (ft)...........1175 | Summit (ft) .....................1475 |
| Vertical Drop (ft)...............300 | Skiable Acres....................50 |

Avg Snowfall (in)...............60
Runs:...Green 20% Blue 60%
Date Open.......Late November
Hours.............10 a.m.-10 p.m.
Tickets: Adult Wkdy ........$20
Tickets: Child Wkdy/Night$10
Tickets: Over 65 Wkdy .....$15
Main.................419-774-9818
Lodging...........419-756-7669
Snow Report .....800-332-7669

*1*

Number of Lifts.....................6
Black 20% DoubleBlack-
Date Close ............Mid March
Night Skiing?.....................Yes
Adult/65+ Wkend.............$32
Child Wkend ....................$15
Adult/65+ Night ..............$18
Toll Free .........800-OHIO SKI
Fax ...................419-756-8031

Location: 27m S of Chilcothe
Latham, Ohio 45646
Base Elevation (ft)...................
Vertical Drop (ft)..............600
Avg Snowfall (in)...............35
Runs:...Green 3%   Blue 3%
Date Open .............December
Hours .................9:30-9:30pm
Tickets: Adult Full ...........$30
Tickets: Child/65+ Full .....$25
Tickets: Under 6 .................$0
Main.................614-493-2599
Snow Report .....888-774-2978

Summit (ft) .............................
Skiable Acres......................32
Number of Lifts....................3
Black 47% DoubleBlack 47%
Date Close...................March
Night Skiing? ....................Yes
Adult Half/Night .............$25
Child/65+ Half.................$20

Fax ...................614-493-2651

1

Photo © Vail Resorts/ Breckenridge. Used by permission.

# Oregon

## *Anthony Lakes Mountain Resort*

Location: 19m W of N Powder Exit on I-84, Oregon

| | |
|---|---|
| Base Elevation (ft)...........7100 | Summit (ft) .....................8000 |
| Vertical Drop (ft)............900 | Skiable Acres.................360 |
| Avg Snowfall (in)................... | Number of Lifts...................2 |
| Runs:...Green 23% Blue 30% | Black 47% DoubleBlack- |
| Date Open.......Late November | Date Close ..............Mid April |
| Hours................9 a.m.-4 p.m. | Night Skiing?.....................No |
| Tickets: Adult Full ............$24 | Adult Half .......................$16 |
| Tickets: Stdt/Sr Full .........$18 | Stdt/Sr Half.......................$16 |
| Tickets: Child ...................$11 | |
| Main................503-963-4599 | Fax ...............541-562-5253 |
| Snow Report .....541-856-3277 | |

*Open Thurs- Sun only*

## *Cooper Spur*

Location: 27m S of Hood River off Hwy 35
Oregon

| | |
|---|---|
| Base Elevation (ft)...........4000 | Summit (ft) .....................4500 |
| Vertical Drop (ft)............500 | Skiable Acres.................100 |
| Avg Snowfall (in).............140 | Number of Lifts...................2 |
| Runs:...Green 40% Blue 40% | Black 20% DoubleBlack- |
| Date Open.......Late November | Date Close............Late March |
| Hours................9 a.m.-10 p.m. | Night Skiing? ...................Yes |
| Tickets: Adult...................$12 | Jr .......................................$8 |
| Tickets: Night......................$5 | |
| Main................503-352-7803 | Fax ...................541-230-1161 |
| Snow Report .....541-352-7803 | |

*Open Fri-Sun only*

## *Hoodoo Ski Area*

Location: 43m W of Bend, 88m SE of Salem
Sisters, Oregon 97759

| | |
|---|---|
| Base Elevation (ft)...........4668 | Summit (ft) .....................5703 |
| Vertical Drop (ft).............1035 | Skiable Acres.................600 |
| Avg Snowfall (in).............260 | Number of Lifts...................4 |
| Runs:...Green 30% Blue 30% | Black 40% DoubleBlack- |
| Date Open.........Thanksgiving | Date Close ....................Easter |
| Hours................9 a.m.-10 p.m. | Night Skiing? ...................Yes |
| Tickets: Adult Full ............$23 | Adult Half .......................$18 |
| Tickets: Adult Night.........$14 | 6-12 Full .........................$16 |
| Tickets: 6-12 Half.............$12 | 6-12 Night ......................$10 |
| Main................514-822-3799 | Fax ...................541-822-3398 |
| Snow Report .....541-822-3337 | |

## Mount Bailey

Location: Oregon

| | |
|---|---|
| Base Elevation (ft)...........5363 | Summit (ft) .....................8363 |
| Vertical Drop (ft)............3000 | Skiable Acres...................6000 |
| Avg Snowfall (in)..............600 | Number of Lifts....................1 |
| Runs:...Green-      Blue- | Black 50%   DoubleBlack 50% |
| Date Open..........Thanksgiving | Date Close .............Mid May |
| Hours.......................7am-6pm | Night Skiing?.....................No |
| Tickets: Daily .................$130 | |
| Main.................541-793-3348 | |
| Fax ...................541-793-3221 | |

*Snowcat skiing only*

## Mt Ashland Ski Area

Location: 18m To Ashland, 28m To Medford
PO Box 220, Ashland, Oregon 97520
Web Site: www.mtashland.com

| | |
|---|---|
| Base Elevation (ft)...........6350 | Summit (ft) .....................7500 |
| Vertical Drop (ft).............1150 | Skiable Acres.....................200 |
| Avg Snowfall (in)..............110 | Number of Lifts....................4 |
| Runs:...Green 15%  Blue 35% | Black 50%   DoubleBlack- |
| Date Open...........Thanksgiving | Date Close ...........Mid April |
| Hours.................9 a.m.-10 p.m. | Night Skiing? ...................Yes |
| Tickets: Adult Wkday ......$23 | Adult Wkend ....................$27 |
| Tickets: 9-12 Wkdy.........$16 | 9-12 Wkend .....................$19 |
| Tickets: Night ...................$15 | Under 8 ...............................$0 |
| Main.................541-482-2897 | Lodging.............541-482-2897 |
| Fax ...................541-482-3644 | Snow Report ....541-482-2754 |

## Mt Bachelor Ski And Summer Resort

Location: 22m from Bend, 162m To Portland
PO Box 1031, Bend, Oregon 97701-1031
Web Site: www.mtbachelor.com

| | |
|---|---|
| Base Elevation (ft)...........5800 | Summit (ft) .....................9065 |
| Vertical Drop (ft)............3265 | Skiable Acres...................3686 |
| Avg Snowfall (in) .............25' | Number of Lifts..................13 |
| Runs:...Green 15%  Blue 25% | Black 35%   DoubleBlack 25% |
| Date Open....Mid November | Date Close .............Early July |
| Hours.................9 a.m.-4 p.m. | Night Skiing?.....................No |
| Tickets: Adult Wkday ........$33 | Adult Wkend ....................$33 |
| Tickets: 13-17 Full ...........$25 | 7-12 Full ...........................$18 |
| Tickets: Over 65 Full........$19 | Under 6 ...............................$0 |
| Main.................503-382-2607 | Toll Free ...........800-547-6858 |
| Lodging.............503-382-8334 | |
| Snow Report .....541-382-7888 | |

## Mt Hood Meadows Ski Resort

Location: 67m from Portland, I-84 To Hwy 26 To Hwy 35
Mt Hood, Oregon 97041

| | |
|---|---|
| Base Elevation (ft)...........4523 | Summit (ft) ......................7300 |
| Vertical Drop (ft)............2777 | Skiable Acres..................2150 |
| Avg Snowfall (in)..............360 | Number of Lifts ..................12 |
| Runs:...Green 15% Blue 50% | Black 20% DoubleBlack 15% |
| Date Open ......Mid November | Date Close ................Mid May |
| Hours................9 a.m.-10 p.m. | Night Skiing? ....................Yes |
| Tickets: Adult Day ............$36 | Adult Half ........................$28 |
| Tickets: Jr/Sr All ................$21 | Night All ..........................$15 |
| Main...................503-337-2222 | |
| Lodging .............800-929-2SKI | |
| Fax ....................503-246-1722 | |
| Snow Report ...503-227-SNOW | |

## Mt Hood Ski Bowl

Location: 53m E of Portland on Hwy 26
Ski Bowl, Oregon 97028

| | |
|---|---|
| Base Elevation (ft)...........3600 | Summit (ft) ......................5100 |
| Vertical Drop (ft)............1500 | Skiable Acres....................620 |
| Avg Snowfall (in)..............300 | Number of Lifts ....................9 |
| Runs:...Green 20% Blue 50% | Black 30% DoubleBlack- |
| Date Open..........November 15 | Date Close ...............Mid April |
| Hours................9 a.m.-10 p.m. | Night Skiing? ....................Yes |
| Tickets: Adult Wkdy .......$15 | Adult Wkend ....................$20 |
| Tickets: Child Full............$18 | Child Night ......................$11 |
| Tickets: Adult Night.........$14 | |
| Main...................503-272-3206 | |
| Snow Report .....503-222-2695 | |

## Summit Ski Area

Location:
Hood River, Oregon

| | |
|---|---|
| Base Elevation (ft)...........4000 | Summit (ft) ......................4300 |
| Vertical Drop (ft)..............300 | Skiable Acres......................50 |
| Avg Snowfall (in)..............150 | Number of Lifts ....................2 |
| Runs:...Green 75% Blue 25% | Black- DoubleBlack- |
| Date Open.......Late November | Date Close............Late March |
| Hours...................9 a.m.-4 p.m. | Night Skiing?....................No |
| Tickets: Adult Wkend .......$15 | Adult Half ........................$12 |
| Main...................503-272-0256 | |
| Lodging............541-386-2200 | |
| Fax ....................503-272-0186 | |
| Snow Report .....503-272-0256 | |

## Timberline Ski Area

Location: 6m from Government Camp, 60m from Portland
Timberline Lodge, Oregon 97028

| | | |
|---|---|---|
| Base Elevation (ft)..........4340 | Summit (ft) ..................8500 | |
| Vertical Drop (ft)...........4260 | Skiable Acres.................2500 | |
| Avg Snowfall (in).............300 | Number of Lifts...................6 | |
| Runs:..Green 30% Blue 60% | Black 10% DoubleBlack- | |
| Date Open ......Mid November | Date Close ....Early September | |
| Hours.................9 a.m.-9 p.m. | Night Skiing? ..................Yes | |
| Tickets: Adult Wkdy ........$31 | Adult Wkend ..................$34 | |
| Tickets: Night .....................$11 | Jr..................................$19 | |
| Main................503-272-3311 | Lodging............800-547-1406 | |
| Fax ..................503-622-0710 | Snow Report .....503-222-2211 | |

## Willamette Pass

Location: 70m from Eugene, 71m from Bend
Cascade Summit, Oregon 97401

| | | |
|---|---|---|
| Base Elevation (ft)..........5120 | Summit (ft) ..................6683 | |
| Vertical Drop (ft).............1563 | Skiable Acres.................220 | |
| Avg Snowfall (in).............300 | Number of Lifts...................5 | |
| Runs:..Green 4%  Blue 13% | Black 12% DoubleBlack- | |
| Date Open ......Mid November | Date Close..............Late April | |
| Hours.................9 a.m.-9 p.m. | Night Skiing? ..................Yes | |
| Tickets: Adult Full ............$25 | 6-10 Full ...........................$15 | |
| Tickets: Over 65 Full........$13 | | |
| Main................541-484-5030 | | |
| Snow Report ...541-345-SNOW | | |

# Pennsylvania

## Alpine Mountain

Location: 1.5 Hrs from NYC. 2 Hrs from Philadelphia
Analomink, Pennsylvania 18320

| | | |
|---|---|---|
| Base Elevation (ft).............600 | Summit (ft) ..................1150 | |
| Vertical Drop (ft).............500 | Skiable Acres.................60 | |
| Avg Snowfall (in)...............50 | Number of Lifts...................3 | |
| Runs:..Green 17% Blue 55% | Black 28% DoubleBlack- | |
| Date Open.....Early December | Date Close..........Late March | |
| Hours......................8am-5pm | Night Skiing?....................No | |
| Tickets: Adult Wkdy ........$23 | Adult Wkend ..................$30 | |
| Tickets: Jr Wkdy ...............$19 | Jr Wkend .......................$26 | |
| Main................717-595-2150 | Toll Free ...........800-233-8240 | |
| Fax ..................717-595-2803 | | |

## Big Boulder Ski Area

Location: 30m from Stroudsburg/2 Hrs from Philadelphia
Lake Harmony, Pennsylvania 18624

Photo Courtesy of Loveland Ski Area, Colorado

With a base elevation of 10,800 feet, Loveland is one of the highest elevation ski areas in the country.

| | | | |
|---|---|---|---|
| Base Elevation (ft) | 1700 | Summit (ft) | 2175 |
| Vertical Drop (ft) | 475 | Skiable Acres | 55 |
| Avg Snowfall (in) | 50 | Number of Lifts | 7 |
| Runs:...Green 40% Blue 35% | | Black 25% DoubleBlack- | |
| Date Open | Mid December | Date Close | Late March |
| Hours | 9 a.m.-10 p.m. | Night Skiing? | Yes |
| Tickets: Adult wkdy | $32 | Adult Wkend | $40 |
| Tickets: Jr Full | $22 | Student Full | $30 |
| Tickets: Senior Full | $20 | Adult Night | $25 |
| Main | 717-722-0100 | Fax | 717-443-8479 |
| Snow Report | 800-475-SNOW | | |

## *Blue Knob Four Seasons*

Location: 25m from Bedford/Pittsburgh 100m
Claysburg, Pennsylvania 16625
Web Site: http://www.nb.net/~blueknob

| | | | |
|---|---|---|---|
| Base Elevation (ft) | 2080 | Summit (ft) | 3152 |
| Vertical Drop (ft) | 1072 | Skiable Acres | 82 |
| Avg Snowfall (in) | 100 | Number of Lifts | 7 |
| Runs:...Green 29% Blue 33% | | Black 24% DoubleBlack 14% | |
| Date Open | Late November | Date Close | Late March |
| Hours | 9 a.m.-10 p.m. | Night Skiing? | Yes |
| Tickets: Adult Wkdy | $25 | Adult Wkend | $35 |
| Tickets: Jr Wkdy | $20 | Jr Wkend | $25 |

Tickets: Sr Wkdy..............$17
Main..............814-239-5111
Fax ...................814-239-8754
Snow Report .....800-458-3403

Sr Wkend..........................$22
Toll Free ...........800-822-3045

## *Blue Marsh Ski Area*

Location: 10m N of Redding on PA 183/Harrisburg 40m
PO Box 609, Bernville, Pennsylvania 19506

Base Elevation (ft).............290
Vertical Drop (ft).............300
Avg Snowfall (in) ..............24"
Runs:......Green 35%  Blue 35%
Date Open.......Mid December
Hours................9 a.m.-10 p.m.
Tickets: Adult Wkdy ........$16
Main.................610-488-7412
Fax ...................610-488-7978

Summit (ft) .......................590
Skiable Acres......................30
Number of Lifts....................5
Black 30%  DoubleBlack-
Date Close...............Mid March
Night Skiing? .....................Yes
Adult Wkend .....................$24

## *Blue Mountain Ski Area*

Location: 17m from Allentown
Palmerton, Pennsylvania 18071

Base Elevation (ft)............457
Vertical Drop (ft).............1083
Avg Snowfall (in)...............50
Runs:...Green 39%  Blue 32%
Date Open......Early December
Hours...........8:30 a.m.-10 p.m.
Tickets: Adult Full ............$31
Tickets: Adult Night .........$23
Tickets: Jr Half ..................$20
Main.................610-826-7700
Fax ...................610-826-7828
Snow Report .....800-235-2226

Summit (ft) ......................1540
Skiable Acres......................74
Number of Lifts....................7
Black 29%  DoubleBlack-
Date Close.............Late March
Night Skiing? .....................Yes
Adult Half.........................$25
Jr Full...............................$26
Jr Night.............................$18

## *Boyce Park Ski Area*

Location: Pennsylvania

Base Elevation (ft)............1072
Vertical Drop (ft)...............160
Avg Snowfall (in)................70
Runs:...Green 75%  Blue 25%
Date Open........Mid December
Hours...................Varied
Tickets: Adult Wkdy ...........$8
Tickets: Jr Wkdy .................$6
Tickets: Sr Wkdy .................$6
Main.................724-733-4656
Fax ...................412-325-9164
Snow Report .....412-733-4665

Summit (ft) ......................1232
Skiable Acres......................25
Number of Lifts....................5
Black-       DoubleBlack-
Date Close .............Mid March
Night Skiing? .....................Yes
Adult Wkend .....................$12
Jr Wkend ..........................$12
Sr Wkend ..........................$10

## Camelback Ski Area

Location: 5 Mins from Tannersville on I-80/NYC 90m
Tannersville, Pennsylvania 18372

| | |
|---|---|
| Base Elevation (ft)...........1239 | Summit (ft) ......................2050 |
| Vertical Drop (ft)...............811 | Skiable Acres.....................139 |
| Avg Snowfall (in)................60 | Number of Lifts ..................12 |
| Runs:...Green 39% Blue 39% | Black 22% DoubleBlack- |
| Date Open .............December | Date Close..........Late March |
| Hours..........8:30 a.m.-10 p.m. | Night Skiing? ....................Yes |
| Tickets: Adult Wkdy ........$33 | Adult Wkend ....................$39 |
| Tickets: Jr Wkdy ..............$27 | Jr wkend...........................$33 |
| Tickets: Sr Wkdy...............$25 | Sr wkend...........................$25 |
| Main .............717-629-1661 | Fax ....................717-620-0942 |
| Snow Report .....800-233-8100 | |

## Crystal Lake Ski Center

Location: 27m from Williamsport. NYC/Wash. DC 200m
Hughesville, Pennsylvania 17737

| | |
|---|---|
| Base Elevation (ft)..........1850 | Summit (ft) ......................2100 |
| Vertical Drop (ft)...............250 | Skiable Acres.........................7 |
| Avg Snowfall (in) .............50" | Number of Lifts ....................3 |
| Runs:...Green 40% Blue 20% | Black 40% DoubleBlack- |
| Date Open........Mid December | Date Close..........Late March |
| Hours....................9 a.m.-5pm | Night Skiing?......................No |
| Tickets: Adult Wkday .......$10 | Adult Wkend ....................$15 |
| Tickets: Jr Wkdy ................$8 | Jr Wkend ..........................$13 |
| Main .................717-584-2698 | Fax ....................717-584-0169 |
| Snow Report .....717-584-4209 | |

## Doe Mountain Ski Area

Location: 12m from Allentown, 50m N of Philly
Macungie, Pennsylvania 18062

| | |
|---|---|
| Base Elevation (ft)............600 | Summit (ft) ......................1100 |
| Vertical Drop (ft)...............500 | Skiable Acres......................90 |
| Avg Snowfall (in) .................. | Number of Lifts ....................7 |
| Runs:...Green 30% Blue 40% | Black 30% DoubleBlack- |
| Date Open........Mid December | Date Close ............Mid March |
| Hours.................9 a.m.-10 p.m. | Night Skiing? ....................Yes |
| Tickets: Adult Wkdy ........$27 | Adult Wkend ....................$35 |
| Tickets: Adult Night.........$24 | 6-12/62+ Wkdy .................$18 |
| Tickets: 6-12/62+ Wkend..$24 | 6-12/62+ ngte ...................$20 |
| Main .................610-682-7100 | Fax ....................610-682-7110 |
| Snow Report .....800-I-SKI-DOE | |

## Eagle Rock Ski Area          *(Unverified data)*

Location: 30 Mins from Wilkes/Barre on I-81
1060 Valley of Lakes, Hazleton, Pennsylvania 18201
Web Site: www.eaglerok.com

| | |
|---|---|
| Base Elevation (ft)............1300 | Summit (ft) ..................1825 |
| Vertical Drop (ft)...............525 | Skiable Acres.......................43 |
| Avg Snowfall (in) ............70" | Number of Lifts.....................4 |
| Runs:..Green 50%  Blue 10% | Black 40%  DoubleBlack- |
| Date Open ..............December | Date Close.....................March |
| Hours...................varied | Night Skiing? ..................Yes |
| Tickets: Adult.....................$0 | |
| Main.................717-384-3223 | Toll Free ..........888-384-6660 |
| Lodging...........717-384-6616 | Fax ...............717-384-6605 |

*Open Fri - Sun only*

## Elk Mountain Ski Resort

Location: 26m from Scranton on I-81 North.
Union Dale, Pennsylvania 18470

| | |
|---|---|
| Base Elevation (ft)...........1693 | Summit (ft) ..................2693 |
| Vertical Drop (ft)............1000 | Skiable Acres....................140 |
| Avg Snowfall (in) .............60" | Number of Lifts.....................6 |
| Runs:..Green 25%  Blue 30% | Black 45%  DoubleBlack- |
| Date Open......Early December | Date Close............Late March |
| Hours...........8:30 a.m.-10 p.m. | Night Skiing? ..................Yes |
| Tickets: Adult Wkday ......$31 | Adult Wkend ....................$39 |
| Tickets: Adult Night..........$20 | 6-12/65+Wkdy ...............$25 |
| Tickets: 6-12/65+Wked.....$31 | 6-12/65+nite ....................$16 |
| Main.................717-679-4400 | |
| Fax...................717-679-4409 | |
| Snow Report .....800-233-4131 | |

## Fernwood Resort

Location: 30 Mins from Rt 80. NYC 90 Mins.
Rt 209, Bushkill, Pennsylvania 18324
Web Site: www.resortsusa.com

| | |
|---|---|
| Base Elevation (ft)............500 | Summit (ft) ....................700 |
| Vertical Drop (ft)...............200 | Skiable Acres.......................13 |
| Avg Snowfall (in) .............60" | Number of Lifts.....................1 |
| Runs:..Green 50%  Blue 50% | Black-          DoubleBlack- |
| Date Open .......Late December | Date Close ..........Early March |
| Hours...........9 a.m.-4:30 p.m. | Night Skiing?......................No |
| Tickets: Adult Full ............$18 | Jr Full..............................$12 |
| Main.................717-588-6661 | Toll Free ..........800-233-8103 |
| Lodging.............717-588-9500 | Fax ...............717-588-7112 |
| Snow Report .....717-588-9500 | |

## Hidden Valley Resort

Location: 12m W of Somerset, Donegal 8m East
Hidden Valley, Pennsylvania 15502

| | |
|---|---|
| Base Elevation (ft)..........2390 | Summit (ft) .....................3000 |
| Vertical Drop (ft)..............610 | Skiable Acres.....................88 |
| Avg Snowfall (in)..............160 | Number of Lifts ..................8 |
| Runs:...Green 35% Blue 35% | Black 30% DoubleBlack- |
| Date Open ..............December | Date Close..............March |
| Hours...................9 a.m.-6pm | Night Skiing? ..................Yes |
| Tickets: Adult Wkdy ........$20 | Adult Wkend ................$34 |
| Tickets: Adult Night .........$25 | 6-12/65+Wkdy .................$15 |
| Tickets: 6-12/65+Wked.....$26 | 6-12/65+nite .....................$20 |
| Main..................814-443-2600 | Toll Free............800-443-SKII |
| Fax ....................814-445-3214 | |
| Snow Report .....800-443-7544 | |

## Jack Frost Resort

Location: 25mi from Scranton/Wilkes Barre. Allentwn 55m
Blakeslee, Pennsylvania 18610

| | |
|---|---|
| Base Elevation (ft)..........1400 | Summit (ft) .....................2000 |
| Vertical Drop (ft)..............600 | Skiable Acres.....................97 |
| Avg Snowfall (in) ..............50" | Number of Lifts ..................7 |
| Runs:...Green 20% Blue 40% | Black 40% DoubleBlack- |
| Date Open......Early December | Date Close..............Late March |
| Hours.............8:30 a.m.-4 p.m. | Night Skiing?....................No |
| Tickets: Adult Wkdy ........$32 | Adult Wkend ................$40 |
| Tickets: Adult Night .........$25 | Jr Full..............................$22 |
| Tickets: Student Full ........$30 | Sr Full..............................$20 |
| Main..................717-443-8425 | |
| Fax ...................717-443-8479 | |
| Snow Report ...800-475-SNOW | |

## Montage Ski Area

Location: Located In NE Pocono Mtns. I-9 To I-81
Scranton, Pennsylvania 18505

| | |
|---|---|
| Base Elevation (ft)............940 | Summit (ft) .....................1940 |
| Vertical Drop (ft)............1000 | Skiable Acres.....................140 |
| Avg Snowfall (in) ..............60" | Number of Lifts ..................7 |
| Runs:...Green 38% Blue 29% | Black 19% DoubleBlack 14% |
| Date Open .......Mid November | Date Close............Late March |
| Hours...............9 a.m.-10 p.m. | Night Skiing? ..................Yes |
| Tickets: Adult Wkdy ........$28 | Adult Wkend ................$35 |
| Tickets: Jr Wkdy ..............$23 | Jr Wkend ........................$30 |
| Tickets: Sr Wkdy ..............$14 | Sr Wkend ........................$18 |
| Main..................717-969-7669 | |
| Fax ...................717-963-6621 | |
| Snow Report...800-GOT-SNOW | |

## *Mount Tone Ski Area*

Location: 3 Hrs from NYC off Rt 17
PO Box 766, Moscow, Pennsylvania 18444
Web Site: ww.mttone.com

| | | |
|---|---|---|
| Base Elevation (ft)...........1480 | Summit (ft) .....................1930 |
| Vertical Drop (ft)...............450 | Skiable Acres .................10 tr |
| Avg Snowfall (in) .............63" | Number of Lifts .....................3 |
| Runs:...Green 40%  Blue 40% | Black 20%  DoubleBlack- |
| Date Open ..............Christmas | Date Close ............Mid March |
| Hours...............9 a.m.-10 p.m. | Night Skiing? ...................Yes |
| Tickets: Adult Full ...........$18 | Jr full ...............................$13 |
| Main.................717-842-2544 | Toll Free ..........800-747-2754 |

Photo courtesy of Descente Skiwear

Lodging...............800-74-2754  Fax ....................717-842-0410
Snow Report .....717-842-2544

*Open weekends, holidays & Weds. evenings*

## Mountain View Ski Area          (Unverified data)

Location: Pennsylvania

| | | |
|---|---|---|
| Base Elevation (ft)...........1230 | Summit (ft) .....................1550 |
| Vertical Drop (ft)...............320 | Skiable Acres.....................25 |
| Avg Snowfall (in)..............120 | Number of Lifts .....................3 |
| Runs:...Green 10% Blue 70% | Black 20%  DoubleBlack- |
| Date Open........Mid December | Date Close............Mid March |
| Hours ................................varied | Night Skiing? ....................Yes |
| Tickets: Adult Wkdy .........$20 | Adult Wkend ....................$24 |
| Tickets: Adult Night .........$20 | Student Wkdy ...................$15 |
| Tickets: Student Wkend ....$17 | Student Nite .....................$15 |
| Main..................814-734-1641 | Fax ..................814-734-1641 |

## Mystic Mountain

Location: 60m S of Pittsburgh
1001 Lafayette Dr, Farmington, Pennsylvania 15437

| | |
|---|---|
| Base Elevation (ft)...........2200 | Summit (ft) .....................2600 |
| Vertical Drop (ft)...............400 | Skiable Acres....................400 |
| Avg Snowfall (in)..............80" | Number of Lifts .....................1 |
| Runs:...Green 90% Blue 10% | Black-         DoubleBlack- |
| Date Open..........Thanksgiving | Date Close......................April |
| Hours ................7am-10 p.m. | Night Skiing? ....................Yes |
| Tickets: Adult Full ............$20 | Jr Full...............................$10 |
| Main..................724-329-6979 | Toll Free ...........800-422-2736 |
| Lodging............800-422-2736 | Fax ..................724-329-6098 |

## Resort At Split Rock

Location: 15m from Hazelton
Lake Harmony, Pennsylvania 18624
Web Site: www.SplitRockResort.com

| | |
|---|---|
| Base Elevation (ft)...........1870 | Summit (ft) .....................2120 |
| Vertical Drop (ft)...............250 | Skiable Acres....................40 |
| Avg Snowfall (in).............. | Number of Lifts .....................2 |
| Runs:...Green 80% Blue 20% | Black-         DoubleBlack- |
| Date Open........Mid December | Date Close ............Mid March |
| Hours.............9 a.m.-4:30 p.m. | Night Skiing?......................No |
| Tickets: Adult Wkdy .........$18 | Adult Wkend ....................$22 |
| Tickets: Jr Wkdy .............$16 | Jr Wkend .........................$18 |
| Main..................717-722-9111 | Toll Free ...........800-255-7625 |
| Lodging............800-255-7625 | Fax ..................717-722-8831 |
| Snow Report ....800-255-7625 | |

## Seven Springs Mountain Resort

Location: 55m from Pittsburgh on The PA Turnpike

Champion, Pennsylvania 15622
Web Site: www.7springs.com

| | | | |
|---|---|---|---|
| Base Elevation (ft) | 2240 | Summit (ft) | 2990 |
| Vertical Drop (ft) | 750 | Skiable Acres | 540 |
| Avg Snowfall (in) | 95 | Number of Lifts | 18 |
| Runs:...Green 50% Blue 35% | | Black 12% DoubleBlack 3% | |
| Date Open......Early December | | Date Close......End March | |
| Hours | 9 a.m.-10 p.m. | Night Skiing? | Yes |
| Tickets: Adult Wkdy | $32 | Adult Wkend | $39 |
| Tickets: Jr Wkdy | $25 | Jr Wkend | $32 |
| Tickets: Adult Night | $24 | Jr Night | $18 |
| Main | 814-352-7777 | Toll Free | 800-452-2223 |
| Fax | 814-352-7911 | | |

## *Shawnee Mountain*

Location: 4m from Stroudsburg. Allentown 40m.
Shawnee on Delaware, Pennsylvania 18356
Web Site: www.shawneemt.com

| | | | |
|---|---|---|---|
| Base Elevation (ft) | 650 | Summit (ft) | 1350 |
| Vertical Drop (ft) | 700 | Skiable Acres | 125 |
| Avg Snowfall (in) | 60" | Number of Lifts | 9 |
| Runs:...Green 25% Blue 50% | | Black 25% DoubleBlack- | |
| Date Open......Late November | | Date Close......Late March | |
| Hours | 9 a.m.-10 p.m. | Night Skiing? | Yes |
| Tickets: Adult Wkdy | $35 | Adult Wkend | $39 |
| Tickets: Youth Wkdy | $25 | Youth Wkend | $30 |
| Tickets: Over 70 | $0 | | |
| Main | 717-421-7231 | Lodging | 800-SHAWNEE |
| Fax | 717-421-4795 | Snow Report | 800-233-4218 |

## *Ski Denton*

Location: 5 Hrs from Balt/Wash. Buffalo 2.5 Hrs
Couldersport, Pennsylvania

| | | | |
|---|---|---|---|
| Base Elevation (ft) | 1750 | Summit (ft) | 2400 |
| Vertical Drop (ft) | 650 | Skiable Acres | 75 |
| Avg Snowfall (in) | 100 | Number of Lifts | 5 |
| Runs:...Green 35% Blue 35% | | Black 20% DoubleBlack 10% | |
| Date Open | December | Date Close | March |
| Hours | 9 a.m.-9 p.m. | Night Skiing? | Yes |
| Tickets: Adult Wkdy | $18 | Adult Wkend | $25 |
| Tickets: Adult Night | $14 | Jr Wkdy | $14 |
| Tickets: Jr Wkend | $16 | Jr Night | $12 |
| Main | 814-435-2115 | | |
| Fax | 814-435-2441 | | |
| Snow Report | 814-435-2115 | | |

## *Ski Liberty*

Location: 9m from Gettysburg. Baltimore 70m.

Carroll Valley, Pennsylvania 17320

| | |
|---|---|
| Base Elevation (ft)............800 | Summit (ft) .....................1400 |
| Vertical Drop (ft)..............600 | Skiable Acres....................100 |
| Avg Snowfall (in) ..............45" | Number of Lifts.................8 |
| Runs:...Green 40% Blue 35% | Black 25% DoubleBlack- |
| Date Open......Early December | Date Close............Late March |
| Hours................9 a.m.-10 p.m. | Night Skiing? ...................Yes |
| Tickets: Adult Wkdy .........$29 | Adult Wkend ...................$37 |
| Tickets: Adult Night..........$24 | Jr Wkdy ...........................$24 |
| Tickets: Jr Wkend.............$33 | Jr Night ............................$19 |
| Main................717-642-8282 | Lodging............717-642-8288 |
| Fax ...................717-642-6534 | Snow Report .....717-642-9000 |

## *Ski Roundtop*

Location: 30 Mins from Harrisburg Or York. Wash DC 2.5hr
Lewisberry, Pennsylvania 17339

| | |
|---|---|
| Base Elevation (ft)............800 | Summit (ft) .....................1400 |
| Vertical Drop (ft)..............600 | Skiable Acres....................100 |
| Avg Snowfall (in) ..............35" | Number of Lifts.................10 |
| Runs:...Green 35% Blue 30% | Black 25% DoubleBlack 10% |
| Date Open..........Thanksgiving | Date Close............Late March |
| Hours................9 a.m.-10 p.m. | Night Skiing? ...................Yes |
| Tickets: Adult Wkdy .........$30 | Adult Wkend ...................$37 |
| Tickets: Adult Night..........$25 | Jr Wkdy ...........................$26 |
| Tickets: Jr Wkend.............$33 | Jr Night ............................$21 |
| Main................717-432-9631 | |
| Fax ...................717-432-2949 | |
| Snow Report .....717-432-7000 | |

## *Ski Sawmill*

Location: 15m from Wellsboro/Williamsport 35m.
Morris, Pennsylvania 16938

| | |
|---|---|
| Base Elevation (ft)..........1700 | Summit (ft) .....................2215 |
| Vertical Drop (ft)..............515 | Skiable Acres....................15 |
| Avg Snowfall (in) ..............45" | Number of Lifts.................3 |
| Runs:...Green 33% Blue 34% | Black 33% DoubleBlack- |
| Date Open.......Late November | Date Close............Late March |
| Hours................10 a.m.-10 p.m. | Night Skiing? ...................Yes |
| Tickets: Adult Wkdy .........$13 | Adult Wkend ...................$25 |
| Tickets: Adult Night..........$20 | Jr Wkdy ...........................$13 |
| Tickets: Jr Wkend.............$15 | |
| Main................717-535-7521 | Toll Free ..........800-532-7669 |
| Lodging............717-353-7731 | Fax ...................717-533-7542 |
| Snow Report ...800-532-SNOW | |

## *Spring Mountain Ski Area*

Location: Rt 29-N to Schwenksville
Spring Mount, Pennsylvania 19478

| | |
|---|---|
| Base Elevation (ft)............108 | Summit (ft) ........................528 |
| Vertical Drop (ft)...............420 | Skiable Acres.....................125 |
| Avg Snowfall (in)................... | Number of Lifts.....................4 |
| Runs:...Green 40% Blue 40% | Black 20% DoubleBlack- |
| Date Open.......Mid December | Date Close ...........Mid March |
| Hours.............10 a.m.-10 p.m. | Night Skiing? ...................Yes |
| Tickets: Weekday/Nite.....$17 | Adult Wkend ....................$22 |
| Tickets: Jr Wkend..............$10 | Sr Wkdy.............................$8 |
| Tickets: Sr Wkend............$22 | |
| Main.................610-287-7300 | Fax ...................610-287-1301 |
| Snow Report ....610-287-7900 | |

## Tanglewood Ski Area

Location: Take Rt 390, N of Exit 7 off I-84
Tafton, Pennsylvania

| | |
|---|---|
| Base Elevation (ft)............1335 | Summit (ft) ........................1750 |
| Vertical Drop (ft)...............415 | Skiable Acres.....................35 |
| Avg Snowfall (in) .............45" | Number of Lifts.....................5 |
| Runs:...Green 30% Blue 50% | Black 20% DoubleBlack- |
| Date Open......Early December | Date Close ...........Mid March |
| Hours.............9 a.m.-10 p.m. | Night Skiing? ...................Yes |
| Tickets: Adult Wkdy ........$18 | Adult Wkend ....................$29 |
| Tickets: Adult Night.........$20 | Jr Wkdy .............................$15 |
| Tickets: Jr Wkend.............$24 | Jr Night.............................$15 |
| Main.................717-226-3000 | |
| Fax ...................717-226-0429 | |
| Snow Report .....717-226-9500 | |

## Tussey Mountain

Location: 5m E of Penn State Campus/Harrisburg 1.5 Hrs
Boalsburg, Pennsylvania 16827

| | |
|---|---|
| Base Elevation (ft)............1310 | Summit (ft) ........................1810 |
| Vertical Drop (ft)...............500 | Skiable Acres.....................72 |
| Avg Snowfall (in) .............48" | Number of Lifts.....................5 |
| Runs:...Green 30% Blue 45% | Black 25% DoubleBlack- |
| Date Open ..............December | Date Close ....................March |
| Hours .............................varied | Night Skiing? ...................Yes |
| Tickets: Adult Wkdy ........$20 | Adult Wkend ....................$24 |
| Tickets: Adult Night.........$18 | Jr Wkdy .............................$17 |
| Tickets: Jr Wkend.............$21 | Jr Night.............................$15 |
| Main.................814-466-6810 | Toll Free ..........800-733-2754 |
| Fax ...................814-466-6810 | |
| Snow Report .....814-466-6810 | |

## Whitetail Ski Resort

Location: 6m from Mercersburg
Mercersburg, Pennsylvania 17236

| | |
|---|---|
| Base Elevation (ft)............835 | Summit (ft) ........................1800 |

| | |
|---|---|
| Vertical Drop (ft)............935 | Skiable Acres....................108 |
| Avg Snowfall (in) .............40" | Number of Lifts....................6 |
| Runs:...Green 22% Blue 53% | Black 25% DoubleBlack- |
| Date Open........Mid December | Date Close ............Mid March |
| Hours..........8:30 a.m.-10 p.m. | Night Skiing? ....................Yes |
| Tickets: Adult Wkdy ........$30 | Adult Wkend ....................$42 |
| Tickets: Adult Night..........$25 | Jr/Sr Wkdy........................$23 |
| Tickets: Jr/Sr Wkend.........$35 | Jr/Sr Night ........................$18 |
| Main.................717-328-9400 | Fax ...................717-328-5529 |
| Snow Report .....717-328-9400 | |

Photo by T.R. Youngstrom, courtesy of Telluride Ski & Golf Company

# Rhode Island

## *Yawgoo Valley*

Location: 25 Mins S of Providence off Rt 2
Exeter, Rhode Island 02822

| | |
|---|---|
| Base Elevation (ft)..............70 | Summit (ft) ........................315 |
| Vertical Drop (ft)..............245 | Skiable Acres......................36 |
| Avg Snowfall (in)...............48 | Number of Lifts ....................4 |
| Runs:...Green 50%  Blue 30% | Black 20%  DoubleBlack- |
| Date Open......Early December | Date Close............Late March |
| Hours..............10 a.m.-10 p.m. | Night Skiing? ....................Yes |
| Tickets: Adult Wkdy ........$20 | Adult Wkend ...................$25 |
| Tickets: Child Wkdy ........$18 | Child Wkend ....................$23 |
| Tickets: Night All............$16 | |
| Main.................401-294-3802 | Fax ....................401-295-7112 |
| Snow Report ...401-295-5366 | |

# South Dakota

## *Deer Mountain*

Location: 2m from Lead, 45m from Rapid City
Box 622, Deadwood, South Dakota 57732

| | |
|---|---|
| Base Elevation (ft)..........6000 | Summit (ft) ......................6600 |
| Vertical Drop (ft)............600 | Skiable Acres....................200 |
| Avg Snowfall (in).............150 | Number of Lifts ....................4 |
| Runs:...Green 9%   Blue 4% | Black 9%   DoubleBlack- |
| Date Open..............November | Date Close......................April |
| Hours..............9 a.m.-9:30pm | Night Skiing? ....................Yes |
| Tickets: Adult Wkdy ........$13 | Adult Wkend ...................$18 |
| Tickets: Child Wkdy ........$9 | Child Wkend ....................$13 |
| Tickets: Adult Night...........$9 | Child Night ........................$7 |
| Main.................605-584-3230 | Fax ....................605-584-1146 |

## *Terry Peak*

Location: 3m W of Lead, 45m from Rapid City
PO Box 774, Lead, South Dakota 57754

| | |
|---|---|
| Base Elevation (ft)..........5900 | Summit (ft) ......................6952 |
| Vertical Drop (ft)............1052 | Skiable Acres...................20 tr |
| Avg Snowfall (in).............150 | Number of Lifts ....................5 |
| Runs:...Green 20%  Blue 50% | Black 30%  DoubleBlack- |
| Date Open..........Thanksgiving | Date Close......................April |
| Hours..............9 a.m.-4 p.m. | Night Skiing?.....................No |
| Tickets: Adult Full ........$32 | Adult Half .......................$27 |
| Tickets: Child Full............$21 | CHild Half .......................$18 |
| Tickets: 13-17 Full............$25 | 13-17 Half .......................$22 |
| Main.................605-584-2165 | Lodging............605-342-7609 |
| Fax ...................605-584-1025 | Snow Report .....800-456-0524 |

# Tennessee

## *Ober Gatlinburg*

Location: 40m from Knoxville on I-40
Gatlinburg, Tennessee 37738
Web Site: www.obergatlinburg.com

| | |
|---|---|
| Base Elevation (ft)...........2700 | Summit (ft) ......................3300 |
| Vertical Drop (ft)..............600 | Skiable Acres ..................7 tra |
| Avg Snowfall (in)................50 | Number of Lifts....................3 |
| Runs:...Green 25%  Blue 50% | Black 25%   DoubleBlack- |
| Date Open........Mid December | Date Close ..........Early March |
| Hours..........8:30 a.m.-10 p.m. | Night Skiing? ....................Yes |
| Tickets: Adult Wkday .......$25 | Adult Wkend ....................$33 |
| Tickets: Age 6-11, Wkdy ..$23 | Age 6-11, Wkend .............$26 |
| Tickets: Over 65, Full.......$26 | Night................................$12 |
| Main.................423-436-5423 | |
| Fax ..................423-430-3920 | |
| Snow Report .....800-251-9202 | |

# Utah

## *Alta Ski Area*

Location: 28 Miles from Salt Lake City, I-80 To I-215
P.O. Box 8007, Alta, Utah 84092-8007
Web Site: www.altaskiarea.com

| | |
|---|---|
| Base Elevation (ft)...........8530 | Summit (ft) ....................10550 |
| Vertical Drop (ft).............2020 | Skiable Acres.................2200 |
| Avg Snowfall (in)..............500 | Number of Lifts...................13 |
| Runs:...Green 25%  Blue 40% | Black 35%   DoubleBlack- |
| Date Open .......Mid November | Date Close ...............Mid April |
| Hours ...............9:15-4:30 p.m. | Night Skiing?......................No |
| Tickets: Adult Full ............$28 | Adult Half .........................$21 |
| Tickets: Beginner ............$20 | Over 80 ...............................$0 |
| Main.................801-742-3333 | Lodging.............801-942-0404 |
| Snow Report .....801-572-3939 | |

### NEW:"Ono Easy Chair"

*Skiing the way you remember it. Laid back & unhurried. Endless powder, outstanding steeps & no crowds. No fru-fru here. Skiing, plain and simple, just the way it used to be...and still is, here.*

## *Beaver Mountain Ski Area*

Location: 12m from Garden City, 27m from Logan
Box 3455, 1045 1/2 N Main/ Su #4, Logan, Utah 84323

| | |
|---|---|
| Base Elevation (ft)...........7200 | Summit (ft) ......................8800 |
| Vertical Drop (ft).............1600 | Skiable Acres....................464 |

Avg Snowfall (in)............400  
Runs:...Green 35%  Blue 40%  
Date Open ..............December  
Hours................9 a.m.-4 p.m.  
Tickets: Adult Full ...........$22  
Tickets: Child Full............$17  
Tickets: 65-69 Full ...........$17  
Main..................801-753-0921  
Lodging............801-946-3364  
Snow Report ....801-753-4822  

Number of Lifts.....................3  
Black 25%   DoubleBlack-  
Date Close......................April  
Night Skiing? ...................Yes  
Adult Half..........................$17  
Child Half..........................$14  
Over 70................................$0  

Fax ....................801-753-0975  
Road Report ........dial 530 AM  

## Brian Head Resort

Location: 30m from Cedar City, Las Vegas 195m  
P.O. Box 190008, Brian Head, Utah 94761  
Web Site: www.brianhead.com  

Base Elevation (ft)..........9600  
Vertical Drop (ft)............1707  
Avg Snowfall (in)..............400  
Runs:...Green 30%  Blue 40%  
Date Open .....Early November  
Hours................9 a.m.-10 p.m.  
Tickets: Adult Full ...........$35  
Tickets: Child Full............$28  
Tickets: 6-12/65+ Full ......$20  
Main..................801-677-2035  
Fax ....................801-677-3883  

Summit (ft) ...................11307  
Skiable Acres....................500  
Number of Lifts...................6  
Black 30%  DoubleBlack-  
Date Close......................April  
Night Skiing? ...................Yes  
Adult Half..........................$27  
Child Half..........................$24  
6-12/65+ Half ....................$16  
Lodging............800-272-7426  
Snow Report ....800-272-7426  

*NEW:2 surface lifts, tubing area, Wild Ride terrain park*

## Brighton Ski Resort

Location: 25m from Salt Lake City, I-15 South to I-215 E  
Star Route, Brighton, Utah 84121  
Web Site: www.skibrighton.com  

Base Elevation (ft)..........8755  
Vertical Drop (ft).............1745  
Avg Snowfall (in)..............500  
Runs:...Green 21%  Blue 40%  
Date Open .......Mid November  
Hours................9 a.m.-9 p.m.  
Tickets: Adult Full ...........$29  
Tickets: Night....................$20  
Main..................801-532-4731  
Lodging............801-532-4731  
Snow Report .....801-943-8309  

Summit (ft) ...................10500  
Skiable Acres....................850  
Number of Lifts...................7  
Black 39%  DoubleBlack-  
Date Close......................April  
Night Skiing? ...................Yes  
Adult Half..........................$26  
Over 70................................$0  
Toll Free ...........800-873-5512  
Fax ....................801-649-1787  

*NEW:$2 million in capital improvements, terrain park*

## Deer Valley Resort

Location: 35m from Salt Lake City, I-80 to Hwy-224
PO Box 3149, Park City, Utah 84060
Web Site: www.deervalley.com

| | |
|---|---|
| Base Elevation (ft)..........7200 | Summit (ft) .....................9400 |
| Vertical Drop (ft)..............2200 | Skiable Acres....................600 |
| Avg Snowfall (in)..............300 | Number of Lifts.................14 |
| Runs:...Green 15% Blue 50% | Black 35% DoubleBlack- |
| Date Open ............December 6 | Date Close................April 12 |
| Hours.........9 a.m.-4:15pm | Night Skiing?.....................No |
| Tickets: Adult Full ...........$54 | Adult Half.........................$38 |
| Tickets: 12 & under...........$29 | Child Half.........................$22 |
| Tickets: Seniors 65+..........$38 | Senior Half........................$25 |
| Main................801-649-1000 | Toll Free ..........800-424-3337 |
| Lodging.........800-424-3337 | Fax ...................801-645-6939 |
| Snow Report .....801-649-2000 | |

*NEW:triple chair, 200 acres glade skiing, increased fleet of snowcats.*

*1st class, top-quality resort. Terrific groomed terrain & family ski experience. Stein Erickson is the man here. A great skier and consummate story teller. A living legend on skis.*

## Elk Meadows Ski And Summer Resort

Location: 17m E of Beaver on Hwy 153
PO Box 511 Dept SP, Beaver, Utah 84713
Web Site: www.elkmeadows.com

| | |
|---|---|
| Base Elevation (ft)..........9100 | Summit (ft) ...................10400 |
| Vertical Drop (ft)..............1300 | Skiable Acres....................400 |
| Avg Snowfall (in)..............400 | Number of Lifts...................5 |
| Runs:...Green 14% Blue 62% | Black 24% DoubleBlack- |
| Date Open.........Thanksgiving | Date Close.....................April |
| Hours.........9 a.m.-4 p.m. | Night Skiing?.....................No |
| Tickets: Adult Full ...........$30 | Adult Half.........................$22 |
| Tickets: Child Full............$15 | Child Half.........................$12 |
| Tickets: 65+........................$0 | |
| Main................801-438-5433 | Lodging.........888-881-SNOW |
| Fax ...................801-438-2598 | Snow Report .....801-438-5433 |

*NEW:quad lift, double chair, base area lodge, 3 snowcats & shuttle buses*

## Nordic Valley Ski Mountain

Location: 15m NE of Ogden
Eden, Utah 84403

| | |
|---|---|
| Base Elevation (ft)..........5400 | Summit (ft) .....................6400 |
| Vertical Drop (ft)............1000 | Skiable Acres......................85 |
| Avg Snowfall (in)..............300 | Number of Lifts...................2 |
| Runs:...Green 30% Blue 50% | Black 20% DoubleBlack- |

Photo courtesy of Loveland Ski Area

| | |
|---|---|
| Date Open .......Mid November | Date Close .............Mid March |
| Hours...............9 a.m.-10 p.m. | Night Skiing? ....................Yes |
| Tickets: Adult Full ............$15 | Adult Night.......................$10 |
| Tickets: Child Full...............$8 | Child Night ........................$8 |
| Tickets: Senior, under 5 ......$5 | |
| Main..................801-392-0900 | Lodging.............801-745-2621 |
| Fax ...................801-392-1293 | Snow Report .....801-521-8102 |

## *Park City Mountain Resort*

Location: 27m from Salt Lake City, I-80 to Hwy 224
PO Box 39, Park City, Utah 84060
Web Site: www.pcski.com

| | |
|---|---|
| Base Elevation (ft)...........6900 | Summit (ft) ...................10000 |
| Vertical Drop (ft)............3100 | Skiable Acres...................2200 |
| Avg Snowfall (in).............350 | Number of Lifts..................15 |
| Runs:...Green 16%  Blue 45% | Black 39%  DoubleBlack- |
| Date Open..........November 14 | Date Close.................April 19 |
| Hours.................9 a.m.-9 p.m. | Night Skiing? ...................Yes |
| Tickets: Adult Full ............$52 | Child Full.........................$23 |

| | |
|---|---|
| Tickets: Adult Half............$37 | Child Half............................$18 |
| Tickets: Adult Night..........$18 | Over 70 ................................$0 |
| Main..................801-649-8111 | Lodging.............800-222-7275 |
| Fax ...................801-647-5374 | Snow Report .....801-647-5449 |

*NEW:$7 million in improvements, 2 hi-spd 6 pass chairs, 4 runs, lighted terrain park & halfpipe, 25 acres expanded snowmaking*

## Powder Mountain Ski Resort

Location: 19m from Ogden, 55m from Salt Lake City
P.O. Box 450, Eden, Utah 84310
Web Site: http://members.aol.com/powdermtn/

| | |
|---|---|
| Base Elevation (ft)...........7600 | Summit (ft) ......................8900 |
| Vertical Drop (ft)..............1300 | Skiable Acres...................4000 |
| Avg Snowfall (in)..............500 | Number of Lifts....................7 |
| Runs:...Green 10% Blue 60% | Black 30% DoubleBlack- |
| Date Open .......Mid November | Date Close .........................May |
| Hours.................9:30am-10 p.m. | Night Skiing? .....................Yes |
| Tickets: Adult Full ...........$27 | Adult Half...........................$22 |
| Tickets: Child Full............$16 | Child Half............................$15 |
| Tickets: Adult Night..........$14 | Over 65 ..............................$21 |
| Main..................801-745-3772 | Lodging.............801-745-3772 |
| Fax ...................801-745-3619 | Snow Report .....801-745-3771 |

## Snowbasin Resort

Location: 52m from Salt Lake City, 17m E of Ogden
PO Box 460, Huntsville, Utah 84317
Web Site: www.snowbasin.com

| | |
|---|---|
| Base Elevation (ft)...........6400 | Summit (ft) ......................8800 |
| Vertical Drop (ft)..............2400 | Skiable Acres...................1800 |
| Avg Snowfall (in)..............400 | Number of Lifts....................5 |
| Runs:...Green 20% Blue 50% | Black 30% DoubleBlack- |
| Date Open..........Thanksgiving | Date Close .......................April |
| Hours.................9 a.m.-4 p.m. | Night Skiing?.....................No |
| Tickets: Adult Full ..........$29 | Adult Half...........................$24 |
| Tickets: Child Full............$20 | Child Half............................$17 |
| Tickets: Over 65 Full.........$21 | Over 65 Half.......................$19 |
| Main..................801-399-1135 | Lodging.........801-ALL-UTAH |
| Fax ...................801-399-1138 | Snow Report .....801-399-0198 |

*NEW:beginning construction of 2002 Olympic Downhill Course*

## Snowbird Ski & Summer Resort

Location: 25m from Salt Lake City, I-80 E to I-215 S
P.O. Box 929000, Snowbird, Utah 84092-9000
Web Site: www.snowbird.com

| | |
|---|---|
| Base Elevation (ft)...........7760 | Summit (ft) ...................11000 |

| | |
|---|---|
| Vertical Drop (ft)............3240 | Skiable Acres..................2500 |
| Avg Snowfall (in)............500 | Number of Lifts...................9 |
| Runs:...Green 20% Blue 35% | Black 40% DoubleBlack 5%% |
| Date Open..........November 23 | Date Close ................May 10 |
| Hours................9 a.m.-4:30 p.m. | Night Skiing?........................No |

Tickets:

| | |
|---|---|
| Adult Full w Tram.......$47 | w/o Tram ..........................$39 |
| 65+, -12 Full w Tram ...$34 | w/o Tram ..........................$27 |
| Adult Half w Tram.......$39 | w/o Tram ..........................$32 |
| Main................801-742-2222 | Toll Free ..........800-453-3000 |
| Lodging............800-640-2002 | Fax ..................801-742-3344 |
| Snow Report .....801-742-2222 | |

*NEW:Hi speed quad, 400 acres of snowcat skiing, night skiing*

*One of the top spots for skiing anywhere! Has a great variety of terrain. Renowned for powder, steeps and bumps. Owned by "7 Summits" author, Dick Bass, a passionate skier and storyteller. If you get a chance to ski with him, take it. He is a gas!*

## Solitude Ski Resort

Location: 23m from Salt Lake City, I-215 S to Exit 6
12000 Big Cottonwood Canyon, Solitude, Utah 84121
Web Site: www.skisolitude.com

| | |
|---|---|
| Base Elevation (ft)...........7988 | Summit (ft) ...................10035 |
| Vertical Drop (ft)............2047 | Skiable Acres..................1200 |
| Avg Snowfall (in)............450 | Number of Lifts...................7 |
| Runs:...Green 20% Blue 50% | Black 30% DoubleBlack- |
| Date Open.............November 1 | Date Close ..........Late April |
| Hours................9 a.m.-4 p.m. | Night Skiing?........................No |
| Tickets: Adult Full ............$36 | Adult Half .......................$30 |
| Tickets: 60-69 ..................$29 | Over 70, under 10 ...............$0 |
| Main.................801-534-1400 | Toll Free ..........800-748-4754 |
| Lodging............801-536-5700 | Fax ..................801-649-5276 |
| Snow Report .....801-536-5777 | |

*NEW:electronic ticket*

*Skied here for the 1st time in '96/97. Great terrain for all abilities. Has some surprisingly steep terrain for experts. Family oriented.*

## Sundance

Location: 50m from Salt Lake City, 13m from Provo on Hwy 89
RR3 Box A-1, Sundance, Utah 84604
Web Site: www.skiutah.com

| | |
|---|---|
| Base Elevation (ft)..........6100 | Summit (ft) ....................8250 |
| Vertical Drop (ft)............2150 | Skiable Acres..................450 |
| Avg Snowfall (in)............320 | Number of Lifts...................3 |
| Runs:...Green 20% Blue 40% | Black 40% DoubleBlack- |
| Date Open ..........December 1 | Date Close ......................April |

| Hours | 9 a.m.-4:30 p.m. | Night Skiing? | No |
| Tickets: Adult Full | $35 | Adult Half | $27 |
| Tickets: Child Full | $22 | Child Half | $16 |
| Tickets: Over 65 | $0 | | |
| Main | 801-225-4107 | Toll Free | 800-892-1600 |
| Lodging | 801-225-4107 | Fax | 801-226-1937 |
| Snow Report | 801-225-4100 | | |

*Created by Robert Redford in 1969*

## *The Canyons*

Location: 28m from Salt Lake City, I-80 to Hwy 224
4000 Park West Drive, Park City, Utah 84098
Web Site: www.thecanyons.com

| Base Elevation (ft) | 6800 | Summit (ft) | 9380 |
| Vertical Drop (ft) | 2580 | Skiable Acres | 2000 |
| Avg Snowfall (in) | 300 | Number of Lifts | 9 |
| Runs:...Green 16% Blue 38% | | Black 46% DoubleBlack- | |
| Date Open | December 20 | Date Close | April 19 |
| Hours | 9 a.m.-4:30 p.m. | Night Skiing? | No |
| Tickets: Adult Full | $32 | Adult Half | $24 |
| Tickets: Over 70 | $0 | 10 & under | $0 |
| Main | 801-649-5400 | Toll Free | 800-754-1636 |
| Fax | 801-649-7374 | Snow Report | 801-521-8102 |

**NEW:Almost everything! American Skiing Co. owned w/ $18 million to spend.** *Check out "Doby," one of the area's top instructors, who's certified in Harald Harb's Primary Movement Teaching System.*

Photo courtesy of Nordica (Prince Sports Group)

**Many families have fun skiing together**

# Vermont

## *Ascutney Mountain Resort*

Location: 6m from Exit 8 off I-91
PO Box 699, Rt. 44, Brownsville, Vermont 05037

| | |
|---|---|
| Base Elevation (ft)............720 | Summit (ft) .....................2250 |
| Vertical Drop (ft)............1530 | Skiable Acres.................47 tr |
| Avg Snowfall (in) .............48" | Number of Lifts....................4 |
| Runs:...Green 35% Blue 30% | Black 35% DoubleBlack- |
| Date Open......Late November | Date Close...........Mid April |
| Hours............8:30 a.m.-4 p.m. | Night Skiing?......................No |
| Tickets: Adult Wkdy ........$34 | Adult Wkend ...................$39 |
| Tickets: Adult Half...........$29 | 7-16/ 65+, Full...............$26 |
| Tickets: 7-16/ 65+, Half .....$20 | 6 & under/70+ .................$0 |
| Main................802-484-7711 | Fax .................802-484-3925 |
| Snow Report .....800-243-0011 | |

## *Bolton Valley Resort*

Location: 20m from Burlington, Boston 197m
Bolton, Vermont 05477

| | |
|---|---|
| Base Elevation (ft)...........1525 | Summit (ft) .....................3150 |
| Vertical Drop (ft)............1625 | Skiable Acres....................150 |
| Avg Snowfall (in) .............250 | Number of Lifts....................6 |
| Runs:...Green 28% Blue 49% | Black 23% DoubleBlack- |
| Date Open..........Thanskgiving | Date Close ..............Mid April |
| Hours..............9 a.m.-10 p.m. | Night Skiing? ...................Yes |
| Tickets: Adult Wkdy ........$32 | Adult Wkend ...................$36 |
| Tickets: Adult Half...........$24 | 6-12/65+ Wkdy .............$22 |
| Tickets: 6-12/65+ Wkend..$24 | Adult Night ....................$18 |
| Main................802-434-2131 | Toll Free ..........800-451-3220 |
| Lodging............800-451-3220 | Snow Report .....800-451-3220 |

*6 & under/72+, Free*

## *Bromley Mountain*

Location: 6m from Manchester, Albany 70m
Box 1130, Manchester, Vermont 05255
Web Site: www.bromley.com

| | |
|---|---|
| Base Elevation (ft)..........1950 | Summit (ft) .....................3284 |
| Vertical Drop (ft)............1334 | Skiable Acres....................175 |
| Avg Snowfall (in).............150 | Number of Lifts....................9 |
| Runs:...Green 35% Blue 34% | Black 31% DoubleBlack- |
| Date Open .......Mid November | Date Close......................April |
| Hours.................9 a.m.-4 p.m. | Night Skiing?......................No |
| Tickets: Adult Wkdy ........$35 | Adult Wkend ...................$46 |
| Tickets: 7-12 Wkend ........$30 | 65+ Wkdy .......................$25 |
| Tickets: 65-69 Wkend .......$30 | 6 & under/70+ (Wkend) ......$0 |
| Main................802-824-5522 | Lodging............800-865-4786 |

Fax .................802-824-3659    Snow Report .....802-824-5522

## *Burke Mountain*

Location: 25 Mins from St Johnsbury, Boston/Spgfld 3 Hrs
PO Box 247, E Burke, Vermont 05832
Web Site: www.burkemountain.com

| | |
|---|---|
| Base Elevation (ft)..........1200 | Summit (ft) ......................3200 |
| Vertical Drop (ft)............2000 | Skiable Acres...................178 |
| Avg Snowfall (in).............200 | Number of Lifts ...................4 |
| Runs:...Green 14%  Blue 40% | Black 44%  DoubleBlack- |
| Date Open.........Thanksgiving | Date Close ....................Easter |
| Hours.................9 a.m.-4 p.m. | Night Skiing?......................No |
| Tickets: Wkday Full..........$25 | Adult Wked ....................$42 |
| Tickets: Halfday.................$-8 | Teen/Sr Wked ................$37 |
| Tickets: Jr Wkend.............$28 | |
| Main..................802-626-3305 | Toll Free ...........800-541-5480 |
| Lodging ............877-BURKEVT | Fax ...................802-626-1323 |
| Snow Report...877-SKI-BURKE | |

## *Cochran Ski Area*

Location: 12m from Burlington on I-89, Montpelier 25m
910 Cochran Rd, Richmond, Vermont 05477

| | |
|---|---|
| Base Elevation (ft)............350 | Summit (ft) ......................850 |
| Vertical Drop (ft)..............500 | Skiable Acres.....................30 |
| Avg Snowfall (in) .............90" | Number of Lifts ...................4 |
| Runs:...Green 20%  Blue 60% | Black 20%  DoubleBlack- |
| Date Open .........December 15 | Date Close.................March 30 |
| Hours.................Varied times | Night Skiing?......................No |
| Tickets: Adult Wkend ......$12 | Child Wkend ....................$10 |
| Tickets: Wkend Half ..........$9 | |
| Main..................802-434-2479 | |

## *Jay Peak Resort*

Location: off Rt 242 in Jay VT.
Route 242, Jay, Vermont 05859
Web Site: www.jaypeakresort.com

| | |
|---|---|
| Base Elevation (ft)............1815 | Summit (ft) ......................3968 |
| Vertical Drop (ft)............2153 | Skiable Acres...................385 |
| Avg Snowfall (in).............325 | Number of Lifts ...................7 |
| Runs:...Green 20%  Blue 40% | Black 40%  DoubleBlack- |
| Date Open .........November 15 | Date Close ........................May 1 |
| Hours.................9 a.m.-4 p.m. | Night Skiing?......................No |
| Tickets: Adult Full ...........$44 | Adult Half ........................$32 |
| Tickets: 14 & under Full ...$32 | 14 & under Half................$25 |
| Main..................802-988-2611 | Toll Free ...........800-451-4449 |
| Lodging............800-451-4449 | Fax ...................802-988-4049 |
| Snow Report....802-988-9601 | |

*150 acres of glade skiing, maximizes use of natural snow*

### Killington Ski Area

Location: 16m from Rutland, Albany 110m, Boston 150m
Killington, Vermont 05751
Web Site: www.killington.com

| | |
|---|---|
| Base Elevation (ft)..........1065 | Summit (ft) .....................4241 |
| Vertical Drop (ft).............3176 | Skiable Acres..................1200 |
| Avg Snowfall (in)..............250 | Number of Lifts................32 |
| Runs:...Green 36%  Blue 32% | Black 32%  DoubleBlack- |
| Date Open .........Early October | Date Close ........................June |
| Hours................9 a.m.-4 p.m. | Night Skiing?......................No |
| Tickets: Adult Full ...........$49 | Adult Half ........................$39 |
| Tickets: Jr Full...................$39 | Child/65+ Full .................$31 |
| Tickets: Child Half ............$23 | 65+ Half ...........................$30 |
| Main................802-422-3333 | Lodging............800-621-6867 |
| Snow Report .....802-422-3261 | |

### Mad River Glen

Location: 5m from Waitsfield, Boston 204m
Waitsfield, Vermont 05859
Web Site: www.madriverglen.com

| | |
|---|---|
| Base Elevation (ft)..........1600 | Summit (ft) .....................3600 |
| Vertical Drop (ft).............2000 | Skiable Acres....................115 |
| Avg Snowfall (in)..............250 | Number of Lifts..................4 |
| Runs:...Green 25%  Blue 40% | Black 35%  DoubleBlack- |
| Date Open ...............December | Date Close ..............Mid April |
| Hours................9 a.m.-4 p.m. | Night Skiing?......................No |
| Tickets: Adult Wkdy .........$29 | Adult Wkend ....................$34 |
| Tickets: 6-16/65-69 Wkdy $29 | 6-16/65-69 Wkend............$24 |
| Main................802-496-3551 | |
| Lodging............802-496-3551 | |
| Snow Report .....802-496-2001 | |

### Middlebury College Snow Bowl

Location: 12m from Middlebury
Middlebury, Vermont 05753

| | |
|---|---|
| Base Elevation (ft)..........1600 | Summit (ft) .....................2650 |
| Vertical Drop (ft).............1050 | Skiable Acres....................105 |
| Avg Snowfall (in)..............130 | Number of Lifts..................3 |
| Runs:...Green 30%  Blue 30% | Black 40%  DoubleBlack- |
| Date Open ...............December | Date Close ........................April |
| Hours................9 a.m.-4 p.m. | Night Skiing?......................No |
| Tickets: Adult Wkdy .........$20 | Adult Wkend ....................$26 |
| Tickets: Stud/Sr Wkdy ......$20 | Stud/Sr Wkend .................$20 |
| Tickets: Half .....................$15 | |
| Main................802-388-4356 | Lodging............802-388-7951 |
| Fax ...................802-388-2871 | Snow Report .....802-388-4356 |

## Mount Snow/Haystack Resort

Location: 10 Mins from Wilmington, NYC 4.5 Hrs
Mount Snow, Vermont 05356
Web Site: www.mountsnow.com

| | | |
|---|---|---|
| Base Elevation (ft)..........1880 | Summit (ft) .....................3580 |
| Vertical Drop (ft).............1700 | Skiable Acres....................750 |
| Avg Snowfall (in).............153 | Number of Lifts....................23 |
| Runs:...Green 21% Blue 61% | Black 18% DoubleBlack- |
| Date Open .....Early November | Date Close .............Early May |
| Hours.................9 a.m.-4 p.m. | Night Skiing?.....................No |
| Tickets: Adult Wkdy ........$45 | Adult Wkend ...................$47 |
| Tickets: Jr/65+ Wkdy ........$26 | Jr/65+ Wkend ...................$28 |
| Main.................802-464-3333 | |
| Lodging.........800-245-SNOW | |
| Snow Report .....802-464-2151 | |

## Okemo Mountain

Location: In Ludlow, Rutland 25m
Ludlow, Vermont 05149
Web Site: www.okemo.com

| | | |
|---|---|---|
| Base Elevation (ft)..........1194 | Summit (ft) .....................3344 |
| Vertical Drop (ft).............2150 | Skiable Acres....................500 |
| Avg Snowfall (in).............200 | Number of Lifts....................13 |
| Runs:...Green 30% Blue 50% | Black 20% DoubleBlack- |
| Date Open .....Early November | Date Close.............Late April |
| Hours.................9 a.m.-4 p.m. | Night Skiing?.....................No |
| Tickets: 19-64 Wkdy ........$46 | 19-64 Wkend ...................$50 |
| Tickets: 13-18 Wkdy ........$39 | 13-18 Wkend ...................$42 |
| Tickets: 7-12/65+ Wkdy....$29 | 7-12/65+ Wkend...............$31 |
| Main.................802-228-4041 | Toll Free.......800-78-OKEMO |
| Lodging............802-228-5571 | |
| Snow Report .....802-228-5222 | |

## Quechee Lakes

Location: 5m from Rt 89, 10m from White River Junction
PO Box 1301, Quechee, Vermont 05059

| | | |
|---|---|---|
| Base Elevation (ft).............600 | Summit (ft) .....................1250 |
| Vertical Drop (ft)...............650 | Skiable Acres....................150 |
| Avg Snowfall (in).............110 | Number of Lifts.....................3 |
| Runs:...Green 40% Blue 60% | Black- DoubleBlack- |
| Date Open .........December 15 | Date Close.............March 15 |
| Hours.................9 a.m.-4 p.m. | Night Skiing?.....................No |
| Tickets: Adult Daily .........$22 | Adult Half........................$18 |
| Tickets: Under 14 Daily ....$18 | Under 14 Half ...................$14 |
| Tickets: Under6/ 70+...........$0 | |
| Main.................802-295-9356 | |
| Fax ..................802-295-1527 | |

## Smugglers' Notch Resort

Location: 25m from Stowe, Burlington 30m, Rt 15 to 108S
4323 Vermont Rt 108S, Smuggler's Notch, Vermont 05464
Web Site: www.smuggs.com

| | |
|---|---|
| Base Elevation (ft)............1030 | Summit (ft) ....................3640 |
| Vertical Drop (ft)............2610 | Skiable Acres................1000 |
| Avg Snowfall (in)..............283 | Number of Lifts..................8 |
| Runs:..Green 21%  Blue 56% | Black 23%  DoubleBlack- |
| Date Open.........November 28 | Date Close .............Mid April |
| Hours.................8:30 a.m.-4 p.m. | Night Skiing?......................No |
| Tickets: Adult Wkdy ........$40 | Adult Wkend ....................$44 |
| Tickets: Adult Half...........$34 | 7-17/65+ Wkdy ..............$28 |
| Tickets: 7-17/65+ Wkend..$28 | 7-17/65+ Half ..................$22 |
| Main ..................802-644-8851 | Toll Free ..........800-451-8752 |
| Fax ...................802-644-2713 | |
| Snow Report .....802-644-1111 | |

## Stowe Mountain Resort

Location: 40 mins from Burlington, N on Rt 100
5781 Mountain Road, Stowe, Vermont 05672
Web Site: www.stowe.com

| | |
|---|---|
| Base Elevation (ft)...........2033 | Summit (ft) ....................4393 |
| Vertical Drop (ft)............2360 | Skiable Acres................480 |
| Avg Snowfall (in).............260 | Number of Lifts................11 |
| Runs:..Green 16%  Blue 59% | Black 25%  DoubleBlack- |
| Date Open .......Mid November | Date Close.............Late April |
| Hours..................8am-10 p.m. | Night Skiing?...................Yes |
| Tickets: Adult 2 Day Reg..$87 | Adult 2 Day Hol ..............$99 |
| 6-12/65+ 2 Day Reg ......$45 | 6-12/65+ 2 Day Hol........$52 |
| Main..................802-253-3000 | Toll Free ..........800-253-4754 |
| Lodging........800-253-4754 | Fax ...................802-253-3439 |
| Snow Report ....802-253-3600 | |

***NEW:3 new grooming machines, Burton Riding Ctr, Advance Ticket Sales***

## Stratton Mountain

Location: 4m from Bondville, Brattleboro 35m
Stratton Mountain, Vermont 05155
Web Site: http://stratton.com

| | |
|---|---|
| Base Elevation (ft)..........1872 | Summit (ft) ....................3936 |
| Vertical Drop (ft)............2064 | Skiable Acres................563 |
| Avg Snowfall (in).............196 | Number of Lifts................12 |
| Runs:..Green 34%  Blue 38% | Black 28%  DoubleBlack- |
| Date Open .......Mid November | Date Close.............Late April |
| Hours.................8:30 a.m.-4 p.m. | Night Skiing?......................No |
| Tickets: Adult Wkdy ........$40 | Adult Wkend ....................$46 |
| Tickets: Adult Half...........$39 | 7-12 Full ........................$30 |

Tickets: 6 & under...............$0
Main.................802-297-2200      Toll Free .........800-STRATTON
Lodging..........800-787-2886
Snow Report .....802-297-4211

## Sugarbush Ski Resort

Location: 3m from Warren, 45m from Burlington Airport
Warren, Vermont 05674

| | |
|---|---|
| Base Elevation (ft)...........1495 | Summit (ft) .....................4135 |
| Vertical Drop (ft).............2640 | Skiable Acres....................435 |
| Avg Snowfall (in)..............282 | Number of Lifts..................18 |
| Runs:...Green 23%  Blue 48% | Black 29%  DoubleBlack- |
| Date Open .....Early November | Date Close...............Mid May |
| Hours.................9 a.m.-4 p.m. | Night Skiing?......................No |
| Tickets: 14-64 Full ...........$47 | 14-64 Half .......................$35 |
| Tickets: 7-13/65-69 .........$28 | 6 & under/70+ ...................$0 |
| Main.................802-583-2381 | |
| Lodging ..........800-53-SUGAR | |
| Snow Report .....802-583-7669 | |

## Suicide Six Ski Area

Location: 3m N of Woodstock
Woodstock, Vermont 05041

| | |
|---|---|
| Base Elevation (ft).............550 | Summit (ft) .....................1200 |
| Vertical Drop (ft)...............650 | Skiable Acres....................100 |
| Avg Snowfall (in)................80 | Number of Lifts...................3 |
| Runs:...Green 30%  Blue 40% | Black 30%  DoubleBlack- |
| Date Open........Mid December | Date Close.............Late March |
| Hours.................9 a.m.-4 p.m. | Night Skiing?......................No |
| Tickets: Adult Wkdy .........$20 | Adult Wkend ....................$36 |
| Tickets: Adult Half ............$16 | Child Wkdy ......................$16 |
| Tickets: Child Wkend........$23 | Child Half ........................$13 |
| Main.................802-457-6661 | Toll Free ..........800-448-7900 |
| Lodging............802-457-1100 | Fax ....................802-475-3830 |
| Snow Report .....802-457-6666 | |

# Virginia

## Bryce Resort

Location: 12m From Mt Jackson/Wash DC 110m
Basye, VA 22810

| | |
|---|---|
| Base Elevation (ft)...........1250 | Summit (ft) .....................1750 |
| Vertical Drop (ft)..............500 | Skiable Acres......................25 |
| Avg Snowfall (in) .............30" | Number of Lifts....................5 |
| Runs:...Green 34%  Blue 33% | Black 33%  DoubleBlack- |
| Date Open......Early December | Date Close.............Mid March |
| Hours.................9 a.m.-9:30pm | Night Skiing? ...................Yes |
| Tickets: Adult Wkdy .........$23 | Adult Wkend ....................$37 |

| | |
|---|---|
| Tickets: Jr/SrWkdy............$23 | Jr/SrWkend......................$32 |
| Tickets: Night....................$15 | |
| Main.............540-856-2121 | Toll Free ...........800-821-1444 |
| Lodging.............540-477-2911 | Fax ....................540-856-8567 |
| Snow Report .....800-821-1444 | |

## *Massanutten Resort*

Location: Harrisonburg 15m/Wash DC 125m
Harrisonburg, VA 22801

| | |
|---|---|
| Base Elevation (ft)...........1770 | Summit (ft) ......................2880 |
| Vertical Drop (ft).............1110 | Skiable Acres......................68 |
| Avg Snowfall (in) ..............50" | Number of Lifts.....................5 |
| Runs:...Green 31% Blue 29% | Black 40% DoubleBlack- |
| Date Open......Late November | Date Close ............Mid March |
| Hours.................9 a.m.-10 p.m. | Night Skiing? ....................Yes |
| Tickets: Adult Wkdy..........$30 | Adult Wkend ....................$42 |
| Tickets: Adult Night..........$20 | Jr Wkdy ............................$25 |
| Tickets: Jr Wkend..............$34 | Jr Night..............................$15 |
| Main.................540-289-4954 | |
| Fax ...................540-289-6414 | |
| Snow Report ....800-207-MASS | |

## *The Homestead Ski Area*

Location: 65m from Roanoke/Wash DC 200m
Hot Springs, VA 24445

| | |
|---|---|
| Base Elevation (ft)...........2500 | Summit (ft) ......................3200 |
| Vertical Drop (ft)..............700 | Skiable Acres......................45 |
| Avg Snowfall (in) ..............50" | Number of Lifts.....................5 |
| Runs:...Green 34% Blue 33% | Black 33% DoubleBlack- |
| Date Open........Mid December | Date Close ............Mid March |
| Hours.................9 a.m.-10 p.m. | Night Skiing? ....................Yes |
| Tickets: Adult Wkdy ........$25 | Adult Wkend ....................$34 |
| Tickets: Adult Night..........$15 | Jr WkdyNite ......................$10 |
| Tickets: Jr Wkend..............$15 | |
| Main.................540-839-7721 | Toll Free ...........800-838-1766 |
| Fax ...................540-839-5954 | |
| Snow Report .....800-838-1766 | |

*Night Skiing Fri & Sat only*

## *Wintergreen*

Location: 43m SW of Charlottesville/Richmond 113m
Wintergreen, VA 22958

| | |
|---|---|
| Base Elevation (ft)...........2512 | Summit (ft) ......................3515 |
| Vertical Drop (ft).............1003 | Skiable Acres......................86 |
| Avg Snowfall (in) ..............40" | Number of Lifts.....................5 |
| Runs:...Green 20% Blue 42% | Black 21% DoubleBlack 17% |
| Date Open........Mid December | Date Close............Late March |

Photo by Ron Dahlquist, used courtesy of Steamboat Powdercats

| | |
|---|---|
| Hours.................9 a.m.-11pm | Night Skiing? ....................Yes |
| Tickets: Adult Wkdy.........$32 | Adult Wkend .....................$40 |
| Tickets: Wkend Night ......$20 | Jr/Sr Wkdy........................$26 |
| Tickets: Jr/Sr Wkend.........$33 | Jr/Sr Night ........................$18 |
| Main.................804-325-2200 | |
| Fax ..................804-325-7500 | |
| Snow Report .....804-325-2200 | |

*Fri & Sat Night skiing 'til 11pm*

# Washington

## *49 Degree North Ski Resort*

Location: 10m from Chewelah
Chewelah, Washington 99109

| | |
|---|---|
| Base Elevation (ft)..........3930 | Summit (ft) .....................5774 |
| Vertical Drop (ft)............1844 | Skiable Acres....................900 |
| Avg Snowfall (in).............120 | Number of Lifts....................4 |
| Runs:...Green 30%  Blue 40% | Black 30%   DoubleBlack- |
| Date Open.......Late November | Date Close......................April |
| Hours.................9 a.m.-4 p.m. | Night Skiing? ...................Yes |
| Tickets: Wkdy/ All Ages...$19 | Adult Wkend ....................$27 |
| Tickets: Adult Half/62+ ....$21 | 7-12/Jr Wkend ..................$19 |
| Tickets: Under 7 .................$0 | |
| Main.................509-935-6649 | Snow Report .....509-880-9208 |

## Badger Mountain

Location: 4m S of Waterman, Wenatchee 30m, Spokane 140m
Waterville, Washington 98858

| | |
|---|---|
| Base Elevation (ft)..........3000 | Summit (ft) .....................3800 |
| Vertical Drop (ft).............800 | Skiable Acres...................20 |
| Avg Snowfall (in)..............100 | Number of Lifts.................3 |
| Runs:...Green 33% Blue 34% | Black 33% DoubleBlack- |
| Date Open ......Late December | Date Close ......Early March |
| Hours..................11am-4 p.m. | Night Skiing?.......................No |
| Tickets: All Times...........$6 | Season Pass ......................$40 |
| Main................509-745-8409 | |
| Snow Report .....509-745-8409 | |

## Crystal Mountain

Location: 76m from Seattle, Enumclaw 39m, Tacoma 64m
Crystal Mountain, Washington 98022

| | |
|---|---|
| Base Elevation (ft)..........4400 | Summit (ft) .....................7002 |
| Vertical Drop (ft).............2602 | Skiable Acres...................2300 |
| Avg Snowfall (in)..............340 | Number of Lifts.................11 |
| Runs:...Green 13% Blue 57% | Black 30% DoubleBlack- |
| Date Open .......Mid November | Date Close ...............Mid April |
| Hours..................9 a.m.-4:30 p.m. | Night Skiing? ..................Yes |
| Tickets: 7-69 Full ...........$25 | 7-69 Night .......................$15 |
| Tickets: Under 6/70+...........$5 | |
| Main................206-663-2265 | Lodging.............206-663-2558 |
| Snow Report ..206-634-3771 | |

*Night Skiing: Fri-Sun & Holidays, 4-10 p.m.*

## Echo Valley Ski Area

Location: 8m W of Chelan, Wenatchee 45m, Spokane 172
Po Box 99, Chelan, Washington 98816

| | |
|---|---|
| Base Elevation (ft)..........2800 | Summit (ft) .....................3200 |
| Vertical Drop (ft).............400 | Skiable Acres...................10 tr |
| Avg Snowfall (in) ..............24" | Number of Lifts.................4 |
| Runs:...Green- Blue- | Black- DoubleBlack- |
| Date Open........Mid December | Date Close ..............February |
| Hours................10 a.m.-9 p.m. | Night Skiing? ..................Yes |
| Tickets: 6 & Over..............$15 | Under 5 Free......................$0 |
| Main................509-682-4002 | |

*Open: Sat, Sun. & Hol.*

## Loup Loup Ski Bowl

Location: 10m E of Twisp on Hwy 20, Chelan 45m
Omak, Washington 98841

| | |
|---|---|
| Base Elevation (ft)..........4040 | Summit (ft) .....................5240 |
| Vertical Drop (ft).............1200 | Skiable Acres...................550 |

| | | | |
|---|---|---|---|
| Avg Snowfall (in) | 50" | Number of Lifts | 3 |
| Runs:...Green 20% Blue 40% | | Black 30% DoubleBlack 10% | |
| Date Open | December | Date Close | March |
| Hours | 9:30 a.m.-4 p.m. | Night Skiing? | No |
| Tickets: Wed/All | $16 | Wkend/Hol. | $18 |
| Tickets: Friday/All | $12 | Night | $10 |
| Main | 509-826-2720 | | |
| Fax | 509-826-5469 | | |
| Snow Report | 509-826-2720 | | |

## Mission Ridge Ski Area

Location: 12m from Wenatchee @ Hwy 2 & 97, Seattle 138m
PO Box 1765, Wenatchee, Washington 98807-1765

| | | | |
|---|---|---|---|
| Base Elevation (ft) | 4570 | Summit (ft) | 6770 |
| Vertical Drop (ft) | 2200 | Skiable Acres | 2100 |
| Avg Snowfall (in) | 170 | Number of Lifts | 6 |
| Runs:...Green 10% Blue 60% | | Black 20% DoubleBlack 10% | |
| Date Open | Late November | Date Close | Mid April |
| Hours | 9 a.m.-4 p.m. | Night Skiing? | No |
| Tickets: Adult Wkend | $32 | Adult Wkday | $24 |
| Tickets: 16-20 Wkend | $26 | 16-20 Wkdy | $21 |
| Tickets: 7-15/65+ | $17 | Under 6 | $0 |
| Main | 509-663-6543 | Toll Free | 800-374-1693 |
| Fax | 509-663-1838 | | |
| Snow Report | 509-663-3200 | | |

## Mount Baker Ski Area

Location: 56m from Bellingham on Rt 542, Seattle 2 Hrs
Bellingham, Washington 98226

| | | | |
|---|---|---|---|
| Base Elevation (ft) | 3500 | Summit (ft) | 5050 |
| Vertical Drop (ft) | 1550 | Skiable Acres | 1000 |
| Avg Snowfall (in) | 595 | Number of Lifts | 10 |
| Runs:...Green 30% Blue 42% | | Black 20% DoubleBlack 8% | |
| Date Open | Mid November | Date Close | End April |
| Hours | 9 a.m.-3:30pm | Night Skiing? | No |
| Tickets: Adult Wkdy | $20 | Adult Wkend | $29 |
| Tickets: Jr/60-69Wked | $22 | Jr/60-69 Wkdy | $15 |
| Tickets: Over 70 | $5 | Under 6 | $0 |
| Main | 360-734-6771 | | |
| Fax | 360-734-5332 | | |
| Snow Report | 360-671-0221 | | |

## Mount Spokane Ski Area

Location: N of Spokane Hwy 2 To Hwy 206 E
Spokane, Washington 99021

| | | | |
|---|---|---|---|
| Base Elevation (ft) | 3818 | Summit (ft) | 5883 |
| Vertical Drop (ft) | 2065 | Skiable Acres | 2500 |
| Avg Snowfall (in) | 100 | Number of Lifts | 5 |

Runs:...Green 20%  Blue 50%  Black 30%  DoubleBlack-
Date Open......Early December  Date Close............Late March
Hours..................9 a.m.-4 p.m.  Night Skiing?.......................No
Tickets: Adult Wkday ......$12  Adult Wkend ....................$20
Tickets: Jr Wkday.............$12  Jr Wkend .........................$16
Tickets: Child Wkdy ........$12  Child Wkend ....................$14
Main..................509-238-6281
Lodging............509-238-4543
Snow Report .....509-443-1397

## *Ski Bluewood*

Location: 30 Mins from Dayton, Walla Walla 1hr
PO Box 88, Dayton, Washington 99328
Base Elevation (ft)..........4545  Summit (ft) ......................5670
Vertical Drop (ft)............1125  Skiable Acres.....................430
Avg Snowfall (in)..............300  Number of Lifts....................3
Runs:...Green 25%  Blue 40%  Black 35%  DoubleBlack-
Date Open .....Early November  Date Close .............Early April
Hours................9 a.m.-4 p.m.  Night Skiing?.......................No
Tickets: Adult Full ...........$25  Adult Half.........................$19
Tickets: Jr Full.................$21  Jr Half...............................$17
Tickets: Child/65+ Full .....$19  Child/65+ Half...................$16
Main.................509-382-4725
Fax .................509-382-4726
Snow Report .....509-382-2877

## *Stevens Pass*

Location: 37m from Leavenworth, 78m from Seattle
Leavenworth, Washington 98826
Base Elevation (ft)..........4000  Summit (ft) ......................5800
Vertical Drop (ft)............1800  Skiable Acres...................1125
Avg Snowfall (in)..............105  Number of Lifts.................14
Runs:...Green 11%  Blue 54%  Black 35%  DoubleBlack-
Date Open .......Late November  Date Close .............Early April
Hours................9 a.m.-10 p.m.  Night Skiing? ...................Yes
Tickets: Adult Wkdy ........$23  Adult Wkend ....................$34
Tickets: 7-12/Sr Wkdy .....$18  7-12 Wkend .....................$24
Tickets: Sr Wkend............$26  Night All............................$20
Main.................360-973-2441
Lodging............360-677-2261
Snow Report .....206-634-1645

## *The Summit At Snoqualmie*

Location: 20m from N Bend/46m E of Seattle on I-90
3010 77th Avenue SE #201,
Snoqualmie Pass, Washington 98068
Base Elevation (ft)..........3000  Summit (ft) ......................5400
Vertical Drop (ft)............2400  Skiable Acres...................1916

| Avg Snowfall (in)..............405 | Number of Lifts.....................34 |
|---|---|
| Runs:...Green 34% Blue 36% | Black 20% DoubleBlack 10% |
| Date Open .....Early November | Date Close................Mid April |
| Hours.........9:30 a.m.-10:30pm | Night Skiing? ....................Yes |
| Tickets: Wkend Full..........$28 | Wkend Half ......................$24 |
| Tickets: Mon & Tues.........$15 | Wed - Fri ..........................$18 |
| Tickets: FriSatNgt............$18 | Over 70 ..............................$0 |
| Main................206-232-8182 | Lodging............800-826-6124 |
| Fax ...................425-434-6160 | Snow Report .....206-236-1600 |

## White Pass

Location: 52m W of Yakima on US 12, Seattle 135m S
White Pass, Washington 98937

| Base Elevation (ft)...........4500 | Summit (ft) ......................6000 |
|---|---|
| Vertical Drop (ft)..............1500 | Skiable Acres.....................635 |
| Avg Snowfall (in)..............250 | Number of Lifts.....................5 |
| Runs:...Green 20% Blue 60% | Black 20% DoubleBlack- |
| Date Open .......Mid November | Date Close.................End April |
| Hours.........8:45am-10 p.m. | Night Skiing? ....................Yes |
| Tickets: Adult Wkend .......$31 | Adult Wkday .....................$19 |
| Tickets: Child/65+ Wkend $19 | Child/65+ Wkday ..............$14 |
| Tickets: Night All ..............$10 | Under 6 ..............................$0 |
| Main.................509-672-3100 | |
| Snow Report .....206-634-0200 | |

# West Virginia

## Alpine Lake Resort                    (Unverified data)

Location: 2m from Terra Alta, 120m S of Pittsburg
Rt 2, Box 99D 2, Terra Alta, West Virginia 26764
Web Site: www.alpinelake.com

| Base Elevation (ft)...........2500 | Summit (ft) ......................2852 |
|---|---|
| Vertical Drop (ft)...............352 | Skiable Acres.........................4 |
| Avg Snowfall (in)..............200 | Number of Lifts.....................2 |
| Runs:...Green 50% Blue 50% | Black- DoubleBlack- |
| Date Open ..............December | Date Close....................March |
| Hours.........8am-4 p.m. | Night Skiing?.....................No |
| Tickets: Adult Wkdy ..........$0 | |
| Main.................304-789-2481 | Toll Free ..........800-752-7179 |
| Lodging............304-789-2481 | Fax ...................304-789-3026 |

## Canaan Valley Resort

Location: Take I-66W To Strasburg
Davis, West Virginia 26260
Web Site: www.canaanresort.com

| Base Elevation (ft)...........3430 | Summit (ft) ......................4280 |
|---|---|
| Vertical Drop (ft)...............850 | Skiable Acres.......................79 |
| Avg Snowfall (in)..............160 | Number of Lifts.....................3 |

Runs:...Green 25% Blue 50% Black 25% DoubleBlack-
Date Open......Late November
Date Close ............Early April
Hours................9 a.m.-10 p.m.
Night Skiing? ....................Yes
Tickets: Adult Wkdy ........$27
Adult Wkend ....................$36
Tickets: AdultWkendNgt ..$23
Jr Wkdy ...........................$22
Tickets: Jr Wkend............$28
JrWkendNgt .....................$18
Main................304-866-4121
Lodging............800-622-4121
Fax ..................304-866-2172

## *Oglebay Park Ski Area*

Location: 3m from Wheeling on Rt 88
Wheeling, West Virginia 26003
Base Elevation (ft)..........1000
Summit (ft) ......................1200
Vertical Drop (ft)...............200
Skiable Acres......................40
Avg Snowfall (in)..................
Number of Lifts ...................2
Runs:...Green 100% Blue-
Black-        DoubleBlack-
Date Open ......Late December
Date Close........Late February
Hours..................Noon-9 p.m.
Night Skiing? ....................Yes
Tickets: Adult.................$16
Adult Half ........................$12
Tickets: Student.............$13
StudentHalf.......................$10
Main................304-243-4049
Fax ..................304-243-4111

## *Snowshoe/Silver Creek Ski Area*

Location: 26m S of Marlington on US 219/Elkins 48m

Photo © Ben Blankenburg, courtesy of Vail Resorts/Keystone

**Keystone is opening more than 1200 vertical feet of new expert gladed terrain this year.**

Snowshoe, West Virginia 26209
Web Site: www.snoeshoemtn.com

| | |
|---|---|
| Base Elevation (ft)............3348 | Summit (ft) .....................4848 |
| Vertical Drop (ft)............1500 | Skiable Acres....................200 |
| Avg Snowfall (in)..............180 | Number of Lifts..................11 |
| Runs:...Green 41% Blue 41% | Black 18% DoubleBlack- |
| Date Open .......Mid November | Date Close ............Early April |
| Hours............8:30 a.m.-9 p.m. | Night Skiing? ....................Yes |
| Tickets: Adult Wkdy ........$33 | Adult Wkend ....................$40 |
| Tickets: Jr Wkdy ...............$21 | Jr Wkend ...........................$25 |
| Tickets: Sr Wkdy ..............$25 | Sr Wkend ...........................$40 |
| Main..................304-572-1000 | Lodging............304-572-5252 |
| Fax ...................304-572-3590 | Snow Report ....304-572-4636 |

*Night skiing Fri-Sun 'til 9 p.m.*

## Timberline Four Seasons Resort

Location: 10m S of Davis on Rt 32/Elkins 35m NE
Canaan Valley, West Virginia 26260

| | |
|---|---|
| Base Elevation (ft)............3268 | Summit (ft) .....................4268 |
| Vertical Drop (ft)............1000 | Skiable Acres....................92 |
| Avg Snowfall (in)..............150 | Number of Lifts..................3 |
| Runs:...Green 34% Blue 32% | Black 18% DoubleBlack 16% |
| Date Open......Early December | Date Close ............Early April |
| Hours..................9 a.m.-9 p.m. | Night Skiing? ....................Yes |
| Tickets: Adult Wkdy ........$32 | Adult Wkend ....................$42 |
| Tickets: Adult Wkendngt ...$20 | Jr/Sr Wkdy .......................$22 |
| Tickets: Jr/Sr Wkend .........$30 | Jr/SrWkendngt..................$15 |
| Main..................304-866-4801 | Toll Free ...........800-SNOWING |
| Lodging............800-448-0074 | Fax ...................304-866-4600 |
| Snow Report ....304-866-4828 | |

## Winterplace Ski Resort

Location: 14m from Beckley/ 2 Mins off I-77 @ Ext 28
Flat Top, West Virginia 25841
Web Site: http://wvweb.com/www/winterplace.html

| | |
|---|---|
| Base Elevation (ft)............2997 | Summit (ft) .....................3600 |
| Vertical Drop (ft)..............603 | Skiable Acres....................80 |
| Avg Snowfall (in)..............100 | Number of Lifts..................9 |
| Runs:...Green 41% Blue 44% | Black 15% DoubleBlack- |
| Date Open......Early December | Date Close............Late March |
| Hours..................9 a.m.-10 p.m. | Night Skiing? ....................Yes |
| Tickets: Adult Wkdy ........$27 | Adult Wkend ....................$39 |
| Tickets: AdultWkendnt ......$27 | Jr Wkdy ...........................$19 |
| Tickets: Jr Wkend.............$28 | Jr Wkendngt .....................$20 |
| Main..................304-787-3221 | Lodging............800-607-7669 |
| Fax ...................304-787-9885 | Snow Report .....800-258-3127 |

# Wisconsin

## *Alpine Valley Resort*

Location: 5m To E Troy, 35m To Milwaukee
PO Box 615, East Troy, Wisconsin 53120

Base Elevation (ft)................
Vertical Drop (ft)..............388
Avg Snowfall (in)..............80
Runs:...Green 40%  Blue 40%
Date Open .....Early November
Hours.............10 a.m.-11 p.m.
Tickets: Adult Wkdy ........$21
Tickets: Adult Night.........$19
Tickets: Child Wkend.........$24
Main ...............414-642-7374
Fax ...................414-642-9873
Snow Report .....414-642-7374

Summit (ft) ...................
Skiable Acres..................90
Number of Lifts................16
Black 20%  DoubleBlack-
Date Close............Late March
Night Skiing? ...................Yes
Adult Wkend ...............$27
Child Wkdy .................$18
Child Night....................$16
Toll Free ..........800-227-9395

## *Bruce Mound Winter Sports Area*

Location: 12m from Neillsville, 100m from La Crosse
Neillsville, Wisconsin 54456

Base Elevation (ft).................
Vertical Drop (ft)..............325
Avg Snowfall (in)..............45"
Runs:...Green 35%  Blue 35%
Date Open........Mid December
Hours...........11 a.m.-4 p.m.
Tickets: Adult.....................$9
Tickets: Student...................$8
Main ...............715-743-5140
Fax ...................715-743-5154
Snow Report .....715-743-2296

Summit (ft) ....................
Skiable Acres..................85
Number of Lifts................4
Black 30%  DoubleBlack-
Date Close.................March
Night Skiing?....................No
Child ............................$5

## *Cascade Mountain Inc*

Location: 10 mins from Portage, 30 mins from Madison
W 10441 Cascade Mtn Rd, Portage, Wisconsin 53901

Base Elevation (ft)............817
Vertical Drop (ft)..............460
Avg Snowfall (in)..............42
Runs:...Green 37%  Blue 22%
Date Open..........November 23
Hours................9 a.m.-10 p.m.
Tickets: Adult Wkdy ........$25
Tickets: Under 12 Wkdy ...$18
Tickets: All Nighters .........$20
Main................608-742-5588
Snow Report ...608-742-SNOW

Summit (ft) ...................1277
Skiable Acres..................130
Number of Lifts................9
Black 41%  DoubleBlack-
Date Close................March 24
Night Skiing? ...................Yes
Adult Wkend ...............$30
Under 12 Wkend ...........$20
Over 55 Wkend ............$30
Toll Free..........800-992-2SKI

## Christie Mountain Ski Area

Location: 8m from Bruce, 55m from Eau Claire
Bruce, Wisconsin 54819

| | |
|---|---|
| Base Elevation (ft)...........1300 | Summit (ft) ......................1650 |
| Vertical Drop (ft)..............350 | Skiable Acres......................14 |
| Avg Snowfall (in) .............60" | Number of Lifts ....................3 |
| Runs:...Green 25% Blue 40% | Black 35%  DoubleBlack- |
| Date Open.......Late November | Date Close...............March 20 |
| Hours................10 a.m.-9 p.m. | Night Skiing? ...................Yes |
| Tickets: Adult Wkend ......$22 | Adult Night.......................$12 |
| Tickets: 12-18 .................$17 | 13-18 Night .....................$10 |
| Tickets: 7-11 ...................$14 | Over 65 .............................$11 |
| Main.................715-868-7800 | Toll Free..........800-373-SNOW |
| Fax ...................715-868-7800 | |
| Snow Report ...800-373-SNOW | |

## Christmas Mountain Village

Location: 4m W of Wisconsin Dells, 1 Hr from Madison
Wisconsin Dells, Wisconsin 53965

| | |
|---|---|
| Base Elevation (ft)...........1000 | Summit (ft) ......................1250 |
| Vertical Drop (ft)..............250 | Skiable Acres......................40 |
| Avg Snowfall (in) .............40" | Number of Lifts ....................3 |
| Runs:...Green 40% Blue 40% | Black 20%  DoubleBlack- |
| Date Open........Mid December | Date Close.....................March |
| Hours..............10 a.m.-10 p.m. | Night Skiing? ...................Yes |
| Tickets: Adult Wkdy .........$18 | Adult Wkend ....................$22 |
| Tickets: Under 13 Wkdy ..$14 | Under 13 Wkend ..............$16 |
| Tickets: Night ....................$8 | |
| Main.................608-253-1000 | |
| Fax ...................608-254-3983 | |
| Snow Report .....608-254-3971 | |

## Crystal Ridge Ski Area

Location: 10 Mins from Downtown Milwaukee, Hwy 36 & 894
Milwaukee, Wisconsin 53132

| | |
|---|---|
| Base Elevation (ft)...............90 | Summit (ft) ........................290 |
| Vertical Drop (ft)..............200 | Skiable Acres......................75 |
| Avg Snowfall (in) .............50" | Number of Lifts ....................5 |
| Runs:...Green-  Blue- | Black-  DoubleBlack- |
| Date Open......Early December | Date Close...........Mid March |
| Hours................10 a.m.-10 p.m. | Night Skiing? ...................Yes |
| Tickets: Adult Wkday .......$14 | Adult Wkend ....................$18 |
| Tickets: Child Wkday........$11 | Child Wkend ....................$15 |
| Tickets: Over 65 .................$0 | |
| Main.................414-529-7676 | Fax ...................414-529-7660 |
| Snow Report .414-529-SNOW | |

*Daily Times: 3:30 p.m. -10 p.m., Weekends-10 a.m.-10 p.m.*

## Devil's Head Resort

Location: 10m from Baraboo, 40m from Madison
S6330 Bluff Rd, Merrimac, Wisconsin 53561
Web Site: www.devils-head.com

| | |
|---|---|
| Base Elevation (ft)............495 | Summit (ft) .......................995 |
| Vertical Drop (ft)..............500 | Skiable Acres....................200 |
| Avg Snowfall (in)..............78" | Number of Lifts..................15 |
| Runs:...Green 30% Blue 40% | Black 30% DoubleBlack- |
| Date Open......Late November | Date Close ............Early April |
| Hours...........9:30 a.m.-10 p.m. | Night Skiing? ...................Yes |
| Tickets: Adult Wkday ........$32 | Adult Wkend ....................$36 |
| Tickets: Child Wkday.......$27 | Child Wkend ....................$32 |
| Tickets: Adult Night........$18 | Under 13 Night .................$15 |
| Main................608-493-2251 | Toll Free ..........800-472-6670 |
| Fax ..................608-493-2176 | |
| Snow Report ....800-472-6670 | |

*Over 72, Under 5, Free*

## Grand Geneva Resort

Location: 1m from Lake Geneva, 40m from Milwaukee
Lake Geneva, Wisconsin 53147

| | |
|---|---|
| Base Elevation (ft)...........1085 | Summit (ft) .....................1296 |
| Vertical Drop (ft)..............211 | Skiable Acres....................14 |
| Avg Snowfall (in)..............36 | Number of Lifts..................5 |
| Runs:...Green 35% Blue 40% | Black 25% DoubleBlack- |
| Date Open ............December | Date Close ...............March 15 |
| Hours..............10 a.m.-10 p.m. | Night Skiing? ...................Yes |
| Tickets: Adult Wkdy ........$21 | Adult Wkend ....................$27 |
| Tickets: 4-11 Wkdy...........$18 | 4-11 Wkend .....................$23 |
| Tickets: Adult Night...........$19 | 4-11 Night .......................$16 |
| Main................414-249-4726 | Toll Free ..........800-558-3417 |
| Snow Report ....414-249-4790 | |

## Highlands of Olympia

Location: 30 Mins from Milwaukee on I-94 to WI 67
965 Cannon Gate Rd, PO Box 1018,
Oconomowoc, Wisconsin 53066

| | |
|---|---|
| Base Elevation (ft).................. | Summit (ft) ....................... |
| Vertical Drop (ft)..............188 | Skiable Acres....................18 |
| Avg Snowfall (in)..............60" | Number of Lifts..................3 |
| Runs:...Green 50% Blue 30% | Black 20% DoubleBlack- |
| Date Open......Early December | Date Close ..........Early March |
| Hours..............10 a.m.-10 p.m. | Night Skiing? ...................Yes |
| Tickets: Adult Wkdy ........$14 | Adult Wkend ....................$19 |
| Tickets: Child Wkdy .......$12 | Child Wkend ....................$17 |
| Tickets: Adult Night.........$12 | Under 6 ............................$7 |
| Main................414-567-2577 | |

Fax ..................414-567-5934
Snow Report .....800-558-9573

## *Kettlebowl Hill*     *(Unverified data)*

Location: 15m NE of Antigo on Hwy 52
1633 Neva Rd, Antigo, Wisconsin 54409

| | |
|---|---|
| Base Elevation (ft)................. | Summit (ft) ............................ |
| Vertical Drop (ft)...................0 | Skiable Acres........................... |
| Avg Snowfall (in)............... | Number of Lifts......................5 |
| Runs:...Green-   Blue- | Black-   DoubleBlack- |
| Date Open ..............December | Date Close....................March |
| Hours..................Noon-4 p.m. | Night Skiing?......................No |
| Tickets: Unavailable..........$0 | |
| Main.................715-627-6300 | Fax ...................715-627-6276 |

*Sat, Sun & Holidays only*

## *Keyes Peak Ski Area*

Location: 15m from Iron Mtn, MI on Hwy 2, Green Bay 100m
Florence, Wisconsin 54121

| | |
|---|---|
| Base Elevation (ft)................. | Summit (ft) ............................ |
| Vertical Drop (ft)...............230 | Skiable Acres ...................5 tra |
| Avg Snowfall (in)...............60 | Number of Lifts.....................3 |
| Runs:...Green 20%  Blue 60% | Black 20%  DoubleBlack- |
| Date Open........Mid December | Date Close ............End March |
| Hours .....................Thurs-Sun | Night Skiing? ...................Yes |
| Tickets: Adult.....................$6 | Child ....................................$3 |
| Tickets: Student.................$4 | |
| Main.................715-528-3228 | |

*Open Christmas*

## *Little Switzerland*

Location: 20m NW of Milwaukee, off Hwy 41
Slinger, Wisconsin 53086

| | |
|---|---|
| Base Elevation (ft)................. | Summit (ft) ............................ |
| Vertical Drop (ft)...............200 | Skiable Acres.......................35 |
| Avg Snowfall (in)............45" | Number of Lifts.....................7 |
| Runs:...Green 30%  Blue 40% | Black 30%  DoubleBlack- |
| Date Open.......Late November | Date Close ............Mid March |
| Hours.............10 a.m.-10 p.m. | Night Skiing? ...................Yes |
| Tickets: Adult Wkend ......$20 | Adult Wkday ....................$10 |
| Tickets: Adult Night.........$14 | |
| Main.................414-644-5020 | |
| Fax ...................414-644-9012 | |
| Snow Report .800-358-SNOW | |

Photo © Dann Coffey, courtesy Vail Resorts/Beaver Creek

## *Mont Du Lac Ski Area*

Location: 16m from Duluth on Hwy 23
Hwy 23W, Superior, Wisconsin 54880

| | | | |
|---|---|---|---|
| Base Elevation (ft)............617 | Summit (ft) ......................917 |
| Vertical Drop (ft)..............300 | Skiable Acres......................55 |
| Avg Snowfall (in)................95 | Number of Lifts....................3 |
| Runs:...Green 33% Blue 34% | Black 33% DoubleBlack- |
| Date Open..........November 20 | Date Close................March 31 |
| Hours...........9:30 a.m.-10 p.m. | Night Skiing? ....................Yes |
| Tickets: Adult Wkdy ...........$8 | Adult Wkend ....................$13 |
| Tickets: Under 10, 65+ Wkdy$4 | Under 10, 65+ Wkend ........$7 |
| Tickets: Night ....................$5 | |

Main..................218-626-3797

## Mount Ashwabay

Location: 3m from Bayfield on Hwy 13; Duluth, MN 90m
Bayfield, Wisconsin 54814

| | |
|---|---|
| Base Elevation (ft)............963 | Summit (ft) .....................1280 |
| Vertical Drop (ft)..............317 | Skiable Acres......................65 |
| Avg Snowfall (in)..............120 | Number of Lifts...................5 |
| Runs:...Green 30% Blue 30% | Black 25% DoubleBlack 15% |
| Date Open......Early December | Date Close ............Early April |
| Hours.............9:30 a.m.-10 p.m. | Night Skiing? ...................Yes |
| Tickets: Adult Wkday ........$8 | Adult Wkend ....................$12 |
| Tickets: Child Wkday ........$4 | Child Wkend ......................$7 |
| Tickets: Adult Night...........$6 | Under 12 Night ...................$3 |
| Main..................715-779-3227 | |

*Open Sat, Sun & Xmas vacation; Wed-Sat Nights, 6:30-10 p.m.*

## Mount La Crosse

Location: 2m from La Crosse, 270m from Chicago
PO Box 9, La Crosse, Wisconsin 54602

| | |
|---|---|
| Base Elevation (ft)............594 | Summit (ft) .....................1110 |
| Vertical Drop (ft)..............516 | Skiable Acres....................100 |
| Avg Snowfall (in)..............50 | Number of Lifts...................4 |
| Runs:...Green 20% Blue 50% | Black 30% DoubleBlack- |
| Date Open.........Thanksgiving | Date Close ............Mid March |
| Hours.................10 a.m.-9 p.m. | Night Skiing? ...................Yes |
| Tickets: Adult Wkend ......$30 | Adult Wkday ....................$27 |
| Tickets: Junior Wkend ......$26 | Junior Wkday ...................$23 |
| Tickets: Child Wkend ......$24 | Child Wkdy ......................$21 |
| Main..................608-788-0044 | Toll Free ...........800-426-3665 |
| Snow Report .....608-788-0044 | |

*NEW:Night: Adult, $20; Ages 6-17, $19*

## Nordic Mountain

Location: 8m from Wautoma, 40m from Oshkoshon Hwy 21
Mt Morris, Wisconsin 54984

| | |
|---|---|
| Base Elevation (ft)............872 | Summit (ft) .....................1137 |
| Vertical Drop (ft)..............265 | Skiable Acres....................80 |
| Avg Snowfall (in)..............80 | Number of Lifts...................6 |
| Runs:...Green 15% Blue 50% | Black 35% DoubleBlack- |
| Date Open .............December | Date Close ............Mid March |
| Hours .................Varied Hours | Night Skiing? ...................Yes |
| Tickets: Adult Wkday ......$10 | Adult Wkend ....................$18 |
| Tickets: Child Wkday.........$8 | Child Wkend ....................$14 |
| Tickets: Adult night..........$10 | Child, 65+ Night..................$8 |
| Main..................920-787-3324 | Toll Free ...........800-787-3324 |
| Lodging............920-787-3324 | |

Snow Report .....920-787-3324

## Potawatomi State Park

Location: 5m SW of Sturgeon Bay off Hwy 42 & 57
Sturgeon Bay, Wisconsin 54235

| | |
|---|---|
| Base Elevation (ft)................. | Summit (ft) ............................. |
| Vertical Drop (ft)................110 | Skiable Acres.........................3 |
| Avg Snowfall (in)................... | Number of Lifts ....................3 |
| Runs:...Green 33% Blue 34% | Black 33% DoubleBlack- |
| Date Open .............December | Date Close ......................March |
| Hours .................Wed/Sat/Sun | Night Skiing? .....................Yes |
| Tickets: Adult Daily .........$12 | Student...................................$7 |
| Tickets: Night ..................$7 | Beginner Hill ......................$5 |
| Main.................414-743-7033 | |

## Powers Bluff Winter Recreation Area

Location: 17m from Wisconsin Rapids
Wisconsin Rapids, Wisconsin

| | |
|---|---|
| Base Elevation (ft)...........1222 | Summit (ft) ......................1472 |
| Vertical Drop (ft)............250 | Skiable Acres.........................40 |
| Avg Snowfall (in) .............25" | Number of Lifts ....................1 |
| Runs:...Green 70% Blue 30% | Black- DoubleBlack- |
| Date Open .............December | Date Close......................March |
| Hours..................Noon-8 p.m. | Night Skiing?.....................No |
| Tickets: Adult ..................$4 | Student................................$3 |
| Main.................715-421-8422 | |
| Fax ..................715-421-8808 | |
| Snow Report ...715-421-8480 | |

*Open weekends only, 10 a.m.-5pm. No snowmaking*

## Rib Mountain Ski Area

Location: 3m from Wausau, 275m from Chicago
Wausau, Wisconsin 54402

| | |
|---|---|
| Base Elevation (ft)...........1242 | Summit (ft) ......................1942 |
| Vertical Drop (ft)............700 | Skiable Acres..................13 sl |
| Avg Snowfall (in)...............60 | Number of Lifts ....................4 |
| Runs:...Green 20% Blue 60% | Black 20% DoubleBlack- |
| Date Open......Early December | Date Close .............Mid March |
| Hours..................9 a.m.-10 p.m. | Night Skiing? .....................Yes |
| Tickets: Adult Wkday ......$18 | Adult Wkend ....................$27 |
| Tickets: Child Wkday .....$12 | Child Wkend ....................$17 |
| Tickets: Adult Night.........$18 | Child Night .......................$12 |
| Main.................715-845-2846 | |
| Lodging.............715-845-2846 | |
| Snow Report .....800-236-9728 | |

## *Ski Skyline*

Location: 30m from Wisconsin Rapids, 80m from Madison
Friendship, Wisconsin 53934

| | |
|---|---|
| Base Elevation (ft)..........1242 | Summit (ft)...................1942 |
| Vertical Drop (ft)..............700 | Skiable Acres.....................35 |
| Avg Snowfall (in) .............50" | Number of Lifts....................3 |
| Runs:...Green 25%  Blue 45% | Black 30%  DoubleBlack- |
| Date Open......Early December | Date Close......Early March |
| Hours.................Varied hours | Night Skiing? ...................Yes |
| Tickets: Adult...................$17 | 11-17..............................$11 |
| Tickets: Under 11 .............$15 | Night...................................$9 |
| Tickets: 65+.......................$0 | |
| Main.................608-339-3421 | Fax ..................608-339-4909 |
| Snow Report.....888-SKI-3811 | |

## *Standing Rocks*

Location: 10m from Stevens Point
Stevens Point, Wisconsin 54481

| | |
|---|---|
| Base Elevation (ft).............. | Summit (ft)..................... |
| Vertical Drop (ft)..............125 | Skiable Acres...............5 trails |
| Avg Snowfall (in) .............45" | Number of Lifts....................3 |
| Runs:...Green 25%  Blue 75% | Black-        DoubleBlack- |
| Date Open......Early December | Date Close.........Mid March |
| Hours.................11a.m.-4 p.m. | Night Skiing?.....................No |
| Tickets: Adult.....................$6 | 13-21..................................$5 |
| Tickets: 9-12.......................$4 | Under 9...............................$0 |
| Main.................715-346-1433 | Fax ..................715-346-1486 |
| Snow Report .....715-824-3949 | |

## *Sunburst Ski Area*

Location: 5m from W Bend, 30m from Milwaukee
Kewaskum, Wisconsin 53040

| | |
|---|---|
| Base Elevation (ft)............886 | Summit (ft) .....................1100 |
| Vertical Drop (ft)..............214 | Skiable Acres.....................35 |
| Avg Snowfall (in) .............50" | Number of Lifts....................7 |
| Runs:...Green 20%  Blue 35% | Black 35%  DoubleBlack 10% |
| Date Open.......Late November | Date Close ............Mid March |
| Hours.................4 p.m.-10 p.m. | Night Skiing? ...................Yes |
| Tickets: Adult Wkend ......$24 | Child Wkend ....................$14 |
| Tickets: Adult Night.........$15 | Child Night ......................$14 |
| Main.................414-626-8404 | Fax ..................414-626-2742 |

## *Sylvan Hill Park*

Location: 12m from Wausau
Wausau, Wisconsin 54401

| | |
|---|---|
| Base Elevation (ft)..........1190 | Summit (ft) .....................1300 |
| Vertical Drop (ft)..............110 | Skiable Acres.....................54 |

| Avg Snowfall (in) ............50" | Number of Lifts .....................3 |
|---|---|
| Runs:...Green 60% Blue 40% | Black-       DoubleBlack- |
| Date Open........Mid December | Date Close ..........Early March |
| Hours...........10 a.m.-4:30 p.m. | Night Skiing? ....................Yes |
| Tickets: Adult Daily ...........$5 | Adult Night ........................$4 |
| Tickets: Child Daily ...........$3 | Child Night ........................$2 |
| Main .................715-842-5411 | Fax ...................715-848-9210 |

## *Telemark Resort*

Location: 4m from Cable, 80m from Duluth
Cable, Wisconsin 54821

| Base Elevation (ft)...........1400 | Summit (ft) .....................1770 |
|---|---|
| Vertical Drop (ft)..............370 | Skiable Acres.....................120 |
| Avg Snowfall (in)................70 | Number of Lifts .....................5 |
| Runs:...Green 20% Blue 50% | Black 30% DoubleBlack- |
| Date Open........Late November | Date Close.............Late March |
| Hours...........9 a.m.-4:30 p.m. | Night Skiing?.....................No |
| Tickets: Adult Wkday ......$15 | Adult Wkend ....................$18 |
| Tickets: Junior Wkday ......$13 | Junior Wkend ...................$15 |
| Tickets: Child Wkdy ......$11 | Child Wkend ....................$13 |
| Main .................715-798-3811 | Toll Free ..........800-472-3001 |
| Lodging ...........715-798-3811 | Fax ...................715-798-3790 |
| Snow Report .....715-798-3811 | |

## *Trollhaugen Ski Area*

Location: .5m from Dresser, 60m from Minneapolis/St Paul
Dresser, Wisconsin 54009

| Base Elevation (ft)...........920 | Summit (ft) .....................1200 |
|---|---|
| Vertical Drop (ft)..............280 | Skiable Acres.......................80 |
| Avg Snowfall (in) .............50" | Number of Lifts ...................10 |
| Runs:...Green 29% Blue 43% | Black 28% DoubleBlack- |
| Date Open........November 1 | Date Close.............March 30 |
| Hours.............10 a.m.-10 p.m. | Night Skiing? ....................Yes |
| Tickets: Adult Wkend .......$26 | Adult Wkdy ......................$20 |
| Tickets: 6-12/62+ Wkend...$19 | 6-12/62+ Wkdy ...............$15 |
| Tickets: 6-12/62+ Night ...$14 | Adult Night ......................$17 |
| Main .................715-755-2955 | Toll Free ..........800-826-7166 |
| Fax ...................715-294-4091 | |
| Snow Report .....612-433-5141 | |

## *Tyrol Basin*

Location: 5m from Mt Horeb, 20m from Madison
Mount Horeb, Wisconsin 53572

| Base Elevation (ft)...........860 | Summit (ft) .....................1160 |
|---|---|
| Vertical Drop (ft)..............300 | Skiable Acres.......................24 |
| Avg Snowfall (in)................50 | Number of Lifts .....................5 |
| Runs:...Green 32% Blue 28% | Black 40% DoubleBlack- |
| Date Open........Mid December | Date Close .............Mid March |

| Hours | 10 a.m.-10 p.m. | Night Skiing? | Yes |
| Tickets: Adult Full | $26 | Adult 4 hr | $20 |
| Tickets: Jr Full | $22 | Jr 4 hr | $16 |
| Tickets: Adult Night | $16 | Jr Night | $13 |
| Main | 608-437-4143 | Fax | 608-437-8665 |
| Snow Report | 608-437-4386 | | |

## *Whitecap Mountains*

Location: 10m from Hurley, 200m from Minn/St Paul
Montreal, Wisconsin 54550

| Base Elevation (ft) | 1350 | Summit (ft) | 1750 |
| Vertical Drop (ft) | 400 | Skiable Acres | 500 |
| Avg Snowfall (in) | 200 | Number of Lifts | 8 |
| Runs:...Green 33% Blue 34% | | Black 33% DoubleBlack- | |
| Date Open | Late November | Date Close | Early April |
| Hours | 9 a.m.-9 p.m. | Night Skiing? | Yes |
| Tickets: Adult Wkday | $26 | Adult Wkend | $33 |
| Tickets: Adult Night | $15 | Sr Wkend | $18 |
| Tickets: Jr Wkend | $26 | Child Wkend | $20 |
| Main | 715-561-2227 | Toll Free | 800-933-7669 |
| Fax | 715-561-4442 | Snow Report | 800-272-7000 |

## *Wilmot Mountain*

Location: .5m from Wilmot, 10m from Antioch, IL/Chicago 50m
Wilmot, Wisconsin 53192

| Base Elevation (ft) | | Summit (ft) | |
| Vertical Drop (ft) | 230 | Skiable Acres | 120 |

Photo by Cynthia Hunter used courtesy of Steamboat Ski and Resort Corp.

Avg Snowfall (in)....................
Runs:...Green 30%  Blue 30%
Date Open.......Late November
Hours....................9:30 a.m.-11p.m.
Tickets: Adult Wkday ......$22
Tickets: Child Wkday....$16
Tickets: Adult Night.......$22
Main.................414-862-2301
Fax ...................414-862-2660

Number of Lifts .................14
Black 40%  DoubleBlack-
Date Close............Late March
Night Skiing? ..................Yes
Adult Wkend .................$27
Child Wkend .................$22
Child Night .....................$16
Lodging............414-862-2301
Snow Report .....312-736-0787

## Woodside Ranch

Location: 5m E of Mauston, 20m NW of Wisconsin Dells
Mauston, Wisconsin 53948

Base Elevation (ft)..................
Vertical Drop (ft)..............100
Avg Snowfall (in)............50"
Runs:...Green 10%  Blue-
Date Open .......Late December
Hours ..........................Fri-Sun
Main.................608-847-4275
Snow Report .....608-847-4275

Summit (ft) ........................
Skiable Acres.........................4
Number of Lifts .....................1
Black-        DoubleBlack-
Date Close ............Mid March
Night Skiing? ..................Yes
Toll Free ..........800-626-4275

# Wyoming

## Antelope Butte Ski Area

Location: 35m E of Greybull, 60m W of Sheridan on US 14
Dayton, Wyoming 82836

Base Elevation (ft)..........8400
Vertical Drop (ft)..........1000
Avg Snowfall (in)............200
Runs:...Green 20%  Blue 50%
Date Open........Mid December
Hours ........................Wed-Sun
Tickets: Adult Full ...........$20
Tickets: Jr Full ................$12
Tickets: Sr Full ................$18
Main.................307-655-9530
Snow Report .....307-655-9530

Summit (ft) .....................9400
Skiable Acres.....................250
Number of Lifts .....................3
Black 40%  DoubleBlack-
Date Close............Early April
Night Skiing?.......................No
Adult Half .....................$16
Jr Half ..........................$10
Sr Half ..........................$14
Fax ..................307-655-9529

## Grand Targhee Resort

Location: 42m from Jackson Hole, 87m from Idaho Falls
Box SKI, Alta, Wy C/O Driggs, ID, Wyoming 83422
Web Site: www.grandtarghee.com

Base Elevation (ft)..........8000
Vertical Drop (ft)..........2200
Avg Snowfall (in)............504
Runs:...Green 10%  Blue 70%
Date Open .......Mid November

Summit (ft) ...................10200
Skiable Acres.................1500
Number of Lifts .....................4
Black 20%  DoubleBlack-
Date Close...............Late April

| Hours | 9:30 a.m.-4 p.m. | Night Skiing? | No |
|---|---|---|---|
| Tickets: Adult Full | $39 | Adult Half | $28 |
| Tickets: 6-14/65+ | $24 | Under 5 | $0 |
| Main | 307-353-2300 | Toll Free | 800-827-4433 |
| Lodging | 307-353-2300 | Fax | 307-353-8148 |
| Snow Report | 307-353-2300 | | |

*Offers Rapid Skier Development Program based on Harald Harbs "Accelerated Skier Performance System*

## Hogadon Ski Area

Location: 11m S of Casper on WY 251
1800 East "K" Street, Casper, Wyoming 82601

| Base Elevation (ft) | 7400 | Summit (ft) | 8000 |
|---|---|---|---|
| Vertical Drop (ft) | 600 | Skiable Acres | 90 |
| Avg Snowfall (in) | 140 | Number of Lifts | 3 |
| Runs:...Green 20% Blue 40% | | Black 40% DoubleBlack- | |
| Date Open | Late November | Date Close | Early April |
| Hours | 9 a.m.-4 p.m. | Night Skiing? | No |
| Tickets: Adult Daily | $20 | Adult/Child Half | $13 |
| Tickets: Under 12/65+ Daily | $14 | | |
| Main | 307-235-8499 | Fax | 307-235-8498 |
| Snow Report | 307-235-8369 | | |

## Jackson Hole Ski Resort

Location: 12 miles NW of Jackson, Hwy 390 to Hwy 22
PO Box 290, Teton Village, Wyoming 83025
Web Site: www.jacksonhole.com/ski e-mail: info@jackson

| Base Elevation (ft) | 6311 | Summit (ft) | 10450 |
|---|---|---|---|
| Vertical Drop (ft) | 4139 | Skiable Acres | 2500 |
| Avg Snowfall (in) | 402 | Number of Lifts | 10 |
| Runs:...Green 10% Blue 40% | | Black 50% DoubleBlack- | |
| Date Open | December 6 | Date Close | April 12 |
| Hours | 9 a.m.-4 p.m. | Night Skiing? | No |
| Tickets: Adult Full | $48 | Under 14/65+ Full | $24 |
| Tickets: Adult Half | $36 | Under 14/65+ | $18 |
| Main | 307-733-2292 | Toll Free | 888-DEEP SNO |
| Lodging | 800-443-6931 | Fax | 307-733-2660 |
| Snow Report | 307-733-2291 | | |

*NEW:Bridger Gondola, Children's Moving Carpet, Outdoor Ice Rink*

## Powder Pass Ski Area

Location: Between Buffalo & Worland on US 16
Worland, Wyoming 82401

| Base Elevation (ft) | 8400 | Summit (ft) | 9000 |
|---|---|---|---|
| Vertical Drop (ft) | 600 | Skiable Acres | 110 |
| Avg Snowfall (in) | 160 | Number of Lifts | 3 |

Runs:...Green 50%  Blue 33%   Black 22%  DoubleBlack-
Date Open..........Thanksgiving   Date Close ..............Mid April
Hours .....................Thurs-Sun   Night Skiing?.....................No
Tickets: Adult Full ...........$15   Adult Half.........................$10
Tickets: Under 12 Full.......$10   Under 12 Half....................$7
Main.................307-366-2600   Toll Free ..........800-873-1859
Snow Report .....307-347-9831

Courtesy of Crested Butte Mountain Resort, Tom Stillo photographer

## Sleeping Giant Ski Area

Location: 46m W of Cody on US 14/16/20
349 Yellowstone Hwy, Cody, Wyoming 82414

| | |
|---|---|
| Base Elevation (ft)..........6700 | Summit (ft) .....................7200 |
| Vertical Drop (ft)............500 | Skiable Acres....................120 |
| Avg Snowfall (in)............300 | Number of Lifts....................2 |
| Runs:...Green 20% Blue 60% | Black 20% DoubleBlack- |
| Date Open......Early December | Date Close.............Late March |
| Hours...........9 a.m.-4 p.m. | Night Skiing?....................No |
| Tickets: Adult Full ...........$18 | Adult Half...........................$14 |
| Tickets: Child Full............$8 | Child Half............................$6 |
| Main ....................307-587-4044 | |
| Fax ....................307-587-2681 | |
| Snow Report .307-527-SNOW | |

*Open Fri-Sun & holidays only*

## Snow King Ski Area

Location: 1/8 m from Jackson, 100m from Idaho Falls, ID
Jackson Hole Ski Corporation, PO Box 290,
Teton Village, Wyoming 83001

| | |
|---|---|
| Base Elevation (ft)..........6237 | Summit (ft) .....................7808 |
| Vertical Drop (ft)............1571 | Skiable Acres....................110 |
| Avg Snowfall (in)............150 | Number of Lifts....................4 |
| Runs:...Green 15% Blue 25% | Black 60% DoubleBlack- |
| Date Open.........Thanksgiving | Date Close.............Late March |
| Hours................10 a.m.-8 p.m. | Night Skiing? ....................Yes |
| Tickets: Adult Full ...........$28 | Adult Half...........................$20 |
| Tickets: Child/60+ Full .....$18 | Child/60+ Half...................$12 |
| Tickets: Adult Night..........$14 | Child/Over 60+.....................$9 |
| Main ...................307-733-5200 | Toll Free ...........800-522-KING |
| Lodging............307-733-5200 | Fax ...........307-733-4086 |
| Snow Report .....307-734-2020 | |

## Snowy Range

Location: 32m W of Laramie
Wyoming

| | |
|---|---|
| Base Elevation (ft)..........9000 | Summit (ft) .....................9990 |
| Vertical Drop (ft)............990 | Skiable Acres....................250 |
| Avg Snowfall (in)............250 | Number of Lifts....................5 |
| Runs:...Green 30% Blue 40% | Black 30% DoubleBlack- |
| Date Open.........Thanksgiving | Date Close .............Mid April |
| Hours................9 a.m.-4 p.m. | Night Skiing?....................No |
| Tickets: Adult Full ...........$28 | Adult Half...........................$21 |
| Tickets: Jr/Sr Full............$14 | Jr/Sr Half............................$10 |
| Main ...................307-745-5750 | |
| Fax ....................307-745-4113 | |
| Snow Report ...800-GO2-SNOW | |

# Index

Accelerated Skier Performance System ...45 - 50, 72, 98
    Alignment and Ski Boots ........................................49
    Primary Movements ...............................................72
Acknowledgments................................................................6
Advanced Skiing.......................................................118 - 119
Afton Alps............................................................................362
Al Quaal Recreation...........................................................347
Alabama...............................................................................298
Alaska.........................................................................298 - 299
Alignment...................................................................47, 50 - 52
Alignment and Ski Boots....................................................49
    Alignment .............................................................50
    Custom Insoles ....................................................62
    Feeling Unsure ............................................68 - 69
    I Can If I Cant .............................................65 - 67
    Ski Boots ..............................................................53
    The Right Boots: Rotary vs. Lateral.....................57
    The Worse for Wear..............................................60
Alpenglow...........................................................................298
Alpine Lake Resort.............................................................443
Alpine Meadows Ski Area..................................................302
Alpine Mountain..................................................................412
Alpine Valley (MI)..............................................................348
Alpine Valley Resort (WI)..................................................446
Alpine Valley Ski Area (OH).............................................406
Alta Ski Area.......................................................................425
Altitude Sickness................................................................294
Alyeska Resort....................................................................298
Andres Tower Hills Ski Area.............................................362
Angel Fire............................................................................382
Antelope Butte Ski Area.....................................................456
Anthony Lakes Mountain Resort........................................409
Appalachian Ski Mountain..................................................401
Apple Mt. Resort.................................................................348
Arapahoe Basin....................................258, 267 - 268, 312
Arizona........................................................................300 - 301
Arizona Snowbowl..............................................................300
Ascutney Mountain Resort.................................................432
Aspen ........................................................46, 276, 304, 313, 365
Aspen Highlands.................................................................313
Aspen Mountain..................................................................313

Attitash Bear Peak.................................................374
Attitude......................................................161 - 163
Avalanche Awareness.............................280 - 281
avalanche control ...................................................281
Badger Mountain ...................................................440
Badger Pass Ski Area.............................................302
Balance........................................47, 75 - 79, 101, 109
Balance in the Turn.....................................98 - 101
Bald Mountain .......................................................326
Be Kind to Yourself......................................152 - 153
Be Present in the Moment ..........................144 - 145
Bear Mountain Ski Resort....................................302
Bear Paw Ski Bowl.................................................368
Bear Valley Ski Area ............................................303
Bears Den Mt ..........................................................405
Beaver Creek Resort ............................................314
Beaver Mountain Ski Area....................................425
Beginner Exercises
    Circular Movement ............................................87
    Side Stepping......................................................81
    Stepping up the slope ........................................90
    The S Line ...............................................82 - 85
    Tipping or Tilting..............................................80
    Traverse.....................................................90 - 91
    with Skis..............................................................86
    without skis..........................................................80
Beginner Skiing......................................................29
Belle Mountain Ski Area .....................................381
Belleayre Mountain...............................................385
Berkshire East Ski Area .......................................342
Berthoud Pass .......................................................314
Big Air Winter Park ..............................................303
Big Birch Ski Area .................................................385
Big Boulder Ski Area ............................................412
Big Powderhorn Mountain....................................348
Big Rock Ski Area .................................................336
Big Sky Ski And Summer Resort .........................368
Big Squaw Mountain .............................................337
Big Tupper Ski Area ..............................................386
Bindings .................................................................61
Bittersweet Ski Area .............................................349
Black Mountain Of Maine .....................................337

Black Mountain................................................374
Blackjack Ski Resort........................................349
Blandford Ski Area ..........................................342
Bleeding...........................................................289
   internal, signs of ......................................289
Blue Hills Ski Area ..........................................342
Blue Knob Four Seasons...................................413
Blue Marsh Ski Area........................................414
Blue Mountain Ski Area ...................................414
Bogus Basin .....................................................327
Bolton Valley Resort ........................................432
Boreal Ski Area................................................303
Boston Mills/Brandywine Ski Resorts................406
Bottineau Winter Park.......................................405
Bousquet Ski Area............................................343
Boyce Park Ski Area.........................................414
Boyne Highlands...............................................349
Boyne Mountain ...............................................350
Bradford Ski Area ............................................343
Brantling Ski Slopes .........................................386
Breakable Crust.................................................250
Breathing......17 - 18, 20, 132 - 135, 147, 169, 288 - 289
Breckenridge Ski Area.........................5, 220, 263, 268,
   281, 299, 314, 408
Bretton Woods Ski Resort .................................375
Brian Head Resort............................................426
Bridger Bowl....................................................369
Brighton Ski Resort ..........................................426
Bristol Mountain Ski Area.................................386
Brodie Mountain ..............................................343
Bromley Mountain ...........................................432
Bruce Mound Winter Sports Area ......................446
Brundage Mountain Ski Area ............................327
Bryce Resort.....................................................437
Buck Hill Ski Area ...........................................363
Buena Vista Ski Area........................................363
Burke Mountain ...............................................433
Buttermilk Mountain.........................................315
Butternut Ski Area ...........................................344
Caberfae Peaks Ski Resort ................................350
California.............................................302 - 311
Camden Snow Bowl ..........................................337

Camelback Ski Area .................................................415
Campgaw Mountain Ski Center.................................381
Canaan Valley Resort .............................................443
CANI ..............................................................23 - 25
Cannon Mountain ...................................................375
Cannonsburg Ski Area ............................................351
Canting ...................................................................65
Carve or Slide? .............................................115 - 117
Cascade Mountain Inc............................................446
Cataloochee Ski Area.............................................402
Catamount Ski Area ...............................................387
Chester Bowl Park .................................................363
Chestnut Mountain Resort ......................................331
children ..........................................44, 266 - 278, 315
Christie Mountain Ski Area.....................................447
Christmas Mountain Village....................................447
Clear Fork Ski Area ...............................................407
Cloudmont Ski Resort.............................................298
Cochran Ski Area ..................................................433
Cockaigne Ski Area ...............................................387
Coffee Mill Ski Area...............................................363
Cold Water Survival Times, chart ............................296
Cold Weather Safety and First Aid ..........................287
    Altitude Sickness............................................294
    Cold Water Survival Times..............................296
    First Aid Priorities..........................................288
    Frostbite........................................................290
    Hypothermia..................................................291
    Ice Thickness - Safety ....................................295
    Wind Chill Temperature Chart.........................293
Colorado ................69, 224, 237 - 238, 242, 251 - 252,
    258 - 259, 266 - 268, 280, 282, 285, 312 - 324
Common Problems In Intermediate Skiing .......189, 191
Connecticut ...................................................324 - 326
Control Your Speed ......................................128 - 131
Cooper Spur ..........................................................409
Copper Mountain ...5, 40, 143, 203, 224, 250, 268, 278,
    285, 315, 317, 359, 379
Cottonwood Butte ..................................................327
Craigmeur Ski Area ...............................................381
Cranmore ..............................................................375
Crescent Hills........................................................334

Crested Butte......................130, 237, 316, 330, 402, 458
Crook, Adrian.................................................39 - 41
Crystal Lake Ski Center.......................................415
Crystal Mountain (WA).......................................440
Crystal Mountain Resort (MI)..............................351
Crystal Ridge Ski Area........................................447
Cuchara Mountain Resort.....................................316
Custom Insoles.............................................62 - 63
DalBello Ski Boots................................................49
Dartmouth Skiway................................................376
Deer Mountain.....................................................424
Deer Valley Resort..............................................427
Detroit Mountain Ski Area....................................364
Devil's Head Resort.............................................448
Diamond Peak Ski Resort.....................................373
Discovery Basin Ski Area......................................369
Dodge Ridge........................................................304
Doe Mountain Ski Area........................................415
Donner Ski Ranch...............................................304
Dry Hill Ski Area.................................................387
Eagle Rock Ski Area.............................................416
Eaglecrest Ski Area.............................................299
Early Season Lesson.......................................20 - 21
Easy Run, Hard Run.............................................175
Eaton Mountain Ski Area......................................338
Echo Valley Ski Area...........................................440
Eldora Mountain Resort..............................267, 317
Elevation
  effect on snow..................................................258
Elk Meadows Ski And Summer Resort.....................427
Elk Mountain Ski Resort.......................................416
exercise program.........................18, 24, 39, 286
Exhale on Every Turn.....................................132 - 135
Expert Improvement.......................................156 - 157
Extreme Conditions..............................................245
  Breakable Crust...............................................250
  Hard Snow.......................................................251
  Keys to the Steep..............................................246
49° North Ski Resort............................................439
fall line...........................86, 91, 119, 131, 226
Fat Skis For Powder.......................................234 - 235
Feeling Unsure............................................68 - 69

Fernwood Resort............................................416
Figures and Illustrations...................................8
First Aid
    Altitude Sickness.......................................294
    Frostbite..................................................290
    Hypothermia............................................291
    Priorities.................................................288
Four Lakes Village.........................................332
Four Seasons Ski Center..................................388
From Intermediate to Expert............................186
    Common Problems in Intermediate Skiing...189 - 191
    Intermediate Skier.....................................187
    The Pole Plant..........................................192
Frost Ridge Ski Area......................................388
Frostbite......................................................290
Frostfire Mountain.........................................405
Gems of the Rockies.......................................267
Georgia.......................................................326
Getting the Kids Started..................................266
Giants Ridge Resort.......................................364
Gladstone Sports Park....................................351
Gore Mountain Ski Area.................................388
Grand Geneva Resort......................................448
Grand Targhee Resort.....................................456
Granlibakken Ski Resort..................................305
Great Divide Ski Area.....................................370
Greek Peak Ski Resort....................................389
groomed.......................33, 36 - 38, 147, 173, 187 - 188,
    208, 213 - 214, 227, 256, 278, 427
Gunstock Ski Area.........................................376
Hanson Hills Recreation Area..........................352
Harb Ski Systems...........................................45
Harb, Harald.......................3, 8, 45 - 48, 72, 99, 109,
    182, 320, 323, 431
Hard Snow....................................................251
Harness Systems............................................274
Hawknest Golf & Ski Resort............................403
Heavenly/Lake Tahoe......................................305
helicopter skiing............................................241
Heliskiing...........................................241 - 243
Hermon Mountain..........................................338
Hickory Hills................................................352

Hickory Ski Center ......................................389
Hidden Valley Resort (PA) .........................417
Hidden Valley Ski Resort (NJ) ...................381
Highlands of Olympia ................................448
Highmount Ski Center ................................389
Hilltop Ski Area ........................................300
Hogadon Ski Area ......................................457
Hole In The Mountain ................................364
Holiday Mountain Ski Area ........................390
Holiday Valley Resort ................................390
Hoodoo Ski Area .......................................409
Hourglass Skis .................96, 111 - 120, 180, 221,
  234, 238, 240, 250, 277
    Advanced Skiing ..........................118 - 119
    Making them Work for You ...................113
    My Kids and .........................................275
    To Carve or Slide? ...............................115
    What Are They ....................................112
Howelsen Hill Ski Area .............................318
Huff Hills .................................................406
Hunt Hollow Ski Area ...............................391
Hunter Mountain Ski Bowl .......................391
Hyland Ski & Snowboard Area ..................365
Hypothermia ............................................291
I Can if I Cant ....................................65, 67
Ice Thickness - Safety ..............................295
Idaho ...............................................326 - 330
Illinois ....................................................331
In Closing ...............................................279
    Avalanche Awareness ...........................280
    It's Not Too Late to Ski ........................283
Inconsistent Spring Snow ..................261 - 263
Indiana ....................................................333
Indianhead Mt & Bear Creek Resort ...........352
Inflex ................................................39 - 41
Injury
    How to Avoid .......................................38
Insoles, Custom ..................................62 - 63
Intention ..........................................26 - 27
Intermediate Lessons ................................170
    Sliding Right .............................179, 181
    Smooth Transitions ..............................171

Unlock the Leg ............................................................177
Use Your Hips ........................................182 - 183, 185
Work Into Your Skiing ................................173, 175
Intermediate Skier ......35, 48, 63, 68, 91, 105, 109, 114, 118, 122, 127, 131, 136, 164, 170 - 171, 175, 177, .180, 186 - 187, 189 - 190, 204, 227, 236, 240
Internal Bleeding ........................................................289
Iowa ..............................................................334 - 335
Jack Frost Resort ........................................................417
Jackson Hole Ski Resort ............................................457
Jay Peak Resort ..........................................................433
Jericho Ski Area ..........................................................344
Jiminy Peak ................................................................344
June Mountain ............................................................305
Keep Your Rhythm ......................................217 - 219
Keep Your Rhythm Constant ......................138 - 141
Kelly Canyon Ski Area ................................................328
Kettlebowl Hill ..........................................................449
Keyes Peak Ski Area ..................................................449
Keys to the Steep ........................................................246
Keystone ......................................19, 21, 36, 268, 318
Kid Slope ....................................................................266
Killington Ski Area ....................................................434
Kinetic Chain ............................72 - 73, 182, 184, 193
King Pine Ski Area ....................................................376
Kirkwood Ski Resort ..................................................306
Kissing Bridge ............................................................391
Labrador Mountain ....................................................392
Las Vegas Ski & Snowboard Resort ..........................373
lateral boot ............................................................57 - 59
Lesson ......................20 - 22, 24, 27, 29, 31, 34 - 35, 43, 117, 122, 154, 159, 175, 266, 284
    Beginner ..............................................................29
    Intermediate ......................................................170
Lift and Tilt ......................47, 95, 97, 102 - 103, 105, 123 - 127, 147, 167, 169, 171 - 172, 182 - 183, 185, 210, 222, 246, 248, 262
Little Switzerland ........................................................449
Look Ahead ..................................................136 - 137
Lookout Pass Ski Area ................................................328
Loon Mountain ..........................................................377
Lost Trail Powder Mountain ......................................370

Lost Valley Ski Area.............................................338
Loup Loup Ski Bowl.............................................440
Loveland Ski Area.............................258, 267, 318
Lutsen Mountains .................................................365
Mad River Glen.....................................................434
Mad River Mountain............................................407
Magic Mountain Ski Area....................................328
Maine...........................................................336 - 339
Making Breakthroughs.........................................155
    Attitude..............................................................161
    Expert Improvement.........................................156
    Overcome Your Fear.........................................158
    Relaxation..............................................167 - 169
    Think Ahead...........................................164 - 165
Mammoth Mountain Ski Area ..............................306
Maple Ski Ridge ...................................................392
Marquette Mountain..............................................353
Marshall Mountain................................................370
Maryland...............................................................341
Massachusetts...............................................342 - 345
Massanutten Resort...............................................438
Maverick Mountain...............................................371
McCauley Mountain..............................................392
McIntyre Ski Area.................................................377
Mentoring............................................148 - 149, 151
Michigan.......................................................347 - 362
Middlebury College Snow Bowl ..........................434
Minnesota.....................................................362 - 368
Mio Mountain Ski Area ........................................353
Missaukee Mountain.............................................353
Mission Ridge Ski Area........................................441
mogul .................37, 108, 135, 141, 146, 157, 166, 171
Mogul Skiing, ABCs of .......................................199
    Keep Your Rhythm............................................217
    Keys to Success....................................200 - 203
    Phantomizing in the Bumps .............................221
    Ski the Line.......................................................213
    Skiing on the Edge...............................205 - 209
    Turning in Moguls................................210 - 211
Mohawk Mountain Ski Area.................................324
Monarch Ski Resort ......................................267, 319
Mont Du Lac Ski Area..........................................450

Mont Ripley ...............................................354
Montage Ski Area ........................................417
Montana ..........................................368 - 371
Montana Snowbowl .......................................371
Moose Mountain Ski Resort ............................300
Mott Mountain ...........................................354
Mount Ashwabay ..........................................451
Mount Bailey ............................................410
Mount Baker Ski Area ...................................441
Mount Frontenac Ski Area ...............................366
Mount Kato Ski Area .....................................366
Mount La Crosse .........................................451
Mount Snow/Haystack Resort .............................435
Mount Spokane Ski Area .................................441
Mount Tone Ski Area .....................................418
Mountain High Resort ...................................306
Mountain View Ski Area .................................419
Mt Ashland Ski Area ....................................410
Mt Bachelor Ski And Summer Resort ......................410
Mt Baldy Ski Area ......................................307
Mt Holly Ski Area .......................................355
Mt Hood Meadows Ski Resort .............................411
Mt Hood Ski Bowl ........................................411
Mt Jefferson ...........................................339
Mt Lemmon Ski Valley ...................................301
Mt McSauba ..............................................356
Mt Peter Ski Area .......................................393
Mt Rose Ski Area ........................................373
Mt Shasta Ski Park ......................................307
Mt Southington ..........................................325
Mt Sunapee Ski Area .....................................377
Mt Tom Ski Area .........................................346
Mt Waterman .............................................307
Mt Zion Ski Area ........................................355
Mulligan's Hollow Ski Bowl .............................356
Mystic Mountain .........................................419
Nashoba Valley Ski Area ................................346
Nevada ..................................................373
New Hampshire ....................................374 - 380
New Jersey .......................................381 - 382
New Mexico .......................................382 - 384
New York .........................................385 - 400

Nordic Mountain ............................................451
Nordic Valley Ski Mountain ...........................427
Nordica..........................................................55
Nor-Ski Runs .................................................334
North Carolina .....................................401 - 404
North Dakota ........................................405 - 406
Northstar At Tahoe Ski Area ..........................308
Nubs Nob ......................................................356
Oak Mountain Ski Center ..............................393
Ober Gatlinburg .............................................425
off-piste..................109, 227, 243 - 244, 261, 308, 319
Oglebay Park Ski Area....................................444
Ohio .....................................................406 - 407
Okemo Mountain ...........................................435
Open Your Mind.............................................143
   Be Kind to Yourself .....................152 - 153
   Be Present in the Moment ....................144
   Mentoring ............................................148
   Start Your Day .....................................146
Orange County Ski Area..................................393
Oregon .................................................409 - 412
orthotic...........................................56, 62, 64, 201
Otis Ridge .....................................................346
Overcome Your Fear .............................158 - 159
Pajarito Mountain ..........................................383
Pando ...........................................................357
parabolic skis
   See hourglass skis
Park City Mountain Resort .............................428
Pats Peak Ski Area.........................................378
Pebble Creek Ski Resort .................................329
Peek'n Peak....................................................393
Pennsylvania ........................................412 - 423
Perfect North Slopes ......................................333
Petoskey Winter Sports Park ...........................357
Phantom Move ...................47, 92 - 97, 100 - 105,
   110, 123, 128, 177, 180, 183 - 184, 190, 193,
   208-210, 213, 222, 227, 229 - 230, 247, 249, 262
Phantom Turn..................73, 103 - 105, 107 - 110, 172,
   182, 184 - 185, 195, 197, 201, 210 - 211,
   213, 218, 222, 228, 246, 253, 262, 277
Phantomizing .105 - 107, 109 - 110, 119, 222 - 223, 248

Phantomizing In The Bumps .............................221 - 223
Phantomizing on Advanced Terrain ................107 - 110
Physical Preparation.............................................31
Pine Knob Ski Resort.........................................357
Pine Mountain ...................................................358
Plumas-Eureka Ski Bowl ...................................308
Pole Plant ...............................192 - 197, 212
Pomerelle Mountain Resort ................................329
Porcupine Mountains .........................................358
Potawatomi State Park .......................................452
Powder Mountain Ski Resort ..............................429
Powder Pass Ski Area .......................................457
Powder Ridge Ski Area .............................325, 366
Powder Skiing ...................................................224
    Advanced ..........................................229 - 233
    Advanced Powder Skiing ................................229
    Fat Skis for Powder .......................................234
    Heliskiing ......................................................241
    Powder Skiing for Beginners ..........................225
    Sno-Cat Powder Skiing ..................................237
Powder Skiing for Beginners ..............................225
Powderhorn Ski Resort ...............................267, 319
Powers Bluff Winter Recreation Area ...................452
Preparation ........................................................13
    Beginner Skiing ..............................................29
    CANI .......................................................23 - 25
    Early Season Lesson ...................................20 - 21
    Inflex ......................................................39, 41
    Intention .................................................26 - 27
    Ski Awareness ..........................................42 - 43
    Ski Legs ...................................................17 - 19
    Ski Safety .................................................31 - 38
    Starting a New Season ...............................14 - 15
Primary Movements ............47, 71, 108 - 109, 116, 277
    Balance .........................................................75
    Balance in the Turn .........................................98
    Beginner Exercises .........................................80
    Beginner Exercises With Skis ...........................86
    Introduction ..............................................72 - 73
    Phantom Turn ...............................................102
    Phantomizing ................................................105
    Phantomizing on Advanced Terrain....................107

The Phantom Move ...................................................92
Pulse ........................................................................289
Purgatory .................................................................320
Quadna Mountain Ski Center ..................................367
Quechee Lakes .........................................................435
Ragged Mountain .....................................................378
ramp angle .........................................57 - 59, 115
Red Lodge Mountain Resort .....................................371
Red River Ski Area ...................................................383
References and Trade Marks .........................................8
Relaxation .......................................................167 - 169
Resort At Split Rock .................................................419
Rhode Island ............................................................424
Rib Mountain Ski Area ............................................452
Right Boots, The ...............................................57 - 59
Right Ski, Left Ski ...........................................126 - 127
Riverside Hills .........................................................334
Robbins, Tony ...................................................23, 26
Rocking Horse Ranch ...............................................395
rotary boot .........................................................57 - 59
Royal Mountain .......................................................395
Saddleback Ski Area ................................................339
safety .............................16, 31, 43 - 44, 138, 239,
   242 - 243, 273, 282, 288, 295
Sandia Peak ..............................................................383
Santa Fe Ski Area ....................................................384
Sapphire Valley ........................................................403
Scaly Mountain ........................................................403
Schweitzer Mountain Resort ....................................329
Scotch Valley Resort ................................................395
Seven Oaks Recreation Park .....................................335
Seven Springs Mountain Resort ...............................419
Shanty Creek ............................................................358
shape skis .............................................112, 274, 277
   See Also Hourglass Skis
sharp edges ...................................14, 252 - 253
Shawnee Mountain ...................................................420
Shawnee Peak ..........................................................339
Showdown Ski Area .................................................372
Shu-Maker Mountain ...............................................396
sideslip .............................................................180, 210
Sierra At Tahoe ........................................................308

Sierra Summit Mt Resort ...................................309
Silver Creek Ski Area ...........................267, 320
Silver Mountain Ski & Summer Resort ...................330
Sipapu Ski Area .....................................384
Six Steps to Effortless Skiing .......................121
    Control Your Speed .........................128 - 131
    Exhale on Every Turn .......................132 - 135
    Introduction ...............................122
    Keep Your Rhythm Constant ..................138 - 141
    Lift and Tilt ..............................123 - 125
    Look Ahead .................................136 - 137
    Right Ski, Left Ski ........................126 - 127
Ski Apache ..........................................384
Ski Areas of the United States ......................297
Ski Beech Mountain ..................................404
Ski Bluewood ........................................442
Ski Boots ...........................................53 - 55
    Custom-fit .................................56
    Fit ........................................54
    Rotary vs. Lateral .........................57
    Worn out ...................................60
Ski Brule Mtn/Ski Homestead .........................358
Ski Cooper ....................................267, 320
Ski Denton ..........................................420
Ski Homewood ........................................309
Ski Legs ............................................17 - 19
Ski Liberty .........................................420
Ski Mt Abram ........................................340
Ski Paoli Peaks .....................................333
ski patrol .............31, 150, 281 - 282, 288 - 289, 294
Ski Plattekill ......................................396
Ski Roundtop ........................................421
Ski Safety ..........................................31 - 38
Ski Sawmill .........................................421
Ski Skyline .........................................453
Ski Snowstar ........................................332
Ski Sundown .........................................325
Ski Tamarack ........................................396
Ski Valley Club .....................................397
Ski Ward ............................................347
Ski Windham .........................................397
Ski World ...........................................333

Skier's Responsibility Code .............................................42
Skiing on the Edge...................................205 - 209
Skiing With the Kids.........................................269
Sky Valley Ski Resort...................................326
Skyline Ski Area...........................................360
Skyline Skiway..............................................406
Sleeping Giant Ski Area................................459
Sleepy Hollow Sports Park............................335
Sliding Right.......................................179 - 181
Smooth Transitions.......................................171
Smugglers' Notch Resort................................436
Sno-Cat Powder Skiing.........................237 - 239
Snow...............................37, 187 - 188, 225, 227,
237 - 238, 242 - 243, 264, 281 - 282, 284
    breakable crust.................................250 - 251
    Early Season..............................................33
    hard conditions...............................251 - 254
    spring conditions.............................256 - 258, 261
Snow Crest At Kratka Ridge............................309
Snow Hill.....................................................378
Snow King Ski Area.......................................459
Snow Ridge Ski Area......................................397
Snow Summit Mountain Resort........................310
Snow Trails Ski Area......................................407
Snow Valley Mountain Sports Park...................310
Snowbasin Resort..........................................429
Snowbird Ski & Summer Resort.......................429
Snowhaven....................................................330
Snowmass Ski Area........................................321
Snowshoe/Silver Creek Ski Area......................444
Snowsnake Mountain.......................................360
Snowy Range.................................................459
Soda Springs.................................................310
Soldier Mountain Resort..................................331
Solitude Ski Resort.........................................430
Something for Everybody.................................265
    Getting the Kids Started.................................266
    Shape Skis for Kids.......................................274
    Skiing With The Kids.....................................269
Song Mountain...............................................398
South Dakota.................................................424
Spirit Mountain..............................................367

Spring Conditions ............................................................255
   Inconsistent Spring Snow ...................................261
   Spring Skiing .......................................................256
   Spring Skiing Preparations ...............................259
Spring Mountain Ski Area ..............................................421
Spring Skiing ...................................................................283
Squaw Valley USA ..........................................................311
Standing Rocks ................................................................453
Start Your Day ..................................................146 - 147
Starting A New Season .........................................14 - 15
Steamboat .........................................................................321
Steamboat Powder Cats .................................................240
Sterling Forest Ski Center .............................................398
Stevens Pass .....................................................................442
Stowe Mountain Resort ..................................................436
Stratton Mountain ...........................................................436
structural imbalance .............................................51 - 52
   bow legged ............................................................50
   knock kneed ..........................................................51
Sugar Bowl Resort ..........................................................311
Sugar Loaf Resort (MI) ..................................................360
Sugar Mountain Resort ..................................................404
Sugarbush Ski Resort ......................................................437
Sugarloaf/USA (ME) .......................................................340
Suicide Six Ski Area .......................................................437
Summit Ski Area .............................................................411
Sun Valley ........................................................................331
Sunburst Ski Area ...........................................................453
Sundance ...........................................................................430
Sunday River Ski Resort .................................................340
Sundown Mountain ..........................................................336
Sunlight Mountain Resort ................................267, 322
Sunrise Ski Resort ...........................................................301
Sunset Ski Area ...............................................................336
Swain Ski & Snowboard Center ....................................398
Swiss Valley Ski Lodge ..................................................361
Sylvan Hill Park ..............................................................453
Table of Contents ................................................................9
Tahoe Donner ...................................................................311
Tanglewood Ski Area ......................................................422
Taos Ski Valley ...............................................................385
Tecnica ................................................................................53

Telemark Resort..............................................454
Telluride Ski Resort.....................46, 48, 153, 168,
  199, 203, 231, 322
Temple Mountain............................................379
Tennessee......................................................425
Tenney Mountain Ski Resort...........................379
Terry Peak.....................................................424
The Balsams/Wilderness.................................380
The Big Mountain...........................................372
The Canyons..................................................431
The Homestead Resort (MI)............................361
The Homestead Ski Area (VA).........................438
The Summit At Snoqualmie.............................442
Think Ahead...........................................164 - 165
Timber Ridge Ski Area....................................361
Timberline Four Seasons Resort (WV)..............445
Timberline Ski Area (OR)................................412
Titcomb Mountain...........................................341
Titus Mountain...............................................399
TLH Heliskiing........................................241 - 242
Toggenburg Ski Center....................................399
Treetops Sylvan Resort...................................362
Trollhaugen Ski Area......................................454
Turner Mountain.............................................372
Turning in Moguls....................................210 - 211
Tussey Mountain.............................................422
Tyrol Basin...................................................454
unconscious...................................................288
Unlock The Leg..............................................177
Use of the Hands............................................110
Use Your Hips........................................182 - 185
Utah.......................................................425 - 431
Vail...............................203, 268, 280, 323
Vermont..................................................432 - 437
Vernon Valley/Great Gorge Ski Area................382
Villa Olivia Ski Area.......................................332
Villa Roma Ski Area........................................400
Virginia...................................................437 - 438
Volant Chubb.........................................235, 244
Wachusett Mountain........................................347
Warm-Up Runs...............................................173
Washington.............................................439 - 443

Waterville Valley Resort............................................380
Welch Village Ski Area .............................................367
West Mountain Ski Area............................................400
West Virginia........................................443 - 445
White Pass...............................................................443
Whitecap Mountains .................................................455
Whiteface Mt Ski Center ...........................................400
Whitetail Ski Resort..................................................422
Wild Mountain Ski Area............................................368
Wildcat Mountain .....................................................380
Willamette Pass........................................................412
Willard Mountain Ski Area........................................401
Williams Ski Area.....................................................301
Wilmot Mountain.....................................................455
Wind chill................................................................293
Winter Park ..............................................46, 203, 269
Winter Park/Mary Jane ..............................................324
Wintergreen..............................................................438
Winterplace Ski Resort ..............................................445
Wisconsin................................................446 - 456
Wisp Ski Resort .......................................................341
Wolf Creek...............................................................324
Wolf Laurel Slopes ...................................................404
Woodbury Ski Area ..................................................326
Woods Valley Ski Area .............................................401
Woodside Ranch........................................................456
Work Into Your Skiing...............................173 - 174
Worse for Wear, The .................................60 - 61
Wyoming................................................456 - 459
Yawgoo Valley .........................................................424

Notes